Brands & Advertising

Brands & Advertising

How advertising effectiveness influences brand equity

Giep Franzen

With the assistance of:
Cindy Goessens
Mary Hoogerbrugge
Cees Kappert
Reint Jan Schuring
Marnix Vogel

Admap Publications

First published 1999 by Admap Publications
Farm Road, Henley-on-Thames
Oxfordshire RG9 1EJ, United Kingdom
Telephone: +44 (0) 1491 411000
Facsimile: +44 (0) 1491 571188

A CIP catalogue record for this book is available from the British Library

ISBN 1-84116-042-3
Copyright © Giep Franzen
Typographic and cover design: Annelies van der Ploeg (FHV/BBDO)/Kluwer

Translated by Wendy van Os

Typeset by Admap Publications in 10.5/12 pt Bembo
Printed and bound in Great Britain by Biddles Ltd, Guildford and King's Lynn

CONTENTS

INTRODUCTION

For many years the academic world has displayed little interest in efforts by advertising practitioners to affect the behaviour of consumers on the basis of subjective, intuitive and often random hypotheses. Advertising practitioners, for their part, have largely ignored any offers of assistance from academics.

Meanwhile, scholars have made great progress in the field of the processing of information by individuals. However, the advertiser is not primarily concerned with such information processing. The advertiser aims to build a strong brand, enlarge market share and achieve return on investment, and is concerned with the effectiveness of advertising in influencing buying behaviour in favour of the brand. So the perspective of the academic, whose approach is based mainly on the processing of the individual advertisement in the individual brain, differs greatly from the perspective of the marketer, who pursues mass behavioural effects in the marketplace. This difference probably accounts for the fact that advertising and academic circles have never achieved more than a 'marriage of convenience'. Or, to be more precise, a series of 'affairs of convenience'. The advertiser is primarily interested in the persuasive effect of advertising: how to influence consumers' choices and buying behaviour most effectively. And academics do not, as yet, have much to contribute in that context.

In this situation of relative ignorance, there has been a growing tendency in recent years for advertisers and advertising agencies to base their relationship on the principle of accountability. 'Accountability' is an umbrella term covering efforts aimed at giving advertisers more certainty about the effectiveness of their advertising campaigns, as well as efforts to make agencies more accountable for their performance in selling the brand. Accountability means forming a relationship between a certain activity and a certain effect, in such a way that the activity can be justified in advance and the effect verified in retrospect.

If one looks at the academic state of play on the one hand, and the know-how of practitioners on advertising effectiveness on the other, one will realise that such an aspiration is a decade too soon. Advertising people are called 'brand builders' these days – correctly so, in principle. But they build their bridge to consumers in a somewhat haphazard way. They select their tools, often at random, take whatever material happens to be available, and start building on one bank in the hope of reaching the other a little later. And then they look back and say: 'Look, a bridge.' They succeed surprisingly often, thanks to experience and intuition, but, as the first chapter of this book details, they probably fail just as often.

In recent years the communication studies faculty of the University of Amsterdam has carried out considerable research into the question of how advertisers and agency people deal in practice with advertising frameworks. We have been especially intrigued by the question of involvement in the effectiveness of campaigns. Our findings, in brief, have been that, in general:

- no clear, specific communication objectives are formulated;
- advertising frameworks are generally seen as a 'black box';
- measurements of brand associations are almost always carried out qualitatively;
- measurement of advertising effects does not take any priority;
- effects research is not conducted systematically but *ad hoc*, particularly in times of uncertainty.

At the same time, there is a growing realisation that this state of affairs cannot continue. Brands are far too important to companies for them to be managed largely on the basis of subjective opinions and 'gut feeling'. The same applies to the huge investments in advertising with a view to building and maintaining brands.

It is not long since the publication of the first book taking the brand as its subject (John Philip Jones (1987) *What's In a Name?*). Since then, many more have been published, but, compared with other fields – marketing in general, for instance – work on brands is still at the pioneering stage. The same applies to the effects of advertising from the 'brand-building' point of view.

The authors of this book seek to contribute to developing knowledge for the benefit of brand policy and advertising, and we emphasise the research methods at the industry's disposal.

However, the book is not only intended as a practical advertising manual. An additional guideline for us has been its usefulness in advanced education, and we hope it will serve to narrow the gap between academics and practitioners.

Finally, a few words about the structure of the book. Advertising frameworks can only properly be understood from the essence of brands and the knowledge, attitude and behaviour of consumers towards brands. Throughout the book we have sought to tie in advertising frameworks with these 'brand responses'. Although advertising effectiveness is the book's starting point, brands are its main subject.

The first chapter contains an overview of what is known on the effectiveness of advertising campaigns in general. In Chapter 2 the methods for researching advertising effectiveness are charted. Chapter 3 defines and delineates all the effects of advertising, and is intended for reference use, while Chapter 4 deals with brand equity and the methods of equity research. Chapter 5 explains advertising framework models, Chapter 6 deals with pre-testing and Chapter 7 with tracking. Chapter 8 discusses modelling methods and also contains an analysis of the results of a simulation study. Finally, Chapter 9 concludes with views on an evolutionary approach to accountability.

This book has been written by six authors, but is not a collection of separate papers. Every chapter is based on the same ideas, starting points and constructs. The authors have done their best to provide readers with a state-of-the-art review of the subject, but needless to say, we would welcome any comments and criticism.

Giep Franzen   **Naarden Vesting, April 1999**

1 Research into advertising effectiveness

Giep Franzen

1.1 GROWING CONCERN ABOUT ADVERTISING EFFECTIVENESS

Interest in the effectiveness of advertising has been growing in recent years, due, in part, to the general trend towards securing and, where possible, raising companies' profitability. The necessity and contribution to the end result of all cost items in a company must be evaluated, and all policy decisions financially justified. It is becoming increasingly difficult for advertising to avoid this accountability requirement.

In many countries awards are presented for the most effective advertising campaigns – the 'Effies', as they are called in the US, or the IPA (Institute of Practitioners in Advertising) Advertising Effectiveness Awards in the UK. From these, it is known that some campaigns have a strong influence on the sale of the brands and products to which they apply. However, until the early 1990s little was known about the effectiveness of advertising campaigns in general. It was not clear how many campaigns were effective, or upon what effectiveness depended. In the past decade new research techniques have enabled us to expose the direct correlations between advertising activities and consumer buying behaviour. Meta-analyses of large numbers of campaigns, using standard effectiveness measures, have gradually provided an idea of the general state of advertising effectiveness.

These analyses show that a good number of the campaigns have no short-term positive effect on buying behaviour, while with other campaigns the short-term effects evaporate within a year. In countries where such research is carried out (the US, Germany and, since 1996, the UK and France) these findings are leading to growing concern about the effectiveness of campaigns and to increasing interest in pre-testing.

This book seeks to provide an overview of the research and analysis methods available to advertisers, so that they can gain an insight into the effectiveness of their advertising campaigns.

1.2 ADVERTISING AND BUYING BEHAVIOUR

So what can be said about the effectiveness of campaigns in general? The results of the following three large-scale research projects, based on the single-source method, give an indication. This method records and compares advertising exposure and brand purchases in the same households.

- The *How Advertising Works* project set up by Lodish (1991) and Lodish *et al.* (1995) is an analysis of 389 campaigns in the US which were examined by means of the IRI Behaviour-Scan Method, based on split-cable testing. (For a general description of split-cable testing, see Exhibit 2.1, page 35.)
- The *When Ads Work* project mounted by John Philip Jones (1995) looks at 78 campaigns in the US which were examined using the Nielsen Household Panel.
- An analysis by Colin McDonald (1996b) of 67 campaigns in England, which made use of the Adlab panel, run by Taylor Nelson from September 1985 to March 1990.

Before reviewing the results of the above studies, let us take a look at the problem of effectiveness in general. The crucial question is to what extent a direct correlation can be demonstrated between advertising and buying behaviour. Since buying behaviour depends on far more marketing variables than advertising alone, it is often claimed to be impossible to link the two directly, and that advertising effectiveness can be determined only in terms of realised mental responses, such as brand awareness, brand attitude and buying intentions.

'Effie' awards

In all the countries where effectiveness awards are granted, market effects (like sales and market share) are used as the chief criterion of advertising effectiveness. The widespread acceptance of the institution of the Effies and IPA awards, and the large numbers of advertising agencies and advertisers taking part, suggest that in practice there is a general consensus as to the direct connection between advertising and sales. The authors, too, assume that the aim of advertising (with the exception of social and institutional campaigns) is to influence buying behaviour, and that the only hard and fast measure of campaign effectiveness is how advertising affects that buying behaviour.

But how should we determine that behaviour? Should we use data at a consumer level, or advertisers' national sales figures?

Market response modelling

One of the methods applied in research into the correlation between advertising and sales is that of market response modelling. In this method developments in sales or market shares are the dependent variables. The influence on these of input variables (advertising, promotions, distribution or price, for instance) is then checked. This requires numerical time series for a great many marketing variables and external variables covering a longer period. This method is gradually being used on a wider scale but progress is slow – numeric series are a stumbling block and few firms seem to have properly organised statistics at their disposal. After all, it is generally an arduous and time-consuming job to compile such material. Few meta-analyses of market response models are in fact available. The few publications that exist on the subject do indicate that the influence of advertising on sales is measurable and significant (Tellis and Weiss, 1995), though according to McDonald (1992) it is generally slight.

In Chapter 8 of this book, Schuring and Vogel describe an analysis of the market simulations they have produced for 100 brands in the food sector, for national markets within Europe. The analysis relates to developments in the 1993–96 period. It reveals that 5–11% of the fluctuations in market shares of these brands can be explained by changes in media expenditure, and that, on average, media influence is 7.6%. It is worth bearing in mind that these are short-term effects. In situations in which it is impossible or inappropriate to relate buying behaviour directly to advertising activities, only market response modelling can give an insight into the connection between the two.

1.3 SINGLE-SOURCING

Sales figures result from three variables: the number of users of a brand ('penetration'), average buying frequency by these users and, of course, the average amount purchased.

The analyses which we shall be describing here are based on recording purchases by a representative household panel using hand-scanners. This enables us to follow the course of individual buying behaviour during a longer period, and, accordingly, the buying frequency of the different brands within a product group. If exposure of the same households to advertising for the brands in question is recorded (the single-source principle) we can now establish at a household level direct correlations between advertising exposures and buying behaviour. For this purpose, electronic methods are used to register television viewing behaviour. The number of 'opportunities to see' (OTS) per household per time unit can be worked out from viewing behaviour data. Purchases per household per time unit are then compared with the number of received OTS in the household in question. In particular, buying behaviour in households with one or several OTS is compared to that of households without exposure to advertising.

It is assumed that household panel members are exposed to the same market influences, so that the only variations are in advertising input or advertising consumption. Although this is probably correct when research is carried out in specific test areas, as is the case in France and Germany, this supposition comes in for some criticism (see Exhibit 1.1 on page 18). In the STAS (short-term advertising strength) approach, the noted differences in buying behaviour with different advertising communications or advertising pressure are ascribed directly to specific advertising. It is less a matter of isolating the effects of advertising from the other variables in the marketing mix than is the case in market modelling.

A second advantage of the STAS approach is that advertising effectiveness is not measured in isolation, but under normal market conditions, and in relation to the activities of competing brands. For instance, negative campaign effectiveness is quite often observed. This may well be caused by a difference in advertising pressure between the brand in question and its competitors.

One drawback of the single-source method is that it provides little information on the reasons why a campaign is or is not effective, making it difficult to carry out the necessary adjustments. We have, for instance, discovered that a campaign does not work, or is below par in its effect, but cannot trace this to the message or the creative strategy.

Behavioural effects

What are the behavioural effects involved? In the context of the individual brand and the principle of effectiveness, the following can be differentiated:
- Effects on brand penetration
  - *New use*. New product category users who start using the brand for the first time.
  - *Switching-in*. Inclusion of a brand in their repertoire by existing category users.
  - *Consolidation*. Prevention of switching-out by present brand users.
- Effects on buying frequency of category users
  - *Higher buying frequency of category users*.
  - *Higher share of customer (SOC) or share of requirements (SOR) of a brand*. This stands for the share of a brand in a household's category purchases.
  - *Consolidation of the SOC*. Prevention of a lowering of the SOC.

The behavioural effects aimed for in both categories are evident in the number of households purchasing a brand within a certain period, and are usually measured and analysed per week or per purchasing interval.

A brand's market position partly decides the growth potential of penetration and/or usage frequency of that brand. When a new brand is launched, its status is quite different from that of an established market leader with a high market share. Nevertheless, almost every practitioner equates effectiveness with growth, and it is the most important criterion for practically all the Effie awards. Similarly, the interpretation of the three single-source studies mentioned earlier implicitly assumes that 'effective' means a positive trend in the number of purchases. So it is hardly surprising that a strong correlation can be found between effectiveness and a brand's assumed growth potential. After all, not every brand can grow. In stable, established markets of many product categories the growth of one brand is bound to be at the expense of other brands. So effectiveness might also be defined as the prevention of a decline in penetration and buying frequency, as listed in the third and sixth points in the effects listed on the previous page.

If the effectiveness of advertising campaigns is to be properly analysed, they should really be classified according to the characteristics of the product category and brand. However, the available analyses only partly distinguish between new and established brands. It is absolutely essential to subdivide the latter category into market positions. Two subcategories suffice:
- smaller established brands with growth potential;
- larger established brands in the consolidation stage.

Results
The main results of the three analyses based on single-source research, as listed in section 1.2, can be summarised for new and for established brands.

Lodish/IRI: new brands
- Fifty-five per cent of the brands showed a rise in sales if the number of gross rating points (GRPs) was increased by 55% on average. For brands that reacted positively, the higher sales volume averaged 22%, and the increase in market share was 20%.
- Sixty per cent of the brands reacted positively to a change in campaign content. For brands in which there was growth, the average increase was 23% in volume and 19% in share.

Lodish/IRI: established brands
- Thirty-three per cent of these brands reacted positively to an average increase of 85% in the number of GRPs. Average increased purchases were 22% in volume and 20% in share.
- For 36% of the brands a positive effect was apparent in families exposed to advertising, compared to families that were not.
- Twenty-five per cent of the established brands reacted positively to a change in campaign content. The average volume growth was 23%, and the share growth 12%.
- For 44 brands that reacted positively to an increase in budget, sales development was followed for two years after the test year. Of the 22% volume growth of the test year, 14% was retained in the year that followed, and 7% in the year after that.

Jones/Nielsen: established brands
- A positive short-term effect (within one week) was seen among 70% of the brands and a negative effect among 30%.
- There is considerable difference in the extent to which campaigns are effective in generating short-term effects.

- For 24% of brands for which there was a positive short-term effect, no positive long-term effect could be determined (after one year). So in all, no positive long-term effect was ascertained for 54% of the brands.
- Forty-six per cent of the brands displayed a positive short-term and a positive long-term effect on market share within a year.
- Eleven of the twenty major established brands in this survey exhibited a positive short-term effect. Only five of them demonstrated that effect in the long term.

McDonald/Adlab: new and established brands
- For 63% of the brands a positive short-term effect was observed (within one week).
- For 27% there was a negative short-term effect; these brands proved unable to withstand advertising pressure from their competitors. This corresponds with Jones' findings.
- Even if the short-term effect is defined as applying to the first two or three weeks, the number of brands with positive STAS results remains practically the same.
- For 56% of the brands the effect on repeat purchases was positive, and for 59% the effect on penetration was also positive (the two may, of course, go together).

Further analyses

In Table 1.1, Jones (1998) gives a comparative analysis of STAS data (see Exhibit 1.1 for a clarification of the STAS formula) in the US, UK and Germany. (Exhibit 1.3 and Tables 1.2 and 1.3 also offer an example of the use of STAS analysis in Germany – see pages 22 and 23.) Average STAS scores were calculated for ten deciles of the total samples of campaigns. The scores of the individual campaigns vary from +200 percentage points (positive) to −56 percentage points (negative).

Jones established a diminishing return with several exposures in one week. However, McDonald (1997b) noted that there was definitely a positive effect on the STAS from the number of OTS (based on Adlab panel data) if the natural sales interval was used instead of a fixed period. He also found that this effect was more pronounced among light than heavy buyers.

	United States Jones STAS	United Kingdom McDonald Adlab	Germany Jones STAS
1st decile	236	184	154
2nd decile	164	129	127
3rd decile	139	119	116
4th decile	121	114	108
5th decile	116	110	106
6th decile	108	107	101
7th decile	103	102	100
8th decile	97	98	98
9th decile	89	93	92
10th decile	73	73	83

Table 1.1 STAS deciles (Jones, 1998)

Millward Brown (Hollis, 1994) used the modelling approach to examine the effect of 235 commercials on the sales trends of 70 brands. It was only possible to ascertain short-term effects from 54% of these commercials.

STAS: short-term behavioural response

In order to analyse short-term behavioural response with single-source research, Jones devised the concept of STAS. This stands for *short-term advertising strength*, and, basically, reproduces the effect on buying behaviour of one or more exposures in the week prior to purchase of the product in question. Jones calculates it by dividing the buyers of a category into two groups for that week. The first group contains all buyers who did not see a commercial for the particular brand in the week preceding purchase. The share of the brand within this group of buyers is called the *baseline STAS* and has an index of 100.

The second group is made up of all the buyers of a product in the category who saw at least one commercial for the brand in the week preceding purchase. Here, too, Jones calculates the share of the brand in all the category purchases, calling this the *stimulated STAS*. The difference between the stimulated STAS and the baseline STAS is the *STAS differential*, which is expressed as a percentage change compared with the baseline STAS (indexed at 100).

In his study, based on 78 brands, Jones arrived at an average STAS differential of 124. This means that a brand's share in purchases by panel members who saw one or more commercials increased by an index of 24 on average. Dispersion of the STAS differential runs from 44 (lower share of 56 percentage points) to 300 (higher share of 200 percentage points). McDonald (1996b) comes up with an average STAS differential of 110 in his analysis of 67 campaigns. However, individual results range from 38 to 315!

The link between advertising viewing and buying behaviour is convincing proof that campaigns can have a short-term effect. A small number of buyers in the category react to advertising exposure almost immediately, with changed buying behaviour. This does not mean that others, whose behaviour has not changed within a week, will not respond. There may well be a mental response, resulting, a little later, in a brand behavioural response. But current single-source research does not give any indication that, with a total absence of short-term behavioural response, there will be a positive effect on purchases within a year.

The chief objection to Jones' analyses is that the STAS measure assumes that all the differences between the exposed and non-exposed groups are due to contacts with the brand's television advertising. It would have been especially useful to have analysed differences between the groups as regards exposure to competitive pricing and promotion activity, in conjunction with differences in television exposures (Lodish, 1997; Schroeder *et al.*, 1997).

Neither has Jones allowed for distortion due to the *a priori* connection between brand usage and viewing behaviour (Broadbent, 1996). Viewing intensity (heavy versus light) also correlates with buying behaviour. Another comment relates to the fact that only the effect of exposures in the week prior to purchase was analysed. In McDonald's opinion, STAS overlooks the carry-over effect from previous exposures. STAS is a sign that there is a positive response to advertising, but it is not a means of forecasting an increase or a decrease in total sales. Thus a high STAS score can coincide with either the presence or the absence of a long-term development, as Jones' analyses also demonstrate (McDonald, 1996b).

Exhibit 1.1

One of the biggest advertisers in the US (General Mills) carried out 63 large-scale experiments (see Exhibit 1.2) to determine the short-term effects of television commercials on the 'share of choice' of its brands (Gibson, 1996). ('Share of choice' refers to the percentage of people who state that they would choose the brand in question as their next purchase within the product category.) As was the case with the single-source analyses described above, considerable differences in effectiveness were noted, varying from an increase of over 50% of the share of choice, to a decrease of 60%.

Marder (1997) describes an analysis of 65 surveys on the influence of very high advertising pressure (250 GRPs per week for 8 to 12 weeks) on brand choice. The latter was measured with an advanced variant of the constant sum method. In the constant sum method, consumers are asked to express their brand preference by allocating points to the various brands. In this case consumers were presented with a series of pages, each containing a verbal and visual representation of a brand, and asked to distribute ten adhesive stickers across the brands, based on the likelihood of their buying them. In 30% of the cases a strong positive effect was found; in 20% slight positive effects were noted,

The effects of one exposure

One of the biggest food sector advertisers in the US, General Mills, has been conducting experiments since 1976 in order to determine the effects of television commercials. This project is called TRI-NET. General Mills collected pre-test scores for most of the commercials in the test, which were established in a laboratory setting, under enforced exposure to the ad.

One of the questions related to the validity of the pre-test scores, and whether they properly predict the effects of advertising under natural conditions.

The test commercials were broadcast around the three major, national networks' news programmes. The morning after the broadcast, brand attitudes and buying intentions were measured in national samples (N = 7600 per test). These were taken as the basis for calculations of the 'share of choice', and viewing behaviour was then determined for the previous evening. The sample was split into consumers who could or could not have seen the commercials, and brand attitude and buying intention scores for the subsamples were then compared.

General Mills' experiments established that one evening's exposure to television commercials had a tremendous impact, in line with the findings of the single-source studies mentioned earlier. After some commercials, the share of choice was up 25%, 50%, or even more. However, negative effects were also revealed for some commercials, in that the share of choice after exposure had dropped by between 5% and 60%! From a total of 63 studied commercials, 19% displayed a strongly positive effect, 54% a moderately positive effect and 8% a strongly negative effect. A pronounced correlation was established with the pre-test scores.

The TRI-NET method underpinned the validity of General Mills' pre-testing methods (based on the pre-post brand attitude shift).

Analysis of the 63 studied commercials revealed a tremendous difference in effectiveness, from very strongly positive to very strongly negative. Lawrence Gibson, who reported on these findings, refers to Irwin Gross, who had already announced in 1972 that expenditure for developing and testing campaigns should be five to eight times what it was at that time.

Exhibit 1.2

and in the remaining 50% the effects were negligible, positive, or negative. Some campaigns actually revealed strongly negative effects.

In Chapter 8 Schuring and Vogel examine in more detail the contribution of advertising to the development of market share, using 60 brands out of an analysis of 100 (20 market leaders, 15 'upwardly-mobile' brands and 25 secondary brands). There was no significant effect on market share for 35% of these brands, while 10% (secondary brands only) showed a negative effect. It can be assumed that the 35% will rise sharply if the other brands are also taken into consideration, since the remaining 40 brands are mainly premium brands with a limited market share, secondary brands, private labels, 'losers' and shadow brands. The contribution of media weight to the market share of this group of brands is expected to be considerably lower than the 60 brands that were analysed individually.

Campaigns with no effect

All these studies demonstrated that there was no effect displayed for a large percentage of campaigns:

- Lodish/IRI – new brands. Forty-five per cent did not react to a considerable increase in budget.
- Lodish/IRI – established brands. Sixty-seven per cent of brands did not react to an increase of 85% in the number of GRPs; 75% did not react to a considerable increase in budget.
- Jones/Nielsen – established brands. Fifty-four per cent of brands did not show a positive long-term effect, and 30% showed a negative short-term effect.
- McDonald/Adlab. There was no positive short-term effect for 37% of brands; no effect on repeat purchase for 44%; and no effect on penetration for 41%.
- Millward Brown (Hollis, 1994). Forty-six per cent of the commercials did not have any short-term effects.
- Marder. Fifty per cent of brands did not react to a considerable advertising boost.
- Schuring and Vogel. Advertising did not have a positive effect on the market share of 45% of brands.

In a competitive marketplace a brand can gain share of choice or share of market only at the expense of other brands. Where one brand wins, one or more others must lose. It is not, therefore, surprising that successful and ineffective campaigns exist in a balance of somewhere around 50:50. Marketers usually have difficulties in accepting that advertising campaigns can even have negative effects. There are different causes for this phenomenon. One of them is that in the competition between brands, the advertising campaign for a specific brand may not be strong enough to maintain the brand's position under the pressure of competitors' campaigns.

General conclusions

A number of conclusions can be drawn from these results regarding the effectiveness of campaigns in general.

The results show that:

- campaigns *can* be very effective in influencing consumer purchases in the period directly after exposure to a television commercial;
- there is substantial difference in the degree of effectiveness of the campaigns in this respect;

- a positive effect within one year can still influence sales volume positively in the two following years.

However, the results also show that many campaigns have no positive influence whatsoever on buying behaviour in the period immediately following advertising exposure. Lastly, they reveal that a large proportion of the campaigns which have a positive short-term effect have lost this effect before the test year is over (probably mainly because there is insufficient continuity).

Marder (1997) defined the advertising effectiveness principle, based on his findings, as follows:

Advertising is a game of chance. Even if you are a major marketer, served by a major advertising agency, you have around a 50% chance of running advertising that won't do anything for you and in some cases will actually hurt your brand.

Use of STAS analysis in Germany

In Germany Nielsen uses a panel of 6,000 households. The service applies the single-source method and has introduced the STAS approach. The following description of one of its uses dates from December 1995 and relates to two competing detergent brands. The results of the STAS analysis are summarised in Tables 1.2 and 1.3.

Advertising pressure for brand A was considerably greater than for brand B, resulting in 102,532 OTS in the panel for brand A, compared with 68,243 for brand B. However, the campaign for brand A did not meet expectations. The STAS score after one or more OTS was only 104: the share in category purchases only increased by 4%. Brand B's share in purchases, on the other hand, rose by 26%. The analysis also shows that the first exposure for both brands had practically the same effect (STAS of 104 for brand A, 106 for brand B).

However, two exposures or more within the seven days preceding a product purchase did not result in a higher share for brand A, whereas the STAS for brand B rose to 141. Higher advertising pressure for brand A did not lead to a higher share in purchases; this campaign was clearly far less effective than brand B's.

Brand A's campaign consisted of a series of commercials with very different creative approaches. For brand B the campaign also contained different commercials, though based on the same theme: everyday family life, with children playing and their mother doing the laundry. The explanation for the difference in effect might lie in the fact that the commercials for brand B were better lodged in the memory and so could be recalled more easily at a subsequent exposure.

The analysis resulted in an adjustment to brand A's campaign.

Exhibit 1.3

Brand A	Total number of contacts	Total number of purchases	Purchases without exposure	Purchases after 1 exposure	Purchases after 1 or more exposures	Purchases after 2 exposures	Purchases after 2 or more exposures
Total category	299,454	3,347	1,554	626	1,793	369	1,167
Brand A	102,532	568	258	108	310	62	202
Share brand A (%)	34.2	17	16.6	17.3	17.3	16.8	17.3
STAS				104	104	101	104

Table 1.2 STAS analysis of brand A (Source: 'Advertising short-term effects, findings from the German market', Commercial Communications, March 1996).

Brand B	Total number of contacts	Total number of purchases	Purchases without exposure	Purchases after 1 exposure	Purchases after 1 or more exposures	Purchases after 2 exposures	Purchases after 2 or more exposures
Total category	299,454	3,347	1,893	644	1,454	304	810
Brand B	68,243	621	316	114	305	57	191
Share brand B (%)	22.8	18.6	16.7	17.7	21	18.8	23.6
STAS				106	126	112	141

Table 1.3 STAS analysis of brand B (Source: 'Advertising short-term effects, findings from the German market', Commercial Communications, March 1996)

1.4 THE NECESSITY OF SHORT-TERM EFFECTS

The burning question is still whether effectiveness exists when no positive influence is noted, either in the very short term (within a purchasing cycle) or in the longer term (within a year). Can advertising have the effect of a time bomb, so to speak?

Jones (1995) found no indication of this so-called 'sleeper effect' in his analyses. However, in theory, campaigns with no positive short-term effects might well have helped prevent a decline in penetration and/or purchasing frequency (consolidation effects). In some situations there might even be some influence on the mental brand response, which only makes itself felt in brand behavioural response after more than a year. This is thought to be especially true for campaigns that work according to the principle of classical conditioning, which requires a large number of repetitions before certain brand associations develop.

Experts in this field differ in their opinions on this subject. Of course, tracking studies ascertain that mental brand responses can be reinforced as time goes by, under the influence of advertising campaigns. But how does the development of mental brand responses tie in with that of brand behavioural responses in the course of time? Ongoing time series for a great many campaigns, covering a good many years, would be required to establish this.

Various experts have been very much involved with the correlation between short and long-term effects. McDonald (1996b), for instance, has observed that in Jones' study, no single brand with a negative short-term effect managed to achieve growth in the number of purchases in the longer term. He believes that this confirms the need for a positive short-term response if advertising is to be effective. A long-term effect is no more, and no less, than the continuation, in time, of short-term responses.

He rejects the idea that a long-term effect might differ, in qualitative terms, from a short-term effect. In his view, advertising, if it is to be at all effective, must produce a direct effect; long-term effects are, he believes, accumulations or prolongations of the same short-term effects.

In Jones' opinion (1995), there are experienced researchers who refuse to accept that a positive short-term effect might be a condition for a positive long-term effect, believing that advertising can work in mysterious ways, possibly by achieving a delayed or 'sleeper' effect. He has little faith in research that seeks to justify this type of delayed effect (such as tracking research).

Hollis (1995a) is also of the opinion that it is unlikely that, in the absence of any short-term response, a real long-term effect might occur. He is, however, concerned that current modelling techniques do not enable short-term responses to be ascertained satisfactorily. To this end, a combination of different research techniques is needed, including, in his view, tracking and sales modelling.

1.5 LONG-TERM EFFECTS

Although there are a variety of research techniques which measure the short-term effects of advertising, such as single-source analysis, tracking and modelling techniques, it has as yet been almost impossible to establish long-term effects satisfactorily. The long-term effects of advertising on consumer behaviour are reflected, among other things, in market share, its trend, a price premium relative to comparable brands, and price elasticity. Advertising has played a vital part in the development of almost all the current major brands. Year after year they retain their sales value and gross profit, thanks, in part, to the brand values they have built up in consumers' minds over the decades.

The primary goal of advertising for these brands is often not to alter behaviour, but to consolidate existing behaviour. The long-term trend of these brands can be an indication of the effectiveness of advertising in consolidating behaviour. It should be remembered though that completely different variables in the marketing mix can also play an important part. Usually, historical data, covering long periods, is not available for either advertising activities or brand developments, neither for one's own brand nor for competitors' brands. Such information would enable us to discover the links between advertising and behaviour and to isolate the influence of advertising.

So although the long-term behavioural response is frequently the most important response, the advertising profession is at a loss when it comes to tracking it down.

Chris Baker (1984) wrote:

In practice I believe that it is impossible to quantify longer-term (behavioural) effects of advertising with any confidence. Because of this, wrongly, longer-term effects are often completely ignored in an evaluation. They are being assumed to be some sort of 'invisible bonus', which automatically accrues whatever the advertising!

And Paul Feldwick (1989) said:

All evaluation techniques are aimed at short-term trends or immediate response. This creates the illusion that the effects of sustained defensive advertising over long periods of time do not have any real existence. It never explains why the current position of the brand is as it is!

Nigel Hollis (1995a) is also alert to the problem:

The challenge of identifying long-term effects is problematic – only the convergence of results from different data sources is ever likely to do more than allow us to hypothesise about the long-term influence of advertising on sales.

However, the long-term behavioural response does not suddenly manifest itself after a long period. It is in fact the cumulative effect of activities over a succession of years. Total penetration of a brand at a certain moment is, for instance, the result of a development in the course of time in which new users are gradually won and other users are lost. However, this development can be measured from one period to another, and so is referred to as 'short-term effects'. In these cases, the long-term effect is nothing but the build-up of a series of short-term effects.

The same applies to price premium and price elasticity. They result from the gradual change in the perception of the brand's value compared with that of the alternatives, a change which can also be measured.

Yet all these measurements and analyses proceed from the present situation, or that of a few years back, and subsequently seek to discover the effect of recent or current campaigns. For example, a certain level of awareness, attitude or behaviour is taken as the starting point, and from that the short-term advertising effect is determined. This fails to take into account the role that advertising has played to reach that level and its influence on maintaining it. We must not lose sight of the fact that the 'holding effect' (confirmation of positive attitudes and buying behaviour of already brand-loyal buyers) of advertising with established brands is often the most important. In such cases it is a matter of establishing that the behaviour of loyal users does not change. The success of advertising campaigns need not always be apparent in rising sales trends. The chief objectives are often actually to prevent a downturn in sales and to maintain the premium price. Colin McDonald (1996a) rightly states:

The real long-term effect may have nothing to do with increasing share at all: success may mean keeping things level, the absence of change. I do not think Jones is saying, or could say, that 24% of his cases which had positive STAS, but no long-term effect, according to his narrow measure were therefore failures, necessarily.

In spite of the apparent consensus on the conditional nature of positive short-term effects for advertising effectiveness in the long term, it would be wrong to conclude that the absence of growth in market share in the longer term means that advertising does not work.

Jones (1995) ascertained a positive short-term effect with 70% of the campaigns he researched, while a positive trend in market share over a one-year period was measured with only 46%. So with 24% the positive short-term effect did not generate market share growth in the somewhat longer term. However, this merely indicates that more is needed than a positive response immediately following exposure to an advertisement (the STAS effect). Campaign continuity is probably the most important requirement – as Jones himself never fails to emphasise.

2 Advertising effects and research methods

Giep Franzen

2.1 THE ADVERTISING RESPONSE MATRIX

If we wish to describe methods of research into advertising effectiveness and place them in the overall process of advertising effect, a diagram of the process is helpful.

Figure 2.1 is a highly simplified representation, and divides the advertising effect process into three main levels.

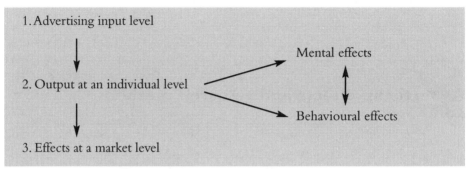

Figure 2.1 The advertising effect process

Advertising input level

Level 1 represents communication activities and can be further divided into two components. The qualitative component relates to campaign content, while the quantitative is expressed in relative opportunities to see (OTS), or gross rating points (GRPs), share of voice (SOV), and so on.

If effectiveness research is to be performed systematically, it is essential to determine the input level in time dimensions (weeks, months, quarters, years).

Output at an individual level

Level 2 depicts the responses at an individual level which form three main groups: mental advertising response, mental brand response and brand behavioural response.

Mental advertising response

This response category comprises, firstly, the individual consumer's mental reactions to the individual advertisement during and immediately after exposure, and secondly the individual consumer's aggregated reactions to the series of advertisements or campaigns to which he/she has recently been exposed (the campaign response).

Mental brand response

This category is made up of brand awareness, brand associations, brand values, brand positioning, brand relationship, attitude and behaviour intentions regarding the brand which can be partly generated by exposure to advertisements.

Brand behavioural response

This response category covers behaviour in the search for information at the fact-finding stage, actual buying behaviour, the level of brand-loyal buying behaviour and sometimes usage behaviour (frequency, usage moments) and/or ending of usage behaviour.

Effects at a market level

Level 3 is formed by the aggregate effects at a market level – the market response.

Market response

This response category relates to turnover, market share, average price, price premium the consumer is prepared to pay, price elasticity, stability of turnover, profit margin, profit, ROI (return on investment) and cash flow. In fact, market response is the aggregate of individual brand responses at the market level.

Time dimension

A time dimension in advertising effects also has to be identified.

Direct effects

Direct effects apply to the responses during and immediately after exposure to one individual advertisement. Since the response need not necessarily occur immediately after exposure (lag effect), a period of zero to two months is used in the response matrix.

Short-term effects

These effects relate to responses brought about by exposure to one or more advertisements (within one campaign), up to the moment when no further effects are noted. A period of one year is often taken. However, empirical research shows that in the second year after a campaign has ended, effects relating to that campaign can still be measured.

Long-term effects

These are a continuation and accumulation of short-term effects which are the result of exposures to different advertising campaigns for the brand over the years. It should be borne in mind that a period of one year to several years – sometimes even 15 to 20 – is needed to build up a strong brand.

No consensus of opinion exists as to exactly what periods of time the definitions short and long-term cover. Some authors take short-term to mean the direct effects, describing what happens within a year as the long-term effect. Others set a lower limit of two to three years for long-term effects. Since market responses, in particular, tend to develop slowly, it is sensible to divide effects into three periods (direct, short-term and long-term).

Creating the Advertising Response Matrix

In this way a matrix can be designed to comprise all advertising effects, which is called the *Advertising Response Matrix* (see Figure 2.2 overleaf). It contains a list and definitions of all these effects, which are described in Chapter 3. For each level in the Advertising Response Matrix there are various sources of information or research methods. Figure 2.3 contains an overview of some of the important ones. Obviously the whole series of techniques is not applicable to every brand. Neither are all the techniques available as standard practice in all markets; nor necessarily possible for practical or financial reasons. In such cases it is important to be able to place findings in a wider context and to bear in mind their significance for the entire advertising process.

The next section outlines the chief methods of effectiveness research.

2.2 RESEARCH METHODS

Pre-testing

This entails ascertaining consumer responses to individual advertisements. It usually only relates to the level of mental advertising responses (likeability, recall, personal relevance) and to a few mental brand responses (persuasion, intention to buy). The main questions concern the relevance of the measured mental brand responses in influencing buying behaviour at an individual level. Another issue is to what extent the results might forecast later effects in the market. For instance, is there a connection between pre-test results and findings from tracking and single-source research?

Can one mental response be isolated which can tell us whether advertising will be effective in influencing behaviour, regardless of the market in which and the brand for which this response is measured? Experts' opinions differ considerably on the subject. Jones (1996a) strongly advocates measuring persuasion (the pre-post attitude shift, the

Advertising input

A	Characteristics of advertisement or campaign
	    a. message and presentation characteristics
	    b. choice of media type and media weight

B	Exposure to advertisement/campaign (GRPs, OTS, SOV)

Output at an individual level

	Time dimension / Response category	Direct effects	Short-term effects	Long-term effects
C	Mental advertising responses			
D	Mental brand responses			
E	Brand behavioural responses			

Effects at a market level

F	Market responses			

Figure 2.2 Advertising Response Matrix

	Advertising input variables	Sources / research methods
A	Advertisement (campaign) characteristics Choice of media and means	Basic format variables Creative execution variables Physical variables (spot length, format, colour, etc.)
B	Advertising expenditure (in monetary terms) Exposure and reach	Advertising Association, NTC GRPs, SOV

	Output at an individual level	
C	Mental advertising responses	Concept testing Copy testing Advertising tracking
D	Mental brand responses	Brand tracking Brand monitoring
E	Brand behavioural responses	Consumer panel Single-source research

	Effects at a market level	
F	Market responses	Retail panel

Figure 2.3 Sources and/or research methods

difference between respondents' brand choices before and after seeing an advertisement). Biel (1996) declares this is outmoded and makes out a case for measuring 'self-relevance' (using cognitive response analysis, where respondents are asked to give their reactions to advertising and subsequently to classify them as positive, neutral or negative). Du Plessis (1994a, 1994b), on the other hand, swears by likeability measurements. The various mental responses, and the views of the above experts are summarised and compared in Chapter 6.

The point here is that before a particular pre-testing method is used, there must be clarity on the intended campaign effects and the objectives of the pre-test. If one wants to establish how recipients deal with an advertisement, diagnostic methods such as likeability or relevance measurements are appropriate. If one is aiming at influencing buying behaviour directly, attitude shift and/or buying intention measurements are a more likely choice.

The predictive value of pre-testing

Opinions also differ greatly on the predictive value of pre-testing. A study conducted by the Advertising Research Foundation (Haley and Baldinger, 1991) into the validity of pre-testing methods showed that likeability scores for 87% of the tested commercials resulted in a correct prediction of their effect in the marketplace. However, only five brands were included in that study, with two different commercials for each. This limited base came in for a great deal of criticism.

In a similar analysis by Kuse (1990), carried out with seven different cases, no relationship was found between likeability and effectiveness in the marketplace! However, it did establish a 100% correlation between persuasion scores and the empirically ascertained effectiveness in the marketplace.

The ARF carried out extensive research in 1993, in which pre-test scores and market development data were available for 103 cases; however, no convincing relationship was found. The great problem would seem to be the unpredictability of the behavioural response (Lodish *et al.*, 1995).

Following a validation analysis of RSC's (Research Systems Corporation) ARS Persuasion Technique, Jones (1996b) came to the conclusion that:

There is indeed good evidence for the predictive power of this technique; and there is also evidence of a progressive relationship between the size of the ARS Persuasion score and the sales results, both within brands and across brands and categories. The higher the score, the higher the sales that are likely to follow.

Thus all the above attempts to determine the predictive value of pre-testing have had varying results. Broadbent and Colman (1986) analysed 18 campaigns in the confectionery market, and concluded:

The only sure way to assess advertising is by testing and careful monitoring in the field. Experienced managers in the industry find it difficult to judge advertising without such information. It seemed to be rare for laboratory research and expert judgement to get better than random results in evaluating advertising.

The problem with all the cited studies aimed at validating pre-testing methods is that one single measuring technique has been sought to correctly predict subsequent effectiveness in the marketplace – regardless of the type of campaign or the desired response. In view of the great variety of communication strategies and basic formats, this is unrealistic. It is only possible to choose an appropriate pre-test method rationally when one knows what one wants to achieve with a specific campaign. Testing methods should be validated to some extent based on the objectives of the campaigns in question – and to my knowledge this has not been the case so far.

Hall (1997) quite rightly states:

If you do not know how you want or expect people to respond, then you cannot evaluate whether you have achieved that response, or what to do to get it.

McDonald (1992) is also of the opinion that:

Pre-testing is concerned not with prediction, but with diagnosis. How will potential buyers take to this ad: will it support the strength of the brand-image? Is it likely, other things being equal, to attract the response and/or support the image that we want, maintain the equity we have established in the brand? We have previously decided what we want our advertising to do, now we check to see whether it is capable of doing it. All the problems about how to interpret pre-tests should fall into place if we view them this way: will it do the job we set for it?

It is this approach that the authors wish to promote in this book.

Tracking research

Tracking is intended to establish whether consumers have reacted to advertising as was hoped or expected in view of the pre-test results.

Tracking research measures continuously and uses the same sets of questions over longer periods, thus producing time series of the development of what are considered to be the most essential mental responses. 'Continuous' measurement entails interviewing every week or every two weeks a large enough sample from the target group to enable appropriate representation of smaller brands with lower penetration as well. The results are analysed per measuring period, but also over longer periods (per month or two months, for instance). Such continuous measurements mean the results can be tied in with the advertising input per time unit (weeks, months), expressed as expenditure, OTS (opportunities to see) or SOV (share of voice) (Level B in the Advertising Response Matrix, Figure 2.2). Some form of intermediary response modelling can also be applied.

Tracking usually consists of measuring advertising recall (Did you see this advertising? Where did you see it?), sometimes supplemented with message recall (What did it consist of?) and likeability. In addition, elementary mental brand responses are measured: brand awareness, brand attitude and brand buying behaviour, sometimes supplemented with a few core associations (positioning).

Opinions differ on what can and cannot be measured with tracking. Since most tracking research is conducted by phone, the questions must be limited (if interviews last longer than 10 to 15 minutes, respondents tend to become irritated. Although it is limited as regards diagnostic scope, it is often a good means of checking whether advertising is effective.

Tracking does not enable us to measure the development of mental brand responses (associations, emotions, attitudes, brand relationships) in all their subtleties either. In that respect we must rely on larger-scale usage and attitude measurements which are determined every one or two years. This restriction makes it difficult to ascertain the influence of advertising on brand image through tracking. It is generally a short cut: has the advertising penetrated and has it led to a change in brand awareness and brand attitude?

A combination of pre-testing of individual advertisements and tracking of advertising effects in time can, however, provide more in-depth insight into advertising effectiveness, thus facilitating adjustment of both content and media weight.

Market response modelling

At the end of the day, an advertiser is interested in discovering to what extent advertising input influences market responses. With market response modelling, time series are developed of the explanatory variables in the marketing mix, such as trends in advertising investments, price, promotions, distribution, and the dependent market responses, like sales volume, market share and total sales value.

Statistical analyses help to pinpoint the influence of explanatory variables on dependent variables. What, for instance, is the influence of advertising expenditure on market share?

If sales is the dependent variable, we refer to sales response modelling. If the variable is a mental brand response, such as brand awareness, we refer to intermediary response modelling. The latter uses advertising tracking in particular, because tracking focuses on isolating the influence of ad awareness or brand awareness and brand attitude rather than including sales as a variable.

'True' market response modelling seeks to identify all the variables which might influence the development of the individual brands, and then to develop time series of these variables. Econometric analysis and time series analyses can be used to determine the correlations between the variables and, on that basis, a model can be designed to provide the best possible representation of the way the market works. This process should be seen as the trying out of hundreds of models, with different combinations of variables, in search of a model which fits, statistically and logically.

Obviously if this type of market model is to be designed, historical and well-organised numerical data is required. Such a model needs time series of many possible, explanatory variables, relating both to the factors which affect the market as a whole, and to the development of each brand in that market. The lack of such data and the tremendous effort required to collect this kind of numerical material systematically are two important reasons why market response modelling is still used relatively little.

Not surprisingly, modelling with a view to determining advertising effects usually amounts to sales response modelling using a limited set of explanatory variables. Generally connections between levels B and F in the Advertising Response Matrix (Figure 2.2, page 30) are involved.

As sales responses depend on far more variables than advertising alone, modelling used solely to establish advertising effectiveness often only applies to intermediary responses, such as brand awareness and brand attitudes. In fact, it amounts to revealing correlations between results of tracking research and input variables which are relatively easy to chart. For example, the connection between the number of GRPs and spontaneous awareness relates to levels B and D in the Advertising Response Matrix.

Objective yet limited modelling like this is preferable to the assumption, based merely on intuition, that there is some correlation between the variables. However, it must always be remembered that we can only ascertain the ultimate effectiveness of advertising by determining its effect on buying behaviour. Only sales response modelling can provide such an insight.

Modelling may have enabled us to identify the variables which influence sales, but it has not yet told us which advertising characteristics make a campaign successful or unsuccessful. This requires research into the response to individual advertisements.

Sales response modelling is based on short-term fluctuations in sales (it usually applies to one or two-month periods), thus disregarding the real long-term effects. Modelling begins at a certain level of sales, after which the short-term influence of explanatory variables on those sales is determined. Such modelling thus ignores the function advertising had in achieving this level – and which it probably also has in maintaining it. Sales response modelling can give insight into the variables which have recently influenced sales, but not into the contribution of advertising a little longer ago to the development of a brand's market position. It can be a very useful tool for analysing advertising effectiveness in the short or medium term, but is not very useful with regard to long-term effects.

Advertising effect is more than an 'echo' in short-term sales figures. It is apparent in the longer-term sales trend. It may well be possible to eliminate the short-term effects of certain marketing activities (for instance, advertising and promotions) from the trend, but not, as yet, to establish a connection between advertising activities and basic sales in the longer term.

Single-source research

Single-source research, as applied in Germany, the US and, since 1996, in the UK, for instance, makes use of electronic devices to register the television advertising exposures and brand purchases, and compare them directly (Levels B and E in the Advertising Response Matrix). Comparison of the buying responses at various levels of exposure enables us to ascertain the influence of advertising directly.

No interviews are held, and so we do not know what happens in consumers' minds. Such single-source research is based on the 'stimulus response' model and so provides hardly any insight into why a certain effect occurs (or not), or pointers for the adjustment of campaign content. These require different research methods.

A special application of single-source research is what is termed 'split-cable' testing, in which the sample is divided into two subsamples. In one, advertising input is varied (different advertisements, change in the number of GRPs) and the effects are compared with those in the control sample, in which the 'normal' programme was carried out. This method is widely applied in the US (see Exhibit 2.1).

Single-source research is the only valid method for determining the influence of advertising on individual buying behaviour. Its application is also the most relevant in situations in which a short-term effect is expected or aimed for. The more one pursues a delayed effect in the longer term, the longer one should carry out single-source testing.

Although the underlying basic idea is simple, single-source research is highly complicated to carry out. It entails compiling extensive information and extremely complicated analyses. If, for instance, one wishes to establish whether there has been an opportunity to see a specific commercial at an individual level, it is not only necessary to register long-term viewing behaviour (a year or longer) from one second to another (or per 10 seconds) (ie, which channel was watched), but it is also necessary to register

Split-cable testing

Alternative television campaigns can be tested as to both content and intensity by means of a household panel, split into two subgroups.

The way the sample is split is based on demographic characteristics, past buying behaviour and shopping behaviour. Care is taken that the two subgroups represent these characteristics to the same degree, which makes it possible to relate the observed differences in advertising effectiveness directly to advertising input.

The use of the split-cable technique means advertising input can be varied in the two subsamples. For example, one half does not receive any ads for the brand in question, the other receives a number which coincides with the average number of GRPs at a national level. Alternatively, the number of GRPs in one subgroup is doubled; or the two subgroups are exposed to the same advertising pressure, but with a different campaign content.

The differences in effectiveness are analysed from week to week, and the study usually lasts a year. Reception (OTS, message) of competing brands' campaigns is also carefully monitored, as are the concomitant promotional activities.

When the analyses are carried out, the effects of these different activities are identified and isolated from the advertising effects of the brand that is the focus of the research.

Exhibit 2.1

what could be seen on every channel. In view of the ever-growing number of available channels and the concomitant fragmentation of viewing behaviour, the problems of data collection and coding are considerable. One wonders if the method is still viable, even in the US. The Adlab panel in the UK was closed down because the industry was not prepared to pay for it. In 1996, however, Taylor Nelson AGB, in a joint venture with Meridian Broadcasting, commenced a new single-source service: TVSPAN. It remains to be seen whether it will find sufficient industry support.

In smaller countries, where television advertising is often less dominant than in the US, for instance, market research agencies do not offer single-source testing of this type. Nor is it likely to become available in the future, in view of the growing problems it is encountering. It is, however, still being applied in Germany, in a geographical test market, which lends itself to split-cable testing. An example of a single-source application in Germany can be found in Chapter 1 (see Exhibit 1.3, page 22).

2.3   GENERAL PRINCIPLES

A central place for brand equity

Advertising is always a means, never an end. The end is the brand. Whether or not, and to what extent, advertising works can never be deduced from mental advertising responses alone – research at a brand level is always needed. At best, we can seek to ascertain which advertising responses are appropriate for achieving certain brand responses, using as our starting point empirical, established relationships between, for example, pre-test results and brand measurements.

The development of brand equity must also have a central position in effectiveness research. We use the term brand equity to describe the meaning which a brand has in a specific market for consumers, and which is reflected in their buying behaviour and attitude towards that brand, as well as in the results the brand achieves in the market as a consequence. In particular, an effort must always be made to tie advertising input in with buying behaviour. All research which is limited to measuring mental responses only is in danger of being based on incorrect assumptions concerning their influence on buying behaviour.

A systematic and consistent approach

Effectiveness research requires a systematic approach. It is essential to determine as accurately as possible which variables affect communication effectiveness, and this development should then be followed consistently in time. It is usually difficult to formulate a reliable research programme based only on subjective hypotheses regarding the correlations between the variables. This implies that, when effectiveness research is initiated, a broad-based approach is needed; after which, the relevant variables can be identified, if possible by modelling.

It is important to apply the measuring tools consistently. Only then will it be possible to understand how a brand develops, and how new advertisements score compared with older ones. Only then can we begin a process of 'cumulative learning'.

Advertising frameworks as the point of departure

Advertising campaigns are worked out from a view shared by all involved on the nature of the intended brand responses, and the advertising characteristics which are instrumental in achieving those responses. The parties involved think implicitly in terms of a specific advertising framework, but if the response to individual advertisements is to be researched, these assumptions must be made explicit. This will facilitate appropriate attuning of the questions and evaluation of the results.

The significance of recall, persuasion, likeability and relevance scores does, after all, depend directly on the intended or assumed effect of the campaign in question.

Competing brands

Advertising for a brand never works in isolation. Buying behaviour within a category is influenced by all the brands operating in that category, and the closer the relative positioning of brands, the more they interact. If we wish to discover the effect of an advertising campaign on a brand, we must involve the activities of competing brands in the measurements. When quantitative input variables are involved (GRPs, OTS, SOV) this is generally adhered to, but when mental responses are measured (as with copy testing and tracking research), the major competitors should be researched and analysed in relation to one another as well.

Understandability

Decisions on advertising campaigns are usually taken by many involved parties together, and 'go/no go' decisions tend to be taken by managers who are little involved in the processes of advertising policy development and advertising research. Whatever the research and analysis methods, it is important to make them accessible in conceptual terms for these 'involved outsiders'. Findings should be presented in such a way that they are consistent with the marketing team's intuitive premises. Obviously they need not coincide with the team members' implicit assumptions, but it should be possible to follow and understand them in that context.

Joining forces

A good researcher not only knows about research methods and techniques, but also has insight into the content of the material to be tested. Advertising research especially often goes wrong because the researchers know too little about communication and persuasion processes. This book will make it clear that the possible research questions are infinite. If researchers are to make a wise selection, they must have a good idea of the relevance of the different variables, and an overall picture of the communication process. They would certainly be advised to spend a great deal of time with the marketing team and advertising experts, including, of course, the advertising agency. Communication research conducted from within an ivory tower or with alleged authority only generates resistance – and that is the last thing that anyone wants.

2.4   CONCLUSIONS

There is no one simple form of advertising research which is generally applicable and which might indicate the degree of effectiveness of an advertisement or campaign, as regards influencing buying behaviour and what this depends on. It just does not exist – and will probably never be found.

Research into advertising effects will always resemble detective work: a matter of slowly piecing together a picture from different research methods and separate bits of information – a picture which also contains quite a few gaps and working hypotheses.

One of the principal things which cannot be ascertained at present is the long-term effect of advertising on sales; one wonders whether it ever will be possible. But knowledge of short-term effects is growing fast, as is that of the research and analysis methods which help to trace these effects and secure them for future use as far as possible.

In view of the revealing results of extensive single-source research in the US mentioned earlier, there is every reason for the individual advertiser to try to work out a programme of systematic effectiveness research. It is not only a matter of precluding the risk of ineffective advertising, but, more especially, of raising effectiveness as much as possible.

McDonald (1992) has said that there is only one way to evaluate advertising better tomorrow, and that is to continue to do one's utmost to fathom out what is happening today. It has been known for around a century, McDonald suggests, that it is difficult, tricky, costly, time-consuming and perhaps even impossible.

However, where there's a will, there's a way. This book is intended to contribute towards finding that way.

3 The Advertising Response Matrix

Giep Franzen
Cindy Goessens
Mary Hoogerbrugge

3.1 INTRODUCTION

The advertising profession is characterised by a lack of communication among those who practise it. A survey among 22 advertising practitioners, on advertiser and agency sides alike, reveals that one cause of this is the fact that each uses different technical jargon, so that none of the effects of an ad or campaign are defined in the same way (Binnendijk, 1995). Consequently, misunderstandings can arise about the course of advertising policy and the desired advertising effects. At the same time, there is no comprehensive, cohesive overview of possible advertising effects. The result is that decisions on objectives, strategies and research programmes are often highly subjective, fragmented and opportunistic in character.

An additional problem is the wide gap in the commercial communication field between the practical and the academic worlds. In academic circles interest is often focused on the psychological processes which occur when recipients process advertising. These processes relate to the individual advertisement or the overall campaign; they are not usually related to the effects which advertisers ultimately aim for – changes in buying behaviour caused by the advertising campaign.

In an effort to facilitate dialogue between practitioners and academics, we have drawn up an overview of all possible advertising effects. Each party can situate their specific field of interest within the spectrum of advertising effects, based on this overview. The effects are placed within the Advertising Response Matrix, as briefly described in Chapter 2 (see Figure 2.2, page 30).

It must be stressed that this is not intended to be a contribution to the theories on the processing or effects of advertising. We do not examine if or how these effects come about, nor do we comment on the validity of defined effects in the light of effective influencing of behaviour. However, the response matrix can enhance readers' awareness of the scope of existing theories on advertising processing.

Each advertising effect/response is defined. The idea is to tie it in with theoretical definitions, as well as with prevailing definitions in marketing and market research practice. As dozens of definitions prove to be in use for many concepts, it was often necessary to make choices.

This chapter describes, on the basis of the Advertising Response Matrix, all the effects/responses which may occur following exposure to advertising or advertising campaigns. The word 'campaign' is used if specific effects are aimed for, within a specific period, in specific target groups, by repeatedly 'inserting' advertisements in the media (Smit, 1994, p 40).

Section 3.2 looks at mental advertising responses, section 3.3 mental brand responses, section 3.4 brand behavioural responses and section 3.5 market responses. With some responses, readers are referred to the appendices for further information on the various forms of response. Each response description uses existing overviews and does not include further comment on the completeness or validity of the response. The description results in a final definition, which is designated by the symbol ○.

Wherever appropriate, available research techniques can be used to measure the effects in question. The intention is not to provide exhaustive information on all the existing research techniques, to discuss them in detail, or to comment on their relevance and validity. The present overview is merely intended as a basis to work from when the significance of specific advertising studies is evaluated.

Readers will soon discover that practically every type of research only casts light on part of the intended effects of advertising or on the factors which are necessary for it to work (see Figure 3.1).

3.2 MENTAL ADVERTISING RESPONSES

Advertising effects can be roughly divided into effects of *processing* and *effectiveness* (Pieters and van Raaij, 1992; Smit, 1994). Processing effects relate to exposure to the ad, while effectiveness effects relate to the mental and behavioural responses to the product and the brand which can be generated by exposure to one or more ads.

This section focuses on the processing effects, which are referred to as 'mental advertising responses' because this term explicitly points to the response in the consumer's mind. Memory plays an important part in these responses.

3.2.1 Memory

The object here is not to ascertain exactly what takes place in people's memories when they are confronted with the things surrounding them in everyday life. Memory experts are still grappling with many questions in this field. The aim instead is to describe succinctly and simply the processes which take place in the memory, in order to give the reader some idea of 'memory activity' when people are exposed to advertisements.

Sensory memory and short-term memory

Before advertising effects can take place, the consumer must have been exposed to the advertising message. The chance of exposure to an ad, opportunity to see (OTS), refers to the fact that consumers find themselves in the proximity of the advertisement, in such a way that one or more senses might be activated. The opportunities to see advertisements are considered to be characteristics of the type of medium, and actual exposure to the ad will depend on whether the senses do in fact 'encounter' the ad or commercial.

Attention

From the moment of exposure to an advertisement, a mental reaction can occur as a result of that exposure. Initially this reaction consists solely of sensory perception and coding.

We are constantly scanning our surroundings, unconsciously and automatically, to determine whether there is something deserving our focused attention. This primary processing is also known as 'pre-attentive' processing, because as yet there is no call for attention as such. During scanning we notice words, images and sounds, and use our sensory memory to code them. The only mental action we perform is to determine the relevance of what we perceive: 'what is it?', 'who is it?' and 'for whom is it?' We do not do much else with these data, because every word and image contains more information than we are inclined to use or process further at this stage (Schiffman and Kanuk, 1987). The reactions (cognitions) which come about are stored briefly in the sensory memory and usually disappear within a second. The attention which, unconsciously, is paid to a stimulus during this 'fact-finding' reaction is termed *primary* or *initial attention*.

Time dimension Advertising response category	Direct effects	Short-term effects	Long-term effects
C **Mental advertising response**	• Primary attention • Secondary attention • Advertising awareness awareness of: – content – presentation • Attitude towards the ad: – content (likeability of message) – presentation (execution likeability)	• Advertising awareness awareness of: – ad content – ad presentation • Emotional responses • Campaign awareness awareness of: – content – presentation • Attitude towards advertising campaign(s) • Advertising involvement	• Campaign awareness • Attitude towards advertising campaign(s)
D **Mental brand response**	• Information intention • Buying intention	• Brand awarenesss • Brand associations: – product-related associations – symbolic associations • Feelings towards brand • Brand positioning • Brand attitude – brand preference – satisfaction • Brand behaviour tendency – buying intention • Brand relationship – involvement • Brand salience	• Brand awareness • Brand associations: – product-related associations – symbolic associations • Feelings towards brand • Brand positioning • Brand attitude – brand preference – satisfaction • Brand behaviour tendency – buying intention • Brand relationship – involvement • Brand salience
E **Brand behavioural response**	• Fact-finding behaviour • Trial purchases	• Trial purchases • Repeat purchases • Share of customer	• Continuation of repeat purchases • Share of customer • Brand loyalty
F **Market response**	• Sales • Turnover	• Sales • Turnover • Distribution • Penetration • Market share	• Sales • Turnover • Distribution • Penetration • Market share • Price • Price premium • Price elasticity • Gross profit • Net profit • Profit margin • Cash flow • Yield on total capital • Financial brand value • Brand equity

Figure 3.1 The Advertising Response Matrix

At some point we may perceive something which stops us in our tracks for a brief moment, for whatever reason, so that we focus on that stimulus (an advertisement, for example). This fact-finding response is also known as PAR (Primary Affective Reaction). The pupils of the eye widen and the lens is focused – we concentrate on the stimulus. At this point attention (we deliberately pay attention) is involved: this is termed *secondary* or *sustained attention*.

While paying secondary attention to a certain stimulus, our senses continue scanning the immediate surroundings, and we process these environmental stimuli 'pre-attentively'. If we happen to perceive something that merits secondary attention, we will then focus our attention on that stimulus.

Secondary or sustained attention is the process in which one sensory input is selected from many others and moved into a person's consciousness (Glass and Holyoak, 1986). Often this fact-finding reaction lasts for less than a second. Within that second we ask ourselves whether the ad is of any importance or interest to us. If we decide we no longer wish to focus our attention on the stimulus, the information is likely to disappear, leaving no trace in the memory.

It should be borne in mind that, in their definition of primary or initial, and secondary or sustained attention, the authors have indirectly taken the working memory (referred to hereafter as 'short-term memory', abbreviated to STM) to represent 'the conscious'. In the working/short-term memory, sensory perceptions of the world around us meet the inner world or long-term memory (LTM) of the individual, where interpretation and evaluation of stimuli take place.

○ *Primary/initial attention*
 The process of sensory perception of an advertisement occurring unconsciously and automatically, and in which the perceived stimuli are stored for a very short time in the sensory memory (unconscious perception).

○ *Secondary/sustained attention*
 The process of sensory perception of an advertisement with a certain deliberate focus and duration in which the perceived stimuli are processed in the working/short-term memory (STM) and possibly stored in the long-term memory (LTM) (conscious perception).

Long-term memory

If someone decides a stimulus is worth paying more attention to, the duration of attention will to some extent determine whether it is stored only in the STM, or in the LTM as well. The STM has a limited capacity, and the information stored there can only be maintained by means of such processing techniques as repetition, coding, transfer, storage and recall (Pieters and van Raaij, 1992; Schiffman and Kanuk, 1987). Repeating information increases the amount of information transferred from the STM to the LTM. Repeating is defined as 'silent, mental repetition of material' (Schiffman and Kanuk, 1987).

Once it is present in the LTM, information can remain there for days, weeks, months, years, even a lifetime. The information in the LTM is constantly being organised and reorganised when new information enters and new links (associations) come about between the different types of information.

Forgetting

Sometimes we fail to find something in our memory bank. It seems as though our recollection of it has disappeared. However, forgetting is more a matter of our having lost our way – of not finding the recollection – than of brain cells dying off. In view of the limited capacity of the STM, forgetting can also result from competition for attention. In order to keep the path to a recollection open, the information must be repeated regularly to enable us to reach the recollection easily and to ward off competition from other information.

Repetition

Countless studies have shown that, with repetition, stimuli which are only processed at the unconscious, pre-attentive level can end up being stored briefly in the STM, and possibly in the LTM. This response does not result from cognitive processing of stimuli and evaluation processes, but from mere exposure. This is particularly important for advertising processing. Many advertisements only attract primary attention.

Measuring attention

It is only really possible to measure the process in which attention is paid at the moment it actually occurs. Since it is almost impossible to directly determine, in natural circumstances, whether and how much attention people pay to ads, such attention can only be measured in laboratory tests. A possible method is that of eye-tracking, electronically measuring the number of eye fixations, the duration of single fixations and the sequence of fixations. It is not possible with this method to measure whether, as a result of the attention paid, information is stored in the STM and/or LTM, and what the content of that information is. And that, when all is said and done, is exactly what interests the advertiser.

3.2.2 Emotional responses

Emotional responses relate to subjective experiences of advertising. The human reaction or response to stimuli is what is experienced as emotions. In general there are two types of stimuli which can trigger emotional responses:
- a displayed emotion;
- persons, objects, situations, actions, animals, sounds or images which evoke an emotion.

The latter category includes stimuli (babies and young animals, for instance) which trigger an emotional response with the majority of recipients, and stimuli which *could* trigger an emotional response, depending on the situation or the individual, such as certain types of music, or colours.

Exposure to an advertisement can also evoke emotional responses. In this case the advertising stimuli (relating to sender, message or presentation) are the triggers.

An emotional response is characterised by three facets (Pieters and van Raaij, 1988, 1992): activation (or arousal), impression and expression.

Activation indicates the intensity of the evoked emotion. *Impression* relates to the inner feeling or awareness (experience) of an emotion. The impression can be split into the direction (approach towards or avoidance of) and content (happiness–anger) of the emotion. And lastly, *expression* covers the perceivable, physical expression of the evoked emotion.

Emotional responses take one of three forms, depending on the degree of physical activation, the impression and expression of the experienced emotion:

- primary emotions;
- specific feelings;
- holistic affect.

Primary emotions are characterised by a high degree of physical arousal, great intensity and specific content. With holistic affect, however, physical arousal is low, intensity slight and the content is general. Specific feelings fall between the two as regards arousal, intensity and content.

When a person is exposed to advertising, primary emotions and specific feelings are chiefly involved. Holistic affect refers to the general attitude towards a person, object or situation (ad, product, brand, and so on). This overall attitude is discussed in section 3.2.6.

The emotions generated by exposure to an advertisement can have a tactical function in that they can facilitate the consumer's processing of the ad. Emotions then lead to activation of attention, sustained attention, more profound processing and better recollection.

In addition, emotions can have a strategic function. This does not entail experiencing emotions oneself, as a result of exposure to an advertisement or brand, but the emotional responses which are connected to/associated with the 'sender' (brand). This linking of the brand to emotional responses is the consequence of repeated exposure to the brand and the concomitant emotions. The strategic function of emotions will be discussed in more detail in section 3.3.4.

Categorising emotions

The emotional responses which people experience are many and varied. Several attempts have been made to classify all manner of emotions into categories or 'basic emotions', but the problem is that emotions do not have one typical symptom or set of symptoms. Each individual experiences emotions in a unique way. However, research has shown that individuals do have a consistent way of describing different emotions (Frijda, 1993).

Russel and Starkman (1990) have drawn up a list of 26 different categories of emotions. They use a two-dimensional field for these categories, these dimensions being active–passive and positive–negative (Franzen, 1994, p 82). The 26 categories of emotions and the perceptual chart can be found in Appendix I.

Mano (1996) carried out a hierarchical cluster analysis with 26 emotions, concluding that eight words representing emotions were enough to measure the emotional response to advertisements. A hierarchical cluster analysis involves combining phenomena (like emotions) into groups or clusters on the basis of their similarities, and constructing a hierarchy of these clusters. (Mano's scales are included in Appendix I.)

Appendix I is completed by the four categories of emotions described by Edell and Chapman Moore (1991), and an overview of the eight basic emotions described by Plutchik in 1958 (Aans, 1996, p 46).

Measuring emotions

The choice of measuring method is determined by the emotional aspect (activation, impression or expression) of interest to the researcher. The different aspects cannot be measured at the same moment using the same method. Each aspect requires an approach of its own. Broadly speaking, there are five different methods:

- behaviour observation;
- physiological;
- verbal;
- projective;
- quasi-physiological.

3.2.3 Advertising awareness

First and foremost, 'advertising awareness' signifies consciousness of advertising and so the presence of cognitions concerning the advertisement in the STM (secondary or sustained attention). It also refers to the respondent's ability to retrieve information stored in the LTM and return it to the STM; to recollect the ad. So awareness involves storage of information in the LTM and the fact that the individual can retrieve it into the STM.

Retrieving information from the LTM to the STM

An individual is not aware of the information stored in the LTM and will have to search actively in order to become aware of it again. The information then returns briefly to the STM (consciousness). Different stimuli can set off a search or retrieval process:

- the person himself/herself;
- another person in his or her immediate surroundings;
- a trigger – words, images or sounds from the immediate surroundings, which do not originate from the person in question or another person (for example, a logo, music or packaging).

Information retrieval can be conscious and deliberate, or unconscious and automatic. Exhibit 3.1 contains a few examples illustrating how different stimuli evoke the recollection of an advertisement.

- ○ *Advertising awareness*
    - The presence of cognitions and/or feelings concerning the advertisement in the STM during perception (secondary or sustained attention, or cognitions and/or feelings which are transferred by a retrieval process (spontaneous or aided) from the LTM to the STM.
    - The presence of cognitions and/or feelings about the ad in the LTM and the capacity to return that information to the STM (the return of that information need not actually take place – yet – contrary to the previous situation).

Retrieval of information from the memory

Person (conscious)
I am making a shopping list, decide I need oranges and try to remember whether I have recently seen an ad for a supermarket where oranges are on special offer.

Person (unconscious)
I am making a shopping list, decide I need oranges and suddenly I recall the Safeway ad I saw on television the day before yesterday.

Other person (conscious)
Someone asks me if I'm familiar with the new ad for Volkswagen. I try to remember whether I am (this generally occurs in research situations).

Other person (unconscious)
I hear the word Volkswagen and immediately think of their fantastic new advertising.

Trigger (conscious)
I hear a tune on the radio and immediately think: 'Where have I heard that before?' I try to remember and realise it's the jingle of the Levi's ad.

Trigger (unconscious)
I see the Hovis logo and automatically think of the ad in which the delivery bike bumps down the cobbled street.

Exhibit 3.1

Explicit and implicit memory

Krishnan and Chakravarti (1993, p 216) distinguish between 'implicit' and 'explicit' memory:

These two forms are seen not as memory 'stores' per se, but as varieties of memory inferred through examination of the patterns of associations and dissociations between various memory tests.

The difference between the implicit and explicit memory is embodied in the question whether the consumer is aware (or not) of the influence exposure to the advertisement has on the behaviour he/she displays towards the advertised product or brand.

With the implicit memory, the consumer is not aware of the behavioural effect the ad has. As a result, he or she cannot attribute the observed behaviour to that exposure – 'traces of the ad-viewing episode are revealed by the consumer without consciously remembering it' (Krishnan and Chakravarti, 1993, p 217). If the consumer does recall the 'ad-viewing episode', these authors refer to explicit memory. Explicit memory contains two categories: *explicit intentional memory* and *explicit involuntary memory*. The former entails a conscious effort on the consumer's behalf to recall the earlier encoding episode (exposure to and processing of the ad), while recollection occurs unconsciously in the latter (see Exhibit 3.1).

Measuring advertising awareness

Advertising awareness can be measured by memory tests, which include techniques measuring recall and recognition. Although these terms are widely used, it would be more appropriate to refer to 'aided' and 'unaided' recall. Recognition can be seen as a form of aided recall.

Aided recall (including recognition) relates to the consumer's capacity to confirm earlier exposure to the advertisement(s) or campaign(s), when given an 'advertising cue', such as a description of the ad, or a key visual. If the advertisement itself is also shown, or an ad which 'personifies' the entire campaign, the term advertising recognition is referred to.

Strictly speaking, recognition is not a criterion of awareness. After all, it means that a consumer has had to be aided in recalling something into his or her consciousness. However, in practice recognition is considered to be and is used as an awareness criterion.

Spontaneous/unaided advertising recall is the consumer's capacity to name or describe the entire advertisement or parts of it, for a particular product group/brand and/or time dimension, plus, possibly, place dimension (medium type).

Top-of-mind advertising awareness (TOMA) is measured when the respondent is asked to name the first advertisement that comes to mind if asked to think of a certain product group. In that way, it will be clear how the advertising for a certain brand stands out in the memory from other ads in the market.

Topicality is the term used to describe how advertisements stand out compared to others.

Indirect tests

Recall and recognition methods refer explicitly in their questioning to exposure to the ad (ad-viewing episode). Krishnan and Chakravarti (1993) call these methods 'direct tests'. The word 'advertising' always features in the questions, meaning that the respondent will consciously search for relevant information in his or her memory.

It is also interesting to see whether advertising exposure has led to storage in the memory without asking the respondent to think back to the ad. This can be done by *indirect tests*, such as the word completion task. Respondents are given a list of words (including the brand name of the ad or ads they have viewed), but with each word missing the final letter. Two groups of respondents (one which has seen the ad and one which has not) then complete all the words as fast as possible. If the group that saw the ads is better than the control group at completing the brand name correctly, this is taken as proof of memory storage as a result of ad exposure.

As Krishnan and Chakravarti stated (1993, p 219), 'ad exposure affected task behavior without conscious awareness of the ad-viewing episode'.

3.2.4 Awareness of the content of the advertisement or campaign

Establishing recognition or recall of an advertisement or campaign is a matter of noting whether consumers have registered the words, images and/or sounds used. What interests us, when memory storage of the ad's content is involved, is the knowledge consumers have acquired and the feelings they have formed and stored, based on that registration.

The content of the advertisement or campaign is threefold:
- The *sender/origin* of the advertisement or campaign ('For what brand/product group/service has the ad or campaign been made?'). So this can be defined as the association between the advertisement and the correct brand.
- The *message* of the advertisement or campaign ('What does the ad say/convey?'). Registration of the advertisement's message is called 'main-copy-point awareness'. It can relate to:
  - *Instrumental stimuli*
    All verbal, visual or auditive information applying to the concrete characteristics, effect and effectiveness of the product/brand/service and its application/use;
  - *Symbolic stimuli*
    Stimuli representing certain types of users, their characteristics and skills (social stimuli); and stimuli associating the use of the product/brand with certain (social) situations or circumstances (situational stimuli).
- The *presentation* of the message ('How is the message conveyed?'). Presentation relates to all the characteristics of an advertisement or campaign concerning the way in which the content (message) is communicated. This includes presentation of the instrumental as well as the symbolic stimuli. It incorporates the technique, persons/actors, situations, actions, music, voices, basic advertising format, executional elements and storyline of the ad.

○ *Awareness of the 'sender' of the advertisement or campaign*
Storage in the STM/LTM of the brand for which the ad or campaign has been made.

○ *Awareness of the message of the advertisement or campaign*
Storage in the STM/LTM of registered words/images/sounds and the meanings associated with them which relate to the content of the ad (message) of a certain brand/product group/service, and the knowledge and/or feelings which are formed and stored based on that registration.

○ *Awareness of presentation of the advertisement or campaign*
Memory storage of registered words/images/sounds and the meanings associated with them, which relate to the way in which the content is presented and/or the knowledge and feelings which are formed and stored based on that registration.

3.2.5 Attitude towards an advertisement or campaign

Attitude stands for a general and lasting (consistent over time) positive, neutral or negative evaluation of an object, person, institution or event. The attitude is the evaluative judgment (favourable/unfavourable; positive/negative) that an individual forms about an object, person or subject based on the information obtained.

Ajzen (1991) describes the term as: 'an individual's disposition to respond favourably or unfavourably to an object, person, institution, or event, or any other discriminable aspect of the individual's world.'

According to the three-component attitude model, attitude is an evaluative state which intervenes between certain stimuli and certain responses. A distinction is made between a *cognitive*, an *affective* and a *conative* component. The *cognitive* component entails knowledge in the form of beliefs concerning the characteristics of the object, person or subject: 'discoveries about the object, person or subject.' The *affective* component relates to the feelings experienced during exposure to the object, person or subject: 'feelings about the object, person or subject.' The *conative* component refers to the aspects that regulate behaviour, such as behavioural intent.

As regards advertisements, the distinction between the cognitive and affective attitude component is important because an individual describing the ad as 'amusing' is not necessarily 'amused' by it. It can be a cognitive judgment, but not necessarily an experienced feeling. Real emotions and experienced feelings can only be measured at the moment they occur. Questions about emotions or feelings usually activate cognitive memories of previously experienced emotions, or cognitive judgments of ads which express certain emotions. The behavioural/conative component is scarcely in evidence in research into attitudes about the advertisement.

○ *Attitude towards the advertisement (AAD)*
The favourable or unfavourable overall evaluation of the advertisement which is expressed as a degree of advertising appreciation.

○ *Attitude towards the advertising campaign*
The favourable or unfavourable overall evaluation of the campaign which is expressed as a degree of campaign appreciation.

Attitude is considered to be an important variable because it steers behaviour and is seen as an inclination towards certain behaviour. According to Fishbein and Ajzen (1975) the social norm and experienced barriers will determine whether or not the behaviour in question is exhibited. However, behaviour can also influence attitude. After all, attitude is based on knowledge and feelings which are acquired from behavioural experience, among other things – 'people buy what they like and grow to like what they buy'.

A consumer's attitude towards an advertisement or campaign is also important in influencing brand attitude. Experimental research has shown that such influence does indeed exist, is in fact not inconsiderable, and affects brand attitude both directly and indirectly.

A positive attitude towards the ad (or advertising appreciation) is termed likeability (Goessens, 1994). Accordingly, 'dislikeability' relates to a negative attitude towards the advertisement.

Measuring attitude

Schlinger (1979a, 1979b) developed the Viewer Response Profile (VRP) (see Appendix III) with which to measure 'attitude to an advertisement'. This measures affective reactions to advertisements, concentrating on the emotional component of the communication effect. A list of statements is used (Likert items) and respondents indicate through a numbered scale to what extent they agree or disagree with the statements. Scales are usually from 1–5 or 1–7. For example: 1 = fully agree, 2 = agree, 3 = neither agree nor disagree, 4 = disagree, 5 = fully disagree (see Chapter 7, section 7.7.2 for more information on Likert scales).

Appendix III also contains Wells' Reaction Profile for printed media (1975) and Leavitt's Commercial Profile for television commercials (1970).

Attitude towards content

Consumers' attitudes towards an advertisement or campaign are also determined by their attitudes towards its message and/or presentation.

○ *Attitude towards the message of an advertisement or campaign*
Evaluative judgments and/or evaluatively experienced feelings focusing specifically on the characteristics of an advertisement's message (instrumental and symbolic stimuli).

○ *Attitude towards the presentation of the advertisement or campaign*
Evaluative judgments and/or evaluatively experienced feelings focusing specifically on characteristics of the presentation of the message.

This split in overall attitude relating either to the message or the presentation is also applied to likeability – *message likeability* and *execution* or *presentation likeability*. Research has shown that the ad content is appreciated if consumers consider it to be meaningful, personally relevant, convincing, credible, effective and worth remembering (Franzen, 1992a, pp 214–224). Variations in the style of execution, such as music, actors, actions and visual effects, arouse affective reactions in the consumer, including 'warm', 'lively' and 'original' (Goessens, 1994).

3.2.6 Advertising involvement

Although dozens of definitions have been provided in the last ten years or so for the term 'advertising involvement', there is still a great deal of confusion about its meaning. The present authors assume that involvement is a characteristic of the individual – entailing involvement with a subject, person or object.

When advertising involvement is being addressed, the important factors are the characteristics relating to the advertisement's content: how is that content presented in the context of the consumer's personal life?

Advertising involvement is determined by other forms of involvement. A list of possible causes of advertising involvement follows:

- The advertised product or brand is important to the consumer.
- The advertisement or campaign emphasises the functional performance of the product/brand (utilitarian or cognitive involvement).
- The advertisement or campaign appeals to the motivation 'to express a self-image', either real or ideal (value-expressive or affective form of involvement) (Park and Young, 1986, in Muehling *et al.*, 1993).
- The advertisement or campaign represents a value. This is the case if advertising involvement is accounted for by performance characteristics (execution and medium involvement).

○ *Advertising involvement*
This relates to the degree of personal relevance of the advertisement or campaign to the consumer. It is the extent to which the ad in some way ties in with values which are important to the consumer (concerns, interests). Advertising involvement is a consumer characteristic.

Measuring involvement

Advertising involvement is generally measured by scale techniques. Generally Likert scales and semantic differentials are used. With semantic differentials, respondents are asked to give their opinion on the ad by means of five or seven-point scales, with pairs of words or statements at either end which relate to the ad (see section 7.7.2).

Since there is no unequivocal definition of the term 'involvement', differing statements and pairs of words are used to establish advertising involvement. With some it is unclear whether they concern antecedents, facets or consequences of involvement.

Several examples of involvement scales can be found in Appendix II. The first is Zaichkowsky's (1985) seven-point scale, which is used in the US. In addition, the Appendix contains scales by McQuarrie and Munson (1986), the Foote, Cone & Belding Involvement Subscale, based on Ratchford (1987) and Vaughn (1986), Laurent and Kapferer's (1985) Consumer Involvement Profiles (CIPs), and the New Involvement Profile (NIP), devised by Jain and Srinivasan (1990).

3.3 MENTAL BRAND RESPONSES

Brand responses are those which occur partly as a result of exposure to an advertisement. Bronner (1993) and Pieters and van Raaij (1992) refer to advertising effectiveness in the context of changes in the response to the brand resulting from exposure to the campaign. But of course there are, in practice, many other factors which affect brand response.

Brand responses are divided into mental brand responses and brand behavioural responses. The former are the effects of advertising on the consumer's knowledge (cognitive effects) of and attitude (affective effects) to the brand. Brand behavioural responses refer to the conative effects (behavioural effects). This section addresses mental brand responses, while brand behavioural responses are dealt with in section 3.4.

3.3.1 The brand as an associative network

A brand only exists in people's minds. It is a network of associations between elements in the memory. These associations are the result of collective, simultaneous processing in space and time of sensory stimuli and of thoughts on different phenomena in relation to one another. Broadly speaking, everything in this network is interconnected; the direct with the indirect, the strong with the weak. In psychology the term 'cognitive structure' is used to describe this network of associations.

Theoretical models, based on the fact that representations of brands in the LTM are organised in interconnected complexes, are termed 'associative network models' (Bouwman, 1996). According to these models, concepts (like brands) can be interpreted as hierarchies of associated elements (interconnected neurons and clusters of neurons), in which each individual element is represented by a node (or neuron) in the brain. These clusters of neurons represent different components or elements of the brand, and our relationship with it.

If this theory is taken as the starting point, a brand can be imagined as a spherical space in which these components are located. So an associative brand network relates to the sum of associations, meanings, feelings, attitudes and behavioural tendencies which a brand name evokes in an individual – in everyday practice this is called 'image'. The core of the system contains the brand name, and the set outward characteristics of the brand, for example, a colour, logo, typeface or design. Figure 3.2 represents in diagram form the associative system of a brand (Franzen and Bouwman, 1999).

The Brand Associative Network (BAN) contains seven components:

- brand awareness/saliency;
- brand meanings;
- brand feelings;
- brand positioning;
- brand attitude;
- brand behavioural tendency;
- brand relationship.

Each component represents a mental brand response, and is briefly discussed in the following subsections.

3.3.2 Brand awareness

The presence of the brand name in the consumer's memory makes it possible for associations to be linked to it which can create brand preference. Thus it hardly needs saying that an advertiser at least wants the consumer to become familiar with and aware of the brand (brand name) which is being advertised.

○ *Brand awareness*
  - The presence of the brand name in the working/short-term memory (STM) during perception of the brand; and which is taken from the LTM to the STM by means of a retrieval process (spontaneous/aided recall).
  - The presence of the brand name in the LTM and the ability to retrieve this information into the STM.

In general, the highest possible level of awareness is aimed at, meaning that the consumer can remember the brand spontaneously (unaided recall). Spontaneous brand recall is usually closely connected with the overall brand attitude and with brand-buying behaviour. With aided brand recall (like recognition) hardly any such connection exists (van Westendorp, 1996), at least in fast-moving consumer product categories.

Measuring brand awareness

The recollection of a brand is not located in one part of the memory, but is spread through different areas. What comes into the consumer's mind when brand recollection is ascertained depends on the moment, the situation and the cue. Moreover, the strength of the connection in the memory between the representation of a cue and the other elements in the network determines whether something is remembered, and what is remembered.

Adherents of the associative network theory maintain that the more recently activation of the brand took place (seen, used, thought about), the greater the chance that it will come back into one's consciousness and be used to process fresh information. This theory also implies that the recollection of specific elements in the brand network can be predicted from the frequency and recency of preceding activations of these associations.

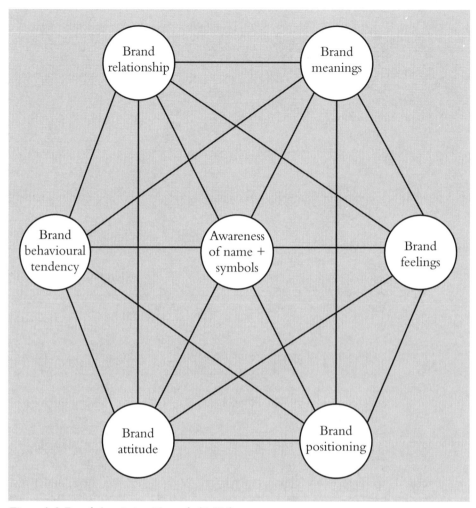

Figure 3.2 Brand Associative Network (BAN)

Brand awareness measuring techniques can be used to measure the probability that consumers will remember the brand name (or not) and the ease with which they do so (spontaneous/aided).

○ *Aided brand recall (including brand recognition)*
   The consumer's ability to confirm earlier exposure(s) to the brand, given the brand name. For example: 'Do you know soft drink brand X?'

Since there is hardly any brand cue other than the brand name, aided brand recall and brand recognition are generally the same.

○ *Unaided brand recall (spontaneous recall/TOMA)*
   The consumer's ability to name the brand, given a product cue (for example, the product group, the needs which the group meets, or the attributes with which

brands in the product group are associated). For example: 'Which brands do you know in category X?' or 'Name all the nappies you know which keep babies dry.'

One problem with ascertaining brand awareness is the extent to which brand recognition or brand recall results from the advertisement or campaign. The researcher can try to solve this problem by continued questioning. Another solution may be to link brand recall or brand recognition data with data from advertising recall and recognition research. However, it will always be hard to establish cause and effect.

Measurement of *brand recognition* is useful if dealing with a (fairly) new brand, or brands for which the decision to buy only occurs in the shop (Farr, 1996). Established/major brands do not always warrant measurement of brand recognition, since in their case aided awareness is often at a very high level. It is important in such cases to know which brand is most prominently established in the memory. Consumers do not consider carefully every buying decision, but try to assemble the daily shopping fast. They usually scan the supermarket shelves to identify the brand they liked last time, and then dump the product absentmindedly in the shopping trolley and focus on the next product group.

If a brand is at the front of the memory, it is likely to be the first one to come to mind when a certain cue is given. This is called brand salience – referring to the intensity of brand representations in memory. It is defined as the probability that someone will think of a brand at some time or another (Sutherland, 1993, p 14). If the consumer immediately thinks of Persil in approaching the detergents shelf, he or she is likely to look specifically for Persil detergent.

Brand salience can be measured by determining 'spontaneous brand awareness'. 'Top-of-mind awareness' (TOMA) indicates which brand is the most salient in the product group. TOMA is the spontaneous – and first – recollection of the brand name relative to other brand names within the product group. Even if the brand name is not mentioned first, it can be of relevance to ascertain its place in the list of recalled brand names, and/or the time needed to remember the brand. In section 3.3.8.2 brand salience will be examined more closely.

3.3.3 Brand meanings

The meaning of 'brand awareness' would appear relatively limited, but the term covers a much wider area than it would immediately suggest. Ultimately, however, the key issue is the meanings with which the brand is associated in the consumer's memory. The meaning of these associations to the consumer is decisive for brand preference and brand loyalty.

○ *Brand meanings*
Mental links between brand names and the images and/or cognitions in the consumer's memory which cause the brand to acquire 'meanings'.

Product categories

Familiarity with the brand is often linked to the need for one or more product categories, something which the advertisers of many extremely familiar brands are inclined to forget. A consumer will probably not recall the Bird's Eye brand spontaneously without being mentally or physically exposed to the need for vegetables. With umbrella or family brands it is important to determine which of the underlying products a brand is associated with. An electric toothbrush made by Philips is not automatically a strongly branded article. This will only be so if consumers think of the Philips brand spontaneously when thinking of electric toothbrushes.

Brand personality

Brand personality displays the brand's core characteristics, as described and experienced in human terms (Gordon and Restall, 1992) (for example, friendly, popular, young, conservative, social, organised, impulsive, dominant, dependent, aggressive). Brand personality may coincide with the perceived brand users and with associations of user types, but this is not necessarily the case.

When brand personality is being researched, the respondent is asked to describe the brand as if it were a person, using personality traits and characteristics. Projective techniques are sometimes used, such as video collages, psycho-drawings and 'photosort' (Gordon and Restall, 1992).

Appendix V contains four personality tests. First there is a comprehensive overview of personality traits as drawn up by Nawas (1986), based on personality theory. This is followed by a short list of the terms devised by Malhorta (1981) for use in marketing, and Aaker's list (1997) which pinpoints five basic dimensions of brand personality.

Lastly, Alt and Griggs' (1988) rating scale of personality items is given. Alt and Griggs isolated and identified three different personality dimensions which consumers use to describe brand personalities, namely extroversion, social acceptability and virtue. There are 15 items in each dimension. The three dimensions can be used to indicate differences in personalities between product categories, as well as between brands.

Relative perceived quality

Perceived quality relative to competing brands is an important distinguishing feature and often a criterion for the consumer to prefer a brand. Aaker (1991) has defined relative perceived quality as the consumer's perception of overall quality or superiority of the brand or product or service in supplying the desired performance compared with competing brands.

The quality the consumer perceives does not always coincide with objective quality as established by experts. Researchers can attach greater or lesser value than consumers to certain attributes. A test carried out by a consumer association may pinpoint a Philips television set as the 'best buy' because of ease of use and a good price:quality ratio. The consumer may select a Sony, because of its modern design and picture quality. Perceived quality among consumers can vary considerably. After all, the demands people make on their brands depend on their personalities, needs and preferences.

Relative, perceived quality is not the same as satisfaction with the brand. A consumer can be satisfied with the brand due to low expectations of its quality.

Apart from the associations with the product group, personality traits and relative, perceived quality, there are several other brand meanings. Exhibit 3.2 contains a list of possible categories of brand meanings, though it is not complete (Appendix IV contains a more comprehensive overview of product attributes and product performance).

Functional and symbolic meanings

Many publications differentiate between product-related brand meanings and meanings which are not product-related, such as symbolic, emotional and hedonistic meanings. The latter are sometimes termed non-attribute or psycho-social associations. It is vital to understand the relative importance of the two different categories of meanings. In Appendix VIII an appropriate measuring tool is given, devised by E.R. Spangenberg (1997).

Core meanings

Associations with brands can vary. By no means all connotations that are linked to a brand have equal influence on the consumer choice process. Core meanings are defined accordingly. They can be described as the associations with some meaning for the consumer, based on which a brand is positioned in the consumer's memory (see section 3.3.5) and on which the consumer can judge whether the brand is relevant to himself/herself (de Vries, 1997). This meaning may come about because the core connotations link up with a personal need or a personal value. Ultimately, core meanings are decisive for a brand's added value for the consumer compared with other brands. The more positively a brand is assessed on account of the core meanings, the greater the likelihood that a consumer will buy that brand.

○ *Core meanings*
  The associations which mean something to a consumer, based on which a brand is positioned in the consumer's memory and on which the consumer can judge whether the brand is relevant to himself/herself.

Measuring brand meanings

It is impossible to avoid asking questions in order to research what is associated with a brand in the memory. However, each individual question triggers off different connections. Researchers must realise that only a small facet of the total brand associations can be perceived.

When a brand is being researched, it is also important to distinguish between matters with which the brand is permanently associated and associations which only occur in a certain (research) situation. There is a tendency, especially in image research, to overlook that dimension and attach equal importance to all associations.

A method which is frequently used for measuring brand meanings is that of direct questioning, such as: 'What do you think of when … ?'

Association tests are another option. They entail asking respondents to associate certain stimuli with a brand; for example, by getting them to complete unfinished sentences or by using methods like 'photosort' (where respondents are asked to match photographs, usually of faces representing different personalities or emotions, with the brands), word-association tests and collage-making.

3.3.3.1 Brand values

People arrange their perceptions, relate them to existing knowledge and make connections between findings in order to form an opinion. We assess persons, objects and situations according to dimensions we consider to be important, in this way developing positive or negative attitudes. The opinions which arise as to what is personally or socially desirable are called 'values'. A value is described as a 'preferred

Categories of brand associations

1 *Brand signals* (the visual, auditive, olfactory characteristics of the brand)
   - Logo, trademark, typeface
   - colour
   - design/form
   - material
   - sound (jingle, voice)
   - smell

2 *Origin*
   - Maker, owner (Yves Saint Laurent, Coco Chanel):
   - place, region, country of origin (Italy, Yorkshire)
   - brand history (age, development)
   - authenticity

3 *Functional brand meanings* (functions)
   Products (washing machines, biscuits):
   - product group (crisps, underwear, confectionery)
   - product variant (chocolate biscuits, waterbeds)
   Outward appearance:
   - design
   - colour
   - material
   Characteristics, attributes and performance:
   - composition, ingredients (natural aromas, flavourings)
   - usage characteristics (useful)
   - experiential characteristics (taste, smell)
   - usage effects (effect, advantages, disadvantages)
   Uses:
   - suitable for microwave, in the car, and so on
   Services:
   - guarantee
   - delivery

4 *Situational meanings* (situations)
   Usage moments:
   - morning
   - evening
   Usage situations:
   - at home
   - at work
   - during sports

5 *Symbolic meanings* (symbols)
   User types (stereotypes):
   - age
   - sex
   - social class (upper/middle class)
   - profession, education (construction workers, housewives, students)
   - personality (kind, caring, macho, dominant)
   - lifestyle
   Personality traits of the brand itself
   Value system (see section 3.3.3.1)
   Feelings, emotions (see section 3.3.4)

6 *Price*
   - absolute price
   - relative price

7 *Quality*
   - objectively ascertained quality
   - relative, perceived quality

8 *Presentation*
   - shops/branches
   - packaging

9 *Advertising* (see section 3.2.5)
   - place/medium
   - content
   - presentation

Exhibit 3.2

way of being'. Values can be arranged at different levels – see Appendix VI. In marketing they are usually classified into instrumental, impressive/expressive and end values (Franzen and Bouwman, 1999).

Brand associations can also be related to values, and these are referred to as 'brand values'.

○ *Brand value*
  A mental link between a brand meaning and a value at an instrumental, impressive/expressive or end level.

The knowledge stored in our memory bank is structured in such a way that we can easily gain access to it. Various models have been designed for describing the 'meaning structures' of brands in our memory (Pieters, 1989). These models identify almost all levels, ranging from concrete to abstract. The lowest level is the most concrete and relates to the representations of sensory perception of the objects (brands) themselves. The highest level is that of the end value positions, such as the pursuit of harmony or power.

These models focus on instrumentality: to what extent do 'lower' meanings contribute to 'higher', and/or which meanings are instrumental in achieving our higher values? The meaning structures are indicated by the term 'means–end hierarchies', or 'means–end chains'. In general, three main levels are recognised within the meaning structures:
• mental and functional characteristics;
• direct functional consequences of the mental and functional characteristics and their pros and cons;
• values to which the consequences are connected.

If the main levels are further divided into sublevels, a means–end hierarchy is produced, comprising the following levels.

Level 1
  This relates to *mental* and *functional characteristics* (see Appendix IV), such as:
• Brand signals (name, colour, mark or logo, sound);
• Products;
• Concrete product attributes (visual, tangible, physical characteristics of the products);
• Abstract product attributes (the 'summary' of the product attributes in umbrella meanings).

Level 2
  This is the level of *functional consequences*: the discernible direct consequences of the use of the product for the consumer.

Level 3
  This applies to *values*, including:
• Psycho-social consequences or impressive value (the feelings the brand or product arouses during use);
• Expressive value (the personality traits with which the brand is associated);

- Terminal (core) value (ideal conceptions of personal life);
- Social value (ideal conceptions of the society in which we live).

The best known value scale is that of the American academic, Rokeach, dating from 1973. This scale does not tie in entirely with European values. However, as yet, most European countries have no generally acceptable list of values and Rokeach's list is the most used. Appendix VI contains Rokeach's scale, as well as the list compiled by Clawson (1994).

Sikkel and Oppenhuisen (Franzen and Bouwman, 1999) developed a list of values for the Netherlands based on in-depth research, which generated 1,382 descriptions of values. These were reduced to 160 different values, which were then factor-analysed. This resulted in six factors, each represented by two opposite groups of values. Appendix VI contains the six factors and underlying values.

Measuring brand values

When people attribute values to a product/brand, they are actually giving the perceived attributes of the product or brand a meaning. But meaning structures are more complex than the hierarchical ranking given above. Researchers rarely rank them in this way, usually arranging them into groups 'after the event'.

The means–end chains are generally studied using the 'laddering technique' (also known as 'Meaning Structure Analysis'). This method boils down to asking respondents why they consider a brand attribute to be important, then why they consider the chosen answer to be important and so on, until the respondent can provide no more answers.

3.3.4 Feelings towards the brand

Emotional responses are individual reactions to stimuli which a person experiences as emotions. They relate to people's subjective experiences. In section 3.2.2 the emotional responses which may result from exposure to an advertisement (primary emotions, specific feelings and holistic affect) were discussed. It was seen that in this context primary emotions and specific feelings play the most important role, thus facilitating the processing of the advertisement. This was termed the role of emotions, in a *tactical* sense.

Similarly, exposure to a brand can arouse emotional responses. In this case the brand itself is the emotional stimulus.

This section examines the emotional responses or feelings which can be linked to the brand (by means of communication through advertising, brand-usage experience or other brand users). In this context, the function of emotions in a *strategic* sense is discussed. This is not a matter of experiencing emotional responses individually as a result of exposure to the brand, but of the emotional responses related to/associated with the brand. This linking of the brand to specific feelings is the outcome of repeated, collective exposure to the brand and the emotion in question (via the process of classic conditioning).

The emotions associated with the brand can be of a 'general' nature, like gladness, joy, happiness, affection, lovingness, friendliness, competence, self-confidence, self-assurance, pride, gratitude, contentedness and satisfaction. In addition, more specific feelings may be involved which coincide with use of the product, such as joviality, excitement and stimulation with beer; serenity, peace and security with tea; and togetherness, solicitousness and conviviality with coffee. These feelings represent 'experiential values'. They are nearly always generic feelings for the product group, but are closely associated with the brand. The brand represents these feelings and arouses associations as regards the usage situation, attendant rituals, the nature of the social relationships which can be expected and the mood experienced with them (Franzen, 1994).

3.3.5 Brand positioning

The knowledge stored in a person's memory bank is sensibly interconnected and well organised. Theories concerning association networks generally assume that knowledge units (persons, objects, situations) are divided into categories of similar units, and that these categories are arranged in a hierarchical structure. A knowledge unit is put into the category with which it has the most characteristic similarities, making it possible to retrieve information from the memory relatively easily.

Categorisation

Consumers also categorise brands according to the most common characteristics (brand associations). So brands are not only associated with all kinds of information (meanings, feelings) in the memory, but are also connected with other brands. The consumer uses these connections between brands to create an overview of the brands in a market, and evaluates them by comparing one with another.

Differentiation

The consumer also arranges competing brands within a category relative to one another (differentiation) in a space (perceptual map), which is determined by the characteristics and most important attributes of that category (Franzen, 1992a, p 6). A perceptual map is a visual expression of perceptual differences among brands expressed by consumers (Keller, 1991). Differentiation is based on the brand associations and results from the fact that the brands have relevant, discernible and characteristic differences for the consumer.

○ *Brand positioning*
   – Classifying a brand into a group/subgroup of other brands on the basis of the most characteristic common features which distinguish the group/subgroup as a whole from brands of other groups/subgroups, and:
   – differentiating a brand from the other brands within the group/subgroup on the basis of the most characteristic differences from the other brands in that group.

Brand positioning is influenced to some extent by brand attitude. A positive attitude contributes to a greater perceived difference in relation to other brands.

Brand positioning can, in theory, be based on all the association categories mentioned earlier. The most usual classifications are:
- structural associations (visual, auditive, gustatory and olfactory characteristics);
- products and product attributes;
- situational associations (applications, usage moments);
- symbolic associations (psycho-social meanings, values).

Makes of cars, for example, are categorised in the first instance according to 'class' and in the second instance according to 'origins'. Research in Austria (Team/BBDO, 1993) shows that consumers categorise detergents firstly according to perceived fields of use ('general' versus 'special', and 'hand wash' versus 'machine wash') and secondly according to their physical characteristics ('powder' versus 'liquid').

3.3.6 Brand attitude

Consumers develop an attitude towards the brand based, among other things, on brand awareness, brand associations and brand values. They evaluate the brand, taking into account all the experiences of the brand in the course of a lifetime. Usage experience plays a particularly important part in the formation of brand attitude. Brands are also assessed as regards status, quality and the price:quality ratio.

The advertiser aims to steer this evaluation in a positive direction with an advertisement or campaign. As a rule, a brand attitude is not an effect or objective as such; the advertiser is usually concerned with creating, maintaining, reinforcing or changing the attitude. A positive attitude contributes to a greater perceived difference in relation to other brands.

The possibilities for changing attitudes are somewhat limited. Attitudes are relatively stable: they do change, but very slowly. Only impact-making experiences would seem to result in fast changes in attitude.

Brand attitude is a response to the brand based on the overall evaluation of all one's impressions and experiences of the brand. It is the expression of the sum of all the underlying values.

The three-component model is based on the assumption that an attitude is expressed in three ways:
* *cognitively* (what the consumer knows about the brand – evaluative opinion);
* *affectively* (what the consumer feels about the brand – an experienced emotion);
* *conatively* (the behavioural tendency based on the evaluation).

The definition below incorporates the cognitive and affective components only, since the behavioural component is not treated as part of brand attitude.

○ *Brand attitude*
  The stable favourable or unfavourable overall evaluation of the brand, expressed as a certain degree of brand preference (brand acceptance or brand rejection) and influencing behaviour regarding the brand.

Attitude can influence behaviour and vice versa. On the one hand, people are inclined to behave in a way which coincides with their judgments (positive/negative) and feelings (positive/negative): 'buy something you like'. On the other hand, behaviour influences attitudes, in the sense of confirmation or change: '(grow to) like what you buy'.

The latter relationship in particular is emphasised by Ehrenberg (1974, 1996). He is of the opinion that trial purchases stem from exposure to the brand or product in the actual shop. The consumer gets to know the brand/product and develops a positive attitude. Advertising then confirms and reinforces that attitude. This is termed the ATRN process: 'awareness–trial–reinforcement–nudging.'

3.3.6.1 Brand preference

In advertising literature the term 'consideration set' is used for the series of brands that a consumer assesses positively and considers for a possible subsequent purchase (Franzen, 1984). The actual purchase of the brand depends partly on the circumstances at the moment of purchase. Rossiter (1993) prefers the term 'acceptance set', which describes the brands that are acceptable to the consumer and are recalled spontaneously or with help.

Consideration set has practically the same meaning as 'evoked set' – a term often used in everyday practice. However, 'evoked set' encapsulates the brands the consumer recalls spontaneously in response to the question: 'What brands do you know in product group X?' Another term used instead of 'evoked set' is 'awareness set'.

○ *Evoked or awareness set*
   The brands that come to mind, with aided or spontaneous recall, when a consumer is exposed to the product group.

○ *Consideration or acceptance set*
   The brands that the consumer evaluates positively in some way or another (overall evaluation) and also contemplates/considers in the buying decision process.

Within the set of brands the consumer takes into consideration, a differentiation can be made between the brand with the greatest preference – the one the consumer 'demands', as it were – the brands which are next in preference, and other brands which are accepted. Levels of preference are referred to in that respect.

○ *Brand preference*
   The preferred brand is the one the consumer likes best of all brands in the consideration set.

In Exhibit 3.3 overleaf Achenbaum's (1972) attitude scale is discussed. The scale is on three levels: an area of acceptance, an area of indifference and an area of rejection.

According to Ceurvorst (1994), brand preference can be defined as 'commitment', a word he uses to represent the psychological ties between a brand and the consumer. In this context, brand loyalty or brand preference relates to the behaviour resulting from commitment, a concept shared by the authors of this book. In Ceurvorst's view, the concept of commitment enables us to differentiate between repeat buying behaviour with mental commitment and other forms of repeat buying behaviour, such as buying as a habit, buying under the influence of external factors (like special-price offers) or because there is no alternative.

3.3.6.2 Satisfaction

For every purchase consumers have certain expectations concerning the product and the service rendered. If performance proves, after use, to have come up to or even surpassed expectations, the purchase has been a success. Consumers are satisfied and there is a good chance they will choose the same brand when next purchasing from that product group. However, if dissatisfied, it is most likely that they will choose a different brand in future, and that they will advise others not to buy the brand in question or complain to a trading standards body. So, in order to augment brand loyalty, the manufacturer or supplier must ensure that the product or service comes up to customers' expectations.

The aim of advertising is often to support and reinforce satisfaction with a purchase. Having bought an expensive item, consumers tend to be uncertain whether they have purchased the right brand. In an effort to reduce this uncertainty, they pay more attention to advertising for the brand in question from which they can obtain information to justify their purchase (Pieters and van Raaij, 1992, p 62). Advertising for other brands is avoided because it can add to their uncertainty. The advertiser can use direct mail and sponsored magazines to maintain a very direct relationship with the consumer. If that relationship is the advertiser's central focus, the outcome may well be more satisfied customers, and so continuity in sales.

3.3.7 Brand behavioural tendency

Brand preference may result in repeat purchases (brand loyalty). In this respect, a mental relationship with the brand (commitment) accounts for brand loyalty. However, many (repeat) purchases of consumer goods do not result from brand preference, but resemble habits. Consumers do not decide, time and again, what brand of coffee, soda, nuts or pasta they want. They primarily select a brand because it is conspicuous in some way. A habit is formed, and because they buy a brand repeatedly, their appreciation of it grows (Ehrenberg, 1974; van Westendorp, 1996). The tendency to keep on buying a brand usually depends on past buying behaviour.

○ *Brand behavioural tendency*
The autonomous inclination a person displays to buy a brand again (and again).

Achenbaum's attitude scale

Achenbaum (1972) devised an attitude scale of three levels: acceptance, unfamiliarity/indifference and rejection. The area of acceptance relates to the brands in the consideration set and the area of rejection contains brands that are considered to be unacceptable or are clearly rejected. There may be a group of brands between the two about which the consumer is uncertain or indifferent.

Area of acceptance
'This is my favourite brand. If it isn't in stock, I'll go to another shop' (demand).
'This is a good brand that I buy regularly myself' (preference).
'This is quite a good brand, but I only buy it if a better one isn't available' (acceptance).

Area of unfamiliarity/indifference
'This brand doesn't mean much to me. I don't know whether it's any good or not. I don't know if I'd buy it' (indifference).
'I've never heard of this brand' (unfamiliarity).

Area of rejection
'This is a brand I don't like. I wouldn't buy it, but there are worse brands' (rejection).
'This is one of the worst brands. I'd never buy it' (condemnation).

Exhibit 3.3

3.3.7.1 Fact-finding and buying intention

The belief that attitude and actual behaviour are closely related encourages practitioners to use attitude to forecast consumer buying behaviour. Accordingly, buying intention is used as an indicator of behaviour with fast-moving consumer goods. To this end, the behavioural intention has to be established. Behavioural intention suggests there is a concrete plan or resolve to display a certain kind of behaviour in the (near) future. However, it must be borne in mind that brand attitude and buying intention both relate to a mental characteristic only, ie, an intention or inclination, and not actual behaviour. In fact, research reveals that measured buying intentions have a stronger correlation with buying behaviour in the past than with buying behaviour that takes place after measurement.

With consumer durables, like cars and washing machines, it is advisable, according to van Westendorp (1996), to determine the 'fact-finding intention' rather than the buying intention, as purchase is often preceded by fact-finding. After all, the purchase of durables is frequently more of a risk.

○ *Fact-finding intention*
The consumer's intention to obtain (more) information about a brand.

○ *Buying intention*
The consumer's intention to buy the brand (at some point).

Fact-finding and buying intentions can be created quite suddenly. The consumer may think 'I've got to know more about that' or 'I'll buy that sometime' while seeing/hearing, or just after seeing/hearing the ad.

3.3.8 Brand relationship

The brand relationship is an important factor in brand loyalty (Ceurvorst, 1994). Loyal behaviour is founded on a certain mental tie with the brand which ensures that the consumer stays loyal to the brand. Ultimately, insight into consumers' knowledge and attitude can explain their motives for buying, and continuing to buy, the brand.

When the brand relationship is described, it is important, first of all, to realise that this relationship is a two-way thing. On the one hand, it is formed by the consumer's attitudes to the brand, and on the other hand by the perceived attitude of the brand to the consumer. The latter relates to what the consumer thinks the brand 'thinks' about him or her, the way the brand is thought to approach the consumer, and the (imagined) comments the brand might make in a conversation with the consumer (Blackston, 1993). For instance, a consumer may imagine that Visa might say: 'you have good taste', 'I can open doors for you', 'don't forget you've got to pay me at the end of the month', or 'you're important to me'.

It is also necessary to understand that a relationship entails a degree of permanence. As time goes by, different interactions between the brand and the consumer occur. A relationship is based on a common 'history' and there are expectations as to the continuation of the relationship in the future.

A relationship is usually characterised by a uniting interest. It may be an instrumental interest, geared to achieving functional goals, or a sociological interest concerning the influencing of the self-image or the pursuit of terminal values.

Lastly, a relationship is characterised by an affective component. A relationship can be positive or negative. In addition, it can be classified according to intensity. The degree of attachment can vary from 'liking' to 'intense love'.

Marketing literature sometimes compares the relationship between a brand and a person as one between good friends. Not all friendships are equally intense, and, similarly, not all relationships between a person and a brand are equally close-knit. Fajer and Schouten (1995) differentiate between:

- potential friends;
- passing friends;
- loyal friends;
- best friends;
- crucial friends.

The ranking according to the closeness of the friendship is determined by:

- the importance of the attitude;
- the replaceability of friends;
- the balance between costs and pleasure.

Fajer and Schouten assume, based on this ranking, that there is a connection between product categories and person-to-brand relationships. Everyday consumer goods do not generally encourage the consumer to invest in maintaining a brand relationship. So the brand has to make a big effort to keep up this type of relationship. And, not surprisingly, not many close-knit friendships are found in the field of fast-moving consumer goods.

However, there can be close ties between a person and a brand in the service sector, partly because personal interaction is generally involved. In such cases the relationship between the person and the brand is on a higher level; it is enduring and worth maintaining, for both sides.

Fournier (1994) describes the ties between a person and a brand as a voluntary or enforced interdependence between a person and a brand, characterised by a unique history of interactions and the anticipation of things to be shared in the future. The aim of this relationship is to help the partners to achieve their instrumental and socio-psychological goals and is characterised by a reinforcing emotional bond.

Fournier believes that a person-to-brand relationship develops sooner in some research categories than in others. Her research shows that there is a greater need for the comfort and reassurance of a long-term relationship if the consumer experiences great uncertainty. The feeling of risk plays an important part in this, in a financial, functional and social sense.

It is Fournier's view that all strong person-to-brand relationships are, essentially, based on confidence in product performance. Reliability can be a reason to maintain a relationship, but its permanence and quality do, in the end, depend on the development of deeper meanings. The brand can, for example, be associated with important moments, memories or people, thus strengthening the person's involvement with the brand. A close-knit relationship is characterised by high involvement and a determination to maintain the relationship in the future.

Fournier designed a tool for measuring the quality of the brand relationship (Brand Relationship Quality). She sees Brand Relationship Quality as a construct (see Appendix VII) consisting of seven aspects:

- personal commitment (loyalty to the brand);
- symbolic connections (self-concept associations);
- nostalgic connections (memories of the past);
- partner quality (what the consumer feels the brand thinks about him/her);
- behavioural interdependence (degree of interaction with the brand);
- love/passion (feelings and attitudes towards the brand);
- intimacy (mutual understanding and trust).

○ *Brand relationship*
The mutual relationship between a consumer and a brand comprising an interaction component and an attitude component. The former is the number and content of the interactions between a person and a brand. The latter is a person's attitude towards a brand and the brand's attitude towards the person, as he or she experiences it.

3.3.8.1 Brand involvement

Brand involvement is a mental brand response reflecting a feeling of emotional proximity and commitment, a 'felt' relationship with the brand.

○ *Brand involvement*
The extent to which a brand is relevant to the consumer because it ties in with the values (concerns, interests) which are important to him or her.

Brand involvement, like advertising involvement, is determined by the values and underlying motives, which are of a cognitive and affective nature. Product and brand involvement are closely interwoven. A consumer can be strongly attracted to a brand because considerable (perceived) functional/financial and considerable psychological risks are involved.

Functional risks chiefly depend on the product attributes and the usage results. Financial risks relate to the possible financial consequences of the purchase. The psychological risk depends on the emotional value of the product/brand for the consumer. A brand not only provides security in a functional sense, but also emotionally. It offers security as regards approval from colleagues or appreciation by friends, and reduces the social risk of the purchase because it has a shared meaning within a group.

Brand involvement is measured in the same way as advertising involvement (see Appendix II).

3.3.8.2 Brand salience

Some brands have a more dominant position in our memories than others. They are more strongly represented and we feel greater involvement with them. The psychological term for this is 'salience'. Sutherland (1993) defines this as the probability that a brand will enter our consciousness at a random moment. It can also be described as the frequency with which we think about a brand. Saliency relates to the prominence of the name and distinguishing features of a brand's representation in our memory, and the strength of its associations with other cues. Salience implies the probability that, when faced with certain cues, we will spontaneously bring the brand to mind, and it will also be the first to be recalled. The cues may be different associations connected to the brand, such as products and product attributes, applications, situations, moments and symbolic associations.

Brand salience affects our perception and buying behaviour considerably. Salience may result from the development of a choice process in the course of time, during which, based on experiences and perceptions, choice becomes narrowed down to one or a few alternatives. Gordon and Corr (1990) suggest that salience is a complex mental phenomenon, comprising experiences (imagined or not) with a brand in the past and the present, or possibly even in the future, the strength of the feelings it arouses, the inclination to buy and use it. Salience, they claim, has motivational components. The consumer feels distant from or emotionally close to a brand; such feelings occur at different levels, from strong to weak, and have a time dimension. The consumer's feelings towards a brand may be related to its present relevance to him or her, or feelings of indifference to it in the past, or even nostalgia.

Again, according to Gordon (1992), salience can best be defined and measured as the emotional distance between a consumer and a brand, as experienced by the consumer.

Brand awareness scores also give an indication of the salience of brands. The most salient brand is probably the first activated – TOMA – when unaided brand recall is measured (see section 3.3.2).

○ *Brand salience*
   The strength of the total mental brand response which comes about in the period in which a brand is activated by inner or exterior cues, and in the emotional distance (proximity) a consumer experiences from the brand.

3.4 BRAND BEHAVIOURAL RESPONSES

The ultimate goal of advertising for branded goods is generally to influence behaviour, in the short or the long term. After all, what is the use of high brand awareness, a positive brand attitude or high advertising involvement for a marketer if no one buys the brand? Many people would love to own a Jaguar, but who actually buys one? Depending on the period in which the marketer wishes to achieve the effects, and on present buying behaviour, various types of buying behaviour (behavioural responses) can be aimed at. This section reviews the various brand behavioural responses.

3.4.1 Fact-finding behaviour

Consumer durables with high involvement are not usually bought on impulse. The purchase tends to be the outcome of an extensive evaluation of the pros and cons of each alternative. The consumer collects information on the 'candidate' brands before the actual purchase is made.

○ *Fact-finding behaviour*
   A consumer's behaviour involving the active collection of information on the product or brand (for example, visiting the shop or showroom, sending in a coupon, ringing a freephone number, consulting an Internet site).

3.4.2 Trial purchases

A consumer finds out about a brand and develops some interest in it. This may be a reason to buy it once, experiment with it and develop experience of it. If it proves to be unsatisfactory, then the consumer will not buy it again.

Sometimes a trial purchase will lead to a second and a third purchase. Even then, this might be the end of the process, because, for instance, the consumer forgets about the brand. He or she does not encounter it again in the shop or is not reminded of it again because advertising for the brand has ceased.

○ *Trial purchase*
The very first time a consumer buys the brand it is usually a trial purchase. This is intended to provide experience of the brand (for durable goods a better term is 'initial purchase', because the item is often bought only once).

3.4.3 Repeat purchases

Trial use sometimes results in a whole series of repeat purchases. An ever-stronger inclination to purchase the brand gradually develops as the consumer is exposed to it. The brand is included in his or her 'repertoire'.

○ *Brand repertoire*
The brand repertoire consists of all the brands which are purchased (at some point) within a certain period. For fast-moving consumer goods a period of one year is usually taken, while for consumer durables, like cars, it can be an entire lifetime.

In practice the terms 'brand repertoire' and 'consideration set' tend to be confused. The former is a behavioural response (brands the consumer sometimes buys), the latter is a mental response (brands the consumer might conceivably buy at some point).

○ *Repeat purchases*
The first purchases following a trial purchase. As yet no preference exists; the consumer is still in the process of forming an attitude.

○ *Continuation of repeat purchases*
The consumer likes the brand, becoming an 'occasional' user, and adds the brand to his or her brand repertoire.

A brand that is occasionally bought by the consumer usually does not account for more than 20% of the share of customer (ie, the share of the brand in all a consumer's purchases in the category in question). Repertoire purchases are those that account for 20–50% of the share of customer (McQueen, 1991; see Exhibit 3.4). The term 'share of customer' is defined more specifically in the next section.

3.4.4 Share of customer (share of requirements)

In many markets it is usual for customers to alternate between two, three or four brands with some regularity. In some markets the number is even bigger, and 'multi-brand' use is then prevalent. In the snacks market, for instance, consumers are in the habit of trying out new options. Trial use is easy to achieve in this market, but such brands will never account for more than a small share of category purchases.

In other markets consumers are geared to one brand, which has a very large share of individual purchases. Products to which this applies are, for example, cigarettes, coffee, razor blades and sanitary towels. In these markets it is very difficult for new brands to achieve trial use, because consumers have a strong preference-relationship with their present brand. If the marketer succeeds in getting consumers to try the brand once, it is quite likely that they will still revert to the old brand.

Six brand behaviour typologies

Group 1 – One-off buyers
Consumers make a trial purchase once only, and not again. This may result from negative brand experience or from the advertising approach: 'try me'.

Group 2 – Repeat trial buyers
Consumers buy the brand a number of times after the first purchase, and then stop buying. This type of buying behaviour may come about because the consumer is unable to assess the brand after one trial use. The untimely conclusion of an introductory campaign may also play a part. New users do not have a real tie with the brand and easily revert to their old habits.

Group 3 – Sporadic buyers
In this group a brand does not usually account for more than 20% of all a consumer's purchases within the product category. There are various possible explanations for sporadic use. It may, for instance, result from the product's attributes, or the product may be a variant, which is especially suitable for special situations. Alternatively consumers may have such a strong tie with their top brand that they only buy another brand in exceptional cases, for instance, if their own brand is out of stock. The brand may still be young and have not yet managed to acquire a preferential position. Consumers' responsiveness to prices may also be a reason for sporadic use.

Group 4 – Repertoire buyers
This group buys the brand in question with the same regularity as several other brands. The brand represents 20–50% of all their purchases in the relevant product category. This buying behaviour frequently occurs in categories in which variation is important, for instance, snacks and desserts. It can also be an intermediate stage in the brand's process of achieving top-brand status.

Group 5 – Top brand buyers
Top brands are those which represent over 50% of a consumer's purchases in the product category in question, even if a great many other brands are available. Top-brand buyers purchase the brand at least 50% more often than any of the other brands they also buy.

Group 6 – 100% brand-loyal buyers
These are the consumers who definitely want nothing else. They are the brand's fan club. If this brand is out of stock, they postpone purchase or go to another shop.

Source: McQueen, 1991 (in Franzen, 1994, pp 204–208).

Exhibit 3.4

The frequency with which people repeat their purchase of a certain brand within total purchases in the product group is described as share of customer.

○ *Share of customer (share of requirements)*
The share of the brand in all an individual consumer's purchases within a certain product group during a certain period.

3.4.5 Brand loyalty

Share of customer can occur to varying degrees: from buying behaviour in which the consumer keeps changing brands, to absolute brand loyalty, where the same brand is repeatedly purchased over a long period. The term 'brand loyalty' is mostly used if the (individual) consumer chooses the brand in at least 50% of cases.

○ *Brand loyalty*
Brand purchasing behaviour that occurs so often that the brand constitutes a top brand for the consumer and has a share of customer of more than 50%.

However, 'true' brand loyalty is claimed to be more than mere repetition of brand choice. True brand loyalty is said to be generated by an emotional tie (commitment) which the consumer has forged with the brand over the course of time. Again, it is worth considering whether brand preference has led to brand loyalty, or whether repeated buying behaviour has contributed to the customer developing a liking for the brand.

Longitudinal research (tracking) conducted for decades and covering buying behaviour of customers in many different markets, in the UK, the US and Germany, has led Ehrenberg (1996) to conclude that brand loyalty is not a function of the brand, but of its market share. All the brands in a product category are characterised by the same degree of brand loyalty. Brands with a bigger market share benefit more, simply because of the size of market share. On average, they are purchased more frequently than small brands, but the main difference between 'big' and 'small' brands is penetration. According to Ehrenberg, brand loyalty is not founded on an emotional tie; it is the result of habit. A summary of Ehrenberg's theories can be found in Chapter 4.

McQueen (1991) describes six brand behaviour typologies: one-off buyers, repeat trial buyers, sporadic buyers, repertoire buyers, top brand buyers and 100% brand-loyal buyers. These are briefly described in Exhibit 3.4.

3.5   MARKET RESPONSE

The market response is actually the aggregate brand behaviour response at market level, involving the financial and economic consequences of brand-buying behaviour for the company. This response is usually established in commercial and marketing terms.

In this section the most prevalent market responses are discussed. In most cases it is not the marketer's aim to create a response as such; it is more a matter of increasing and/or maintaining the existing effect.

3.5.1 Sales and turnover

Sales and turnover are market responses which it should be possible to influence in the short term. In this context, advertisements are intended to lure consumers into the shop in the very near future to buy the brand. The marketer will often try to stimulate purchase directly, by offering a better price-to-quantity ratio.

○ *Sales*
Total sales of the brand expressed in product units. These sales may be ascertained ex-factory or at the sales outlet stage.

○ *Turnover*
The total proceeds from all sales of the brand expressed in monetary units. Again, either ex-factory or at the sales outlet stage.

3.5.2 Distribution, penetration and market share

○ *Distribution*
The inclusion of the brand by the distributive or retail trade in their range. The brand's position in the shop or on the shelf and the attitude of the shopkeeper and/or staff towards the brand can both have an effect.

○ *Penetration*
The total number (or the percentage) of persons/households that have purchased the brand at least once in a certain period.

It is advisable to differentiate between total penetration and 'top brand penetration'. The latter is the percentage of persons/households that has bought the brand more often than one of the other brands in the brand repertoire.

○ *Market share*
The share in sales/monetary units of a brand during a certain period expressed in the percentage of sales of the total defined product category or subcategory.

It should be borne in mind that, with the above definitions, any product category demarcation is arbitrary. Even carefully defined categories/markets consist of several segments, which reflect different patterns of needs and product formulas. The marketer uses different category definitions when working out the market share. So a coffee manufacturer, when calculating the market share, may use the total beverages market, the hot beverages market, the coffee market, the coffee bean market or the decaffeinated bean market.

Market shares can be expressed in absolute shares (percentage of the total defined market) as well as in relative shares (share compared with competing brands). In addition, the market share can be related to that of the biggest competitor, or to the total share of manufacturers' brands in the market. In the latter case, private labels are not taken into consideration.

Changes in market share are caused by changes in penetration or frequency. In markets with high brand loyalty it is often difficult to change penetration.

○ *Penetration change*
The increase or decrease in the numbers of brand users.

○ *Frequency change*
An increase or decrease in use per user of the brand.

In the long run the size of market share is not all that counts – its stability is also an important factor. Ehrenberg (1996) indicates that the market share of an established brand is usually stable – so much so that it is difficult to achieve growth in market share.

Consumers in established markets have set habits concerning the different brands they buy in a certain category. It is the marketer's job to ensure that the brand is included in the consumer's brand repertoire, and stays there. In an established market it is less a matter of augmenting market share than of maintaining the status quo.

Brand loyalty varies little within product categories with respect to the individual brands. On average each brand accounts for 25% of individual purchases (US, Moran, 1994). This percentage is a little higher for brands with a large market share. Similarly, smaller brands are bought by fewer people and also a little less frequently. This is called the 'double jeopardy effect' (Ehrenberg, 1974; Ehrenberg *et al.*, 1990). According to Ehrenberg, brand loyalty is not influenced by the brand, but is the result of the market share. Consequently, in his opinion it is an illusion to think that advertising can directly affect brand loyalty. The market share of established brands can, he believes, basically be increased only by penetration changes, which, in practice, means the competitor will need to decrease in performance.

3.5.3 Price and profit

The market strives, in the long term, to influence a brand's profitability by means of advertising. Consumers' evaluations of the brand are determined by the extent of their brand loyalty and also the price they are prepared to pay for the brand. This means producers can charge higher prices for branded goods than for the same, unbranded, products.

○ *Price*
The average price paid over a certain period for the brand in the marketplace.

○ *Price index*
The average price paid for the brand, expressed as an index, in which the average price paid in the entire product category is set at 100.

○ *Price premium*
The difference between the average price of a brand in the marketplace and the price of an alternative with the same attributes, but unbranded (for example, a good quality private label).
Price premium is also defined as the difference between the average price paid in the marketplace for the whole category and the average price of a brand.

○ *Price elasticity*
The percentage change (increase or decrease) in sales resulting from a 1% change (increase/decrease) in price.

○ *Gross profit*
Ex-factory turnover of the brand less purchase costs.

○ *Net profit*
Financial result of brand operation(s) after manufacturing costs, marketing and sales costs, overheads, interest (on loan capital) and tax have been deducted from the gross profit.

○ *Profit margin*
Net profit expressed as a percentage of turnover.

○ *Cash flow*
The sum of net profit and depreciation on invested capital.

○ *Return on total capital*
Net profit expressed as a percentage of the invested shareholders' equity and long-term loan capital.

3.5.4 Brand value and brand equity

In the past ten years it has been realised, thanks to the effects of brands on the market position and financial results of manufacturers, that brands have a financial value. And this value tends to be greater than that of the material assets on the balance sheet.

Two terms which have emerged in this context in advertising literature, and which are very much in the limelight, are brand equity and brand value. Both relate essentially to the value that a brand represents for a company, and which is the outcome of the position the brand has acquired in the marketplace. However, according to Pauli and de Smeth (1994; de Smeth, 1996), it is worth making a distinction between brand value (what the brand represents for the company in financial terms) and brand equity (the value the brand represents in marketing terms).

Brand value is a term used in financial literature for the actual monetary value of a brand. Brand valuation expresses/assesses the trademark rights of the brand in financial terms. An assessment of the brand value is intended to achieve the effective management of brands, the takeover of brands, or for use when financing an enterprise and/or in damage claims.

○ *Brand value*
Assessment of the value of the brand name, based on:
- cost price (costs involved in 'making' the brand);
- acknowledged market value (takeover price as actually paid);
- the expected proceeds (for example, the sum of five years' net profit).

'Equity' is also a term found in financial literature and relates to shareholders' equity (compared with loan capital, for instance, provided by a bank). However, in everyday and marketing terminology, the term 'brand equity' has acquired a far wider meaning. It often stands for the sum of awareness, preference and buying tendency (all the consumer responses together) linked to the brand, and the concomitant total benefits for the manufacturer. Just to complicate matters, this is sometimes termed 'brand added value' (Riezebos, 1994).

In this book a distinction is made between two types of brand equity – *consumer equity* and *financial/economic equity*. The former is further subdivided into mental brand equity and behavioural equity. Mental brand equity relates to the inclusion of the brand in a consumer's consideration set (so the consumer has a conscious and active preference for the brand based on perceptions and feelings about it). Behavioural equity entails the habitual or deliberately loyal purchasing of a brand by consumers to meet an important part of their category needs.

Financial/economic brand equity is the influence of consumer equity on the brand's financial/economic performance in the marketplace. It is expressed in the level of distribution, sales, market share, premium price and profits achieved by the brand.

'Equity' in these expressions represents the quantitative component: the extent to which a brand succeeds in bringing about positive consumer and market responses.

3.6 POSTSCRIPT

The Advertising Response Matrix contains all the advertising responses which might arise as a result of exposure to advertising, advertisements or advertising campaigns. The aim of this chapter has been to provide a succinct but complete listing of all possible responses, dividing them up into four categories: mental advertising responses, mental brand responses, brand behavioural responses and market responses. The last category is quite different from the other three, relating as it does to aggregated rather than individual effects on the consumer.

Insight into all advertising responses and their definitions can simplify the dialogue between practitioners and academics. The listing within this chapter can enable each interested party to locate their specific field of interest within the overall response 'package', thus clarifying the margins and relative 'lie of the land'.

An overview of all possible responses shows that a great many effects can be pursued with advertising. The Advertising Response Matrix can be used as a starting point for the exact formulation of advertising objectives and the delineation of advertising policy.

CHAPTER 3 APPENDICES

Chapter 3: Appendix I Types of emotional responses

1. Categories of emotions
Russel and Starkman (1990)

Category	Descriptive synonyms
Joy	Joyful, happy, delighted
Surprise	Surprised, astonished, amazed
Sadness	Sad, unhappy, depressed
Anger	Furious, angry, enraged
Disgust	Disgusted, revolted, repulsed
Contempt	Scornful, contemptuous, disdainful
Fear	Afraid, fearful, frightened
Shame	Ashamed, embarrassed, humiliated
Guilt	Guilty, remorseful, regretful
Affection	Loving, affectionate, friendly
Activation	Aroused, stimulated, excited
Counter-activation	Bored, unexcited, disinterested
Competence	Confident, assured, competent
Helplessness	Powerless, helpless, weak
Surgency	Playful, entertained, lighthearted
Scepticism	Sceptical, suspicious, distrustful
Pride	Proud, superior, worthy
Serenity	Restful, serene, comfortable
Conflict	Tense, frustrated, upset
Desire	Desirous, wishful, hopeful
Duty	Virtuous, honest, dutiful
Faith	Reverent, worshipful, spiritual
Gratitude	Grateful, thankful, appreciative
Innocence	Innocent, pure, blameless
Interest	Attentive, curious, interested
Distraction	Distracted, preoccupied, inattentive

2. Mano's eight emotion scales
Mano (1996)

Arousal	Astonished, surprised, aroused
Elation	Elated, active, excited
Pleasantness	Pleased, satisfied, happy
Calmness	Calm, at rest, relaxed
Quietness	Quiet, still, quiescent
Boredom	Sleepy, sluggish, drowsy
Unpleasantness	Unhappy, sad, blue
Distress	Anxious, fearful, nervous

3. Perceptual emotion chart
Russel and Starkman (1990)

Emotions can be situated in a perceptual chart, based on the dimensions of active–passive and positive–negative. There are eight clusters of emotions in the chart.

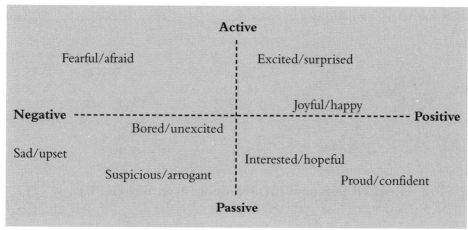

Figure 3.3 Perceptual chart of emotions

4. Four categories of emotions which advertising can arouse
Edell and Chapman Moore (1991)

Upbeat	Cheerful, playful
Warm	Affectionate, hopeful, calm
Uneasy	Anxious, uncomfortable, tense
Negative	Bored, disgusted, dubious, disinterested

5. The eight basic emotions, their functions and dominant behaviour
Plutchik (1958)

Emotion	Function	Dominant behaviour
Acceptance	Affiliation	Connect
Fear	Protection	Escape
Surprise	Fact-finding	Stop, freeze
Sadness	Reintegration	Cry for help
Disgust	Rejection	Surrender
Rage	Destruction	Attack
Anticipation	Discovery	Research
Pleasure	Reproduction	Couple, possess

Chapter 3: Appendix II Involvement scales

1. Personal involvement inventory for advertising (PIIA)
Zaichkowsky (1990)

1 Important – unimportant
2 Boring – interesting
3 Relevant – irrelevant
4 Exciting – unexciting
5 Means nothing – means a lot to me
6 Appealing – unappealing
7 Fascinating – mundane
8 Worthless – valuable
9 Involving – uninvolving
10 Not needed – needed

2. Revised personal involvement inventory (RPII)
McQuarrie and Munson (1986)

1 Important – unimportant
2 Irrelevant – relevant
3 Means a lot to me – means nothing to me
4 Unexciting – exciting
5 Dull – neat
6 Matters to me – doesn't matter
7 Fun – not fun
8 Appealing – unappealing
9 Boring – interesting
10 Of no concern – of concern to me

3. Foote, Cone & Belding involvement subscale (FCBI)
Ratchford (1987); Vaughn (1986)

1 Very important decision – very unimportant decision
2 Decision requires a lot of thought – decision requires little thought
3 A lot to lose if you choose the wrong brand – little to lose if you choose the wrong brand

4. Consumer involvement profiles (CIP)

Laurent and Kapferer (1985)

1   If you choose … it isn't so bad if you make the wrong choice.
2   It's very annoying to buy … which aren't suitable.
3   If I prove to have made the wrong choice after buying … I feel very unhappy.
4   Every time you buy … you don't really know if you should have bought it/them.
5   When I'm standing in front of a shelf of … I always find it a bit difficult to make a choice.
6   It's not easy to choose …
7   When you buy … you're never sure of your choice.
8   You can get to know a lot about a person from which … he/she chooses.
9   The … I buy gives a glimpse of the kind of person I am.
10 The … you buy says something about the person you are.
11 I enjoy buying …
12 Buying … is a bit like giving yourself a present.
13 I quite like …
14 I'm very attached to …
15 You could say that … interests me a great deal.
16 … is a subject that leaves me absolutely cold.

5. New involvement profile (NIP)

Jain and Srinivasan (1990)

1   Essential – not essential
2   Beneficial – not beneficial
3   Unnecessary – necessary
4   I don't find it pleasant – I do find it pleasant
5   Unexciting – exciting
6   Nice – not nice
7   Tells other people something about me – tells other people nothing about me
8   Others use it to judge me by – others don't use it to judge me by
9   Does not depict a picture of me for others – depicts a picture of me for others
10 It's very annoying if you buy something unsuitable – it isn't annoying to buy something unsuitable
11 A poor choice wouldn't upset me – a poor choice would upset me
12 Little to lose if you make the wrong choice – a lot to lose if you make the wrong choice
13 When I buy it I'm sure about my choice – when I buy it I'm not sure about my choice
14 I never know if I've made the right choice – I know for sure I've made the right choice
15 I find it a bit difficult to make that choice – I don't find it difficult to make that choice

6. The Jain and Srinivasan CIP items

Jain and Srinivasan (1990)

1 It doesn't much matter if I make a wrong choice – it matters if I make a wrong choice.
2 It's very annoying if I make an unsuitable purchase – it's not annoying if I make an unsuitable purchase.

3 The wrong choice wouldn't make me unhappy – the wrong choice would make me unhappy.
4 I never know if I'm buying the right thing – I know for sure I'm buying the right thing.
5 I find it a bit difficult to make a choice – I don't find it difficult to make a choice.
6 It's easy to make a choice – it's not easy to make a choice.
7 When I buy something, I'm sure about my choice – when I buy something, I'm not sure about my choice.
8 It says something about a person – it says nothing about a person.
9 What I buy doesn't reflect the kind of person I am – what I buy reflects the kind of person I am.
10 What I buy says something about me – what I buy says nothing about me.
11 I enjoy buying it for myself – I don't enjoy buying it for myself.
12 When I buy it, it's as if I'm giving myself a present – when I buy it, it's not as if I'm giving myself a present.
13 I don't enjoy it – I do enjoy it.
14 I find it important – I don't find it important.
15 I'm not interested in it at all – I'm very interested in it.
16 It means nothing to me – It means something to me.

Chapter 3: Appendix III   Response profiles

1.   Viewer response profile
Schlinger (1979)

Entertainment
1   The commercial was lots of fun to watch and listen to.
2   I thought it was clever and entertaining.
3   The enthusiasm of the commercial is catching – it picks you up.
4   The ad wasn't just selling the product – it was entertaining me and I appreciate that.
5   The characters (or persons) in the commercial capture your attention.
6   It's the kind of commercial that keeps running through your mind after you've seen it.
7   I just laughed at it – I thought it was very funny and good.

Confusion
8   It was distracting – trying to watch the screen and listen to the words at the same time.
9   It required a lot of effort to follow the commercial.
10   It was too complex. I wasn't sure of what was going on.
11   I was so busy watching the screen, I didn't listen to the talk.

Relevant news
12   The commercial gave me a new idea.
13   The commercial reminded me that I'm dissatisfied with what I'm using now and I'm looking for something better.
14   I learned something from the commercial that I didn't know before.
15   The commercial told me about a new product I think I'd like to try.
16   During the commercial I thought how that product might be useful to me.
17   That's a good brand and I wouldn't hesitate recommending it to others.
18   I know that the advertised brand is a dependable, reliable one.

Empathy
19   The commercial was very realistic – that is, true to life.
20   I felt that the commercial was acting out what I feel at times.
21   I felt as though I was right there in the commercial experiencing the same thing.
22   That's my idea – the kind of life that commercial showed.
23   I liked the commercial because it was personal and intimate.

Familiarity
24   This kind of commercial has been done many times … it's the same old thing.
25   I've seen this commercial so many times – I'm tired of it.
26   I think this is an unusual commercial. I'm not sure I've seen others like it.

Alienation

27 What they showed didn't demonstrate the claims they were making about the product.
28 The ad didn't have anything to do with me or my needs.
29 The commercial did not show me anything that would make me want to use their products.
30 The commercial made exaggerated claims. The product would not live up to what they said or implied.
31 It was an unrealistic ad – very far-fetched.
32 The commercial irritated me – it was annoying.

2. Wells' reaction profile (for printed media)
Wells (1975)

1 Beautiful/ugly
2 Pleasant/unpleasant
3 Gentle/harsh
4 Appealing/unappealing
5 Attractive/unattractive
6 In good taste/in bad taste
7 Exciting/unexciting
8 Interesting/uninteresting
9 Worth looking at/not worth looking at
10 Comforting/frightening
11 Colourful/colourless
12 Fascinating/boring
13 Meaningful/meaningless
14 Convincing/unconvincing
15 Important/unimportant to me
16 Strong/weak
17 Honest/dishonest
18 Easy to remember/hard to remember
19 Easy to understand/hard to understand
20 Worth remembering/not worth remembering
21 Simple/complicated
22 New/ordinary
23 Fresh/stale
24 Lively/lifeless
25 Sharp/washed out

3. Leavitt's reaction profile (for TV commercials)

Leavitt (1970)

Energetic factor
1 Lively
2 Exhilarated
3 Vigorous
4 Enthusiastic
5 Energetic
6 Excited

Amusing factor
7 Merry
8 Jolly
9 Playful
10 Joyful
11 Amusing
12 Humorous

Personal relevance factor
13 Important for me
14 Helpful
15 Valuable
16 Meaningful to me
17 Worth remembering
18 Convincing

Authoritative factor
19 Confident
20 Businesslike
21 Consistent in style
22 Responsible
23 Frank
24 Dependable

Sensual factor
25 Lovely
26 Beautiful
27 Gentle
28 Serene
29 Tender
30 Sensitive

Familiarity
31 Familiar
32 Well-known
33 Seen before

Novel
34 Original
35 Unique
36 Imaginative
37 Novel
38 Ingenious
39 Creative

Disliked
40 Phoney
41 Terrible
42 Stupid
43 Irritating
44 Unimportant to me
45 Ridiculous

Chapter 3: Appendix IV Product attributes and performance

Product profiles and performance
Franzen (1994)

AI		*Instrumental values*
1	Original	Traditional, honest, from the farm, home-produced, traditional methods, handmade, non-mechanical, small scale, primitive.
2	Pure	• clear, smells good, odourless, virginal; • hygienic, clean, no dirt and stains; • no damaging substances, mild, soft.
3	Natural	• organic, not artificial, plants, animals, minerals; • primal: sun, earth, water, fire, air, wind.
4	Technological	Hi-tech, composed, constructed, electronic, scientific discovery, invention, advanced.
5	Magic	Mystical, wonders, supernatural, mythical, secret composition.
6	Durable	Good quality, strong, firm, solid, lasting, stable, robust.

AII		*The use*
1	Easy	Handy, easy to use, easy to handle, not complicated, practical, open, accessible, available, easy to repair, comfortable.
2	Safe	• protecting, risk-free, immune to outside influences; • guaranteed, tried and tested, reliable, certain.

AIII		*The effect*
1	Effective	• working properly, fit, functional, efficient; • firm, thorough.
2	Vital	Energy, nutritious, high-spirited.
3	Soft	Mild, careful, non-irritating.
4	Quick	Time saving.

AIV		*The appearance*
1	Aesthetic	Well-designed, beautiful in style, decorative, simple, no frills, tasteful, sober, natural.
2	Refined	Delicate, elegant, sensitive, soft, nice, graceful, stylish, attractive.
3	Robust	Rough.

AV		*The cost*
1	Inexpensive	Economical, money-saving, cheap, inexpensive in use.
2	Expensive	Valuable, luxurious, expensive, rich, priceless.

Chapter 3: Appendix V   Personality characteristics

1.   An overview of personality characteristics
Cattel and Eber (1970, in Nawas, 1986)

A   *Sizia*
Remote, reserved, cool, suspicious, rigid, critical

A   *Affectia*
Affectionate, thoughtful and interested in others, mild, flexible, impulsive, actively participatory attitude

B   *Stupid*
Low intelligence, gives up quickly, no insight into abstract problems

B   *Clever*
High intelligence, persevering, can quickly discover connections between certain things or events

C   *Low ego*
Reacts fast emotionally, not so stable emotionally, easily upset, changeable, melancholy

C   *High ego*
Mature, balanced, emotionally stable, self-controlled, realistic

D   *Subservience*
Subservient, obedient, docile, mild, passive, obliging

D   *Dominance*
Dominant, assertive, aggressive, competitive, stubborn

E   *Desurgency*
Sober, silent, serious, quiet, introspective, concerned, cautious

E   *Surgency*
Carefree, enthusiastic, nonchalant, talkative, cheerful, alert

F   *Low superego*
Not concerned about rules and moral standards, no perseverance, lax, carefree

F   *High superego*
Conscientious, moralistic, responsible, persevering

G   *Threctia*
Shy, timid, inhibited, fearful

G   *Parmia*
Adventurous, thick-skinned, sociable and enterprising in dealings with others

H   *Harria*
Hard, unsentimental, few illusions and expectations, self-reliant, businesslike

H   *Premsia*
Soft, sensitive, dependent, unsure, over-protected, seeks help and sympathy, has an imaginative inner world, intuitive

I Alaxia
Full of confidence, can accept situations as they happen, can easily dismiss difficulties, understanding, tolerant

I Protension
Suspicious, jealous, dogmatic, difficulty dismissing frustrations, tyrannical, irritable

J Praxernia
Practical, concerned with concrete everyday things, conventional, prosaic, focused on objective reality

J Autia
Imaginative, bohemian, preoccupied, unconventional, has artistic, philosophical and theoretical interests, quickly distracted from practical matters

K Naiveté
Ingenuous, unpretentious, authentic but clumsy in social intercourse, spontaneous, genuinely concerned about others, no exact mentality, lack of insight into self and into others (motives), satisfied with the status quo

K Shrewdness
Shrewd, astute, worldly, affected, cunning, ambitious, reserved and self-aware in dealings with others, insight into oneself and into others

L Self-confidence
Self-confident, calm, sure, self-satisfied, resilient, cheerful, insensitive to the opinions of others, unafraid

L Tendency to guilt feelings
Fearful, self-reproaching, unsure, brooding, depressed, touchy, moody, strong sense of duty, scrupulous

M Conservatism
Conservative, cautious, respects traditional values, tolerant of inconvenience and old methods

M Radicalism
Experimental, analytical, free-thinking

N Social dependence
A 'group' person, a 'joiner', a loyal follower

N Autonomy
Complacent, copes well, prefers own decisions

O Low self-sentiment
Uncontrolled, lax, acts of own accord, not integrated, not bothered by social rules

O High self-sentiment
Controlled, strong-willed, sticks closely to social rules, relentless

P Low tension
Relaxed, quiet, slow, calm, not frustrated

P High tension
Tense, petulant, agitated, frustrated, overwrought

2. Self-concepts, person concepts, and product concepts
Malhortra (1981)

1 Rugged – delicate
2 Excitable – calm
3 Uncomfortable – comfortable
4 Dominating – submissive
5 Thrifty – indulgent
6 Pleasant – unpleasant
7 Contemporary – non-contemporary
8 Organised – unorganised
9 Rational – emotional
10 Youthful – mature
11 Formal – informal
12 Orthodox – liberal
13 Complex – simple
14 Colourless – colourful
15 Modest – vain

3. A brand personality scale (BPS)
Aaker (1997)

The big five

Sincerity (Campbell's, Hallmark, Kodak)
Down-to-earth: family-orientated, small-town, conventional, blue-collar, all-American
Honest: sincere, real, ethical, thoughtful, caring
Wholesome: original, ageless, classic, old-fashioned
Cheerful: sentimental, friendly, warm, happy

Excitement (Porsche, Absolut, Benetton)
Daring: trendy, exciting, off-beat, flashy, provocative
Spirited: cool, young, lively, outgoing, adventurous
Imaginative: unique, humorous, surprising, artistic, fun
Up-to-date: independent, contemporary, innovative, aggresive

Competence (Amex, CNN, IBM)
Reliable: hard-working, secure, efficient, trustworthy, careful
Intelligent: technical, corporate, serious
Successful: leader, confident, influential

Sophistication (Lexus, Mercedes, Revlon)
Upper class: glamorous, good-looking, pretentious, sophisticated
Charming: feminine, smooth, sexy, gentle

Ruggedness (Levi's, Marlboro, Nike)
Outdoorsy: masculine, Western, active, athletic
Tough: rugged, strong, no-nonsense

The brand personality scale

Down-to-earth	Contemporary
Family-oriented	Reliable
Small-town	Hard-working
Honest	Secure
Sincere	Intelligent
Real	Technical
Wholesome	Corporate
Original	Successful
Cheerful	Leader
Sentimental	Confident
Friendly	Upper class
Daring	Glamorous
Trendy	Good-looking
Exciting	Charming
Spirited	Feminine
Cool	Smooth
Young	Outdoorsy
Imaginative	Masculine
Unique	Western
Up-to-date	Tough
Independent	Rugged

4. Brand personality rating scale
Alt and Griggs (1988)

Extraversion
- Lively
- Outgoing
- Fun-loving
- Young at heart
- Happy-go-lucky
- Cheerful
- Cheeky
- Modern
- Bold
- Energetic
- Vivacious
- Dynamic
- With it
- Vibrant
- Flamboyant

Virtue
- Graceful
- Thoughtful
- Tidy
- Homely
- Reassuring
- Reliable
- Gentle
- Helpful
- Kind
- Charming
- Hard-working
- Honest
- Clever
- Sincere
- Sympathetic

Social acceptability
- Uncouth
- Coarse
- Gullible
- Insincere
- Slipshod
- Indecisive
- Untruthful
- Devious
- Brutal
- Superficial
- Arrogant
- Childish
- Mean
- Inconsiderate
- Loud-mouthed

Chapter 3: Appendix VI Value listings

1. The Rokeach Value Survey (RVS)
Rokeach (1968, 1973)

End values
- A comfortable life (a prosperous life)
- An exciting life (a stimulating, active life)
- A sense of accomplishment (a lasting contribution)
- A world at peace (free of war and conflict)
- A world of beauty (beauty of nature and the arts)
- Equality (brotherhood, equal opportunity for all)
- Family security (taking care of loved ones)
- Freedom (independence, free choice)
- Happiness (contentedness)
- Inner harmony (freedom from inner conflict)
- Mature love (sexual and spiritual intimacy)
- National security (protection from attack)
- Pleasure (an enjoyable, leisurely life)
- Salvation (saved, eternal life)
- Self-respect (self-esteem)
- Social recognition (respect, admiration)
- True friendship (close companionship)
- Wisdom (a mature understanding of life)

Instrumental values
- Ambitious (hard-working, aspiring)
- Broad-minded (open-minded)
- Capable (competent, effective)
- Cheerful (lighthearted, joyful)
- Clean (neat, tidy)
- Courageous (standing up for your beliefs)
- Forgiving (willing to pardon others)
- Helpful (working for the welfare of others)
- Honest (sincere, truthful)
- Imaginative (daring, creative)
- Independent (self-reliant, self-sufficient)
- Intellectual (intelligent, reflective)
- Logical (consistent, rational)
- Loving (affectionate, tender)
- Obedient (dutiful, respectful)
- Polite (courteous, well-mannered)
- Responsible (dependable, reliable)
- Self-controlled (restrained, self-disciplined)

2. Personal values

Clawson (1994)

Egoistic values
Happiness
Success
Idealism/realism
Motivation
Excitement
Inner harmony
Calmness
Time
Self-esteem
Stability/change
Fun/seriousness
Vicarious experience/participation
Self-improvement
Self-confidence
Enthusiasm

Biogenic values
Athletic skill
Physical energy
Safe life/danger
Pleasure and comfort
Beautiful world
Clean/tidy surroundings
Youth/maturity/old age
Physical health
Good build, strength

Cognitive values
Human wisdom
Information
Understanding (of events, people)
Rationality/impulse
Language skills
Foresight/live for today
Intelligence
Creativity
Memory
Mental energy

Familial values
Romantic love
Family love
Sexual intimacy
Popularity with opposite sex
Romantic stages
Sexual morality
Masculinity/femininity
Child and family care
Home and family life
Physical attractiveness
Sexual capacities

Material values
Material quality of life
Financial security
Living with nature
City life
Wealth and assets
Estate for heirs
Current income
Future retirement income
Liquidity: ready cash
Creditworthiness
Meaningful work
Economical/extravagant
Hard-working, good conditions, employed
Free economy/regulated/controlled
Natural resources
Personal competence

Religious values
Betterment of mankind
Spiritual reward
Religious belief and experience/atheism
Brotherly love and fellowship
Spirituality/worldliness and sin
Natural or supernatural help

Social values
True friendship
Modernity/tradition/social skills
Well-being of others (patriotism, world
view, group loyalty, happiness of others)
Ethical behaviour
Approval, belonging, tolerance
Prestige, glory
Pets' well-being
Fame
Gratitude, appreciation
Helpful, generous
Personal warmth
Humility
Conformity, similarity/individualism
Manners
Good grooming, dress
Self-sufficiency
Honesty
Sociability
Co-operativeness/solo player

Political values
Victory (contest, war)
Peaceful world/violence, war
Happiness
Superior social status
Power/equality/submission
Leadership
Mercy and fair play

3. The SWOCC (Stichting Wetenschappelijk Onderzoek Commerciele Communicatie) value inventory

Sikkel and Oppenhuisen (1998)

Factor 1

Bond   *Relationships*
            Endearing
            Atmospheric
            Cosiness
            Love
            Friendship
            Hugging

Freedom   *Career*
            To climb
            Fanaticism
            Power
            Perseverance
            To be ambitious

Factor 2
Bond   *Other-directed*
To listen to someone
To have understanding for someone
To be helpful
To be responsible
To be a good judge of character
To take others into consideration

Freedom   *Self-directed*
To relax
To be healthy
To stay young
To be carefree
To be attractive
Enjoyment
To be a good judge of character
To take others into consideration

Factor 3
Bond   *Society*
Patriotism
To be dignified
Pride
To be tough
To be attractive

Freedom   *Personal enjoyment*
To be active
To relax
To make something
To have time
To learn
To have a hobby

Factor 4
Bond   *Certainty*
Security
Tranquillity
Luxury
A place of one's own
Frugality
To be self-supporting

Freedom   *Challenge*
To be provocative
To be spontaneous
To go beyond one's own limits
To be fascinating
To have one's own opinion
To be a hero/heroine

Factor 5
Bond   *Family life*
To be a mother
To have children
To hug
To care for
To indulge

Freedom   *Freedom*
To be satisfied
To be carefree
Tranquillity
To be ordinary

Factor 6
Bond   *To make oneself attractive/appealing*
To have authority
To be dignified
Neatness
Prestige
To be attractive
To look smart

Freedom   *To go one's own way*
To believe
To be rebellious
Patriotism
To protect
To be idealistic

Chapter 3: Appendix VII Brand relationships

The brand relationship quality (BRQ) construct
Fournier (1994)

Personal commitment
I feel very loyal to this brand.
I have made a pledge of sorts to stick with this brand.
I will stay with this brand through good times and bad.
This brand can count on me to always be there.
I am willing to make sacrifices for this brand.

Self-concept connection
The brand and I have a lot in common.
This brand's image and my self-image are similar in a lot of ways.
This brand says a lot about the kind of person I am or want to be.
This brand reminds me of who I am.
This brand is a part of me.

Nostalgic connection
This brand reminds me of things I have done or places I have been.
I have at least one fond memory that involved using the brand.
This brand will always remind me of a particular phase in my life.
This brand reminds me of what I was like at a previous stage of my life.
This brand reminds me of someone important in my life.

Partner quality
I know this brand really appreciates me.
I know this brand respects me.
This brand treats me like a valuable customer.
This brand shows a continuing interest in me.
This brand takes care of me.

Behavioural interdependence
I feel like something is missing when I haven't used the brand in a while.
This brand plays an important role in my life.
It would be a shame if I had to start over from scratch with another brand from this category.
Every time I use this brand, I'm reminded of how much I like it.

Love/passion
I would seek out this brand if I moved to a new town where it wasn't readily available.
No other brand can quite take the place of this brand.
I would be very upset if I couldn't find or get in touch with this brand when I wanted it.
I have a powerful attraction towards this brand.
I feel that this brand and I were 'meant for each other'.
I am addicted to this brand in some ways.

Intimacy
I know a lot about this brand.
I know a lot about the company that makes this brand.
I feel as though I really understand this brand.
I know things about this brand that many people just don't know.

Chapter 3: Appendix VIII

HED/UT: a generally applicable scale for measuring hedonistic and utilitarian dimensions of attitude
Spangenberg, Voss and Crowley (1997).

Utilitarian items
Useful/useless
Practical/impractical
Necessary/unnecessary
Functional/not functional
Sensible/not sensible
Helpful/unhelpful
Efficient/inefficient
Effective/ineffective
Beneficial/harmful
Handy/not handy
Unproductive/productive
Problem solving/not problem solving

Hedonistic items
Dull/exciting
Not delightful/delightful
Not sensuous/sensuous
Not fun/fun
Unpleasant/pleasant
Not funny/funny
Not thrilling/thrilling
Not happy/happy
Not playful/playful
Enjoyable/unenjoyable
Cheerful/not cheerful
Amusing/not amusing

4 Brand equity: concept and research

Giep Franzen

4.1 INTRODUCTION

Nothing in the marketing world has been so much the focus of attention in recent years as the significance and value of strong brands for their owners.

Until around 1990 leading standard works on marketing treated brands merely as a means of identifying the products of certain manufacturers. Theories related chiefly to the question of how consumers chose between certain products. There was little interest in the independent role of brands in that process.

Of course, leading manufacturers of branded articles knew better. This was especially apparent in the sums of money they were prepared to pay for companies with strong brands in their portfolios. Listed below are five examples underlining the significance attributed to brands:

- Philip Morris, the largest cigarette manufacturer in the world, paid around twice the market value of both Kraft Inc. and General Foods when they were acquired in 1988. Ninety per cent of the takeover price for Kraft was goodwill. Hamish Maxwell, the chief executive of Philip Morris at the time, said that his company was prepared to spend that sum of money, because it was convinced that the future (in marketing and consumer goods) belonged to the firms with the strongest brands.
- Nestlé acquired Rowntree, also in 1988 (the manufacturer of Kit Kat, After Eight and Rolo) for the then staggering sum of US$4.5 billion.
- Grand Metropolitan, a British food and beverages company, acquired the American food business Pillsbury in 1988 for US$5.5 billion, thus paying 50% on top of its market value.
- Herb Baum, the president of Campbell Soup, explained that his company lived off branded foods, and that a look at its balance sheet would reveal the brands behind the figures. He stated that these brands were the company's true assets (Achenbaum, 1993).
- John Stuart, at one time chairman of the board of Quaker Oats, once said that if ever the company was split up, he would take the brands and trademarks and someone else could have the property, plant and equipment – and he would be better off!

There are plenty more examples to add to these five. Although brands, in the form we know today, originated in the nineteenth century, it has taken until the end of the twentieth century for people to fully appreciate their value.

The need arose for a new term to convey that value: the term 'goodwill', indicating the value of brands, was exchanged for 'brand equity'. *Webster's Dictionary* defines equity as 'the value of a property beyond what is owed on it' (ie, assets minus liabilities). Accountants use the word equity to indicate what a company owns. The new term sounded different, more reliable.

The American Advertising Research Foundation (ARF) organised a whole series of workshops on the brand equity phenomenon. To counterbalance the growth of private labels, a Coalition for Brand Equity was even set up in 1992 in the US. The big issues were: what is it exactly, how does it come about, how can we measure it, and how can we manage it? Numerous researchers threw themselves into the subject – the list of references accompanying this chapter gives some impression of their numbers. It soon became apparent that the precise substance of brand equity was quite unclear. Almost all the authors writing on the subject felt obliged to explain what they were talking about, by first providing a definition. These definitions have been gathered together and added to this chapter in Appendix I (see page 174), which gives a good idea of the confusion that has long prevailed concerning the term.

Consensus would meanwhile seem to be growing as to what the term brand equity conveys. This chapter attempts to unravel the term, in the light of the interpretations of 1998. However, it does not examine how brand equity comes about. Several good books have been written on the subject in recent years (by Aaker, 1991, 1996a; Kapferer, 1995; Keller, 1998, to name a few) and it is to some extent implicit in the text. This chapter reviews the components of brand equity and their interconnection, as well as explaining how to examine them. It also lists as many ways as possible in which successful brands differ from less successful ones.

In the definitions various researchers have formulated of brand equity, four main components can be identified:

- the *presence* of a brand in consumers' minds;
- its *influence* on their buying behaviour;
- its *effects* on a brand's market position and financial results;
- the *financial value* of a brand as one of a company's immaterial assets which could be included in the balance sheet, and finds expression if the company (or the brand itself) is sold.

So gradually a differentiation in the concept of brand equity begins to emerge. The first two components are increasingly referred to as consumer equity, the third as financial equity and the last component as brand value. Taylor (1992) makes a further distinction, within consumer brand equity, between attitudinal equity and behavioural equity. This is in keeping with the classification on which the Advertising Response Matrix is based (see Figure 2.2, page 30).

To tie in with the Advertising Response Matrix, two levels of brand equity, made up of three components, are summarised below:

- *Consumer equity*
  - Mental brand equity: the inclusion of a brand in consumers' consideration sets, ie, the conscious and active preference for a brand based on consumers' perceptions and feelings about it.
  - Behavioural brand equity: habitual or deliberately loyal purchasing of a brand by consumers in order to meet an important part of their category needs.
- *Financial/economic brand equity*
  - The influence of consumer equity on the brand's financial/economic performance in the marketplace, expressed in the level of distribution, sales, market share, price premium and profit it achieves.

The term 'equity' represents the quantitative component here: the extent to which a brand succeeds in generating positive consumer and market responses. It could also be described as the strength of the brand; strong brands have high equity, weak brands low. The three brand equity components can be represented in diagram form, as shown in Figure 4.1 overleaf.

Since the concept of equity originates from accountancy, it is often 'translated' into the financial value a brand represents: the brand value (see, among others, Haigh, 1997). However, this is confusing: brand equity does indeed result in financial brand value, but

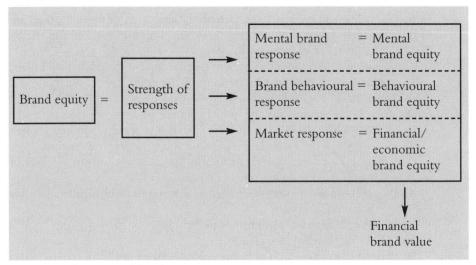

Figure 4.1 The concept of 'brand equity'

is just as 'unequal' to it as the value of real estate is to the commodity itself. The brand value is the financial value of brand equity.

In recent years people have come to realise that brands represent a financial value which sometimes far exceeds that of the fixed assets in the balance sheet. Various methods have been developed to calculate this value. These are, as such, positive developments. But, to my knowledge, this brand value is still not used as a measuring tool for advertising effectiveness – partly because the specification of a brand's financial value largely depends on which assessment method is used. In particular, the different approaches that can be used once brand-related costs and benefits have been separated can produce widely divergent results. The first question that needs to be asked is: what is a brand? Is it the brand name itself, plus the concomitant associations and attitudes, or the combination of brand name and product; the entire branded article? How, for example, can the perceived quality linked with the brand name be separated from the actual quality of the product? With the approach calculating the value of the entire branded article, the value greatly depends on all the costs related to production. Investments in manufacturing capacity considerably influence brand value. An additional complicating factor occurs with so-called 'umbrella brands' (those connected with different product categories), for which the brand value of each item in the assortment has to be worked out separately.

The financial value of a brand also depends on the opportunities it represents for the company that owns it. It is not an entity that can be determined objectively, but depends on the brand's significance in a specific context. This explains why big multinationals are sometimes willing to pay so much more for a brand than its company's share value.

In 1989 the Institute of Chartered Accountants in England and Wales issued an order to its members to refuse brand valuations from formal balance sheets until the consequences of such a procedure were sufficiently clear. In the same year a survey by the London Business School (Haigh, 1997) queried many of the assumptions which were implicit in the financial valuation of brands.

The Financial Reporting Standards (FRS) later issued by the Accounting Standards Board (ASB) deal with intangible assets generally, rather than brands specifically. The treatment of brands remains open to interpretation. There is a difference between the allowed treatment of home-grown brands (their value cannot be included in the official balance sheet) and acquired brands. Inclusion of the latter in the balance sheet (capitalisation) is dependent on whether brands are identifiable assets which can be separated from acquired goodwill. The ASB comments: 'It is not possible to determine a market value for unique intangible assets such as brands and publishing titles.'

The financial valuation of brands for company financial reports is, therefore, still a less suitable means of measuring the effectiveness of advertising campaigns. Financial valuation reflects the effectiveness of all brand activities. Consequently it can be found in brand portfolio policy in the context of the allocation of annual budgets among the various brands produced by a company (see Netelbeek and de Smeth, 1997). Anyone who is specifically interested in methods of brand valuation will find good overviews in Pauli and de Smeth (1994) and Haigh (1997). The focus here is on methods which can be used to establish mental brand equity, behavioural brand equity and financial/economic brand equity.

4.2 MENTAL BRAND EQUITY

Brand equity at a consumer level consists of a mental component (mental brand equity) and a behavioural component (behavioural brand equity). The subcomponents of these are described in the Advertising Response Matrix (see Chapter 3). The various measuring techniques are also briefly reviewed in that chapter.

The many different responses certainly cannot all be involved in a measuring system in detail to determine advertising effectiveness. So what are the main responses which might go into making up that measuring system? It is impossible to answer this question categorically; every measuring system will have to take maximum account of the specific nature of the product category and the position of the individual brand in the market. The following overview of mental responses follows the classification of the Brand Associative Network (see Figure 3.2, page 54) as proposed in the Advertising Response Matrix. As many sets of research questions as possible are indicated for establishing mental responses, but specific research methods (such as the use of scaling techniques) are not examined in detail. The listed questions are, moreover, only intended as examples. Other, possibly better questions are also conceivable.

4.2.1 Brand awareness

The importance of brand awareness almost goes without saying. In the very first models of advertising effectiveness (like AIDA (St. Elmo Lewis, 1898), which stands for Attention, Interest, Desire, Action), awareness of what is being offered was seen as the first effect of advertising communication, and this continues to apply today (ATR&N (Ehrenberg, 1997), which stands for awareness, trial, reinforcement and nudging). Aided awareness of a brand name (ie, brand recognition) is the absolute minimum condition for a brand to play a part in a consumer's choice. A strong brand is at the front of the memory and will spontaneously (without help) come to mind when a consumer thinks of a certain product category associated with the brand.

Brand awareness is easy to measure. A consumer can be asked:
- Give the brand names which first come to mind when you think of category X.
- Name all the brands in category X which you have heard of at some time.
- Which brands in category X do you know; which have you heard of, read about or seen?

Aided brand awareness is established by means of the following questions:
- A number of brands in category X are listed below. Which do you know or which sound familiar?
- Do you know brand X, even if only by name?

When consumers buy products with which they have little involvement, aided awareness has little significance for sales. Spontaneous awareness is a prerequisite in such product categories for a brand to feature prominently in consumers' choice behaviour. There is a strong correlation between spontaneous awareness and a brand's penetration (the brand is bought at least once in a 12-month period). Figure 4.2 gives an impression of this and relates to the correlation between spontaneous awareness and penetration of toothpaste brands in the Dutch market (van Westendorp, 1996).

There would seem to be a connection between the order in which brands are named spontaneously and buying frequency. This mainly helps to establish 'top of mind' awareness (TOMA): the percentage of users in a category who spontaneously give the name of a certain brand first. One problem with TOMA is that only one brand can be named first. It also overestimates the importance of market leaders, particularly when they are brands which are firmly anchored in a country's culture, such as Douwe

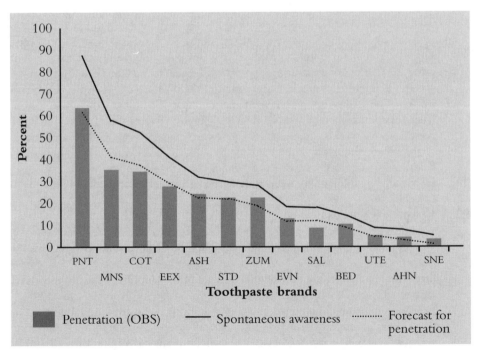

Figure 4.2 Spontaneous awareness and penetration of toothpaste brands (1989)

Egberts, Heineken and Shell in the Netherlands (van Westendorp, 1996). In such cases the position of other brands is systematically underestimated. It is therefore better to record and analyse the *order* in which brands are spontaneously named (or at least establish the first three positions).

'Spontaneous awareness' is more than the two words imply. It is an expression of the total presence of a brand in consumers' minds *and* behaviour – the brands in question are nearly always ones which people have bought at some time in the past, and will, in many instances, buy again in the future. They usually belong to a consumer's consideration set (examined later in reference to brand attitude). So it is necessary to analyse spontaneous awareness to find out whether or not the brand features in the consideration set. Van Westendorp (1996) illustrates this with an analysis of spontaneous awareness of toothpaste brands in the Netherlands in 1989 (Table 4.1 overleaf).

Luyten (1993) outlined awareness (or non-awareness) of brands of low-calorie spreads and diet margarines in the Netherlands. Non-awareness and TOMA scores, as shown in Table 4.2, also provide an indication of the strength (or weakness) of mental brand equity. It is a good idea to arrange awareness scores in order.

It is worth considering supplementing questions on awareness with questions relating to the extent of awareness (brand familiarity), as experienced by consumers themselves. Bronner and van Rooy (1997) categorise consumer reactions as follows:
- I don't know the brand at all.
- I only know the brand by name.
- I know the brand a little.
- I know the brand quite well.
- I know the brand very well.

When a product category is used as a cue, measurement not only covers spontaneous brand awareness, but, more especially, association of the brand with the product category. This is not a problem with product brands (also known as 'mono-brands'), but it is with umbrella brands. The product–brand association affects brands which are brought into the working memory when a brand choice is made within a specific category or subcategory. With umbrella brands, the brand's strength of association usually varies with the various products it covers, quite considerably even, meaning that the equity of a brand also varies in the different market (sub)categories in which it is present. For example, brand awareness for Philips will be high with the cue 'light-bulbs', but lower with the cue 'electric toothbrushes'. So it is vital, with umbrella brands, to measure their strength of association with the various product categories or subcategories they cover. If the product categories concerned are very varied, equity measurement will have to be carried out for the whole, or at least part, of each category. The measurement of brand awareness is a set element of all systems of brand equity research. However, the research agency Millward Brown points out that a measurement of brand awareness alone does not necessarily correlate with a brand's share in the individual consumer's spending within the product category in question (Dyson *et al.*, 1996). Millward Brown believes it is more than a matter of spontaneous awareness alone, and refers to 'brand presence', in which recalled trial use and a realisation of a brand's specific promise are also important.

In Young & Rubicam's Brand Asset Valuator brand knowledge is one of the four basic factors of brand equity (Agres and Dubitsky, 1996). This too stresses that what a brand represents is just as important as mere brand awareness.

Brands	Spontaneous awareness	In consideration set (%)	Awareness only (%)
Prodent	89% (=100)	84	16
Macleans	58% (=100)	71	29
Colgate	53% (=100)	65	35
Elmex	41% (=100)	69	31
Aquafresh	32% (=100)	70	30
Zendium	30% (=100)	64	36
Everclean	18% (=100)	75	25
Signal	18% (=100)	46	54
Blendamed	14% (=100)	74	26
Ultrabrite	8% (=100)	46	54
AH	7% (=100)	53	47
Sensodyne	6% (=100)	74	26
Average	31% (=100)	70	30

Table 4.1 Share of consideration set in spontaneous brand awareness (1989)

Brand \ Awareness (%)	TOMA	Other spontaneous awareness	Aided awareness only	Non-awareness
Becel Light	14	25	59	2
Blue Band halvarine	26	36	23	15
Sense Light	3	7	48	42
Lätta	4	10	72	14
Leeuwezegel halvarine	1	3	55	41
Linera	13	16	68	3
Remia halvarine	2	3	55	40
Wajang Light	2	9	61	28
Zeeuws meisje halvarine	2	14	42	42

Table 4.2 Brand awareness of low-calorie spreads ('halvarines') and diet margarines (Source: GfK; Luyten, 1993)

4.2.2 Defining brand meanings (brand knowledge)

Brands can have many different meanings. The Advertising Response Matrix distinguishes between the following categories (see Exhibit 3.2, page 58):

- brand signals;
- origin;
- company/maker;
- functional brand meanings ;
- situational meanings;
- symbolic meanings;
- price;
- quality;

- presentation;
- advertising.

When analysing a brand's equity, the meanings that affect consumer choice behaviour must be the main focus of attention. The core meanings are those which primarily define the brand. They are the associations which are significant to consumers, from which they assess whether the brand ties in with their personal values, and whether this brand is different from or better than other brands. A brand equity measuring tool will therefore have to be based on preliminary investigation determining the chief associations for the product category and the specific associations applying to the individual brands within that category. Those meanings listed above are analysed in more detail below, and include examples of associated statements.

Origin (country, region)

The origin and history of a brand can occupy an important position in the association network. Some brands spontaneously call to mind a country or region, others the company behind the brand. Consumers can have stereotypical associations with products from different countries which may play an important part in their evaluation of those products. In that case the question is to what extent a country is associated with a specific product category, such as Switzerland with watches and France with wine. These products are part of the specific frame in which the country is represented in our memory. If, in our minds, a brand is connected with a country, it may result in our linking these associations with the brand in question. With cars, for instance, the country of origin is one of the first (and hence foremost) associations which are activated when a brand comes to mind.

Research by Roth and Romeo has shown that consumers are more inclined to buy brands from countries with a good reputation in a relevant category than from countries which have no associations with the category in question. In particular, consumers with little or no product experience are inclined to base their judgment largely on the country of origin. For example, a consumer might say:
- This brand comes from a country where they're good at making category X.

Company/maker

The association of brands with the companies that market them varies greatly from one category to another, and from one brand to another. Two developments are currently taking place. First, companies behind individual brands are coming forward and making a growing effort to get their brands associated with their company. Second, companies which in the past were selling all their products and services under the company brand are switching more and more to 'sub-branding' their individual products or product categories. Aaker (1996a) differentiates between 'driver brands' and 'endorsement brands'. He uses the former term for a brand which primarily reflects what purchasers expect from the brand; ie, the collection of attributes they are looking for and the usage experience they expect. The endorsement brand adds to this the credibility of and confidence in the company, putting the consumer's mind at rest that the driver brand will do what it promises. For example, Mach 3 is a new razor blade from Gillette, which consists of three blades to provide a smooth shave. It is a typical driver brand. 'Gillette' is the endorsement brand in this case – it adds its reputation of being a shaving specialist.

Associated statements might include:
- This brand comes from a well-known company.
- The company behind this brand is good at making category X.

Functional brand meanings

One of the most significant findings relates to the relative importance of functional compared with symbolic characteristics. Spangenberg (1997) has developed a measuring tool for analysing the 'utilitarian' and 'hedonistic' dimension of product and brand attributes (see Appendix VIII of Chapter 3).

The significance of product perceptions is sometimes measured by determining whether the following examples are true:
- You buy this brand more because of its good, special product attributes than because of its 'charisma'.
- People buy this brand mainly because it aims to be a good product rather than aiming for good advertising.

Perceived product attributes

Brand associations influence brand equity in two different ways. Many surveys have shown that brands ensure that product attributes are perceived to be different (and better in the case of strong brands) from what they really are. Table 4.3 demonstrates different preferences for low-calorie versions of Pepsi Cola and Coca-Cola. Brand preference when people did not know which cola they were drinking (blind test) was compared with that when they knew which brand it was (branded test).

Park and Srinivasan call this difference in preference for brands when named the attribute-based component of brand equity. They also refer to the non-attribute based component – brand preference, which cannot be traced to the perception of product attributes. These two components are also referred to using terms like instrumental versus expressive, functional versus symbolic, utilitarian versus hedonistic, and even cognitive versus emotional.

Much research shows that perceived product attributes explain only a small part of brand preference. This is definitely the case with product categories which are primarily selected for their symbolic functions, like clothes and watches. However, Park and Srinivasan's analysis (1994) of the equity of toothpaste and mouthwash brands reveals that, even in these highly 'functional' product categories, the non-attribute based component plays a more dominant role than the attribute-based component. These findings support the conclusion that symbolic brand meanings should always be included in a tool for measuring mental brand equity, even with products which would seem to have a purely instrumental function.

	Blind (%)	Branded (%)
Preference for Pepsi Light	51	23
Preference for Coca-Cola Light	44	65
No preference	5	12
Total	100	100

Table 4.3 Brand preference for different colas (UK) (Source: Chernatony and McDonald, 1992, p 68)

Uses

The specific perceived product attributes of certain brands can mean that they are particularly associated with certain uses. Other brands may be perceived as having a more general use. Research by Millward Brown (Dyson *et al.*, 1996) reveals that when a brand is bought for specific uses, buying behaviour is generally more stable in character than with brands which are felt to have a more general use (and so can be replaced more easily by others).

Millward Brown identifies performance and advantage as key components of brand equity. She takes performance to represent the perception of the branded product's relative achievements compared with those of its competitors. Her analysis highlights perception of the level of innovation as an important criterion. A successful brand offers its users a unique proposition, which they perceive as an advantage over competing brands. As suggested in the section on brand awareness, the main issue is to discover the essential promise a brand represents for its users, and whether that promise is recognised and understood.

Symbolic meanings

Brand personality

It is becoming increasingly difficult to provide really significant and long-lasting product benefits, and so, to a growing extent, the difference between brands is determined by symbolic brand associations, in particular the unique aspects of brand personality. Consequently, it is of vital importance to define the truly distinguishing brand personality features and translate them into a measuring tool. In this context, readers are referred to Jennifer Aaker's (1997) fundamental research in this field. It has culminated in a Brand Personality Scale (BPS) which is included in Appendix V of Chapter 3. Since the whole battery of associations cannot possibly be included in an equity measuring tool, a preliminary study should be set up to isolate those items which best represent a brand's specific personality.

Users' associations

Consumers often have a picture of the kind of people who use a brand. They can describe them in the same terms they use to denote the brand's personality, though the categories of associations differ. Some similarity may exist between the two, but this is not always the case. For example, Marlboro the brand can be directly associated with masculinity, vigour, and ruggedness, but Marlboro smokers may be pictured as mainly women, young people and extrovert types.

A small-scale survey (de Vries, 1997) of Dutch beer drinkers showed that users' associations coincide with some of the most defining meanings of the Heineken and Grolsch brands. Heineken drinkers were seen as ordinary, common, rather 'macho' people, Grolsch drinkers as individualistic, stylish people who reflected on life. Users' associations often reflect more differentiation than functional product attributes.

Situational associations

The situations (places, moments, social contexts) with which brand use is associated can also be characteristic of brands. In the above-mentioned survey, Heineken was mainly associated with places in which groups of people congregate – the pub, the beach or the campsite, whereas Grolsch primarily evokes a domesticated setting, a chic interior or an easy chair.

Values

When referring to 'values' in the context of brands, what is actually meant is psycho-social meanings which can represent 'values' for people. These are symbolic brand associations, which correspond with the ideas these groups of people pursue in their own lives. (Readers are referred to Appendix VI of Chapter 3 which contains lists of values.) However, a connotation which counts as a value for one person, such as status or power, may rank as an anti-value for someone who is more egalitarian in approach.

Values with which a brand is associated may be part of brand personality. However, because current value 'inventories' do not fully correspond with inventories of brand personality features as yet, it is worth treating them as a separate category of associations.

Associated statements might include:

- When you see people using brand X, you get a better idea of what they're like.
- People buy this brand because they want to show who they are.
- With this brand you feel at home with your friends.
- This brand says something about its user.
- This brand matches/does not match my personality.
- This brand has 'charisma'.
- This brand helps me to express who I am.

Price and quality perceptions

Not only are specific functional and symbolic associations important in an equity measurement tool, so are perceptions of price and quality. However, both are primarily relative concepts, which the consumer uses to compare one brand with another. Price and quality evaluations result in a value perception of a brand. They will be examined in more depth in section 4.2.4.

4.2.2.1 Fixed and variable associations

Values represent a higher level of abstraction than product attributes. They are generally measured by means of standardised sets of questions which are used for a wide range of products and brands. Take, for example, the Brand Asset Valuator, designed by Young & Rubicam (see Exhibit 4.8, page 133). Basically, this enables us to compare brands from different categories.

In this context Bronner and Hoog (1979) differentiate between 'fixed' and 'variable' brand values. These 'fixed' brand values are included in an analysis, regardless of the product category. They mark out four clusters:

- *emotional and direct*, such as 'exclusive, modern, familiar, classy brand';
- *emotional and projective*, such as 'for people who think quality is important, for people with style, for people who don't mind spending money, for successful people, for trendsetters' (referred to earlier as users' associations);
- *rational and direct*, such as 'value for money, you see it everywhere, available everywhere';
- *rational and projective*, such as 'for people who think health is important'.

In order to compare brands in a product category properly with one another, the brand-specific associations must be ascertained, and included in the analysis. Bronner calls these assocations the 'variable associations'.

4.2.2.2 Measuring core meanings

When associations are measured quantitatively, verbal and/or numerical scaling techniques are generally used. Three, five, seven or even nine-point scales are used, sometimes with verbally qualified intermediate positions. When a larger number of brands and associations have to be measured, it is a time-consuming process. This need not always be a problem for specific image research. However, brand equity research, in which a larger number of equity components are measured with greater regularity (in the form of tracking studies, for instance), requires the most compact measuring tool possible. According to Bronner and van Rooy (1997), experience has shown that respondents cannot be presented with more than 20 to 25 characteristics and asked to give a scale rating.

The Asspat (short for association patterns) method designed by Research International can be helpful here. It involves presenting all the brands to the respondent at the same time. Statements are then presented one by one, and the respondent is asked to say which statement is most appropriate to which brand, so that their choices are comparative. The simplicity of the method is its strength and, at the same time, its weakness: consumers cannot qualify their opinions, which they can do with scaling techniques. However, considerable interviewing time is saved.

An example of the Asspat method follows, and is illustrated in Figure 4.3.

- Here you see a number of brands (category X). On the left-hand side there is a list of words relating to those brands. Please mark beside each word the brands to which you think that word applies. You may mark more than one brand.

4.2.2.3 The brand ideal

Image research has always rightly occupied an important place in market research, but the relationship between image components and ultimate brand choice has received considerably less attention. Brand image measurement in quantitative research generally entails assessing various criteria of a brand, in which the result of one criterion may be positive, of another negative (Bronner and de Hoog, 1979), so that the importance of the criteria usually varies. The way in which the eventual choice is reached may differ from one consumer to another. The term 'combination rules' is used in this context, distinguishing between compensatory and non-compensatory rules. With the former, less favourable assessments for certain criteria can be 'compensated' by more favourable assessments for others (for example, choice is based on the average of all criteria, or on a weighted average). Non-compensatory rules may involve threshold values which have to be met, or one important property on which choice is based.

It is not relevant to discuss this in more detail here, but the importance of a better understanding of the individual criteria and the concomitant brand associations must be stressed. Good, sound brand equity measurement requires sufficient certainty on the significance of different attributes for the respondents, obtained by prior empirical research. This information is usually provided by ranking and scaling techniques, or conjoint analyses. In conjoint research (or the trade-off approach) consumers have to weigh up two attributes at a time. The ultimate goal is to establish the partial preference

Association	Omo	Persil	Witte Reus	Ariel	Dixan
Washes whiter	☐	☐	☐	☐	☐
Traditional	☐	☐	☐	☐	☐
Old–fashioned	☐	☐	☐	☐	☐
Powerful	☐	☐	☐	☐	☐
Good for coloured washes	☐	☐	☐	☐	☐
Gentle	☐	☐	☐	☐	☐
Rough	☐	☐	☐	☐	☐
Biological	☐	☐	☐	☐	☐
Modern	☐	☐	☐	☐	☐
Good for washing machines	☐	☐	☐	☐	☐
Value for money	☐	☐	☐	☐	☐
Cheaper	☐	☐	☐	☐	☐

Figure 4.3 Asspat method for measuring associations

of every brand attribute. The analysis of brand equity measurements using modelling techniques can also provide useful information.

Another way of finding out the significance of various brand associations for consumers is to ask respondents to what extent their 'ideal brand' in the category has the appropriate attributes, and how important it is for them that a brand possesses those attributes.

When the Asspat method is used, the same statements should be submitted again and respondents asked which attributes the ideal brand ought to have. It will then be possible to make a segmentation according to preference profiles, as expressed in the ideal brand scores, and check to what extent brands, in consumers' views, coincide with their specific values and product expectations of the different segments. It will also be possible to relate this to the scores on attitude and behaviour questions. The degree of correspondence between brand scores and ideal scores gives an indication of the brand's relevance to the respondent.

4.2.3 Differentiation

Defining differences

Differentiation is the distinctiveness of a brand; how different it is from its competitors. Differentiation is a bottom–line characteristic (Aaker, 1996a). If a brand is not seen to be 'different', it is difficult for consumers to reach a decision based on that, and they will certainly not be inclined to pay more for it. In Y&R's Brand Asset Valuator research model, differentiation is the first criterion that a successful brand has to meet. It is even more important than brand awareness.

The extent to which a brand stands out from its competitors can be deduced from the scores on individual questions, such as:

- How different is this brand from other (category X) brands?
- Most brands (category X) are (taste) the same.

Y&R's Brand Asset Valuator test suggests that new brands which are relatively successful often achieve high differentiation scores, and that old brands in particular risk losing in terms of differentiation. This is said to be a sign of the weakening of long-standing brands, which do not invest enough in achieving and communicating brand-differentiating characteristics. These need not be product attributes only, as a brand like Coca-Cola demonstrates: at a product level it is not essentially different, but is perceived as being very distinctive (Agres and Dubitsky, 1996).

Evaluative and differentiating associations

Consumers almost always consider the brands they use to be better in most respects than those they do not use. They adjust their attitudes to their behaviour. This phenomenon brings about a pronounced correlation between the associations of a brand with positive characteristics and the percentage of people who use the brand, and so between the brand associations and with the market share as well. This correlation is very pronounced for more or less 'generic' characteristics of a product category, for example, 'nice taste' with all kinds of foods, beverages and snacks. They are, in a sense, 'evaluative associations'. Evaluative associations reflect attitudes towards the brand – they correlate highly with brand preference/usage. Research by Osgood has shown that 80% of the variance in attributing characteristics to objects is brought about by an evaluative factor (van Westendorp, 1993).

When the brands in question exhibit no clear differences from one another at a product level, the various users' functional associations do not differ much either. For example, great similarity can be observed in Heineken's product attribute associations for a Heineken drinker, in Amstel's associations for an Amstel drinker and in Grolsch's associations for a Grolsch drinker. But for each brand the associations differ greatly between the brand's own users and users of competing brands.

If a brand has a physical attribute or effect which clearly differs from the competing brands, it is usually reflected in the associations. These 'differentiating associations' may also be the result of advertising, which has communicated a distinctive claim consistently over the years. They are found among users and non-users alike.

Brand equity research needs to establish which associations are chiefly 'evaluative' and which are chiefly 'differentiating'. Analysis of brand associations as regards overall brand attitudes and brand purchasing behaviour can provide insight into this.

The double-jeopardy effect

Small brands are mainly small because they are bought by fewer consumers, but also because those who buy them do so somewhat less often than big brands. This is called the 'double-jeopardy' effect. The same effect occurs when associations and attitudes are measured: as previously seen, respondents are more inclined to ascribe more vague evaluative concepts to brands they use than to brands they do not use – something which is further reinforced by higher usage frequency. When research results are not broken down, this is an advantage for larger brands. Small brands tend to do worse, even with their own users, than large brands. Various analysis methods are available for correcting these effects and providing insight into the real differences (see Bronner, 1993). However, they usually require large-scale sampling, in order to represent users of smaller brands adequately.

4.2.4 Price–quality assessment

Perceived quality

Consumers perceive the quality of brands as 'very good', 'less good', 'not so good' or 'poor'. This is more a continuum than a dichotomous judgment. 'Perceived quality' is one-dimensional, an abstraction that cannot be compared to anything. Admittedly it is based on the assessment of individual functional and symbolic characteristics, but consumers integrate these partial assessments in order to reach an overall rating (Steenkamp, 1989).

Perceived quality is a relative concept: perception of the quality of individual brands occurs in a competitive context, so the perceived quality of Pepsi Cola is also influenced by the perceived quality of Coca-Cola and private labels like Real American Cola.

Perceived quality is category-dependent. The quality of a brand can vary from one subcategory to another: perception of Marlboro in the full-flavour cigarette subcategory can differ from its perception in the ultra-light subcategory. This is partly because it is compared with different brands in the various subcategories. Perceived quality of brands is affected by situational variables: the purpose for which brands are used and the physical and social surroundings in which they are used. The same brand can be assessed differently in relation to different usage situations – the question of whether consumption is individual or social is particularly relevant.

Overall quality perception is based on quality cues. These are used to assess the brand's quality characteristics: the functional and psycho-social benefits it offers. Quality characteristics represent what the brand (branded article) offers the consumer in terms of usage. The consumer observes the cues (for example, price, packaging style) and derives quality characteristics from them. Cues are concrete, characteristics are abstract. It is not intended to go into the way in which cues influence quality characteristics or how consumers process the different characteristics in order to reach their overall assessment. Steenkamp (1989) presents an overview of theories in this field.

Perceived quality is partly determined by the extent to which a brand meets users' expectations – in their perception. These expectations vary. With service brands, for

---

The PIMS Database

The Profit Impact of Market Strategy (PIMS) Database was set up in 1972 by the Marketing Science Institute in the US. Some 450 companies participate, reporting on over three thousand business units. Data relating to finance, market, customers and quality is supplied periodically for each unit, and researchers establish correlations and trends. The PIMS Database is the only one in the world containing strategic information on a wide variety of businesses. Different sub-databases are analysed as to the effects of a wide range of strategic variables, including advertising expenditure. Correlations are always made with ultimate financial results, including profit, ROI and cash flow. The PIMS Database is currently maintained by the Strategic Planning Institute.

Exhibit 4.1

instance, they may relate to the characteristics of the service itself, the physical conditions in which service is provided, service reliability, the service-provider's helpfulness, promptness and empathy, guarantees, and so on. Quality perceptions can be measured separately for each of these characteristics. If the relative significance of each quality property can be determined, a total score can be calculated using weighting factors. It can be worthwhile, especially with service brands, to use differentiated measuring techniques for quality perceptions. However, for fast-moving consumer goods, questions into overall evaluation will generally be used within the framework of an equity measuring tool.

- Compared with other brands (category X) the quality of this brand is high/ average/low.
- This brand is the best (category X)/one of the good brands/not so good a brand/ a poor brand.
- No one brand is the best, but two or three are better than the others.
- All brands are about the same.

The significance of perceived quality

Analyses of the PIMS Database (see Exhibit 4.1) show that perceived quality is the single most important variable affecting companies' profitability. Its influence is even greater than that of market share or the volume of marketing activities (Buzzel and Gale, 1987). Figure 4.4 depicts this correlation: on the horizontal axis, relative quality is expressed in five ratings, from low to high. On the vertical axis, profit is expressed in return on sales or ROS (gross margins) and return on investment or ROI.

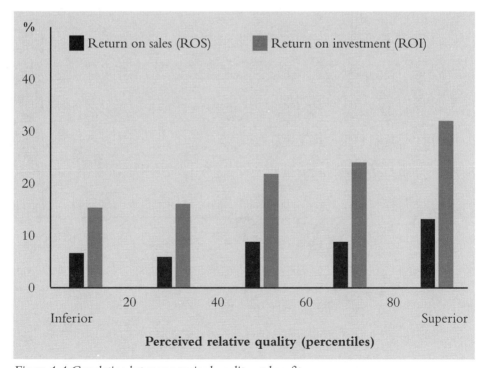

Figure 4.4 Correlation between perceived quality and profit

An important correlation was also noted between perceived quality and the brands' relative market positions. Market leaders score considerably better on perceived quality than brands in second and third place. The more dominant the market leader's position, the greater the difference in perceived quality between the brands below it. There is probably some interaction between the two variables (see Figure 4.5).

Fornell (in Aaker, 1996a) also concluded, on the basis of his analysis of 77 Swedish companies, that perceived quality was the most important factor influencing customer satisfaction and that it had considerable influence on profitability.

High perceived quality of a brand results in customer willingness to pay a price premium, greater satisfaction, greater brand loyalty and less susceptibility to competitors' price discounts.

In addition, PIMS analysis demonstrated that high perceived quality not only leads to higher profit, but also to greater market share.

Differentiation and perceived quality

Analyses of the PIMS Database (Buzzel and Gale, 1987) show that differentiation and perceived quality together greatly influence the profitability of brands (business units).

In markets in which consumers assess the different brands as equal with respect to the relevant dimensions, ie, in which 'perceived parity' can be said to exist, the brands are seen to have relatively low profitability in terms of ROI. The perceived quality of brands in these markets is generally rated as 'average': not much better or worse than

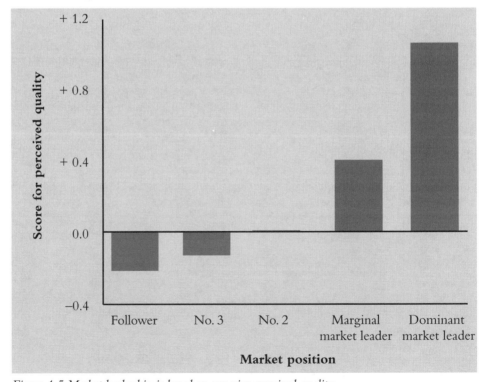

Figure 4.5 Market leadership is based on superior, perceived quality

others. The bigger the difference between the individual brands, the greater the chance of a high score for perceived quality. The combination of a high quality score and a market which is perceived as being highly differentiated leads to higher profitability: 30–40% ROI (see Figure 4.6). The PIMS analyses confirm that perceived differentiation of a market need not be based only on perceived product differences, but can also be caused by symbolic brand associations:

- To what extent do you think the various brands (category X) resemble one another?

Perceived relative price

Consumers do not usually know exactly how much a brand costs, but they do have an idea of whether it is dearer or cheaper than its competitors. This perception of relative price affects consumers' decisions on whether or not to include a brand in their consideration set. Consumer statements tend to be based along the following lines:

- This brand is (much) more expensive, just as expensive, (much) cheaper than other brands in category X.

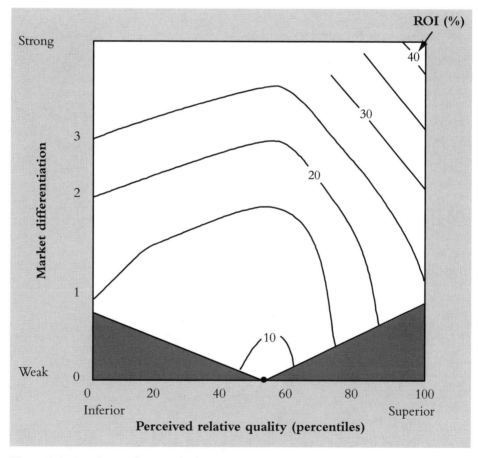

Figure 4.6 Correlation of perceived relative quality, market differentiation and ROI (Source: PIMS Database)

Price premium

An important component in the equity of a brand is the price premium which users are prepared to pay, compared with competing brands or private labels. Ideally this price premium is determined in the marketplace by consumer or retail panels.

Willingness to pay a price premium is reflected to some extent in price elasticity: the change in sales (in percentage terms) resulting from raising or lowering the price by 1% (see section 4.4 on financial/economic brand equity).

However, sales figures do not give proper insight into how willingness to pay a price premium varies in the different attitude groups: how, for instance, do committed brand users compare with potential 'deserters'? In order to get an idea of this, willingness to pay a price premium is established as part of attitude measurement. For example:

- How much more would you be prepared to pay for (brand) instead of (brand)?
- Which brand would you buy if all brands (category X) cost the same?
- Which brand would you buy if your usual brand became 10% or 20% more expensive?

A more reliable method of studying price premium is conjoint analysis. Consumers are faced with a succession of choices between two alternatives, which, in this case, have a different price each time. The research agency Research International uses this kind of conjoint analysis as a direct indication of a brand's value for consumers: BETA, which stands for Brand Equity or Price Trade-Off Analysis (Blackston, 1993b). It argues that this method, used for tracking research among other things, gives a good idea of the range and development of brand equity throughout the product categories.

It is essential, if price premium and price elasticity are to be studied reliably, to identify the competing brands with which the brand in question is to be compared. The object of the exercise is comparison with competitors which users at least see as acceptable alternatives.

According to Aaker (1996a):

The price premium may well be the best single measurement for the strength of brand equity, because in the vast majority of situations whatever equity is based on influences the price a consumer is prepared to pay for the brand. So the price premium is a reasonable reflection of the strength of the brand.

Perceived (relative) value

Perceived value is the outcome of weighing up perceived quality and perceived price. A user who assesses a brand as superior and the price as not too high attributes a high value to the brand. Someone who considers the quality to be merely average and the price relatively high has a low value perception of the brand.

A survey by Total Research in the US (Alleborn, 1994) shows that the influence of perceived quality on perceived value is considerably more than that of perceived price. They conclude that perceived quality accounts for, on average, 80% of the variance in perceived value. Fornell *et al.* (1996) also established that user satisfaction with their brand is influenced more by quality perceptions than by price.

However, research by Y&R (Aaker, 1996a) suggests that 'perceived quality' and 'value' should be seen as two different dimensions. Perceived quality proves, in Y&R's research, to be closely connected to the prestige attributed to the brand, while value largely relates to its functional performance.

Perceived (relative) value is generally assessed with statements like the following:
- This brand offers good/less good/little value for money.
- This brand is worth the money.

Leadership

Analyses of brand equity, measured by Y&R's Brand Asset Valuator, have led to the conclusion that measurement of perceived quality is not always sensitive enough to explain or predict changes in market response (Aaker, 1996a). Consequently Y&R suggest that questions into leadership of brands can be helpful in ascertaining brand equity. Leadership is connected with perception of the brand as the biggest in its market (the 'number one'), but also with its perceived popularity and innovativeness. Consumers often base their brand preferences on what they believe they perceive in their surroundings (the 'social desirability' hypothesis). Usually this relates to larger brands, which they believe are also more popular. Possible lines of inquiry include:
- This brand is the biggest/one of the biggest/smaller than other/one of the smallest brands (category X).
- The popularity of this brand is growing/stays the same/is decreasing.
- This brand leads the way with new products.

4.2.5 Overall evaluation and brand attitude

Evaluation and attitude are closely interconnected. Attitude is sometimes defined as the mental product (outcome) of an evaluation. In the Advertising Response Matrix brand attitude is defined as 'the stable favourable or unfavourable overall evaluation of the brand expressed as a certain degree of brand preference (brand acceptance or brand rejection) and influencing behaviour regarding the brand'. Although there is a very close connection between brand assessment and brand attitude in terms of preference or rejection, the two are usually measured independently in brand equity research.

Overall assessment can be measured by means of direct questions, which respondents can answer verbally or using numbers, for example:
- How well do you assess this brand compared with other similar brands?
- Please give marks out of 10 for each of the following brands.

Esteem, or consumers' respect for a brand, is the third pillar in Y&R's Brand Asset Valuator. Brand esteem is closely linked to the quality and popularity assessment of a brand.

Brand attitude

Measurements of brand attitude (preference, neutrality or rejection) can take many different forms. To start with, it is important to find out whether a brand belongs in a consumer's consideration set:
- If you buy (category X) again, which brands would you consider?
- Are you considering buying (brand x) again?
- Which brand or brands would you buy if your favourite brand were sold out?

Dyson *et al.* (1996) submit that Millward Brown's tracking study demonstrates a strong correlation in many categories between the historical development of consideration scores and development in the brand's sales.

GfK (Luyten, 1993; Luyten and Hulsebos, 1994) suggests that the consideration set is generally limited in scope. It presents the arrangement in Table 4.4 for three product categories based on measurements from the GfK panel.

No. of brands in the consideration set	Low-calorie spread/ diet margarine (%)	Packet soup (%)	Sanitary towels (%)
0	17	7	12
1	37	13	17
2	41	59	47
3	5	19	23
4+	–	2	3

Table 4.4 Size of consideration set for several product categories (Source: Luyten, 1993)

Once it has been discovered which brands belong to the consideration set, relative brand preference must be established. Measurement of attitudes then resembles the measurement of buying intentions (see section 4.2.6). Buying intentions and attitudes both reflect the same mental dispositions. For attitude measurement, scaling techniques are often used, for instance:

- I like this brand a lot/I quite like this brand/I don't like this brand.
- This is the only brand I'd want to buy.
- I'd never buy this brand.
- Which brand would you buy most, if all brands cost the same?
- It doesn't make much difference to me which brand (category X) I buy.
- I have a preference for one brand (category X).

Constant sum methods are also frequently used. They entail asking respondents to express their relative brand preference by allocating points to the brands in their consideration set. There are different ways of applying these methods. Usually a consumer is asked to divide 11 points among two brands at a time. For example:

- We would like to know how you rate brands X and Y in relation to each other. To illustrate this, please divide up 11 points between these two brands.
- We would like to know how you rate the brands you sometimes buy, compared with one another. If you could divide up 11 points among them, based on your esteem for them, how many points would you give brand X, how many brand Y and how many brand Z?

Of course, scaling techniques can also be used to measure the strength of attitudes with respect to alternative brands.

A distinction must be made between brands people say they buy sometimes and the brand they say they buy more often than the other named brands: the consumer's 'top brand'. The top-brand score plays an important part in influencing the market share.

Consumers who only accept one brand do exist. They are generally only a small percentage of users of the relevant category – but for the brand in question they form an important group. So it is worth identifying that group through questioning. Exhibit 4.2 describes the Target Monitor model developed by the Nederlandse Stichting voor Statistiek (NSS) research agency.

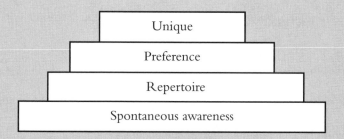

Figure 4.7 NSS Target Monitor model

The Target Monitor model designed by Nederlandse Stichting voor Statistiek (NSS) takes spontaneous awareness as a minimum condition for a successful brand. Aided awareness is of little significance for buying frequency. The model calls spontaneous awareness 'consumer franchise'. Users of a category are divided into five groups in this model.

1   *Not spontaneously aware*
    No consumer franchise

2   *Spontaneously aware*
    Brand not in repertoire, split according to attitude:
    • negative;
    • neutral;
    • positive.

3   *In repertoire*
    The brands the respondent will buy in the future or will consider buying

4   *Preference*
    Relative preference for the brands in the repertoire, measured by the constant sum method

5   *Unique*
    When consumers accept only one brand. This is a small group for many brands. The category can be divided into two groups:
    • traditional (those who have been using the brand for a very long time, out-and-out 'habit' buyers);
    • convinced (consumers with a very positive attitude to the brand).

Not only is consumer franchise measured, but also brand use (with questionnaires). This determines total penetration (brands which have been purchased in a certain period) and top-brand penetration (the brand which has been bought more often than any other during this period).

Total penetration, and top-brand penetration, are systematically greater, the higher the franchise level. But a substantial share of total penetration is accounted for by groups 1) not spontaneously aware, and 2) spontaneously aware/brand not in repertoire.

Links between usage, and size and structure of the franchise provide insight into psychological potential and the extent to which the brander makes the most of it.

Source: van Westendorp, 1996

Exhibit 4.2

The conversion model

To gain some idea of the strength of brand equity and the course it is likely to take, users within a category must be segmented according to the relative strength of their attitudes towards alternative brands. Hofmeyr (1990) developed such a method which he called the Conversion Model. The model is a combination of questions for establishing consumer commitment to a brand compared with the alternatives. Essentially, the system entails determining the strength of consumer preference for each brand in a category compared with brand use. At the analysis stage consumers are first divided into users and non-users, and then the users are divided into four groups based on the strength of their brand attitude. The model is based on four types of questions: assessment, satisfaction of needs, importance, and movement.

- *Assessment*

  Questions concerning the overall assessment of the brand using a seven-point scale, ranging from 'cold' to 'hot' (corresponding with 'emotional distance').

- *Satisfaction of needs*

  Satisfaction with the brand, measured by a ten-point scale, ranging from 'very dissatisfied' to 'perfectly satisfied in every respect'. This question is put to users of a brand only.

- *Importance*

  Measurement of involvement with the product category.

- *Movement*

  Measurement of inertia or inclination to change, and whether reasons for brand loyalty prevail over reasons to change brands.

These four variables are used in a classification procedure in which segments are formed, based on a series of multiple matrices. This results in eight highly practicable segments: 1–4 for users (varying according to degree of commitment) and 5–8 for non-users (varying according to inclination to switch brands or possible 'conversion'), listed below.

1 *Entrenched users*

  Users who are not available for conversion in the near future. They will always remain loyal to the brand.

2 *Average users*

  Secure users who are not immediately available for conversion. They are so committed to the brand that they will not easily abandon it.

3 *Shallow users*

  Users who are beginning to show signs of wavering. Their loyalty is below average and they are starting to consider other brands/organisations.

4 *Convertible users*

  Users who are on the threshold of leaving the brand.

5 *Available consumers*

  Non-users who actually prefer the brand in question to their current choice(s).

6 *Ambivalent consumers*

  Non-users who are equally attracted to the brand in question and to their current choice(s).

7 *Weakly unavailable consumers*

  Non-users whose preference lies with their current brand(s), but not strongly.

8   *Strongly unavailable consumers*
    Non-users who have a strong preference for their current choice(s).

The 'secure users' form the core of consumer equity, while 'vulnerable users' and 'available non-users' are the groups responsible for growth or decline in sales. Comparison of the way the eight segments are divided among the brands gives an idea of which brands in a market are vulnerable and which have little to fear. An important approach of the analysis is to single out the shallow users and convertible users and see whether these people are from the 'available' or 'ambivalent' group of other brands. Movements between convertible users and the available group are of particular interest. They provide insight into which brand battles will be lost and won.

Secure users		Vulnerable users			
Entrenched	Average	Shallow	Convertible		
		Open non-users		**Unavailable non-users**	
		Available	Ambivalent	Weakly unavailable	Strongly unavailable

Figure 4.8 Segments of users in the 'conversion model' (Source: Heath, 1997)

The conversion model (see Table 4.5) is now widely used on an international scale. Switches between the eight segments are claimed to be a good prediction of developments in market shares. For instance, the decline of Marlboro in 1991 in the US, known as 'Marlboro Friday', is said to have been predicted in this way (Heath, 1997).

Feldwick (1996) is of the opinion that brand commitment, measured according to the conversion model, is an important improvement on more traditional buying intention questions.

Satisfaction

The realisation that brand loyalty is the core of brand equity and that existing customers' satisfaction with the purchased product or service is probably the most important condition for brand loyalty, has generated great interest in customer satisfaction research. A series of analyses of the costs of recruiting new customers compared with retaining existing ones (see Hallberg, 1995) has made an important contribution in this respect. It has resulted in a great many tools being developed to measure customer satisfaction (Mosely, 1993). However, they are often more focused on uncovering specific causes of dissatisfaction than assessing the degree of satisfaction as the basis for consumer loyalty.

These analyses can certainly be a useful tool with which to alert management in time to the fact that a problem is developing, but they are invariably too extensive and complex to be part of a tool for measuring brand equity.

Available for:	Deserter users of:			
	Brand A (%)	Brand B (%)	Brand C (%)	Brand D (%)
Brand A	–	38	26	38
Brand B	26	–	24	24
Brand C	28	14	–	25
Brand D	12	7	20	–

Table 4.5 Conversion model: availability of 'deserters' for other brands (Source: presentation by NIPO, Amsterdam)

However, they can supply insight into the main dimensions of satisfaction or dissatisfaction for the specific sector or product category. And, as a result, a decision may be made to include some relevant questions in a brand equity measuring tool. For brands in the services sector this may even become a key component. When fast-moving consumer goods are involved, more general questions on brand satisfaction will usually suffice, such as:

• How satisfied were you the last time you used brand X? (combined with a satisfaction scale).

The American Customer Satisfaction Index is widely used (Exhibit 4.3 contains a brief description).

As it happens, dissatisfied customers by no means always switch to a competing brand, and 15–25% of those who switched brands did not do so because they were dissatisfied with their old brand.

4.2.6 Buying behaviour tendency

Consumer inclination to buy a brand is, of course, a vital component of consumer equity. If actual behaviour is not measured frequently (longitudinally), questions on recent buying behaviour or intended buying behaviour have to be relied upon. The latter, involving questioning consumers about which brand they expect to buy in the future, is particularly problematic. Analyses of buying intention scores compared with actual purchases, established in a consumer panel, show that there is a greater correlation with buying behaviour in the past than with buying behaviour in the future (Barnard, 1990).

Questions concerning intended buying behaviour are in fact more like attitude measurements than measurements of actual intended behaviour. Ajzen and Fishbein (1977) also found a weak correlation between buying intentions and subsequent behaviour. They noted that attitudes and buying intentions should correlate when correctly measured. Consumers cannot tell us what they are going to do in the future, but merely what they think, at the moment they are questioned, they might do. Their answers simply reflect their attitudes at that moment. So are questions on buying intention the best measures of attitude? There are indications that other forms of attitude measurement, as already discussed here, are better at forecasting.

The research service NPD Group in the US devised a tool for measuring brand loyalty, validating it through longitudinal behaviour research with a consumer panel. It called this method the Brand Builder (Baldinger and Rubinson, 1996). It concluded that attitude measurements using a form of constant sum approach correlated well with actual buying behaviour.

In order to divide consumers into brand loyalty groups, Millward Brown (Dyson *et al.*, 1996) uses a combination of questions on satisfaction with the product category and receptiveness to price cuts. This has shown, in almost all product groups, a strong correlation with actual buying behaviour established in a consumer panel.

Bacon (1994) found that buying intention measurements correlated better with measurements of multiple purchases (for instance, as expressed in share of customer) than with measurement of the next individual purchase. He believes that a combination of association and attitude measurements is best at forecasting buying behaviour.

The American Customer Satisfaction Index

Fornell *et al.* (1996) developed a standard tool for measuring customer satisfaction (the American Customer Satisfaction Index, or ACSI for short), which is now widely used in various countries. General Motors uses it in the US for measuring customer satisfaction with cars, and the Deutsche Bank is using it to track satisfaction with all its branches using a sample of 250,000 customers. It is based on the measurement of three antecedents of satisfaction: customer expectations; perceived quality; and perceived value.

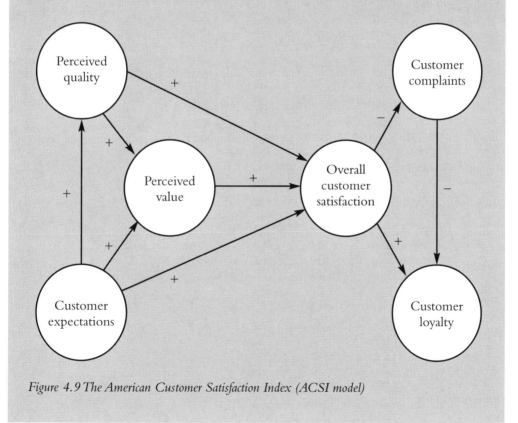

Figure 4.9 The American Customer Satisfaction Index (ACSI model)

Exhibit 4.3; continued overleaf

The ACSI model contains the following measuring variables:

- overall quality expectations;
- expectations relating to the extent to which the brand meets personal requirements;
- expectations relating to reliability (how often the respondent expects something to go wrong);
- overall evaluation of usage experience;
- overall evaluation of the extent to which the brand has met personal requirements;
- overall evaluation of reliability (how often something went wrong);
- assessment of quality in relation to price;
- assessment of price in relation to quality;
- overall satisfaction;
- shortfalls in the light of expectations;
- Achievements in the light of brand ideal.
- Official or unofficial complaints.
- Buying intentions.
- Price tolerance (buying intention with higher price).
- Price tolerance (lower price needed if this brand is to be bought again).

Fornell claims that there is a positive correlation between the ACSI scores and ROI of the brands in question.

Source: Fornell *et al.*, 1996

Exhibit 4.3 continued.

Questions

- Which brands (category X) do you sometimes buy, even if only occasionally?
- Which brand (category X) did you purchase last?
- Do you remember which brand (category X) you bought before that? What was it?
- Do you buy one brand (category X) more than others?
- Which brand (category X) do you buy most?
- Since when have you been buying that brand most?
- Do you regularly change brands (category X)?
- Which brand (category X) do you think you'll buy next time?
- If you were to buy (category X) again today, which brand would you be most likely to buy?
- If that brand was out of stock, which other brand would you buy?
- Which brand do you think you'll be buying more often in the future?
- Which brand do you think you'll be buying less often in the future?

If there is a direct connection between exposure to advertising and equity measurement, it can be advisable to check consumers' fact-finding behaviour. Agreement with the following statements can be checked:

- I obtained further information about this brand.
- I talked to other people about this brand.
- I rang a toll-free number about this brand.
- I sent in a reply coupon about this brand.
- I called at a showroom about this brand.

Brand Watcher: loyalty versus switching

Strong brands are able to generate a relatively high 'share of customer' and have a greater appeal for brand switchers. The strength of brands is primarily apparent when price changes occur. In order to determine the relative strength of brands within a category, Sloot and Bunt (1996) calculate three indices in their Brand Watcher method: a brand loyalty index, a brand switch index and a consumer franchise index. Their calculations are based on the following questions:

- Which brand (category X) do you use most?
- Which brand would you use most if all brands had the same price?
- Which brand would you buy if your regular brand weren't sold anymore?

The second question can be used to analyse whether the consumer is loyal to the brand or to the price. Consumers who continue to buy the brand when the price changes are classified as loyal. Comparison of the score for a certain brand with the average score for all brands in the category gives the brand loyalty index.

$$\text{Brand loyalty index} = \frac{\text{percentage loyal to brand A}}{\text{percentage loyal to all brands}} \times 100$$

If the index is more than 100 it means that the brand can count on relatively loyal consumers.
To compute the brand switch index, the 'switcher share' of the brand is compared with its 'most used' share. In this way it is possible to analyse whether a brand with a high percentage of brand-loyal buyers also has a relatively high appeal for brand switchers. This is expressed in the consumer franchise index, which is calculated by dividing the share of 'same prices' by the share of 'most bought'.

Exhibit 4.4

Exhibit 4.4 contains a description of the Brand Watcher method, devised by Sloot and Bunt, which also assesses brand-buying behaviour.

4.2.7 Brand relationship

In recent years the development of relationships with consumers has become the focal point of branding theory. A good relationship with customers proves to result in greater continuity in sales, less price susceptibility and higher margins. Fournier (1994) came up with three conditions, based on thorough research, which brand–consumer interactions must meet if there is to be a 'relationship':

- Some 'motivation' must exist for interdependence; the relationship must be based on a function.
- A relationship must be 'condition-specific' and result in rewards.
- An 'emotional tie' must exist.

Fournier identified seven aspects of customer–brand relationships which occur to a varying degree in different products and brands. So, in fact, it is impossible to devise one simple set of questions producing satisfactory measurement of a relationship in all situations: a combination of questions is always necessary.

All the writings on customer–brand relationships emphasise in the first instance a 'binding interest'. It may be an instrumental or a socio-psychological interest, or a combination of the two. Instrumental interests focus on achieving functional goals. Socio-psychological interests are about influencing the self-image (the impressive and expressive function of brands), and about pursuing such terminal values as certainty, security, solidarity, adventure and pleasure in life.

Y&R's Brand Asset Valuator uses the term 'relevance' for this binding interest. It implies that consumers see the brand as an instrument with which to achieve their own goals. Possible statements used might be worded:

- This brand meets my own specific product requirements.
- This brand is especially suited to people like me.

A second component is the tie-in with the self-concept: the brand personality coincides with the self-image the consumer aspires to. The consumer might agree that:

- This brand says a lot about the kind of person I should like to be.
- This brand says something about what I consider important in life.
- This brand and I are alike.
- This brand's personality matches mine.

A third aspect is the 'affective emotional feelings' a person has about a brand, which is both an emotion and an attitude. This implies an affinity with the brand, 'adoration' of the brand compared with the alternatives. These feelings are often combined with fascination and a sense of exclusiveness. Relevant statements might include:

- I am extremely fond of this brand.
- I am greatly attracted to this brand.
- I have certain feelings for this brand which I don't have for other brands.
- I really love this brand.

'Intimacy' in the sense of emotional proximity is the fourth component in a brand relationship. Consumers feel they know the brand very well and also believe the brand understands them well.

- I know a lot about this brand.
- This brand is very close to me.
- I feel at home with this brand.
- This brand is reliable.
- I feel as if I've known this brand for a long time.

Intimacy in this context is closely related to the consumer's 'trust' in the brand: it reflects the personal bond the brand has with the consumer (Blackston, 1993a). Trust results in commitment.

- This brand always looks after its clients well.
- This brand is interested in me, does its best for me and treats me like an important client.
- This brand has always been good to me.
- This brand always shows an interest in me.

These measure the perceived partner quality (ie, the consumer views the brand as a 'partner'), an aspect which overlaps the last one to some extent.

'Attachment' refers to the interconnection between actions and reactions in the relationship between consumer and brand. It reflects the extent to which a brand is part of a consumer's daily life. Attachment is mainly expressed in feelings of loss if the customer–brand relationship is threatened:

- This brand plays an important part in my life.
- If this brand were not to exist any more, I'd really miss it.
- I'm addicted to this brand in a way.

Strong customer–brand relationships are primarily marked by strong commitment; the resolve to reinforce the relationship with the brand in the future. In the most extreme cases it results in rejection of any alternative:

- I am very loyal to this brand.
- I can't manage without this brand.
- If one shop doesn't have this brand, I'll go somewhere else to buy it.

Questions geared to measuring commitment must be included in any equity research tool. However, it is worth considering adding questions concerning the relationship which are relevant to specific product categories.

Not all the seven aspects of Fournier's research have the same predictive ability as regards attitude and behaviour. The 'attachment' and 'personal commitment' factors are the most appropriate. Morgan and Hunt have demonstrated empirically that customers with strong commitment also have relatively stable buying behaviour (de Boer and Waarts, 1997). These customers are less easily influenced by competitors. The 'love' factor is also useful in predicting attitude and behaviour, especially with 'hedonistic' products like alcohol and tobacco, cars and designer label goods. Overall, however, each of the seven factors does correlate with certain individual attitude and behaviour scores (Fournier, 1994).

Although 'commitment' is an important component of mental brand equity, it does not necessarily lead to brand-loyal buying behaviour. As will be seen later in this chapter, buying behaviour with fast-moving consumer goods is far less stable than generally supposed. The average share of customer for the average brand is around 25% (Hallberg, 1995). For brands with a relatively large market share it is a little higher, and a little lower with brands with a smaller market share, but these differences are not marked (Ehrenberg and Uncles, 1995).

Substitutability

The degree of substitutability of a brand is also expressed as the acceptance of alternatives. Moran (1993) is an advocate of direct questions concerning consumers' willingness to buy another brand if the brand they last bought is no longer available, and if so, which brand they would prefer. By taking the brand last purchased as the point of departure, the purpose for which the branded article is bought remains constant, implicitly. Different people have different usage situations/applications (for example, tea in the morning or before sleeping). These are implicit in their brand choice (black tea or herbal tea). On this basis Moran has worked out a 'substitutability index', establishing a good correlation (0.73) between this index and the net profit margin made on the brands. The questions are primarily suited to markets which are strongly segmented according to the purpose for which the brand is used.

- If your favourite brand were no longer available, which other brand would you buy?

All the above components of brand equity are summarised in Exhibit 4.5 overleaf.

The components of 'consumer brand equity'

1   *Brand awareness*
    Top-of-mind awareness (TOMA)
    Spontaneous brand awareness (rank)
    Aided brand awareness

2   *Defining brand meanings (brand knowledge)*
    Origin
    Company/maker
    Category associations
    Functional attributes/consumer benefits
    Uses
    Symbolic attributes
    • brand personality
    • user associations
    • situational associations
    • values

3   *Differentiation/positioning*
    Characteristic differences
    Degree of uniqueness
    Degree of innovation/pioneering position

4   *Price/quality assessment*
    Perceived relative quality
    Perceived relative price
    Accepted price premium
    Perceived relative value
    Leadership/popularity

5   *Overall evaluation/attitude*
    Consideration set
    Relative brand preference/
    ambivalence (rejection)
    Level of satisfaction

6   *Buying behaviour tendency*
    Most used brand
    Last/last-but-one purchase
    Buying intention
    Inclination to switch brands

7   *Brand relationship*
    Functional relevance
    Support of self-concept
    Brand affinity/affection
    Emotional distance
    Perceived partner quality/reliability
    Attachment/reliability
    Commitment/substitutability

Exhibit 4.5

4.2.8 Hierarchical correlation

Research by both Millward Brown and Y&R shows that there is, essentially, a hierarchical correlation between the individual components of consumer brand equity. Brand awareness serves as a base for equity, the strongest expression of which is a brand relationship as represented by a strong commitment to the brand. This classification can be taken as the basic structure of the hierarchy, as shown in Figure 4.10.

Brand stages of mind

Mental brand response develops in stages. First you get to know a brand's name, then you become familiar with it. You start using it, gain some initial experience with it, and get to know it better and better. A general liking develops. Then specific brand values and aspects of knowledge start to take shape. The brand may reach top-of-mind awareness, and finally a strong brand commitment may result. The sequence in which these responses occur can vary from one category to another. Readers are referred to the discussion on hierarchies of effects in Chapter 5 (advertising effect models).

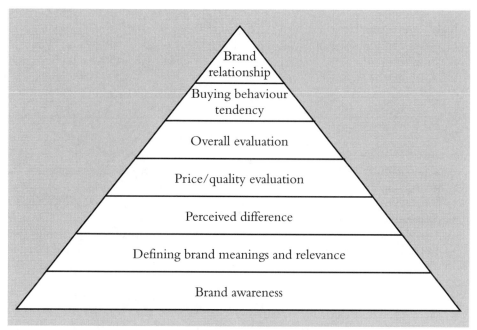

Figure 4.10 Hierarchical correlation of components of brand equity

Bronner based his Stage of Mind theory (in *De Zilveren Standaard – The Silver Standard, 1993*) on this development in stages. It involves segmenting users of a certain category on the basis of their mental brand responses: to what extent have they developed their knowledge, attitude and behaviour concerning the brand? Exhibit 4.6 (page 130) lists the stages of development of customer–brand relationships in more detail. The starting point is buying behaviour – after all, that is the principal criterion for brand equity. The last two stages (most purchased brand or only brand bought) represent the position of the really strong brands, which is reviewed in more detail at the end of this chapter.

The stages of mind as indicated here only reflect a positive development of the brand. Obviously a negative development must also be taken into account, as already indicated in the conversion model.

It is worth segmenting category users according to these brand stages of mind. Comparing the relative size of one segment to another is particularly useful in planning advertising policy. A good example of equity research based on these stages of mind is Millward Brown's Brand Dynamics Pyramid, as described in Exhibit 4.7 (page 131).

Standard research methods

Several standard tools are available for measuring brand equity. They vary in terms of design and analysis of the scores, and so produce different equity hierarchies. In Exhibits 4.7 and 4.8 the arrangement and analysis results of two such methods are explained briefly – those of Millward Brown's research company and of Young & Rubicam, respectively.

Mental brand equity is a complex phenomenon, in which seven main components can be differentiated. Different sets of questions can be used for each component. Ideally, the questions take into account the specific features of the product category and

1 *No brand experience*	4 *Most purchased brand*
• Brand unknown or only known when aided	• Top-of-mind awareness
• Weak associations	• High salience of brand promise or brand benefit
• Brand not relevant	• Strong symbolic brand perceptions
	• Concurrence with brand ideal
2 *Brand tried previously* (trial + retrial)	• Distinctive and relevant
• Brand known spontaneously	• High perceived quality or value
• Remembered trial use	• High overall assessment/trust
• Understanding of brand promise	• Strong preferred position/top brand
• Low relevance	• High satisfaction
• Not included in consideration set (yet)	• Acceptance of bigger difference in price
	• Not inclined to change in the short term
3 *Brand in repertoire*	5 *Only (or almost only) brand purchased* as 'most purchased brand', plus
• Brand spontaneously known; either tried previously, in repertoire or most purchased	• Only brand accepted
• Product meanings taken shape	• High emotional connotation/affection/ attachment/involvement
• Symbolic meanings developing	• Brand supports self-concept
• Included in consideration set	• Emotional proximity
• Positive quality and value perception	• High partner quality
	• Strong brand ties

Exhibit 4.6

special aspects of individual brands. Financial considerations and consumers' objections to long interviews do, however, restrict the scope of questionnaires.

In fact, according to both Feldwick (1996) and Aaker (1996a), there are no simple standard methods for measuring a brand's equity. They suggest that the best course of action is to begin with a broad field, qualitatively – many tests using smaller samples – to gain an idea of the aspects that are relevant for a product category and a brand. A quantitative measuring tool should then be designed, based on these findings, and used in larger samples. Multiple regression analyses can then be used to determine the correlations between the individual scores. (A regression analysis is when the relationship between an output variable, such as market share and explaining variables, such as price, is determined and expressed in a mathematical formula.) After this the measuring tool is reduced as much as possible to the factors most independent from others. This requires an ability to set priorities and a willingness to dispense with subtleties. In the end, the idea is to construct a tool which is reliable enough to measure the really important aspects of brand equity and, at the same time, compact enough to be used regularly to follow the course of brand equity in time.

It is important to establish that what is being measured does indeed influence consumer buying behaviour, and so company turnover and profit. For example, this is by no means certain in the case of slogan-awareness measurement – an issue which regularly crops up in equity measurements.

Millward Brown's 'Brand Dynamics Pyramid'

Millward Brown constructed a measuring tool for consumer brand equity, calling it the 'Consumer Value Model' (Dyson *et al.*, 1996). It was used to construct a hierachy of brand equity – the Brand Dynamics Pyramid – comprising the following five levels.

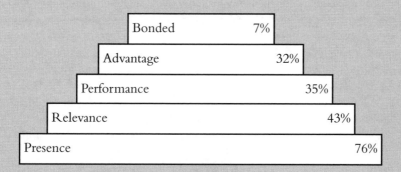

Figure 4.11 The Brand Dynamics Pyramid

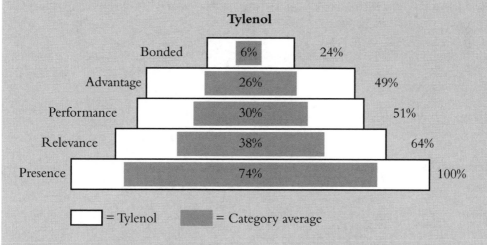

Figure 4.12 Brand Dynamics for Tylenol

The percentages indicate the percentage of category users in the different stages.

1   *Presence*: a factor based on spontaneous awareness, remembered trial use and active understanding of the brand promise.
2   *Relevance*: an assessment of the extent to which the brand meets the consumer's core criteria (functional and/or symbolic) and the extent to which the price is acceptable.
3   *Performance*: an assessment of the product's performance compared with that of its competitors.
4   *Advantage*: an assessment of the extent to which the brand represents a unique proposition in a functional and a symbolic sense, combined with direct questions concerning uniqueness, supremacy and ability to kindle enthusiasm.
5   *Bonded*: the brand in question is the only one the consumer accepts.

Exhibit 4.7; continued overleaf

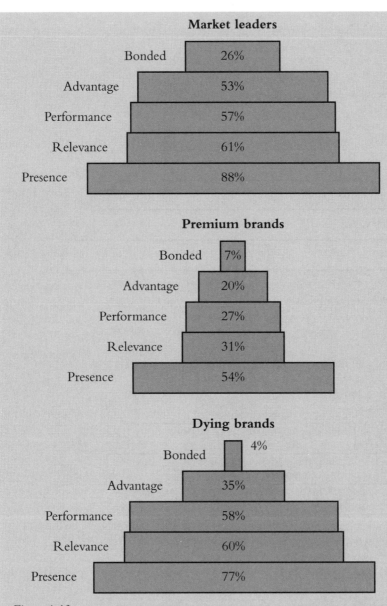

Market leaders

Bonded	26%
Advantage	53%
Performance	57%
Relevance	61%
Presence	88%

Premium brands

Bonded	7%
Advantage	20%
Performance	27%
Relevance	31%
Presence	54%

Dying brands

Bonded	4%
Advantage	35%
Performance	58%
Relevance	60%
Presence	77%

Figure 4.13

In Figure 4.13 the average scores are given for all the brands in the different product categories which have been analysed with this tool. The scores for the individual brands can, of course, diverge considerably from these averages. Figure 4.12 gives the scores for the US painkiller Tylenol, compared with the average scores for the entire painkiller category.

Millward Brown measured average scores for three categories of brands as regards brand mind response, using the Brand Dynamics Pyramid (Dyson *et al.*, 1996). They measured scores for market leaders, premium brands (the brands whose price is at least 50% higher than the average for the category) and dying brands.

Exhibit 4.7; continued on facing page

Comparison of the scores of market leaders and dying brands shows that those relating to presence, relevance and performance barely differ. The great difference is found at the top levels of the pyramid – the advantage was 53% for market leaders compared with 35% for dying brands, and bonded was 26% for market leaders compared with 4% for dying brands.

Source: Dyson *et al.*, 1996

Exhibit 4.7 continued.

Y&R's Brand Asset Valuator

The advertising agency, Young & Rubicam (Y&R), developed a measuring tool for analysing the development of brands called the Brand Asset Valuator. The procedure entails a telephone interview measuring brand awareness, and a written investigation, using a detailed questionnaire, among the same respondents. The questionnaire contains 32 items, including questions regarding current brand use and buying intentions, a psychographic measuring tool termed 'Cross Cultural Consumer Characteristics' and a set of demographic questions.

Measurements relating to 8,500 brands in 24 countries were used to draw up a brand equity hierarchy, made up of four levels. Development of brand perceptions is thought to progress in the following sequence: differentiation, relevance, appreciation and knowledge.

1 *Differentiation*: the perceived distinctiveness of a brand emerges as the basis for the development of a successful brand (what makes this brand different?).
2 *Relevance*: the assessment of the suitability of the brand by the individual consumer (how important is the brand to the consumer?). Y&R discovered a strong correlation between measured relevance and penetration of brands. Brands which are trendsetters in their category are often characterised by a combination of high differentiation and relevance scores (relevant differentiation).
3 *Appreciation*: how much do consumers appreciate a brand? These scores prove to correlate strongly with those for 'how popular is the brand?' and 'how high is this brand's quality?'
4 *Knowledge*: this not only includes brand awareness, but, more especially, knowledge of the brand's specific meanings and the feeling of knowing the brand very well: 'how much is it part of consumers' everyday lives?' Y&R believe this is not the first step in the development of brand equity, but constitutes a clear understanding of what the brand essentially stands for ('core meanings').

Scores for the 'differentiation' and 'relevance' factors are combined in a 'brand strength' (vitality) dimension, those for 'appreciation' and 'knowledge' into a 'brand stature' (authority) dimension. Y&R took this as its base for what it termed a 'power grid', in which every brand can be located. It gives a picture of a brand's present strength and future potential. As Ahlers (1996) suggested, when a brand is highly appreciated and when many consumers are familiar with it, this tells us something about how well established the brand is.

Source: Agres and Dubitsky, 1996

Exhibit 4.8

The measuring tool must also be sensitive: important developments in the market – tactical blunders, for instance (like the Persil Power fiasco in 1995) should be reflected in the equity scores.

Practical research guidelines

When developing a tool for the measurement of consumer brand equity, the following guidelines should be taken into account.

Relevance of factors

Establish what is important to the consumer. There is no point in asking questions on all manner of subjects which do not influence buying behaviour. At the same time, take care not to overlook matters which might at first sight seem less important, but can ultimately influence consumer brand equity. Try to isolate the most relevant factors using factor analysis.

Relevance of questions

Perception and attitudes can be measured in many different ways. Test the various options on a small scale with one another and decide which questions differentiate best.

Filter questions

Add filter questions to isolate category users. For example, there is no point in interviewing a random sample of women about nappies. Good filter questions can cut survey costs considerably.

It is sometimes more efficient to use quota samples (ie, samples of subgroups that buy from the product category) rather than random samples (especially in business markets).

Target group

If a segmented target group has been specified for the brand, the survey must take this into account. When links have to be made with advertising campaigns it is particularly important to attune target group definitions and survey questions.

Conciseness

Make sure the eventual measuring tool is as concise as possible. A great deal of research is conducted on the phone, and experience shows that a telephone interview should be no longer than about 15 minutes.

Validity

Validity indicates whether the research results do what they are supposed to. Ultimately the aim is to understand and forecast buying behaviour, so mental brand responses should always be assessed as to whether they actually do so.

Forecasting capacity

The final test of equity research is the question of how well it forecasts the course of consumer behaviour.

Practical usefulness

Monitor how useful generated data are, and whether they are used at all. Management, especially, will have to understand the results and base decisions on them.

The aim is a better understanding of how the market works and why one's own brand is successful (or not so successful).

Reliability

Do the research methods supply the same results, when the same measurements are repeated, under the same conditions? It is important to avoid coincidences.

4.2.9 Segmentation of brand users

Users of a product category vary greatly in their product consumption, and so in their level of importance for its sales. They also vary a great deal in their attitude and behaviour towards individual brands. In addition, consumers of individual brands display substantial shifts in attitude and behaviour within short time spans.

The consequence of all this is that some users are far more important to a brand than others. To get a good idea of a brand's consumer equity, it is absolutely essential to segment the equity research sample and follow the development within and between the segments from one period to the next. Average scores for a total population or even for all users of a category tell us next to nothing.

Users of a brand can be segmented on the basis of the share the brand has in their total consumption of the product category. This is termed 'share of customer' or 'share of requirements'. Various segmentations, based on buying behaviour patterns, are available. McQueen (1991) came up with a division into six brand behaviour typologies (see Exhibit 3.4, page 70):

- one-off buyers;
- repeat trial buyers;
- sporadic buyers (share of customer < 20%);
- repertoire buyers (share of customer 20–50%);
- top brand buyers (share of customer > 50%);
- 100% brand-loyal buyers.

Hofmeyr's (1990) Conversion Model, with its classification into eight attitude categories, was discussed earlier in this chapter. Baldinger and Rubinson (1996) propose a division of brand users into three groups:

- *Users with high brand loyalty*
  People for whom the brand accounts for at least 50% of consumption (coinciding with McQueen's groups 5 and 6). A share of requirement higher than 50% means that the people in this category cannot also be classed as high brand loyalty users of other brands. They are people who clearly have one top brand.
- *Users with medium brand loyalty*
  Those for whom the brand accounts for 10–50% of their consumption (roughly coinciding with McQueen's groups 3 and 4). These users may be buyers with a larger brand repertoire, or users with high loyalty to another brand.
- *Users with low brand loyalty and non-users*
  Those who hardly ever or never use the brand (share of requirements lower than 10%). This includes those who have tried the brand at some point, but did not become regular users.

Analyses of research data on 27 brands (Baldinger and Rubinson, 1996) confirm yet again the tremendous importance of consumers with high loyalty for a brand. On average they only accounted for 12% of the category users, but they represented 69% of the individual brand's sales (see Figure 4.14).

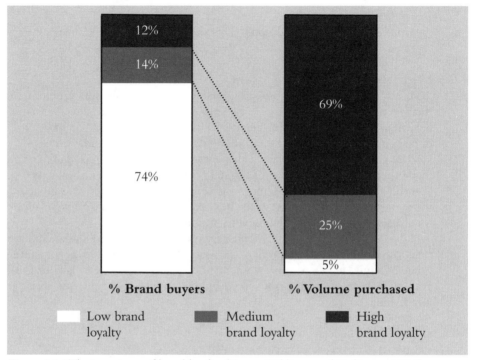

Figure 4.14 The importance of brand loyalty (Source: Baldinger and Rubinson, 1996)

Baldinger and Rubinson did, however, note a considerable shift from year to year between the three groups. Brand growth was mainly due to conversion of users from groups 2 and 3 to the group with high brand loyalty. On average, half the users with high brand loyalty in a particular year proved to have belonged to either group 2 or 3 in the previous year. At the same time, it transpired that almost half the users with high brand loyalty in a certain year slid back to medium or low brand loyalty the following year. So considerable shifts (conversion) were taking place between the three groups. Baldinger and Rubinson (1996) took these findings as the basis for an attitude/behaviour matrix, as depicted in Figure 4.15. This model results in a segmentation into the following four groups:

- *Very loyal users*
  Consumers who exhibit high loyalty to a brand, year in, year out.
- *Vulnerable users*
  Consumers whose attitude towards a brand is weaker than their behaviour. Possible 'deserters'.
- *Prospects*
  Consumers whose attitude to a brand is more positive than their behaviour. Potential new users.

- *Inaccessibles*

  Consumers with a weak brand attitude who rarely, if ever, buy the brand from year to year.

This classification resembles Hofmeyr's Conversion Model. Brands with a positive loyalty 'mix', in the sense of having more prospects than vulnerable users, are more likely to grow. Those with many vulnerables and few prospects are likely to decline.

Sloot *et al.* (1997) divided brand users into five market segments, based partly on their research into the Dutch beer market, as listed below:

- *Ambassadors*

  A small percentage of users, usually the true 'devotees' of the product who use relatively few brands, but who want a wide assortment and are open to information. They talk a great deal to other people about their favourite brand and often buy from specialist outlets (for example, beer at the off-licence or liquor store). They are category opinion leaders.

- *Loyalists*

  A group who perceive great differences between brands, both symbolically and functionally. They have a small brand repertoire, demonstrate relatively high loyalty to their favourite brand and have little urge to switch.

- *Variety seekers*

  These consumers have high product involvement and like trying out new product variants, even if they are satisfied with their current brand. They display low brand loyalty and are not very price-sensitive.

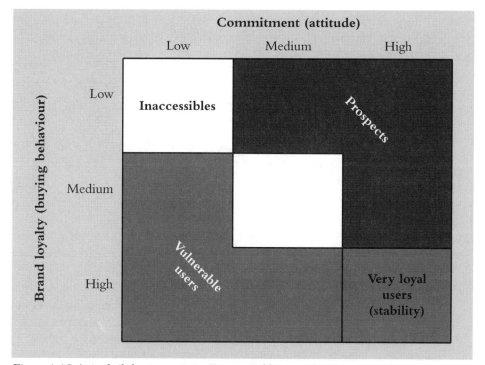

Figure 4.15 Attitude/behaviour matrix (Source: Baldinger and Rubinson, 1996)

- *Habit buyers*

  These usually form the largest segment. They do not see much difference between the brands and have relatively low involvement with the product. They tend to base purchases on habit and to have above-average price susceptibility. Habit buyers use relatively few brands and are easily persuaded.

- *Switchers*

  These use a jumble of different brands (two or three times more brands than other groups). They are price-sensitive, highly focused on others and buy other brands for special situations.

The last four groups correspond with a segmentation made by the Cranfield School of Management in the UK (Lazarus, 1997).

When there is an absence of information on actual buying behaviour, segmentation based on attitude measurements must be used. Baldinger and Rubinson (1996) validated a set of attitude questions, based on the constant-sum method, against buying behaviour measured by a panel method, concluding that good attitude measurement can be an acceptable substitute for the establishment of buying probabilities. In practice, this results in a matrix in which the results of the constant-sum method are plotted against attitude measurements based on brand knowledge and emotions.

A segmentation based on brand loyalty or brand attitude may be useful, but in many cases it is worth segmenting users according to their total category consumption into heavy, medium and light users. For further information, readers are referred to Hallberg (1995), who has demonstrated the great importance of loyal heavy users in particular, with respect to brand sales and especially to brand profitability (see Exhibit 4.13, pages 154–5).

In markets in which temporary price reductions (TPRs) are an important factor (detergents, for instance), it is worth considering carrying out a segmentation based on consumers' price awareness. It can be important to establish whether brand loyalty is brought about by a positive brand attitude or by an active TPR policy. Analysis of buying behaviour (or attitude measurements which are used as a substitute) can produce misleading conclusions if consumer susceptibility to special offers is not taken into account.

Last but not least, it is important for the future of brands that they obtain the highest possible share of new users in the product categories. The main focus for developed and often stable markets is the 'intake' of new generations. The large established brands are especially dependent for their further development on the extent to which they succeed in appealing to and holding on to younger consumers. An age segmentation can be informative.

4.3   BEHAVIOURAL BRAND EQUITY

4.3.1 Behaviour research

Research into mental brand responses boils down to asking consumers questions. Complicated theoretical constructs have to be translated into questions formulated in ordinary, everyday language. The problem is whether these questions properly measure the construct under investigation. Do the correlations assumed to exist between the measured constructs reliably reflect reality? Does, for example, the psychological construct of brand commitment in fact tie in with consumers' actual buying behaviour in terms of brand loyalty? And to what extent?

The vast proportion of research that might be classified as 'brand equity research' belongs in the category of image and attitude research. This is what most market researchers do, and what they prefer to do.

However, it must be stressed how variable consumer behaviour really is, and it is necessary to examine to what extent it correlates with the results of perception research. Some scientific researchers, like Ehrenberg, even see 'image research' as a fairly pointless exercise. Ultimately, the manufacturers of branded articles are most interested in buying behaviour. To discover something about this, it must be researched directly.

The result of this interest is research into buying behaviour with representative panels of consumers or registration of sales at a representative sample of outlets. In countries like the US and Germany, research based on consumer panels is becoming a key element in studies of consumer equity. It is the only type of research that can follow the course of consumer behaviour in time and relate the world of the individual consumer to that of marketing and finance.

The extent and strength of the mental brand response is clearly reflected in consumers' buying behaviour. Exhibited buying behaviour is the litmus test of brand equity measurement. Measurement of mental brand responses can provide information on the underlying factors influencing that behaviour. Certain methods for measuring attitude, like the constant-sum method, might even be an acceptable substitute for behaviour research. But, in the end, research into buying behaviour itself is the soundest method for measuring the strength of brand equity.

In Table 4.6, Donius (1986) gives an example of the differences between buying behaviour measured in a survey, and in consumer panels using hand scanners (as carried out by GfK in the Netherlands and AGB). These measurements cover a period of three months and a number of different product categories.

Survey questions which relate to buying behaviour nearly always result in an overestimation of reality. Moreover, it is practically impossible to follow developments properly in buying behaviour (and so in consumer equity) with a one-off survey or research that is only repeated at fairly long intervals. Although accumulated knowledge on the validity of specific sets of questions and the development of tracking methods probably help to achieve greater validity than ten years ago, survey research still has great limitations for measuring behaviour. It is impossible to determine properly the development of brand equity at an individual level with survey research. Panel research is the only method which effectively illustrates the variability of buying behaviour in

Category	Survey data (Assumed buyers) % of sample	Panel data (Actual buyers) % of sample
Tinned tuna	86	64
Ketchup	82	50
Furniture polish	57	26
Breakfast cereals	93	85

Table 4.6 Buying behaviour: assumed versus actual buyers

different groups of consumers and the development of brand buying behaviour in time. It records all the individual consumer's purchases for a longer period, and can also follow the correlation with other marketing variables, such as price, special offers and competitors' activities.

The three most important dimensions of behavioural brand equity will be discussed in turn. They are:

- the penetration of a brand;
- the level of brand loyalty;
- the price premium.

4.3.2 Penetration

The first important dimension of behavioural brand equity is penetration: the number of persons/households who have bought a brand at least once during a certain period (usually one year). According to Ehrenberg (1996), a brand's sales largely depend on its penetration. Research in a great many markets in different countries shows that average consumption per user varies only slightly between large and small brands. This is termed 'Pareto's law'. Accordingly, Ehrenberg argues that penetration is decisive in the development of brands. He acknowledges the importance of brand loyalty, but believes that average consumption per user cannot be increased so much that it will be substantially higher for one brand than for another. Buying behaviour for different brands largely follows the same patterns. For smaller brands, the average buying frequency is slightly lower than for larger brands: the 'double-jeopardy' phenomenon (see Exhibit 4.11, page 148, for a summary of Ehrenberg's findings).

Consequently, it is important to follow the development of penetration in time. If panel research can be used, it is possible to establish the consumers who stopped buying the brand and those who are actually going to buy a brand for the first time. This enables us to calculate the lost:gained ratio.

Brand repertoire

It has already been shown that consumers have only a limited number of brands in their consideration set. The repertoire of brands they have actually purchased is also limited. Analysis of buying behaviour data, based on the GfK panel in the Netherlands, gives the results shown in Table 4.7 for brands which have been bought at least once in a one-year period (Luyten, 1993; Luyten and Hulsebos, 1994).

No. of brands[1] purchased in 1 year	Low-calorie spread and diet margarine	Packet soup	Sanitary towels
0	43	13	27
1	40	26	31
2	13	26	25
3	3	25	12
4	1	8	4
5	–	2	1

[1] of brand names included in survey

Table 4.7 Repertoire of brands actually purchased

Product categories	One brand	Two brands	Three or more brands
Detergents	33	24	43
Toilet soap	30	25	45
Shampoo	33	24	43
Tissues	18	16	66
Ice cream	31	28	41
Mayonnaise	55	31	14
Peanut butter	48	30	22
Ground coffee	32	22	46
Breakfast cereals	6	7	87
Painkillers	43	29	28

Table 4.8 Brand repertoire of a number of product categories

In Table 4.8 Jones (1995) also gives an overview of the brand repertoire for a number of product categories.

4.3.3 Behavioural brand loyalty

Behavioural brand loyalty is the core dimension of brand equity, according to Aaker (1996a). It is a dimension of buying behaviour. Conceptually it is often confused with the 'commitment' dimension of mental brand response.

In 1971 Jancoby came up with the following definition of brand loyalty, which is still applicable today.

Brand loyalty is: (1) the biased (ie, non-random), (2) behavioral response (ie, purchase), (3) expressed over time, (4) by some decision-making unit, (5) with respect to one or more alternative brands out of a set of such brands, and (6) is a function of psychological (decision-making, evaluative) processes.

He was emphasising even then that brand loyalty can only be measured by means of behavioural research, and that this must cover a sufficiently long period. It is important to follow the purchasing pattern over time rather than merely establishing the next individual purchase.

There are many ways of expressing brand loyalty. The examples below illustrate the complexity of the subject.

Repeat buyers

This entails measuring what percentage of buyers of brand X buy it again the next time. Analysis of this information is very problematic; successive purchases by heavy, medium and light users soon diverge. However, it can be a useful analysis with infrequently purchased consumer goods, like cars.

Variants on this type of measurement are:

- True repeat rate. This expresses the percentage of consumers who bought a brand for the first time and then bought it at least once more within 12 months. The length of the time period between purchases can be related to the buying frequency in a category.
- Equilibrium repeat. The percentage of trial users of a brand who bought the same brand in each of their subsequent category purchases. This percentage gradually

drops, until the buying pattern has become set (has stabilised). Equilibrium repeat measurement discriminates well between successful and unsuccessful brands (Moran, 1993).

Repeat buyers per period

This method examines what percentage of those who bought brand X at least once in the first quarter bought it in the second quarter, again at least once, in combination with the measurement of how often these repeat buyers bought brand X in the first and second quarters. The data can be analysed in periods of varying length (for instance, per week or per year), which will produce different sets of figures.

Repeat buyers per buying cycle

The percentage of buyers of a brand who buy it again when they next make a relevant purchase. This eliminates buying frequency as an interfering factor.

Average buying frequencies

This measures the average frequency with which a brand is bought by each consumer within a certain period of time.

Duplications

The extent to which buyers of brand X also buy other brands in a certain period. This measures the number of consumers who do so, how often they do so, and what other brands they buy (their brand repertoire).

Share of (category) requirements (share of customer)

This establishes the share of a brand during a certain period in all purchases of a brand buyer in a product category. It is the share of a brand at an individual level.

Financial share of requirements (share of wallet)

A brand's share in a brand buyer's spending in a product category in a certain period.

The different criteria for measuring brand loyalty have clear correlations and reflect the same underlying mechanisms.

Ehrenberg and his colleagues took buying behaviour research over a period of more than 30 years, in over 50 product categories and various countries, as the basis for their conclusion that however often people buy a product, it would appear to be largely out of 'habit' (Ehrenberg and Uncles, 1995). A small percentage of people are 100% brand-loyal, but most divide up their purchases within a repertoire, buying one brand more often than the other. Although these buying patterns vary between individuals and between households, it can be seen that the aggregate behaviour at a market level of all buyers presents the same patterns for different products and brands.

This is particularly relevant for markets which are stable and in which market shares remain more or less stable for a year. It not only applies to fast-moving consumer goods, but also to such divergent categories as drugs, store choice, choice of television programmes, paraffin oil and petrol, and cosmetics. Even when purchases of makes of cars are analysed over a longer period, the same patterns emerge. These 'law-like' relationships are expressed in the so-called 'Dirichlet formula' (see Exhibit 4.11 on page 148).

Product category	Penetration	One brand (%)	Two brands (%)	Three or more brands (%)
Coffee				
Jacobs Krönung	34% (= 100)	41	30	29
Dallmayr	15% (= 100)	27	30	43
Tschibo Beste	14% (= 100)	24	24	52
Eduscho Gala	12% (= 100)	32	29	39
Margarine				
Rama	33% (= 100)	55	30	15
Lätta	24% (= 100)	51	32	17
Flora Soft	12% (= 100)	42	32	26
Shower gel				
Nivea	22% (= 100)	27	18	45
Duschdas	21% (= 100)	26	28	46
Cliff	15% (= 100)	29	26	45

Table 4.9 Brand duplication (Source: Verbraucher Analyse in 'Marktreue in Konsumgutermärkten', Schätzendorf, Germany, 1997)

Product category	All users (%)	Light users (%)	Heavy users (%)
Beer	53.4	61	49
Mineral water	35.4	39	35
Soft drinks	27.3	40	21
Coffee	26.6	27	26
Fruit juice	18.3	29	13
Fabric softener	72.2	80	53
Washing-up liquid	57.5	74	53
Fine laundry detergent	56.0	64	54
Fabric detergent	50.3	63	41
Deodorant	41.6	57	35
Toothpaste	38.2	61	34
Shampoo	31.0	31	31
Foam bath	30.6	33	22
Margarine	45.4	58	43
Chocolate bars	15.7	23	6
Ketchup	15.6	26	14

Table 4.10 Percentage of users who only use one brand (Source: Verbraucher Analyse in 'Marktreue in Konsumgutermärkten', Schätzendorf, Germany, 1997)

An analysis of buying behaviour in Germany (Table 4.10) shows that in most categories a majority of users buy two or more brands. This applies to both bigger and smaller brands alike, as is shown in Table 4.9, 'Brand duplication'.

Ehrenberg maintains that brand loyalty does differ according to user, but little according to brand – loyalty for the various brands in a category varies very little. Smaller brands are smaller because they are bought slightly less often by a much smaller group of customers.

Moran (1993) also examined the relationship between market share and brand loyalty, and had similar findings to Ehrenberg.

Exhibits 4.9 and 4.10 (page 147) contain further examples of models based on this relationship, by Parfitt, Collins and Boschloos, and GfK.

Stability of brand loyalty

Practitioners often assume that brand loyalty is a relatively stable characteristic of individual consumers: someone who is loyal to the brand is thought to be so for quite some time. They take this to be especially true of consumers who have a strong commitment to the brand.

However, research has shown that the real-life situation is dramatically different. Ehrenberg has constantly emphasised that consumers are 'polygamous', ie, they buy a mixture of several brands (forming their brand repertoire). The frequency of purchases of individual brands is constantly changing within that repertoire. There are not many 100% brand-loyal users, and most of them are light users at that.

Analysis of panel research in the US (Moran, 1993), covering a large number of fast-moving consumer goods, shows that the average brand has only a 25% share of customer. It is a little higher with major brands, but the differences are rarely substantial.

In an analysis of buying behaviour over a two-year period, using 27 brands in five categories, Baldinger and Rubinson (1996) established that the implicit hypothesis of stable brand loyalty, thought to cover several years, was untenable. Only 53% of the 'high loyals' of the brands in the first year (consumers with a share of customer of 50% or more) continued on into the following year. With 24% of high loyals the share of customer dropped to below 50%, and with 23% it even fell below 10%. This was offset by an increase in new high loyals: 20% of buyers in the first year with a share of customer of between 10 and 50% (moderate loyals) and even 4% of the 'low loyals' (share of customer below 10%) became high loyals in the second year. Large shifts were also noted with the moderate loyals (share of customer between 10 and 50%): with almost half of this group the share of customer dropped in the second year to less than 10%. With 20%, share of customer rose to above 50%; ie, they became high loyals.

So, at an individual level, there were considerable shifts from year to year; moreover, they occurred to about the same extent in all the examined product categories. At a brand level the dispersion was much greater.

Penetration or frequency: where does growth come from?

Healthy brands grow, or are at least stable, while brands whose market share declines have crumbling brand equity. But where does growth come from? To what extent do changes in penetration and/or buying frequency play a part?

The advertising agency Leo Burnett in the US researched this issue with 1,251 brands (Sylvester *et al.*, 1994). With 60% a decline was observed, and with 60% of the growing brands, growth was less than 20% a year. In the end, the analysis was applied to 95 brands, divided into penetration classes. The results are given in Figure 4.17 overleaf.

The market share analysis, according to Parfitt, Collins and Boschloos

Parfitt and Collins (1968) designed a model for breaking down a branded article in a product field into three components. These three components are: the cumulative growth in the number of new users of a brand; how often consumers buy the brand again after their first purchase; and the rate of category purchases of these buyers compared to all category buyers. Their aim was to forecast at an early stage the market share that would eventually be achieved, taking the course of the three components as their point of departure. When, in later years, more emphasis came to rest on the significance of brand loyalty, Boschloos adapted the model somewhat.

A simple example can illustrate the breakdown of a brand's market share, based on product category P and brand X. The starting point is all buyers of P, which are divided into buyers of X (X) and non-buyers of X (NX). The numerical example below is 100 X and 200 NX.

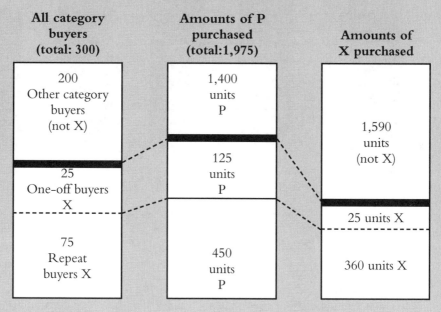

Figure 4.16 Numerical example of market share analysis, according to Parfitt, Collins and Boschloos

So penetration of X is 100/300 x 100 = 33.3%.

All buyers of P together buy 1,975 units of P in one year.

The buyers of X together buy 575 units of P, of which 385 are X units and 190 NX units. X's share of customer is therefore 385/575 x 100 = 67%.

X's market share is 385/1,975 x 100 = 19.

Repeat buyers of X buy 450 units of P, of which 360 are units of X. The share of customers for X with these repeat buyers is 360/450 x 100 = 80%.

The share of repeat buyers of sales of X is 360/385 x 100 = 93.5%

All buyers of P buy on average 1,975/300 x 100 = 6.6 units of P.

All buyers of X buy on average 575/100 = 5.7 units of P.

Repeat buyers of X buy on average 450/75 = 6.0 units of P

Non-buyers of X buy on average 1,400/200 x 100 = 7.0 units of P.

Exhibit 4.9

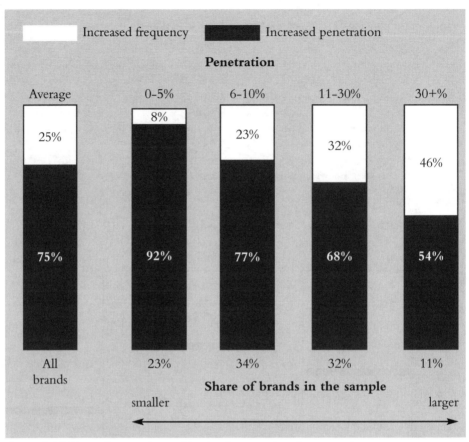

Figure 4.17 Share of penetration and buying frequency in volume growth

On average, 75% of volume growth with these brands could be attributed to penetration growth and 25% to an increase in buying frequency. Part of this frequency increase is a result of the penetration increase; it merely shows the double-jeopardy effect at work. Smaller brands are 95% dependent on higher penetration for their growth. The higher the penetration, the greater the contribution of higher frequency to growth. The very largest brands (penetration above 30%) are the only ones with which higher penetration and frequency make an almost equal contribution to growth. Anschuetz (1997) concludes:

Brand popularity (= the number of households that buy a brand = penetration) leads to greater frequency of brand buying, a greater number of heavier buyers, a greater level of brand loyalty (share of customer) and a greater share of market.

Buyer concentration (percentage of volume accounted for by percentage of buyers) derives from a general pattern of buying behaviour, and is very predictable. The 80/20 rule (where 80% of users are responsible for 50% of purchases and 20% of users are responsible for the remaining 50%) is a regular feature of repeat buying.

Increasing penetration will increase the number of 'profitable households'. Deciding to increase profitability by focusing on a small number of heavy brand buyers instead of raising the number of category users that buy the brand (penetration) will have an effect on total profits that will be the opposite of what is intended. Within any given marketing budget, maximising profitability will require maximising penetration (Anschuetz, 1997).

4.3.4 Price premium

The third important dimension of behavioural brand equity is the price premium consumers are prepared to pay, compared with the price of similar alternatives at the product level. These may be good quality private labels with the same objective product attributes. In the Netherlands, for example, the following prices are paid per litre of lager (Nielsen, October/November 1998):

- Grolsch: Dfl 2.66
- Heineken: Dfl 2.58
- Amstel: Dfl 2.42
- Bavaria: Dfl 2.17

So compared with Bavaria, Grolsch's price premium is Dfl 0.49 per litre, or almost 22.5%. This is with a market share that is almost twice that of Bavaria.

Market share analysis according to GfK

GfK developed a model for analysing market share (based on volume), according to five components. The model is, basically, an elaboration on Parfitt and Collins' well-known model. GfK's version focuses with its starting point more on people who have noted at least two purchases of the brand in the period in question. The five components (applied to consumer panel data) follow.

1 *Pull*: the number of buyers of the brand/the total number of buyers of the product.
2 *Conviction*: the number of loyal buyers of our brand/number of buyers of our brand.
3 *Domination*: average buying volume of the brand per loyal buyer of the brand/average buying volume of the product per loyal buyer of the brand.
4 *Intensity*: average buying volume of the product per loyal buyer of the brand/average buying volume per buyer of the product (all brands). If the loyal buyers of the brand buy just as much on average as the average of all buyers, this index equals 1.
5 *Absorption*: total purchases in volume of the brand by loyal buyers/total purchases in volume of the brand.

The formula is as follows:

$$\text{Market share} = \frac{\text{pull x conviction x domination x intensity}}{\text{absorption}}$$

This model enables us to check which of the five factors affect development of the market share to what degree. It can be used to establish which elements the brand scores well or badly on. The evolution of the market share components can be followed in time.

Sources: GfK Foodscan, 1996, and de Pelsmacker and van Kenhove, 1996

Exhibit 4.10

Although it is possible to measure the price premium at a market level by means of a retail panel, a consumer panel has the advantage of exposing the price premium's correlation with brand loyalty. The price premium that consumers are prepared to pay depends on the strength of their brand preference, and is expressed in the share of customer with different relative price differentials compared to that of competing brands.

Aaker (1996a) is of the opinion that the price premium is perhaps the best 'singular' measure of the strength of brand equity, and that it gives a good indication of the strength of brand preference. However, the price premium is always the result of a comparison of brands, which is influenced by the other brand or group of brands on which it is based. At an individual consumer level, the other brands in the consumer's repertoire can be taken into account. Measurements of consideration sets may suggest other brands that are involved in calculating the price premium.

Buying patterns according to Ehrenberg

Buying patterns in stable markets can be described as follows (Ehrenberg and Uncles, 1995):
- The number of consumers who buy a certain brand in a certain period (a year, for instance) differs from brand to brand. The penetration of different brands varies.
- There is considerable correlation between this penetration and brands' market shares.
- The average frequency with which the various brands are purchased by their buyers differs very little. Major brands are bought on average a little more often than small brands, but the difference is slight.
- Major brands are chiefly big because they have a lot of buyers, and are bought a little more often by them (the so-called double-jeopardy effect – see Exhibit. 4.12).
- Most buyers of a brand buy it infrequently.
- The number of people buying a brand increases with time. Penetration depends on the time frame which is being used.
- Average repeat purchases, measured from one quarter to the next, are relatively low but are fairly similar from brand to brand.
- Levels of repeat purchases are roughly stable in time. This means that individual consumers have stable buying patterns.
- The average amount bought per purchase differs very little from one brand to another. All these variables are reflected in the market shares of the brands. In view of the regularity in the underlying buying patterns, market share is a good reflection of development at a micro-level.
- Big and small brands exist, but as yet there is no proof of the existence of strong and weak brands.

The above patterns do not imply that marketers should focus solely on increasing penetration. They only mean that if sales really are growing it will be displayed in a far greater rise in penetration than in repeat purchases (Ehrenberg, 1997).

Exhibit 4.11

Brand loyalty and market share

The following example is a good illustration of the double-jeopardy phenomenon (derived from Moran, 1993).

Category	Brand with 5% market share	Brand with 20% market share
Toothpaste	6.0	9.0
Washing-up liquid	7.0	8.5
Fabric detergent	5.6	8.0
Margarine	5.8	7.5
Soap	5.4	6.5

Table 4.11 Number of purchases of a brand out of 10 category purchases

If the percentage of category buyers who last bought a brand is compared with the percentage who bought the brand both the last time and the last but one, strong uniformity can be seen between the different brands in a category and even between categories. The toothpaste example above shows that the repeat purchases score is 60% for a brand with a market share of 5% (3% of the 5%) and 90% with a market share of 20% (18% of the 20%). This occurs throughout the categories – the larger the market share, the higher the repeat purchase scores.

The repeat rate for brands with a 20% market share is as follows:

- toothpaste – 90%;
- washing-up liquid – 85%;
- fabric detergent – 80%;
- margarine – 75%;
- soap – 65%.

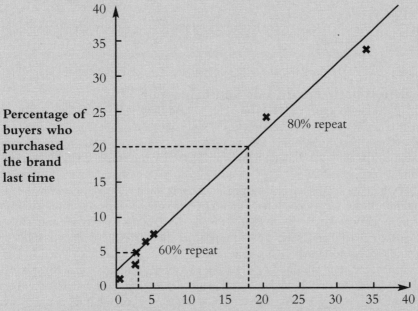

Figure 4.18 Repeat purchases for toothpaste brands (Source: Moran, 1993)

Exhibit 4.12; continued overleaf

149

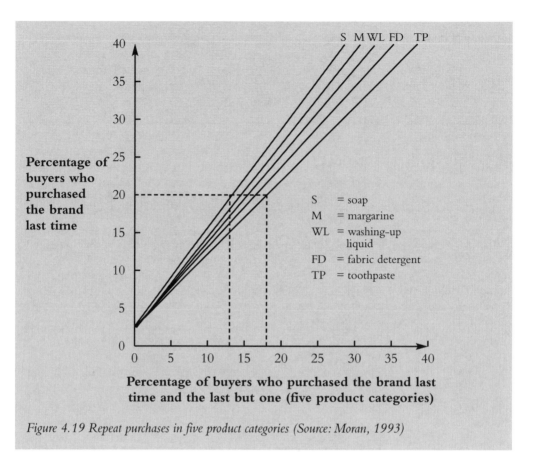

Figure 4.19 Repeat purchases in five product categories (Source: Moran, 1993)

Exhibit 4.12 continued.

4.3.5 Correlation between attitude and behaviour

The burning question concerns the connection between actual buying behaviour and mental brand equity. This can only really be established by measuring the two using the same consumers/households, for example, by measuring mental brand responses in consumer panels alongside buying behaviour. However, this runs the risk of influencing subsequent buying behaviour. GfK in fact provides this option in its 'Dating 2000' concept, where buying behaviour is measured using hand scanners, along with mental responses with the same consumer panel. The tool used for measuring mental brand responses is known as the AGB Brand Profile. In Table 4.12 Luyten and Hulsebos (1994) present several correlations for two product categories, between the AGB Brand Profile indicators and actual buying behaviour.

It can be seen that the questions relating to attitude and buying behaviour in the Brand Profile tool (first preference and generally in the home) have the biggest correlation with actual buying behaviour, and that the correlation between actual buying behaviour and the consideration set is relatively slight.

So, as discussed in the foregoing, it is advisable to relate the measurements of mental brand response with measurements of buying behaviour. Figure 4.20 can be a guide to analysis. If research into actual buying behaviour is not available, survey questions will

Product category	TOMA	Spontaneous awareness	Consideration set	First preference	Usually in home
Sanitary towels					
Always	0.16	0.21	0.37	0.47	0.62
Kotex	0.13	0.16	0.34	0.41	0.45
Libresse	0.19	0.21	0.33	0.45	0.51
Packet soups					
Honig	0.19	0.26	0.36	0.36	0.34
Knorr	0.02	0.10	0.24	0.17	0.16
Royco	0.17	0.17	0.12	0.13	0.14

Table 4.12 Correlations between buying behaviour and AGB Brand Profile indicators (two product categories) (Source: Luyten and Hulsebos, 1994)

be needed which approximate buying behaviour as closely as possible. These questions should, if possible, be verified by consumer panels.

A high degree of commitment to a brand is generally assumed to result in high brand loyalty. Ehrenberg has his doubts. He points out that in many markets he encountered slight differentiation in brand loyalty between the various brands. Brand

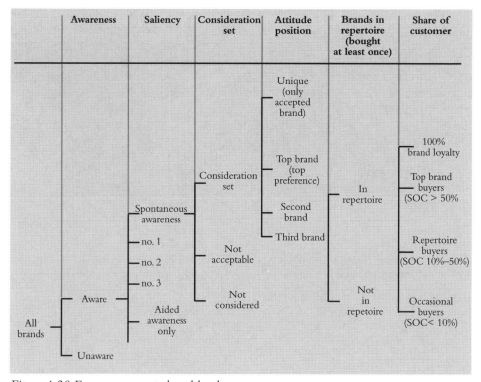

Figure 4.20 From awareness to brand loyalty

loyalty, in his view, is predictable, coincides with regular patterns and consequently need not result from deeper consumer ties with the brand.

Dyson *et al.* (1996) tried to determine the connection between the strength of the mental brand response, measured according to their Consumer Value model (see Exhibit 4.7 and Figure 4.11 *et seq.*) and the behavioural brand response, expressed in financial share of customer. Consumers for whom a brand had not yet reached the stage of 'presence' (spontaneous awareness, understanding of brand promise, recalled trial use) spent on average only 2% of their total expenditure in the product category on that brand. Average expenditure by consumers for whom the brand had achieved the presence status was 13%. The more positive the scores for a brand and the further its penetration to the higher levels of the Brand Dynamics Pyramid, the greater the financial share of customer. With customers in the 'bonded' segment the average expenditure on the brand was 38%. This confirms Ehrenberg's view: although there is a correlation between brand loyalty (expressed in financial share of customer) and strength of attitude, the 38% share of consumers with a pronounced brand 'bond' was much lower than one might expect – for two out of three purchases in the category these 'bondeds' bought another brand.

Figure 4.21 shows, in diagram form, the correlation between the mental brand response and the behavioural brand response for packaged goods in the US, measured using Millward Brown's Brand Dynamics Pyramid method.

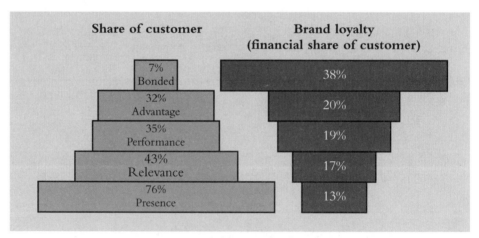

Figure 4.21 Average share of customer and brand loyalty for packaged goods in the US

Recent research (Baldinger and Rubinson, 1996) also shows that both attitude and behaviour and the link between them are far from stable. Commitment to a brand and share of customer prove to fluctuate widely in the course of one year.

Figure 4.22 (based on research by the NPD Group in the US, quoted earlier – Baldinger and Rubinson, 1996) represents the correlation between the development of attitude and behaviour of the 27 brands under investigation. Sixty per cent of the high loyals (with a strong bonding with the brand combined with a share of customer > 50%) in the first year, also proved to belong to this category in the second year. But with 40% of this group there was a decline in the strength of commitment, or the share of customer. Only 37% of the high loyals (share of customer > 50%) with

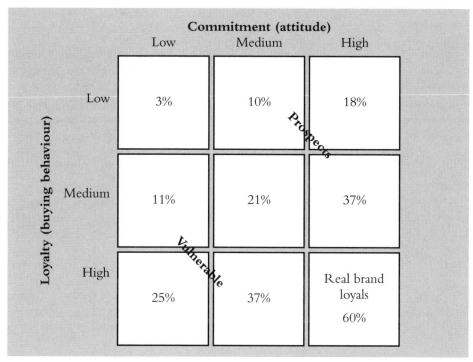

Figure 4.22 Attitude/behaviour matrix (source: Baldinger and Rubinson, 1996)

medium commitment remained high loyals in the second year. For two out of three brands (67%) the connection between attitude strength and share of customer proved to predict the development of market share. When the joint share of prospects (ie, those with medium to high commitment and low to moderate loyalty) exceeded that of the 'vulnerables', market share increased; when the reverse applied, it decreased.

The penetration versus brand loyalty controversy

Not everyone agrees with Ehrenberg's theory that brand loyalty for the various brands in a category develops, in connection with penetration, in a systematic way, and consequently is largely beyond a company's influential scope. However, there is a wide consensus that brand loyalty does develop systematically in connection with penetration in stable markets for frequently purchased low-involvement products and for established (undifferentiated) brands. There are, however, exceptions. Dowling and Uncles (1997) differentiate between three categories of brands (see Figure 4.24 overleaf) for which purchasing frequency differs from the frequency predicted by the Dirichlet formula. (The Dirichlet formula is a mathematical formula that forecasts the average buying frequency of a brand, and its duplication with other brands, on the basis of: its market share; the total number of users of the category in a given year; the average buying frequency of the category; and the number of brands the average household buys during the year.) These are:

- *Super-loyalty brands*
  Some major brands (especially market leaders) have more frequent buyers among their followers. It is unclear what these brands' attributes are.

Hallberg (1995) suggests (based on data from MRCA Information Services) that with fast-moving consumer goods, on average 33% of category buyers account for 67% of the total category volume sold. This implies that the top one-third of all buyers purchase at least four times as much as the bottom two-thirds. This division also applies to brands. MRCA's analysis of 27 well-known, well-established brands in 13 product categories over a period of 15 years (1977–1993) revealed equivalent findings, which also applied, by and large, to clothing, shoes and credit cards. Kuending, the vice-president of Kraft Foods, reported that the top one-third of households that buy the company's brands is responsible for almost 70% of Kraft's total volume; ie, all the brands they sell, from cheese to coffee to desserts.

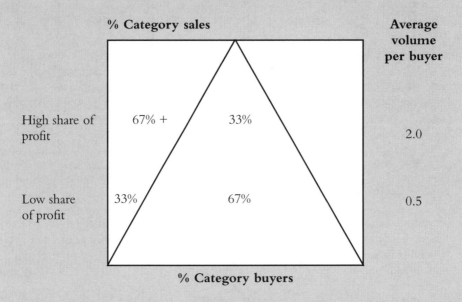

Figure 4.23 Profit matrix for packaged goods (Source: MRCA Information Services)

The most important findings from MRCA's analysis, as reported by Hallberg (1995, p 57), can be summarised as follows:

- The average share of customer of brands among heavy buyers in a category was less than 20%. They bought those brands, on average, less than one in five times of their purchases in that category. The other four times they bought a competing brand.
- Of the heavy buyers in a category who bought a certain brand, only 11% belonged to the loyal buyers category (share of customer > 50%).
- The number of brands bought by medium and heavy buyers (the size of the brand repertoire) increased from 1977 to 1993 from 3.7 to 3.9, and among heavy buyers from 5.3 to 5.7.
- The average share of customer of the average brand dropped among medium and light buyers in that period from 27% to 23%, and among heavy buyers from 23% to 18%.
- With brands in the heavy-buyer category, the percentage with a share of customer of 50% or more (the 'loyals') dropped from 17% to 11%. Nine brands managed to keep their share of customer with this group reasonably intact, while with 17 brands the percentage of heavy buyers was halved.

Exhibit 4.13; continued on facing page

- The percentage of extremely loyal brand users (share of customer > 80%) among the heavy category buyers dropped from 10% to 5%.
- Only 20% of a brand's sales can be ascribed to the heavy category buyers (share of customer > 50%), and only half of that (10%) to the extremely loyal buyers.
- Two-thirds of a brand's sales are bought by customers who buy the brand less than once in every two purchases (share of customer < 50%).

Exhibit 4.13 continued.

- *Niche brands*
  Brands with divergent product attributes often displaying higher buying frequency than predicted by Dirichlet. However, many niche brands which grow do assume a Dirichlet pattern as time goes by.
- *Change-of-pace brands*
  Brands in newly developing segments of product variants attuned to specific usage situations (such as non-alcoholic beer for when people want to drink and drive). They often command less loyalty than predicted by Dirichlet.

Light (1998) is also of the opinion that commitment affects the share of customer, particularly in the longer term. He believes that when commitment is relatively low, share of customer is at risk, and that, on average, the Dirichlet formula applies, but some brands diverge markedly. He also states that slight alterations, of 2 or 3%, in the share of customer covering short periods (a year, for instance) can, over a longer period, be of considerable influence on market share and profitability.

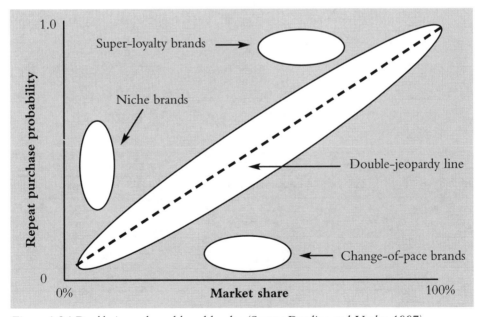

Figure 4.24 Double-jeopardy and brand loyalty (Source: Dowling and Uncles, 1997)

155

If brands and categories are reviewed for the short term (one year, for example), many do indeed appear stable, but unusual developments can occur in the longer term (five to ten years). An analysis by the NPD Group (Baldinger and Rubinson, 1997) of 60 brands in the US covering a five-year period showed that:

- with 75% of the market leaders, market share dropped, with a variance of 4–29%;
- fifty-four per cent of the brands which started out with a market share ranking of 2, 3 or 4 had dropped to a lower position;
- thirty-nine per cent of the brands which started out with a ranking of between 5 and 10 had lost at least 20% of their share.

So, in most categories, a brand's size (penetration, market share) strongly correlated with consumer loyalty. But there are situations in which brands deviate, positively or negatively, from the Dirichlet predictions, due to changing consumer attitudes.

Farr and Hollis (1997) ascertained, from brand equity measurements using Millward Brown's Brand Dynamics system, that brands exist whose mental brand equity scores deviate, positively or negatively, from category averages in the longer term. In their view: 'Ehrenberg is not entirely correct: there are stronger and weaker brands, and it is possible to identify which are which, and which brands are likely to grow.'

Brands *can* apparently break through the status quo in a category, though admittedly this does not often happen with long-established brands. In a 74-brand sample, Farr and Hollis encountered the divisions and developments shown in Table 4.13 (a market share, value-wise, of more than 5% is classified as 'large', below 5% as 'small').

The majority of the large, strong brands exhibited growth, the large, weak brands a decline. Most small brands were stable. The share of 46 of the 74 brands (62%) remained the same, probably in accordance with the double-jeopardy relationships in their category. Ehrenberg commented that only four of the 74 brands rose by 1–2%. That might be very important for those brands, but it is not what mass marketing is all about (Ehrenberg *et al.*, 1998).

The double-jeopardy phenomenon is apparent in the correlation between penetration and share of customer, in that two-thirds of the variation in share of customer can be explained by penetration. However, Baldinger and Rubinson (1997) maintain that share of customer makes an independent contribution to market share growth which is almost as important as that of higher penetration.

Brand classification	Sample		Changes in value share		
	Number	Percentage	Down	Same	Up
Large and weak	15	20	8	4	3
Large and strong	14	19	1	5	8
Small and weak	41	55	4	35	2
Small and strong	4	5	1	2	1
Total	74	100	14 (19%)	46 (62%)	14 (19%)

Table 4.13 Changes in value share for different types of brands

They demonstrate that high loyals for major brands (share of customer 50% or higher) account for 80% of the volume of sales, and smaller brands account for 56%. They note an almost perfect correlation between the high loyals' percentage and market share.

East and Hammond (1996) have also found, on the basis of large-scale research within nine categories of fast-moving consumer goods in three countries, that brands with high market shares achieve a higher share of customer than the Dirichlet formula predicted.

4.4 FINANCIAL/ECONOMIC BRAND EQUITY

As suggested in the introduction, people are starting to realise that the meaning of the term 'brand equity' must be differentiated according to the brand's position at the individual consumer level, and the brand's performance in the market as a whole. Alongside consumer brand equity there is also financial/economic brand equity. The latter coincides with the market response in the Advertising Response Matrix and entails the direct financial results for a company of the aggregated buying behaviour of all the individual consumers. In particular, a distinction is made between:

- distribution;
- sales and the resulting market share;
- price premium;
- price elasticity;
- gross and net profit;
- profit margin.

4.4.1 Distribution equity

In the previous sections, brand equity was examined in terms of the part brands play in consumers' minds and buying behaviour. This took no account of the influence of the brand on other stakeholders in the sales process, the distribution channels in particular. A wider interpretation of the brand equity concept takes this into account.

Srivastava and Shocker (1991) provide such a definition. They describe brand equity as a collection of associations and actions by consumers, the distributive trade and the brand's parent company, which enables the brand to achieve greater volume or greater margins than would have been possible without the brand name. The result, they claim, is a strong, sustainable and differential benefit.

Ambler (1995) also assumes that brand equity is a 'relationship' concept, and includes distribution of the brand in the interpretation. A distinction can be made between consumer brand equity, as described earlier, and distribution brand equity. If the measurement of brand equity is based on market response, particular account should be taken of attitude and behaviour trends among retailers regarding the brand, and the resulting availability (distribution) of the brand at the moment consumers are making their category purchases.

Consumers' selection behaviour is not only influenced by the presence of brands in their minds, but also by the availability of brands at the point of sale. This is probably one of the most important background factors of the variability of buying behaviour and the relatively weak correlations between attitudes and behaviour. In marketing terms, buying behaviour is a result of 'pull' and 'push' factors alike.

It is often hard to determine what is cause and what effect in that process. Reibstein and Farris (1995) suggest that a two-sided causality exists between distribution and market share. Larger brands have a greater chance of better distribution than smaller brands, usually have more shelf space, more in-store promotion and greater likelihood of distribution of line extensions. They also exercise bigger push influence. So they are bought more often by consumers with a strong preference for these brands (the loyals), but also have a greater chance of being bought by the vulnerable buyers of smaller brands who do not find their brand at the point of sale and make a 'compromise' choice. This might explain one of the factors of the double-jeopardy effect. Reibstein and Farris assume that the influence of distribution on market share is greatest in product categories where loyalty is low, brand preferences are less pronounced, and consideration sets and brand repertoires are larger – which would be the case with many dairy products in most countries.

When consumer brand equity is measured, market share and level of distribution should not, therefore, be treated as output variables only. They are also input variables, as the main representatives of the push factors which influence buying behaviour (Dyson *et al.*, 1996,1997).

The shelf-space share

The level of distribution of brands is measured and followed with retail panels such as Nielsen's and GfK's. It is wise not only to establish a brand's mere presence in the shop, but to follow the quality of that presence as well. Nielsen measures the reserved length of the brand on the shelf, as well as the depth and height it takes up. In that way it is possible to determine for each brand in a category the length, surface and content of the shelf space it occupies, and so the shelf-space share of each brand within the category. The distance of products from the floor is measured too, enabling us to determine the influence of position on the shelf on sales.

4.4.2 Market share

A brand's market share and development, together with the price premium it achieves, is the most important output variable of consumer brand equity. Analyses based on the PIMS Database indicate that a very strong correlation exists between the market share of a brand (business unit) and its profitability. Brands with a share of more than 40% achieve 30% higher ROI than brands with a share below 10% (see Figure 4.25). It is hardly surprising that companies follow carefully the course of their market shares when they track the performance of their brands, particularly from one period to the next.

Ehrenberg used research covering many different markets over several decades to establish that the course of individual brands' market shares is a good reflection of changes in the underlying buying behaviour variables, such as penetration, buying frequency, repeat purchases and buying duplication with other brands. In his Dirichlet model (used for static markets) the market share is actually the only element with which to forecast these underlying variables. Ehrenberg goes so far as to suggest that the market share itself is the foremost explanatory factor of all brand performance. In fact, he claims that it is enough to measure market share alone. Although he suggests in more recent publications that the brand's saliency is the driver for market position and its developments, it seems that he sees brand saliency and market share as being closely interwoven.

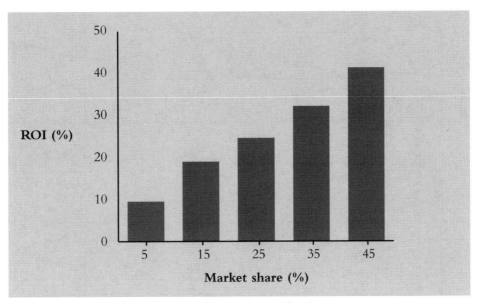

Figure 4.25 Correlation between size of market share and ROI

Ehrenberg actually observes that it is the deviations between reality and the Dirichlet predictions that are of prime interest, rather than the Dirichlet predictions themselves. Accordingly, he advocates a Brand Performance Audit, in which penetration, frequency and duplication scores measured in the marketplace are compared, on a quarterly basis, for instance, with the Dirichlet findings, which serve as the standard. In his view, those deviations warn the manager that something is taking place – in a positive or negative sense. An example of a comparison of that type is shown in Table 4.14.

The market share is, in a sense, a subjective factor, because it is based on the definition of the category or subcategory that is selected as the denominator. It makes a difference whether the share of a special beer (white beer, for example) is expressed as a percentage of comparable white beers or of all beers, and whether private labels should be included or treated as a separate category. It is worth calculating and tracking a market share at several such levels.

It is also worth taking the distribution factors into account in the market share calculations. This would obviously include splitting the share according to outlets that stock the brand and those that do not. Similarly, the connection between changes in trade stocks should be examined, and the extent to which the share is affected by out-of-stock situations.

Size and stability of market share

It is surprising to note how little movement there often is in market shares. Half a percentage point growth or decline per year is often seen as an important development. In many markets the market leaders are those that are especially successful in maintaining their position for decades. Stobart (1994) gives the examples listed in Table 4.15 (page 161).

The exceptional staying power of major brands is probably the best reflection of the effects of consumer equity.

| Instant coffee USA 1981 (Source: MRCA) | 100%-loyal | | | | Average no. of purchases of all brands | | Brand buyers also buying other brands (%) | | | | | | | | | | |
| | % brand buyers | | Average no. of purchases | | | | Maxwell House | | Folgers | | Nescafé | | Brim | | Maxim | | Other brands | |
All brands	O 100	T 100	O (6.7)	T 6.7	O (6.7)	T 6.7	O 24	T 27	O 18	T 17	O 13	T 14	O 9	T 7	O 6	T 6	O 20	T 21
Maxwell House	20	16	4.2	2.1	9.5	9.1	–	–	38	25	26	20	13	11	13	9	36	30
Sanka	20	15	3.2	2.0	9.2	9.3	36	40	25	26	23	21	20	11	11	9	27	30
Tasters Choice	24	15	4.2	2.0	8.8	9.4	31	40	28	26	20	21	17	11	14	9	28	30
High Point	18	14	1.8	1.9	8.5	9.4	34	40	31	26	22	21	18	11	10	9	33	31
Folgers	13	14	3.3	1.9	9.4	9.5	51	41	–	–	25	21	15	11	11	9	35	31
Nescafé	15	13	4.3	1.8	10.5	9.7	48	41	34	26	–	–	15	11	8	9	40	31
Brim	17	12	2.4	1.7	9.4	9.9	33	41	27	26	20	21	–	–	16	10	29	31
Maxim	11	12	3.9	1.7	11.2	10.0	52	41	34	26	17	21	25	11	–	–	35	31
Other brands	20	14	3.0	1.9	9.3	9.4	42	40	31	26	25	21	14	11	10	9	–	–
Average brand	17	14	3.4	1.9	9.5	9.5	41	41	31	26	22	21	17	11	12	9	33	31

O = observed (actually measured), T = theoretically

Table 4.14 Brand performance

United Kingdom			
Brand	*Category*	*Position 1933*	*Postition1993*
Hovis	Bread	1	1
Stork	Margarine	1	1
Kellog's	Cornflakes	1	1
Gillette	Razor blades	1	1
Schweppes	Mixers	1	1
Colgate	Toothpaste	1	1
Kodak	Film	1	1
Hoover	Vacuum cleaners	1	1
United States			
Brand	*Category*	*Position 1933*	*Position 1993*
Eastman Kodak	Cameras/film	1	1
Del Monte	Tinned fruit	1	1
Wrigley	Chewing gum	1	1
Nabisco	Biscuits	1	1
Gillette	Razor blades	1	1
Coca-Cola	Soft drinks	1	1
Campbells	Soups	1	1
Ivory	Soap	1	1
Goodyear	Tyres	1	1

Table 4.15 Market leaders in the UK and the US, 1933–93

The relative strength of brands is best expressed in value shares as they take the relative prices into account. The value shares of the three biggest brands, measured in many markets in various countries, including the US and the Netherlands, are found in a ratio of roughly 4:2:1. Nielsen Netherlands analysed these ratios for 90 product groups in six different sectors (Positioneringsgroep/A.C. Nielsen, 1994). An average figure was encountered over all 90 product groups of 34.4% (No. 1), 17% (No. 2) and 9.5% (No. 3). Sector-wise, the range of the average figure was as shown in Table 4.16.

Sector	Brand No. 1	Brand No. 2	Brand No. 3
Food	4.5	1.6	1.0
Non-food	3.1	1.8	1.0
Total food + non-food	3.8	1.7	1.0
Alcoholic beverages	3,1	1.7	1.0
Small electrical domestic appliances	3.7	2.0	1.0
DIY products	5.5	2.3	1.0
All sectors	3.6	1.8	1.0

Table 4.16 Average market share ratios (value) for the three biggest brands (90 product groups, six sectors)

The average absolute market share for the three largest brands was as shown in Table 4.17.

Sector	No. 1	No. 2	No. 3	Total 1, 2 and 3
Food	37.3	15.1	8.8	61.2
Non-food	28.0	16.5	10.2	54.7
Total food + non-food	32.6	15.8	9.5	57.9
Alcoholic beverages	24.1	11.1	7.9	43.1
Small electrical domestic appliances	43.0	22.9	11.4	77.3
DIY products	39.6	18.9	9.4	67.9
All sectors	34.4	17.0	9.5	60.9

Table 4.17 Average absolute market share (guilders) for the three largest brands (90 product groups, six sectors)

Although no general pattern emerges across all the sectors and the absolute shares of numbers 1 and 2 displayed reasonable dispersion, a general trend can be observed.

The dispersion of shares of the market leaders is the largest: in 18 product groups they had a share of less than 20%, in 58 product groups between 20 and 50%, while the biggest brand in 14 markets generated more than 50% of income.

Not only is there a correlation between profitability and market share, as the PIMS analyses show, but, more especially, the ranking of brands according to size proves to have a strong correlation with profitability. Chernatony and McDonald (1992) noted the correlation shown in Table 4.18 for the food market in the UK.

Market share ranking	Net profit margin (%)
No. 1	17.9
No. 2	2.8
No. 3	– 0.9
No. 4	– 5.9

Table 4.18 Correlation between market share ranking and net profit margin of a brand

An analysis of 2,746 brands in the PIMS Database produced the correlation shown in Table 4.19 between ranking and ROI (Light, 1989).

Market leaders are, on average, twice as profitable as those at positions 3 and 4. Light based his 'law of dominance' on the following: 1 is fantastic, 2 is fine, 3 is vulnerable and 4 is usually fatal.

However, not all market leaders are the same, as the Nielsen analysis also revealed. Light differentiates between dominant and marginal leaders. Dominant leaders have a sales volume which is at least 1.5 times that of number 2. The other market leaders are defined as marginal. The dominant market leaders in the PIMS Database achieve an

Market share ranking	ROI (in %, before interest and tax)
No. 1	31
No. 2	21
No. 3	16
No. 4	12

Table 4.19 Correlation between market share ranking and ROI

average return of 34%, while marginal leaders achieve an average of 26%; the average return of dominant leaders is 52% higher than that of number 2. The pattern is the same for the US and Europe, for industrial and consumer markets, for services and products, and for durable and non-durable products (see Table 4.20).

Market position	US	Europe	Industry	Services	Durables	Non-durables
Dominant leaders	36	34	31	48	38	37
Marginal leaders	25	27	26	37	25	29
No. 2	22	19	20	24	21	24
No. 3	13	17	18	20	10	13
No. 4+	12	10	13	18	11	7

Table 4.20 Market leadership and return

These PIMS database analyses again demonstrate a strong correlation between market position and relative perceived quality (see Table 4.21).

In view of this correlation, multinationals are probably inclined to withdraw from markets in which they have not succeeded in becoming one of the top two brands (Quelch and Harding, 1996).

Market position	Relative perceived quality (index)
Dominant leaders	+ 14.0
Marginal leaders	+ 6.0
No. 2	+ 0.3
No. 3	− 2.7
No. 4+	− 3.1

Table 4.21 Market position and relative perceived quality

Niall FitzGerald, the chairman of Unilever plc, described the company's rationalisation in *Adformatie* (1997, no. 42) as follows:

Unilever seeks to achieve a position of leadership with its brands – that of number one, or at least number two. And we sell off brands in fourth, fifth or sixth place in a market as a commercial proposition. Many brands have meanwhile been disposed of, or been allowed to fizzle out.

This rationalisation is a final step. Unilever still have to part with a billion pounds' worth of brands. Originally, around five billion pounds' worth were to be jettisoned. The result has been an improvement in the quality of the overall portfolio, and a rise in margins. We can plough the resources thus released back into their major brands, thus further increasing their competitive impetus – their punching power.

4.4.3 Price premium and price elasticity

One of the principal advantages of a strong brand for a firm is that it can demand a higher price in the marketplace than less strong brands, and its sales are less sensitive to price rises.

Yasin (in Luik and Waterson, 1996) carried out a comprehensive analysis of the effect of advertising expenditure on the price premium of brands in the UK (1993). He noted that a growth of total advertising expenditure in a product category of 1% of total turnover (advertising to sales ratio) coincides with a 3.9% increase in the market leader's price premium. Table 4.22 contains an overview of both market share and price premium of market leaders compared to private labels, in 42 product categories. The average market share of the market leaders (unweighted) is 34%, the average price premium 39.9% (unweighted).

In a market in which 5% of turnover is spent on advertising, the market leader makes, on average, a price premium of 19.5% compared to private labels. As Yasin comments: 'For this reason it pays to advertise.'

The amount of the price premium, reflected in the price differential between the brand and physically comparable propositions, is an important indicator of the strength of the brand equity. If the price differential increases but market share is retained, this demonstrates an improvement in brand equity. If the price differential has to be cut in order to retain market share, it means that brand equity relative to competing brands has deteriorated.

Reliable information on developments in market shares and relative prices, as supplied by retail panels, theoretically enables us to calculate the price elasticity of a brand. If this information is analysed a 'demand-curve' can be drawn up – see Figure 4.27, page 167. This depicts how brands A and B react to a higher or lower price differential between the two brands from P1 to P2, or vice versa. Brand A is far less sensitive in that respect than brand B. In practice, a direct connection does not usually exist; price elasticity varies with different price levels, resulting in a non-linear correlation.

Optimisation of price policy requires insight into the extent to which the buyers of a brand react to changes in its price, and to changes in the price differentials with competing brands. The graph in Figure 4.26 illustrates this. The price elasticity of the brand in question is -2.12, which means that a 1% price rise results in a decline in purchased volume of -2.12%. This price elasticity consists of two different elements: a drop of 0.17% due to the rise in the brand's own price, and a drop resulting from the devaluation of the brand compared with competitors. So a drop of 0.56% can be ascribed to the devaluation relative to brand B, and so on (Nielsen, 1997).

Market	Leader's share [1]	Price premium [2]
Ales and stout	20	52.0
Batteries	30	60.3
Biscuits	28	8.8
Brandy	18	46.1
Breakfast cereals	45	23.9
Butter	28	5.0
Canned fruit	17	16.4
Chilled desserts	31	15.5
Chocolate/confectionery	31	9.7
Cider	22	8.4
Cigarettes	41	21.4
Clothes-washing products	42	35.9
Concentrated drinks	31	19.2
Conditioner	12	131.1
Crisps	33	16.9
Dark rum	30	30.7
Flour	30	60.2
Frozen desserts	19	−4.7
Frozen ready meals	31	16.8
Fruit juice	14	18.6
Gin	49	19.9
Ice-cream	32	23.9
Instant coffee	55	23.5
Lager	25	59.9
Margarine	25	38.3
Nuts	58	27.3
Photographic film	43	39.5
Rice	23	119.2
Sanitary products	28	18.8
Shampoo	35	63.7
Sherry	28	61.9
Snacks	37	37.1
Suncare products	20	93.8
Tea	28	73.4
Toilet soap	23	88.8
Toothbrushes	26	80.3
Toothpaste	26	80.3
Vermouth	54	44.6
Vodka	51	36.6
Whisky	21	28.5
White rum	90	32.6
Yoghurts	25	8.6

[1]Calculated from Mintel data, [2]The Planning Business, 1993

Table 4.22 Market leaders' market shares and price premiums, compared with private labels in the UK (Source:Yasin, in Luik and Waterson, 1996)

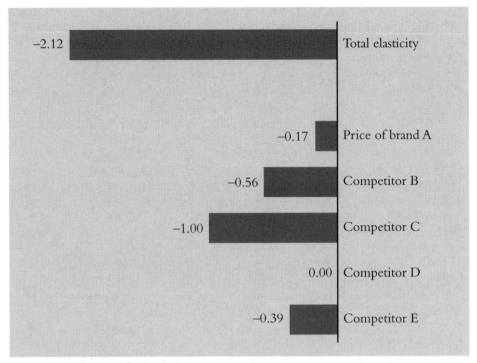

−2.12	Total elasticity
−0.17	Price of brand A
−0.56	Competitor B
−1.00	Competitor C
0.00	Competitor D
−0.39	Competitor E

Figure 4.26 Elements of price elasticity

Broadbent analysed the price elasticity of 105 brands, and arrived at the range shown in Table 4.23.

His analysis revealed that between 65 and 85% of short-term sales fluctuations can be explained by the variation in price differentials.

Buck calculated the price elasticity of a large number of brands, and established the connection with their market positions shown in Table 4.24. Market leaders have stronger brand equity than brands in second place. This is partly reflected in lower price elasticity.

Price elasticity classes	Number of brands
0.00 to −0.49	22
−0.50 to −0.99	20
−1.00 to −1.49	26
−1.50 to −1.99	16
−2.00 and higher	21
Average −1.32	105

Table 4.23 Price elasticity classes

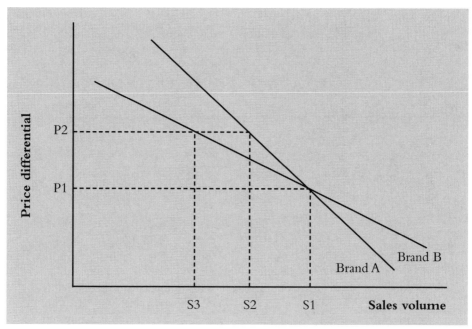

Figure 4.27 Demand curve: the ratio between price differential and sales volume

Although marketers are generally aware of the phenomenon of price elasticity, it is often disregarded in marketing practice. However, it is quite easy to calculate from Nielsen data, or else with econometric market models as described in Chapter 8.

Nielsen (US) (Ellis and Gajula, 1993) defines a brand's price elasticity as the influence of competing brands' price changes on its sales (susceptibility) and of the brand's price changes on competing brands (competitive impetus). As a measure of financial brand equity, a brand's competitive impetus is indexed on the basis of that brand's susceptibility. Nielsen examines price elasticity at the retail level using scanner data, which enables it to isolate promotional effects accurately.

In the day-to-day battle for orders, the prime interest of marketers tends to be developments in sales and market shares. But better insight into the actual course of financial/economic brand equity can be obtained if we also focus on movements in price differentials and calculate price elasticities.

Market position	Price elasticity (index)
Market leader	87
Brand no. 2	100
New brands	140
All brands	100

Table 4.24 Market position and price elasticity

4.4.4　Margin elasticity

The size and strength of consumer brand equity not only affect a brand's demand elasticity. They also have great influence on the gross profit margins distributors can make on one brand. Retailers are willing (or obliged) to work with lower margins on strong brands – for which they have good reason. Brands with strong consumer–brand equity imply:

- greater rate of turnover;
- lower costs per unit;
- faster stock flows, so lower financing costs;
- higher turnover per unit of shelf length;
- higher total gross profit contribution by the brand, despite possible lower margins per unit (after all, gross profit contribution = margin x sales in units).

Strong consumer brand equity not only lowers demand elasticity at the consumer level, but also that of the retailer to the manufacturer. The shopkeeper must (of necessity) accept a lower margin. That lower margin helps to keep the retail price down, which in turn has the effect of increasing sales.

Albion studied this phenomenon. He came up with a theory, which he tested in practice. He devised the concept of 'margin elasticity': the effect of consumer brand equity on trade margins. The term suggests a direct causal relationship between the margin and distributors' demand. But actually it might be more appropriate to call it 'retail-trade demand elasticity'.

In 1978 Albion carried out empirical research on 488 brands in 51 markets of everyday consumer goods. He established a connection between a number of product attributes and the influence of advertising expenditure on retail margins. He designed a model with which he could explain 70% of the variance in margins (see Figure 4.28).

The influence of advertising on the number of consumers buying a brand (brand penetration) in particular has a lowering effect on margins (via the consolidated consumer brand equity) – more so than the frequency with which the individual consumer buys the brand (brand loyalty).

Total advertising expenditure in a product category has a significant influence on trade margins. In addition, there is a connection between the availability of product variants and the retailer's handling costs.

So consumer brand equity has a number of important effects for the manufacturer:

- it (strongly) increases sales volume – large numbers of consumers want the brand;
- it increases the price the consumer is prepared to pay for the brand;
- it lowers trade margins;
- it increases the share of the retail price the manufacturer manages to appropriate (if lower margins result in lower retail prices, this is not entirely valid);
- it lowers the sales price on account of the lower trade margins;
- this in turn increases sales volume.

Low retail-trade price elasticity results, in turn, in high margins. In other words, as soon as retailers have the opportunity to raise their margins (without this greatly affecting sales of the product in question), they will not desist from doing so. So in those product groups, retailers are the ones who appropriate a larger proportion of the retail price. The resulting higher retail price can, in turn, have an adverse effect on sales volume.

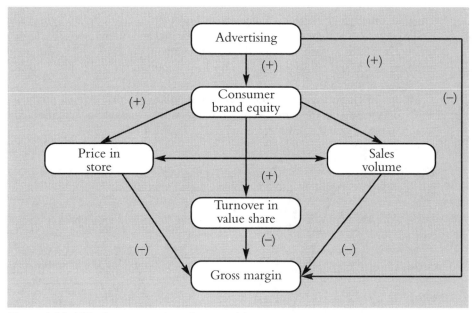

Figure 4.28 Albion's gross margin variance model

4.4.5 A method for calculating financial/economic brand equity

The research service Longman Moran Analytics in the US has developed a method for calculating financial/economic brand equity based on the two most important output variables: market share and price premium (Moran, 1994). Moran also argues that a brand's financial/economic equity for a firm is the result of its value for consumers. This is reflected by the premium that consumers are prepared to pay for a brand compared with competing brands, and how long this situation lasts (durability). His formula for calculating financial/economic brand equity is, briefly: market share x relative price x a durability factor.

This formula seems attractively simple, but is less so in application. Moran actually implies the same thing himself, stating that it is essential to demarcate the market correctly. So all possible relevant market segmentations must be considered to allow market shares and price differences in the various brands to be established and tracked as accurately as possible. Neither is it easy to determine the 'durability factor'. Moran

	a	b	a x b	c	a x b x c	
Brand	Market share (%)	Relative price index	Brand value	Durability	Brand equity	Equity per % market share
Acura	7.0	0.93	6.5	136	8.8	126
Volvo	6.5	0.84	5.5	203	11.2	171
Audi	1.2	0.97	1.2	137	1.6	132
Saab	1.0	0.91	0.9	198	1.8	180

Table 4.25 Brand equity calculation for four imported makes of car, US, 1990–91 (Moran, 1994)

suggests using price elasticity: brands with lower price elasticity are stronger, after all, and so represent a higher value. But it is complicated and often impossible to determine price elasticities within a defined market segment. In Table 4.25 Moran gives an example of a brand equity calculation for four imported car makes in the lower part of the deluxe segment of the American car market (1990–91).

If the development of brand equity can be followed in this way, it might serve as a tool for measuring the effectiveness of alternative marketing activities. The main components of brand equity are combined in Figure 4.29.

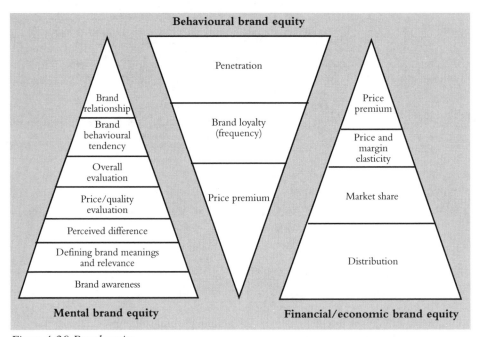

Figure 4.29 Brand equity

4.5   WHAT IS A STRONG BRAND?

It is still necessary to answer the question: what is a strong brand? Or, you might even ask: do strong brands exist? It has been shown that Ehrenberg, who, for a lifetime, has been involved with research and analysis of buying behaviour patterns, thinks that they do not. He believes that there are only big brands and small brands. Big brands are those which are bought by more people, and which are bought by those people a little more frequently. Small brands have fewer buyers, who buy them a little less frequently (the so-called double-jeopardy effect, which McPhee (in Ehrenberg *et al.*, 1990) observed back in 1963). The great difference between big and small brands is the number of buyers, not the average buying frequency. In stable markets the purchase of established brands proves to coincide largely with set patterns, which form the basis for the Dirichlet formula. This formula can predict the duplication of a brand with other brands and the buying frequency, based on a given market share and penetration (see Ehrenberg, 1996). So the question is: can the Dirichlet model be beaten?

Hallberg (1995) thinks it can. He has made an impassioned plea for differential marketing, as it is called: the concentration of marketing activities on the small category of heavy users, who are responsible for the lion's share of turnover and profit of the brand. However, he does not back up his arguments with material to demonstrate that it also has effect. When I asked him what a brand could gain in that group, the essence of his reply was that the next group in order of importance should be addressed: medium-loyal users.

The analysis described in section 4.3.3 (see Figure 4.19) by the Leo Burnett advertising agency in the US shows that brand growth is primarily the result of penetration growth: 75% on average. At the same time, the greater the brand penetration, the greater the contribution of increased frequency – another reflection of the double-jeopardy effect. However, the results suggest that the effect of increased frequency is still greater than one might expect on the strength of that effect alone. The findings of Baldinger and Rubinson were the same. Research by the NDP Group (Baldinger and Rubinson, 1997) and by Millward Brown (Farr and Hollis, 1997) shows that brands do indeed exist which deviate from the Dirichlet patterns, either in a positive or a negative sense.

First of all, it can be concluded that there are large and small brands, which is primarily apparent in the differences in their penetration, and, to a lesser degree, in smaller differences in their average buying frequency. In addition, there are differences in brand strength, in that, given a certain penetration, for a small minority of brands there are greater differences in frequency than Dirichlet patterns might suggest. Some large brands are relatively weak, and very few small brands are relatively strong.

Brands can be observed becoming bigger and smaller, especially as penetration increases and decreases. But is not an increase in a brand's penetration and, concomitantly, in its buying frequency and market share, also proof of its stronger brand equity?

In this context, the characteristics of a strong brand can be summarised as follows.

Mental brand equity

- *High saliency*: the brand has a strong presence in the memory. It scores well on spontaneous awareness (TOMA) and emotional proximity. Consumers feel they know the brand well.
- *Clear product meanings*: consumers know, in essence, what the brand means and how it differs in a functional sense. It is strongly associated with the underlying product category/categories. It has high saliency for relevant product attributes, which consumers are looking for in the product category/categories.
- *Defining symbolic meanings*: the brand has a distinct personality of its own, thus standing out from competing brands in the category. Its symbolic meanings represent important values for users (binding interest).
- *High perceived quality*: compared with other brands, the quality of the brand in question is rated relatively highly within the underlying product category/categories. Consumers have a positive opinion of the brand's performance and see it as a leader in its category. They value and trust the brand highly.
- *Entrenched users*: a relatively large number of the brand users are loyalists, or entrenched users, who have a strong commitment to the brand and little inclination to switch.

- *Attractive to non-users*: the brand is seen by its 'non-users' as an acceptable alternative to the brands they are currently using – it is in their consideration set.

Behavioural brand equity
- *High level of penetration*: compared with other brands, the brand in question has a lot of users (penetration on the increase).
- *Good 'intake'*: the brand is bought by a relatively large number of new category users, especially new generations.
- *Few deserters*: the brand has a stable group of users from year to year; compared with competing brands it has fewer deserters (not so many switch out).
- *High level of brand loyalty*: within the (sub)category/categories, the brand has a relatively high 'share of requirements', particularly for heavy buyers.
- *Good price premium*: consumers are prepared to pay a good premium for the brand compared with its competitors, and are relatively less susceptible to competitors' price offers.

Financial/economic brand equity
- *Good level of distribution*: the brand has a high weighted distribution within the relevant sales outlets for the category and the target group/groups.
- *Relatively high market share*: with respect to the market share within the category or subcategory, the brand is one of the (two) biggest brands.
- *Relatively high price*: the brand commands a relatively high price premium compared with competing brands.
- *Low price elasticity*: the brand is less susceptible than competitors to changes in the price differential compared with competing brands.
- *High financial market share*: the brand has a higher share of the market in sales by value than in sales by volume.
- *High net profit/ROI*: the brand has a high net profit contribution and high ROI.

Brand equity research: no one magic formula
After this extensive discussion, branders may be wondering whether there might not be one simple way of measuring brand equity. Is there not one 'equity gauge'?

It would, of course, be fine if there were. Robert Kaplan of Harvard compared the steering of a brand with flying a plane. He wondered if it might be possible to provide a pilot with an instrument on which he could read all the important factors, including height, speed, course, fuel supply. All the pilot would have to do, with Kaplan's system, would be to keep the pointer of the instrument within the green range of the dial. The answer is obvious. It is just the same with equity research. Although the course of the relative market share and the relative price differential are still, at the end of the day, the most important parameters for expressing brand equity, a good 'brand pilot' will want to know quite a lot more than that. He or she will want to understand why the market share and price differential are what they are, and why they develop the way they do. To this end, the most important components of mental brand equity must be measured periodically – not forgetting a check on connections with behavioural responses.

The significance of the different factors varies from market to market, as well as from brand to brand. Many brand owners carry out research regularly, along the lines described. Brand equity research entails designing tools with which to follow the critical success factors of a brand systematically with time. The tools may consist of measurements carried out with varying frequency: those relating to the components of financial/economic brand equity are ongoing, image measurements are carried out every one or two years, intermediate awareness, attitude and behaviour measurements use tracking methods, supplying bi-monthly or quarterly scores.

Chapter 4 Appendix

Appendix I Definitions of brand equity

1 'Brand equity is the lifetime value of each customer.'
Robert P. Parker, National Geographic Society.

2 'Brand equity is the proportion of revenues due to "beyond-commodity" quality.'
James P. Alleborn, Total Research Corporation.

3 'A set of associations which are most strongly linked to a brand name'.
Andrea Dunham, Unique Value Int.

4 Brand equity is the 'future value of a brand name. This derives from the value
consumers believe the brand offers them. This is expressed by how many
consumers are willing to pay how much for the brand relative to the cost of
alternative brands, and how durable their valuation is likely to be. Durability is the
degree of loyalty at various relative prices.'
William T. Moran, Longman Moran Analytics Inc.

5 'The customer franchise and the loyalty it commands.'

6 'Retained customers in the marketing sense of the corporation's ownership of the
equity in its brands.' (Retained buyers: the accumulated proportion of households
purchasing the brand from year to year.)
David B. Learner, MRCA Information Services

7 'The finance "value" added when a product is sold branded versus unbranded.'
R. W. Ceurvorst, MarketFacts Inc.

8 'Brand equity is the measurable financial value in transactions that accrues to a
product or service from successful programs and activities relating to branding.'
Nigel Hollis, Millward Brown Inc.

9 'Base brand equity is that portion of the existing brand's annual sales that a
comparable new brand could not generate at the same marketing support levels.
Potential equity is the increased level of sales that line and franchise extensions would
have versus comparable new brands that brands would be able to spawn over time.'
Joel Rubinson, NPDG Group Inc.

10 'In case of an acquisition, it is the expectation of the future cash flow that
commends a premium over the cost of developing the plant and infrastructure
required to bring a new, competing brand to the market.'
Alexander Biel

11 'The set of associations and behaviours on the part of a brand's customers, channel
members, which gives the brand a strong, sustainable and differentiated advantage.'
Marketing Science Institute

12 'Brand equity is the set of brand assets and liabilities linked to the brand, its name, and symbol, that adds or subtracts value to a product or service for a firm and/or its customers.'
David Aaker

13 'Brand equity is everything the customer walks into the store with.'
Peter Farquhar

14 'Brand equity is the incremental amount your customer will pay to obtain your brand rather than a physically comparable product without your brand-name.'
Joel Axelrod

15 'Equity is the value that the brand adds to the product.'
Larry Light

16 'Equity is the value of the incremental cash-flows of branded products over and above cash flows of unbranded ones.'
Simon and Sullivan

17 'Brand equity is the set of associations that permits the brand to earn greater volume than it would without the brand name.'
Marketing Science Institute

18 'Brand equity is the differential effect that brand knowledge has on consumer response to marketing-activity.'
K.L. Keller

19 'Brand equity is the incremental utility associated with a brand name, which is not captured by functional attributes.'
Kamakura and Russell

20 'Brand equity is the incremental price premium, compared to a "generic" competitor.'
Muller and Mainz

21 'Brand equity is the collection of all the accumulated attitudes in the extended consciousness of customers, distribution channels and influentials which will increase future profit and long-term cash flow.'
Tim Ambler

22 'Brand equity is the sales share we would get if we were at average price and had average distribution – and average price and distribution elasticities applied.'
Simon Broadbent

23 'Brand equity is the component of overall preference for a branded product, not explained by objectively measured product attributes.'
V. Srinivasan

5
Advertising frameworks

Giep Franzen

5.1 HISTORICAL THEORIES OF ADVERTISING FRAMEWORKS

For almost a century advertising practitioners, market researchers and scientists have been trying to understand exactly how advertising influences consumers' buying decisions. And for just as long, they have been reaching the conclusion that this question, in its general formulation, is unanswerable.

Advertising works in very different ways. It depends on a great number of variables, the most important of which are:

- the recipient's nature and personal relationship with what is being advertised;
- the type of product or service, and the role it plays in people's lives;
- the brand's stage of life;
- the brand equity;
- the content of the advertising itself and the way in which it is presented;
- the context in which the advertising is perceived;
- the advertising pressure that is exercised.

The 'hierarchy of effects' models

It is not hard to imagine that a campaign for Mars ice cream, geared to young people with a sweet tooth, works quite differently from a series of advertisements intended to interest savings-minded citizens in investing in British Telecom shares.

Nevertheless, since 1898, when St Elmo Lewis formulated the AIDA model, academics have been trying to devise general models of the process of how advertising works, applicable to such divergent cases.

That earliest advertising framework model presupposed a succession of effects, the last one of which was the purchase of the product in question. AIDA stands for 'attract attention, maintain interest, create desire, get action'. The model stood its ground for some 60 years. As time went by adaptations were regularly proposed, though the basic idea was never abandoned. That basic idea entailed a 'hierarchy of effects', in which each effect category was considered to be necessary for the next and dependent on the previous one. The idea was to 'pilot' consumers through the hierarchy, step by step, until the final stage – the purchase of the product – had been reached. Logically, it was also known as a transmission model.

Consumers were still largely seen as unresisting recipients of persuasive, even manipulative advertising campaigns. This was the tradition which gave rise to the DAGMAR model (Colley, 1961) which many feel is still applicable today.

DAGMAR stands for 'defining advertising goals for measured advertising results'. Like its predecessor, AIDA, it entailed a four-stage model: ACCA (short for awareness, comprehension, conviction, action).

New ideas

Not long after DAGMAR, Lavidge and Steiner (1961) proposed a model in which five stages precede buying behaviour: awareness, knowledge, liking, preference, conviction, and buying behaviour. And in 1968 McGuire followed with a model comprising the following stages: presentation, attention, comprehension, yielding, retention, and buying behaviour.

All these models were further elaborations on the CAE sequence (cognition, affect, experience).

The peculiar thing about these hierarchical models is that they all finish with 'action'. They totally neglect the fact that all advertising for established brands takes place after action, among highly experienced buyers.

In the 1970s and 1980s these simplistic sequential models were adapted to incorporate new views on consumer choice behaviour and new theories of information processing.

Although March and Simon (1958) had already pointed out that consumer behaviour did not focus on optimising choice but on achieving a satisfactory result, the science of consumer behaviour appeared to assume that people had a kind of built-in computer program – and this assumption lasted into the 1980s. Consumers were thought to weigh up the functional characteristics of all the options and thus reach an optimum choice through a number of logical rules of choice. However, in the 1980s the fact that consumers have emotions and feelings was 'rediscovered', and these, it transpired, are a decisive factor in many choice processes. Consumers often just select what appeals to them emotionally. So advertising frameworks made room for emotional reactions as a primary communication response, alongside cognitive reactions to convincing arguments.

At the same time, people were realising that many products were not bought for their functional attributes but purely for their symbolic function. From then onwards, the world of consumer goods was divided into instrumental and expressive products (in other words, problem-solving and enriching products).

It was found that the development of knowledge and attitudes need not necessarily precede buying behaviour, but that consumers often buy something, prompted by impulse or emotion, and only start to process information after the event, in order to justify their choice. A change in behaviour would appear frequently to precede a change in attitude, rather than result from it.

It became clear that sequences of effects were quite different from the CAE order in traditional learning theory, on which AIDA and DAGMAR were based. The 'new' sequence was: affect, cognition, experience (ACE, for short), and there were also two others in which consumers first buy the brand and gain usage experience, followed by knowledge and feeling, ie, experience, cognition, affect (ECA), and experience, affect, cognition (EAC).

In 1965 Herbert Krugman added involvement to the models, as an important variable. Krugman ascertained that the importance of a product for consumers' egos, and the risks they ran if they made the wrong choice, greatly affected their willingness to pay attention to advertising. Not only was it necessary to take account of situations where interest was great, but also of those where consumers were indifferent.

The advertising agency Foote, Cone & Belding (FCB) (Vaughn, 1980, 1986) integrated the new ideas in a matrix, which has since been dubbed the 'FCB grid' (see Figure 5.1 overleaf).

Rossiter et al. (1991) suggested an alternative to the FCB grid (the Rossiter-Percy grid, Figure 5.2) in which they replaced the cognition/affect dimension with a motivation dimension: (negative) informative motivations versus (positive) transformative motivations. They also introduced a brand awareness dimension, as a prerequisite for the development of brand attitudes.

Psychologists ascertained what advertising practitioners had known for a long time – that recipients are not always attuned to processing the factual content of advertisements, but mainly focus on the way in which they are presented. Consumers

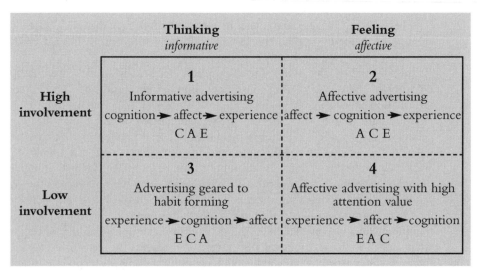

Figure 5.1 The FCB grid (Source: Vaughn, 1980, 1986)

tend to use two different 'routes' or 'highways' for processing information and adapting their attitudes: a central route for factual information and a peripheral route for presentation features (Petty and Cacioppo, 1986). However, they usually combine both routes in some proportion to each other.

Willingness to pay attention to an ad was found to depend on an emotional evaluation at the very first moment of exposure, and on the context in which advertising is 'consumed'. People have a PAR (primary affective reaction) which determines whether or not they want to give something their attention. Obviously that PAR depends chiefly on their involvement with the product or brand.

Whether recipients process an ad (and to what extent) depends on their personal motivation, the opportunities and limitations inherent in the exposure situation and their personal abilities (for instance, existing product knowledge). It depends, in particular, on their 'inclination to consider' the ad. The MOA (motivation, opportunity, ability) model is appropriate here.

It became apparent that there is an interaction between what is present in the memory (associations, affects, beliefs, brand attitudes) and the processing of advertisements. Recipients prove, to some extent, to perceive what they already know and think, which is frequently quite different from what the advertising practitioner is trying to tell them.

Barry and Howard (1990) analysed literature relating to the hierarchy of effects models and concluded:

It is unclear whether the primacy of an initial cognitive or affective response has a significant influence on the processing of advertising-related information. ... No evidence currently exists supporting the contention that the sequential ordering of cognitive versus affective responses to advertising communications ultimately matters in terms of what people purchase or consume.

After a thorough analysis of over 250 scientific studies, Vakratsas and Ambler (1995) proposed an integrated model:

If any combination of think, know and feel into a hierarchy has merit, then that model must be included by CAEA (cognition, affect, experience, affect) ... whilst awareness could well be part of the 'learning' stage, it is not obvious how purchase or affect can take place without any awareness of the brand. In CAEA, awareness is included in the first stage ... It is reasonable to believe that advertising works both before and after purchase experience, or before or after.

On the basis of extensive analysis of empirical research, I (Franzen, 1994) suggested replacing theories proceeding from a hierarchal sequence of effects by the theory of an interactive system (see Figure 5.3).

With the exception of product and brand launches, which, by definition, have a zero-based start, practitioners are always confronted with situations in which existing attitudes, buying behaviour and usage experience also influence advertising effectiveness, and vice versa. In fact, this tends to apply quickly to product launches also.

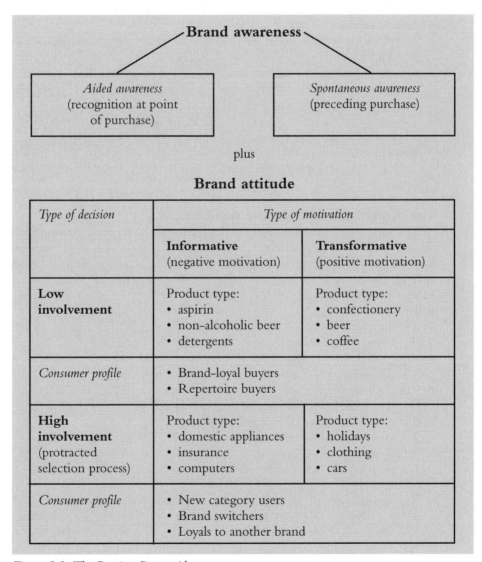

Figure 5.2 The Rossiter-Percy grid

Ferguson (1989) notes that in a system each variable interacts so completely with the other variables that it is not possible to distinguish cause from effect. The proposed system consists of a number of groups of effects, which are parallel to the Brand Associative Network described in Chapter 3 (see Figure 3.2, page 54). The following division applies:

- *Attention*
  Exposure to advertising, and the resulting scanning, focusing, and duration and intensity of attention.
- *Advertising processing*
  The different levels at which advertising stimuli are processed, and the form of processing – cognitive, affective, visual/verbal.
- *Brand awareness*
  Awareness of the brand and the levels of brand awareness.
- *Brand associations*
  The categories of association and storage in the memory, in association networks.
- *Brand positioning*
  Comparison of brands with one another, and the relative position in the memory of one brand in a category/subcategory compared with that of competing brands.
- *Brand evaluation and brand attitude*
  The evaluation of the brand, its inclusion in the consideration set and brand repertoire, and the emergence of brand preference or brand rejection.
- *Brand behaviour and product experience*
  Trial purchase, repeat purchase, product usage experience and the development of degrees of brand loyalty.

The limitations of scientific theories

The variety of different models has not made the theory of advertising frameworks any clearer for advertising practitioners. One problem has been how to single out those elements that are relevant to a specific situation from all the abstract theories and models claiming to be universally valid. And then, in terms of effectiveness, how to influence, effectively and verifiably, consumer buying behaviour in favour of the advertised brand.

The development of scientific theories on advertising frameworks has stemmed chiefly from cognitive psychology. This is biased towards the question of how consumers deal with the individual advertisements to which they have been exposed.

The following aspects have received hardly any attention:

- The *effects* campaigns have over the course of time on perceptions and emotions linked with the brand. Although short and long-term effects are familiar elements, they are not the explicit thrust of the theories.
- The entire *phenomenon of 'the brand'* as the carrier of a wide range of meanings, emotional associations, evaluations and behavioural tendencies.
  For years, any available insights on this have stemmed solely from market research circles.
- The *persuasive effect* of advertising – what motivates people to buy certain products, or not, and what mainly affects their selection behaviour? Hardly any new theories have been developed since those of Ernest Dichter, Abraham Maslov and Milton Rokeach in the 1960s and 1970s, and the main focus since then has been on descriptions of processes. This has meant that advertisers have encountered hardly any points of

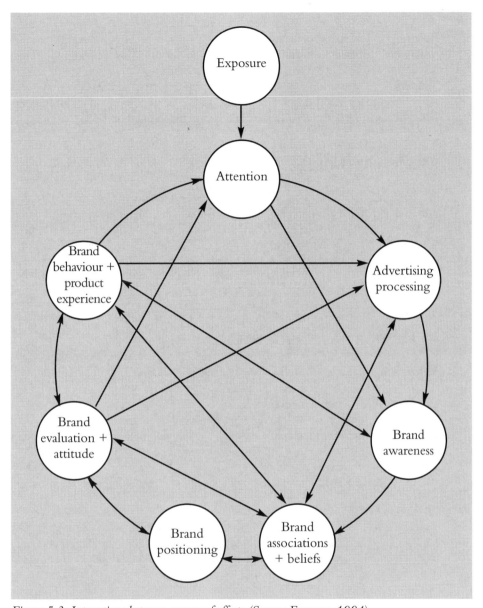

Figure 5.3 Interactions between groups of effects (Source: Franzen, 1994)

contact in the theories about what they should be communicating in order to
influence selection behaviour in favour of their brands.

• The *characteristics of the advertising* itself. Although the formal characteristics of ads and
campaigns do, of course, have a major effect on the entire communication process,
there is little system to the scientific interest in the effects of the various basic forms
of advertising and communication. Each researcher makes a random choice, which
means that there are many disconnected facts available which lack the cohesion of a
good 'blanket' theory or model.

These are the main problems confronting advertisers. It is, of course, highly relevant to the planning of advertising campaigns to discover how consumers deal with an individual ad, but such information provides nothing to go on when advertising strategies have to be developed. The chief problem for advertisers is still how they can influence consumer buying behaviour and which recurring effects they should aim for in the process. Thus they are not primarily concerned about how consumers process advertising, but how advertising influences buying behaviour.

5.2   POLICY THEORIES

Rational decisions on media deployment and creative solutions can be made only when a satisfactory theory has been found on how advertising influences consumer behaviour in specific circumstances, and which intermediate mental reactions occur and are necessary. This, too, is a prerequisite for proper research design into both mental and behavioural responses. As early as 1949 Bernard Berelson summarised the situation as follows:

Some kinds of communication, on some kinds of issues, brought to the attention of some kinds of people under some kinds of conditions, have some kinds of effects.

And, a few decades later, Neville Darby (1979) said:

No single theory or group of theories can explain it all, because advertisements work in such different ways. There is no point in looking for an overall theory.

According to Stephen King back in 1975:

What we need is not a wholly comprehensive theory of advertising, but a slightly more advanced theory of advertisements. A framework for thinking how different sorts of advertisements might work, for different people, in different circumstances, at different stages of time. With such complexity, the framework should be simple enough to be of practical use to the people who have the job of planning and creating advertisements, and those who have the job of evaluating them.

In 1979 Hugh Murray observed:

The most realistic answer to the question: 'How does advertising work?' lies in a family of models, derived from careful empirical studies over a considerable period, reduced to their most basic form by rigorous application of the principle of excluding trivial, insignificant and irrelevant factors. These relate only to certain product market conditions, but are nevertheless better than the alternatives.

Every practitioner makes assumptions or has firm convictions as to the way in which an ad or a campaign works. Such opinions are generally expressed only when the person in question is faced with creative proposals. Then all involved prove to have a personal 'intuitive' model of how advertising works. These intuitive opinions tend to differ considerably between those responsible for developing campaigns. It would be much better, both for harmonious teamwork and communication, and possibly also for the effectiveness of campaigns, if, before campaigns were developed and deployed, there were agreement on *how* they should work. It should be ascertained which behavioural response among which consumers is considered realistic in which circumstances, and what mental responses are expected to make the most effective contribution to behaviour. A conscious choice for a specific advertising framework model results in rational appraisals, which should benefit effectiveness.

The academic community has not yet produced or verified these specific models of advertising effect. Admittedly, much progress has been made in general theories of advertising processing, and there is more insight into consumers' direct mental responses to all kinds of characteristics of individual ads. But few, if any, connections have been made with the long-term persuasive effect of campaigns in the marketplace.

So, all in all, little has been pinpointed to tie in with the specific problems of individual advertisers. They have great difficulty in recognising their own situations and dilemmas in the models couched in general terms.

It is time we looked at the views and experiences of policy makers. This leads on to what are called 'policy theories'. This term is used for the whole gamut of hypotheses on which a policy is based. These hypotheses are concerned with characteristics of phenomena, but, more especially, the relationships between phenomena.

Argyris and Schön (in Hoogerwerf, 1983) define a theory of action which can be represented as a formula: 'if one wishes, in situation S, to achieve result R, under the assumptions $a_1 \ldots a_n$, carry out action D.' They also define a theory of practice, which, they claim, consists of a system of interconnected 'theories of action'. They provide, for specific 'real-life' situations, a description of the actions which are believed to produce the desired results under relevant assumptions. The thrust of this theory is the views on connections between end and means, and between cause and effect.

Lindblom and Cohen (1979) use the term 'policy-making frameworks' in this context. They suggest that:

Policy makers attack specific problems in the light of a general framework or perspective that controls both explanatory hypotheses and a range of solutions that they are willing to consider.

The hypotheses on which policy-makers' actions are based can, of course, be partly derived from scientific insights. They may, to some extent, be based on observations in the marketplace. But this does not mean that policy theories are scientific theories. The failure of many a policy, understood as the failure to achieve desired objectives, can, after all, be partly explained by the fact that policy is often based on incorrect assumptions (Hoogerwerf, 1983).

Advertising campaign decision-makers generally apply greatly simplified representations of reality, within which they try to work as rationally as possible. They are mainly hampered by their own reactions as recipients of advertisements, and the difficulty of putting themselves impartially in the position of the target group.

It is important, both for the evolution of advertising theory and for advertising practice (policy-making, campaign development and research and evaluation of campaigns), to open up the advertising framework models on which these decision-makers implicitly base their assumptions. In addition, greater understanding of the assumed models may also help to improve the whole operation of the advertising process, as well as improving effectiveness. Policy theories can also form a bridge between academic knowledge and advertising practice. Hoogerwerf (1983) expressed it as follows:

Policy people are expected to be prepared to subject their often beloved policy theories to critical study and empirical research. Researchers are expected to be willing to take the policy people's theories seriously enough to make a study of them!

5.2.1 The experienced consumer

Before describing advertising frameworks as they are probably perceived by practitioners, it is worth reflecting on the key question: who is in charge of what is communicated, the sender or the receiver? The answer to this question greatly influences the choice of advertising framework model in a given situation.

The hierarchy of effects models were based implicitly on a passive recipient, who absorbed advertising in the way the sender intended. Active participation by the recipient in the communication process was virtually discounted. He or she was seen as a *tabula rasa* on which messages were imprinted. Consequently, the theory on which this was based was termed the 'hypodermic needle' theory. Meanwhile there are a whole range of views and models at our disposal, all of which represent the independent, active role of the recipient in the processing of information.

Practitioners are alert to the fact that among recipients there is a growing avoidance of advertising, increasingly selective perception, increasingly partial processing, ever-sooner breaking of 'the connection' with the ad, and growing focus on visual images. But, more importantly, they realise that a recipient's existing associations, beliefs and attitudes greatly influence his processing and interpretation of messages. Advertising interacts constantly with the consumer's personal experiences in perceiving and using products and brands. Moreover, the public today are also experienced 'advertising consumers' by now. They see through the advertiser's intentions and, to a growing extent, adopt the attitude of seasoned observers rather than unsuspecting recipients.

Practitioners have learnt to see the people with whom they communicate as individuals, who create meanings for themselves from the sensory stimuli they are offered. This has led to the 'sense-making' theory, which can be summarised as follows (Dervin, 1984, in Windahl *et al.*, 1992).

Sense-making theory starts with the recipient seeing the message only in terms of how it crosses his or her life. It assumes that the message has no autonomous power of penetration, but that recipients themselves decide what impact it will have on them. The theory does not see the characteristics of the context in which a message is received as stimulating or inhibiting factors, but as essential to the way in which recipients use the message to make sense of the world around them. This theory defines information as something which informs, from the recipient's point of view. Since every recipient is unique, it is hard to conduct the process of sense-making uniformly for large groups of people. To some extent, everyone sees their own advertisements and commercials.

Here too, the truth is somewhere in the middle. The consumer does of course react largely individually to advertisements, but content and presentation determine the range of potential responses. Research shows time and again that certain responses to advertisements occur a great deal, others only a little. So consumer response can be steered quite considerably.

5.2.2 Corroborating function

Not only have practitioners acknowledged the independent role of the recipient, but they also now better understand the development of brand preferences and brand-loyal buying behaviour. This has also helped them to see that advertising's prime task is often not to bring about an initial product purchase, but rather to influence the behaviour of existing brand users. The first trial use of a brand is often the result of other marketing activities, such as sampling and special offers in the shop, with advertising focusing on corroborating and reinforcing the initial product experience. Practitioners are frequently communicating with people who use the brand several times a week, and have sometimes been doing so for decades. With these people it is necessary to reinforce and deepen their relationship with the brand and to increase the share of customer by stepping up buying frequency. The STAS effect is particularly relevant in this respect.

All this has brought about new and different views among practitioners as to how advertising works in general and in specific cases. Sometimes former models, like the Unique Selling Proposition (USP) (focusing on one unique product attribute), have been completely rejected as a result. In addition, some practitioners are also simplistically proclaiming a new creed, for instance, that of 'confrontational advertising', which uses extreme means to attract recipients' attention and penetrate their minds.

There is a growing belief that if the recipient is omnipotent and creates highly personal meanings for advertising, it is not so important what is communicated as long as there is communication.

5.2.3 Mechanistic and humanistic advertising

Lannon and Cooper (1983) made a distinction between past and present thinking, using the labels 'mechanistic' and 'humanistic' advertising. With the former, the sender controls the process, while with the latter the receiver is the key player, with advertising itself constituting a consumer product. People 'consume' advertising voluntarily and use it for their own purposes. When applied to media consumption, the 'uses and gratifications' theory is referred to (Stappers *et al.*, 1990). For advertising, the attributes listed below can be taken as uses and gratifications.

- Consumption information (tools for daily living) concerning:
  - (new) products;
  - (new) attributes;
  - (new) uses;
  - brands as 'signposts';
  - shops as 'preselectors'.
- Corroboration of own choices and behaviour.
- Allocation of values.
- Sharing of experiences with others.
- Relaxation and escape:
  - cognitive stimulation;
  - emotional stimulation and release;
  - identification with actors, situations and events.

So, with this theory, advertising, like other consumer goods, must meet needs. It must represent values, and develop usage satisfaction and recipients' loyalty. The importance of this has gradually got through to advertisers and practitioners. However, it does sometimes generate the wrong approach, as in 'confrontational' advertising, where the advertiser tries to force consumers to pay attention by shocking them.

A radical rejection of mechanistic models, and a proclamation of one of the humanistic models of the type to be discussed later, is neither practical nor even wise. The professional communication expert abstains from biased opinions on this subject and considers, within the limits of what is ethical, each of the different models as a theoretically acceptable option. The only relevant question in this respect is which model is most practical in a specific situation. Even the USP approach of the 1960s, based on the DAGMAR model, still proves to be highly effective when practical, instrumental products with a relevant problem-solving attribute are involved. Likeability measurements also indicate that recipients still most appreciate advertising which gives them sensible information in a realistic and credible way, thus arousing in them a feeling of reality (Franzen, 1994). The important thing is to select a model on rational grounds which can be expected to influence behaviour most effectively in the situation in question.

5.3   SEVEN ADVERTISING FRAMEWORK MODELS

To the best of my knowledge, the first research by practitioners into advertising-policy theories was by Hall and Macla, in the UK in 1991. This produced four different models:

- the *sales response* model;
- the *persuasion* model;
- the *involvement* model;
- the *saliency* model.

These models can be seen as 'major influencing highways'. They will be very familiar to an experienced practitioner, but they are incomplete. Their incompleteness may be because the sample used at the qualitative stage of research was too small, meaning that beliefs among the total population did not emerge sufficiently. My own practical experience and theoretical knowledge have led me to add three hypothetical models to the British ones:

- the *emotions* model;
- the *likeability* model;
- the *symbolism* model.

The name of the saliency model has been changed to the *awareness/saliency* model, and that of the involvement model to the *relationship/involvement* model.

When the models identified by Hall and Maclay are described, their descriptions will be adhered to as closely as possible. But they will be arranged in relation to the Advertising Response Matrix, and additional personal viewpoints will be added where useful.

Smit (1998) interviewed in depth 40 advertising policy-makers in the Netherlands, to discover their underlying views on the mechanisms of their campaigns. A very careful analysis of their responses uncovered six of the above models. The relationship/involvement model was not found. No other models surfaced beyond the seven described.

So these seven models probably represent a very large part of advertising practitioners' perceptions of advertising frameworks. However, further research may well reveal that more models can be added or that it might be better to combine some models.

These advertising framework models are primarily defined in terms of the response which is considered most important. This is called the key response – which, as will be

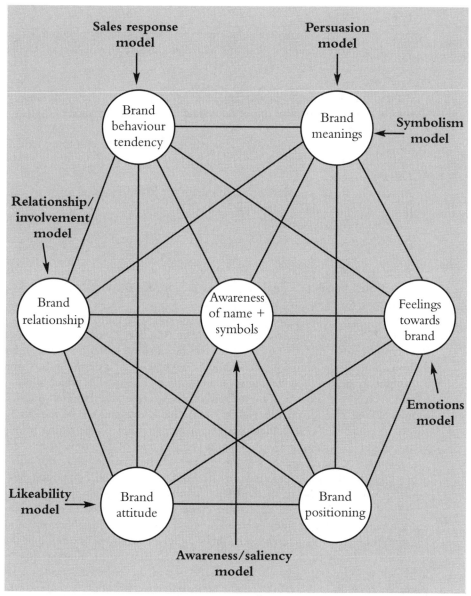

Figure 5.4 Basic elements of brands in the memory and advertising framework models

seen, is not always a behavioural response. In addition, the models are defined in terms of intermediate mental advertising and brand responses.

Each of the seven models is based on the choice of one of the components from the Brand Associative Network. This is illustrated in Figure 5.4.

Briefly, the thrust of the models is as follows:

- *Sales response* model
  Advertising aims to give consumers a direct impulse to buy, usually by announcing special offers.

- *Persuasion* model

  Advertising tries to convince consumers that the product represented by the brand has one or more attributes (benefits) which are important and relevant to them, and in which it differs from alternative brands.
- *Symbolism* model

  Advertising is geared to developing associations between the brand and symbolic meanings which represent important values for the target group.
- *Emotions* model

  Advertising seeks to have the brand associated with specific emotions, which colour usage experience.
- *Likeability* model

  Advertising focuses on developing liking for the brand, by using forms of advertising that the recipient particularly appreciates.
- *Relationship/involvement* model

  Advertising is aimed at developing an intimate relationship between the brand and its user.
- *Awareness/saliency* model

  Advertising pursues the highest possible saliency for the brand, generally using very distinctive forms of advertising.

These advertising framework models are not mutually exclusive. Each model is a prototype, representing the most characteristic attributes of one major influencing highway. Sometimes an unequivocal choice can be made of one model, but more often campaigns are geared to achieving several objectives. The models which apply then are hybrid in character: they are combinations of the described ideal models. So these seven should not be considered too rigidly – possible combinations of responses should always be considered. Nevertheless, their very existence is worth taking into account even without consensus on the number or precise effect of the individual models.

Practitioners have views on advertising characteristics that are effective in generating specific responses, and on the contexts in which advertising framework models are practical. More detailed descriptions of the models appear below, which indicate the most important advertising characteristics displayed in each model. Here again, a cautious interpretation is recommended: the relationships between models and characteristics are by no means always different for each model. For example, the use of humour is not only functional in the awareness/saliency model. Nor should campaigns in which emotions are expressed always be put in the emotions model. Advertising generates a whole series of different responses, by definition. A key response in one model may be a facilitating, secondary response in another. For instance, the relationship model is geared to developing a mental relationship (involvement) between the recipient and the brand (brand involvement). Obviously advertising involvement contributes towards generating different key effects in all other advertising framework models. So it will often be difficult to classify campaigns unequivocally in one of the models. The main point is that advertisers should be aware of the advertising framework model or combination of models on which they base their approach in a given situation. By making the choice explicit, one can steer the advertising development process more easily. Moreover, this approach helps to clarify evaluation criteria and facilitates a practical choice concerning the aspects to be researched.

The seven advertising frameworks are now described in more detail, following the arrangement in the Advertising Response Matrix (see Figure 5.5).

With each individual model the key effects are examined, indicating, as far as possible, which advertising characteristics occur where. However, it will become clear that these are not one-to-one relationships between advertising framework models and advertising characteristics.

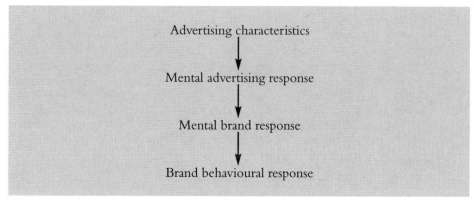

Figure 5.5 Main categories of the Advertising Response Matrix

5.3.1 Sales response model

Key effect

The sales response model focuses on one thing only: the act of purchase as a direct effect of exposure to the ad. An important intermediate effect is fact-finding behaviour (applying for a leaflet, visiting a show/showroom). Most other intermediate effects are usually considered to be irrelevant or completely unimportant.

Mental advertising response

The intended advertising response coincides with achieving, through one or several exposures, all of the AIDA effects: attention, interest, desire and action. The strategy requires high involvement from the recipient during exposure, but neither likeability nor short or long-term advertising response are particularly important.

Sometimes a negative attitude to the ad is accepted as an admittedly less desirable but inevitable side effect.

Mental brand response

The sales response model has three different points of departure:
- the brand is not known and not important. The only concerns are the attributes and instrumental functions of the product;
- brand awareness and brand acceptance are prerequisites, but the brand is selected purely on its merits as a product. Maintenance or increase of brand awareness is sometimes a secondary objective;
- buying and usage behaviour precede the development of the attitude towards the brand. Advertising must focus directly on influencing buying behaviour.

It is not a prime objective in any of these situations to build up brand awareness, specific brand associations and brand attitude through advertising.

The desired response is always an immediate, positive interest in the specific, often moment-related (product) proposition. Price stimuli are frequently used to trigger a direct behavioural response.

Advertising characteristics

Advertising in this model is highly informative in character. It aims at supplying both verbally and visually whatever information is needed to stimulate direct interest in the product proposition. Facts are important. Favourable (often temporary) price:value ratios tend to be strongly emphasised. Repetition within one advertisement is sometimes used. Text is presented in the form of reasoning. Specific aesthetic standards are not usually applied, unless to specify that the advertising should not be in conflict with the general style which the brand (the company, the shop) presents. Clarity, credibility and cogency are important. Advertising need not differ from competing brands in terms of basic format.

Evaluation criteria

Only one evaluation criterion is applied: behaviour. This may be fact-finding behaviour (store visit, vouchers), or, better still, recorded buying behaviour.

Little or no importance is attached to research into intermediate responses.

When ads are evaluated, the chief focus is on empirically established relationships, or general advertising conventions that have developed within the specific sector.

Notes

On the whole, practitioners realise that advertising aiming primarily at the direct buying response will have an effect on associations with the brand (company, shop). Yet they make light of this.

Neither are they particularly interested in exactly how advertising works – as long as it works. The 'stimulus response' model (where behaviour as the result of a stimulus is the only issue) rather than the 'stimulus organism response' (where the mental response of the 'organism' or recipient is important) is their point of departure. They see advertising frameworks as a 'black box', their sole focus of interest being empirically established (or assumed) relationships between advertising characteristics and recorded (buying) behaviour. They are not interested in theories on advertising frameworks. What others think about advertising is not considered important. Research is only carried out in order to remove doubts concerning the message's presentation characteristics.

5.3.2 Persuasion model

Key effect

The main aim of the persuasion model is a short-term effect: to stimulate (trial) purchases by non-users of the brand (to increase penetration). Its secondary aim is to increase the brand's share of customer among existing brand users (repertoire buyers), especially by influencing the following purchase in the series (the STAS effect).

Mental brand response

The advertising within this model seeks to convince its recipients that the brand offers them one or more relevant and important product attributes, in which it differs from competing brands. An effort is made to achieve a direct buying or fact-finding intention and inclusion of the brand in the consideration set. The establishment or reinforcement of brand awareness is a prerequisite.

Mental advertising response

In this model the primary aim of advertising is to communicate the instrumental product benefits, arouse interest in them and create credibility. Brand registration – the perception of the brand and its storage in the memory – is also important.

Advertising characteristics

Advertising takes the form of reasoned argument. It uses direct approaches, including presenters, demonstrations, forms of comparative advertising, user testimonials and authority figures.

It is important to communicate a new product attribute, or one which is, as yet, insufficiently well known. This attribute must represent a value or benefit for the recipients and be credible. Supporting evidence can contribute to the consumer's conviction. Advertisers who adhere to this model are always on the look-out for product improvements.

Branding of the ad is important: pack shots (shots of the brand's packaging, featuring the brand name) or brand signals should be so prominent that the brand and the message are perceived as inseparable.

Evaluation criteria

Advertising recall (spontaneous and aided) of perceived instrumental characteristics, processing and storage of the main message, brand registration and, in particular, attitude change are the most important evaluation criteria. The main message should be understood and judged relevant. The likeability of presentation is a less important criterion.

Brand awareness, cognitive brand associations and brand attitude are leading short-term effects. The development of sales in the short term is an important indicator of advertising effectiveness. Research into advertising frameworks emphasises measuring buying interest and attitude change.

Notes

The persuasion model largely coincides with the DAGMAR model devised in 1960. It too is based on step-by-step rational influencing, a passive recipient and traditional learning processes. It differs from the sales response model in that it pursues a short-term effect, whereas the desired effect of the sales response model is a direct one.

The persuasion model is chiefly used for products with a primarily instrumental function and a problem-solving attribute, such as maintenance products and toiletries. The persuasion model is based on the effect of a campaign, the sales response model on the effect of an individual ad.

5.3.3 Symbolism model

Key effect

The central focus of the symbolism model is the development of the brand's symbolic meanings. It entails a long-term mental brand response.

For users, the brand primarily serves as a means of expressing meanings about themselves: both towards themselves and their social environment. The brand expresses who and what consumers are, or would like to be. The symbolism encapsulated in the brand is the main reason for its selection (or rejection).

An important function of the brand is to keep the user group together. Users recognise and identify one another by way of the brand, which serves as a collective emblem. The brand is a vehicle of expression for minorities. Its symbolic distinctiveness is essential. Users divide people into 'one of us' or 'others'. A brand which has too general a use or user associations loses its ability to serve as a symbol for a certain type of people (subcultures).

Mental advertising response

Advertising aims primarily to represent 'human meanings' and link them to the brand by association transfer.

The product is of secondary importance in this model. Perceived product attributes are mainly for rationalising brand choice.

Mental brand response

The meanings attached to the brand consist largely of associations with user types, defined by socio-economic personality, value and lifestyle characteristics (user image). For the user, these meanings represent expressive values and terminal values. Meanings are expressed in a process which follows the principle of classical conditioning.

Advertising characteristics

Advertising contains little or no product information and does not 'reason'. It embodies brand meanings. Advertising and brand merge together, as it were. Important elements are a large number of exposures and the use of stimuli with which the specific target group can identify (famous actors, sporting jargon, photo models, musicians). Advertising does not communicate much verbally and contains little other than visual and auditive stimuli.

Evaluation criteria

The chief criteria are whether the desired meanings are activated, and whether this occurs quickly and spontaneously. In effectiveness measurements, recognition of the ad and brand registration are desirable. Spontaneous advertising recall is not an important criterion.

The main criterion is the development, over the years, of symbolic associations with the brand. It is difficult to quantify the intensity of these associations in research. Consequently, qualitative research and projective techniques are mainly used.

This model is mainly appropriate for products used in social situations and which, in those situations, are very much in evidence: cigarettes, beverages, clothing, sports equipment, cars, jewellery, watches, newspapers and magazines.

5.3.4 Emotions model

Key effect

The purpose of this model is primarily to develop associations between the brand and specific feelings. Ultimately it entails a long-term mental brand response.

The model is based on the assumption that a positive brand attitude and brand-loyal buying behaviour are mainly the consequence of the specific feelings the brand generates in its users. This can lead to brand involvement, although this is not the prime objective but a positive side effect.

Mental advertising response

Advertising is primarily geared to activating defined brand feelings during processing. Communication of instrumental characteristics is not important, but a strong link between the brand and emotions, followed by good brand registration, is essential. The activated feelings are latently present in every recipient. The development of an associative link with a product and brand follows the process of classical conditioning.

Mental brand response

The emotions associated with the brand may be general, such as happiness, joy, affection, lovingness, kindness, competence, self-confidence, self-assurance, pride, gratitude, contentedness and satisfaction.

More specific feelings may also accompany use of the product, such as cheerfulness, excitedness and stimulation with beer, and serenity, tranquillity and security with tea. These feelings represent 'experience values'. They are almost always generic to the product category, but are also linked closely with the brand. The brand represents these feelings and calls forth associations concerning the usage situation, the concomitant rituals, the nature of the expected social relationships and the mood experienced during use.

Advertising characteristics

The process of classical conditioning requires the use of images and sounds that generate unambiguously the intended emotions in the recipients. With that in mind, the emotions are usually portrayed by people.

Predominantly 'slice-of-life' scenarios tend to be used: minor events from everyday life. Liveliness is important. Classical conditioning usually works most efficiently if the brand signals are perceived before the emotion is activated. A great many exposures are needed. Advertising in this model has usually been consistent in its basic format for many years, sometimes decades.

Evaluation criteria

Emotional response and brand registration during exposure to advertising are the most important evaluation criteria, and likeability is desirable. Recall of the ad is not a functional evaluation criterion.

Notes

The emotions model is particularly appropriate with products performing an 'enjoyment function' or a function in social intercourse. Advertising according to this model contributes especially to a deeper emotional experience of the brand in people who already use it. The emotions experienced during use and during advertising processing are mutually reinforcing. The model is chiefly geared to confirming and strengthening an already positive attitude.

It is often used in markets where the physical difference between brands is slight, and is particularly suitable for brands whose market position is strong to start with.

5.3.5 Likeability model

Key effect

The likeability model seeks to develop and strengthen a positive brand attitude as a long-term effect. It is based on the assumption that likeability of advertising leads straight to likeability of the brand. Much experimental research would seem to support this hypothesis. The model assumes that in certain situations this is a more effective approach than the communication of product attributes or symbolic meanings.

Mental advertising response

Likeability of ads is based on evaluation of the content (information and emotions), and on the way in which it is presented: the 'idea' and the execution of the advertising. The likeability model focuses on the execution characteristics of the advertising.

If an instrumental message is involved, it is more likely to be selected because recipients find it fun, interesting or worthwhile than because it is necessary to associate these cognitions with the brand (as in the persuasion model).

Likeability of the ad's execution is mainly brought about by liveliness, surprise, the use of popular personalities, of popular (ie, well-liked) music, appealing landscapes or settings, the use of children or animals, and humour.

Mental brand response

The intended effect is to develop liking for the brand, not resulting from evaluation of product attributes or brand meanings, but as the direct effect of evaluations and appreciation of the advertising characteristics.

Advertising characteristics

Advertising in this model is primarily a form of entertainment and so uses styles and resources found in the worlds of television, cinema, theatre, cabaret, art and literature. Popular actors, music and situations are used to produce positive reactions.

However, there must be a plausible relationship with the advertised product or brand. Advertising can neither be 'over the top', irrelevant nor pointless, nor activate feelings which do not tally with the product category. The transfer of advertising likeability to brand likeability is a process of classical conditioning. It is therefore a long-term effect. It requires consistent use of the selected style forms over the years.

Evaluation criteria

The chief criterion is of course the recipient's enjoyment of the advertising. It is a short-term advertising response, which in the long term leads or contributes to a positive brand attitude. The likeability of individual ads is researched by looking at perceived body language responses during exposure, and reactions to likeability statements after exposure (funny/nice/interesting/amusing/appealing/original/lively/warm/sensitive).

Notes

This model is used mainly when the brand is included in the brand repertoire on the basis of a general, positive 'feeling' about the brand, and when the choice and purchasing act depend on other marketing variables. This is the case for insurance companies, department stores and products with no important functional or symbolic attributes.

5.3.6 Relationship/involvement model

Key effect

In this model the main issue is the mental brand response: to develop and reinforce the relationship with the user of the brand. To that end, the emphasis is on strengthening brand involvement and the feeling of emotional closeness to the brand. The expression 'brand involvement' is used to describe the degree of importance a person attaches to the brand because it ties in with his or her personal values, concerns or interests. A degree of brand involvement can develop in the short term, but profound brand involvement is a long-term response. The model assumes that this has a positive effect on brand attitude, while the reverse is also true – a positive brand attitude can lead to higher involvement. A relationship is presumed to exist between brand involvement and buying behaviour, but it is felt to be vague and indirect.

Mental brand response

The relationship model seeks to stimulate a feeling of emotional closeness and involvement with the brand, thus gaining attention for it. This is done mainly by building up a significant brand personality, linking recipients' perceptions of likeable, sometimes beloved (human) characteristics to the brand. It is more important 'who' the brand is than what it does.

The perceived brand status can also be important (well-known brand, major brand, important, good, successful, widely appreciated, and so on).

Mental advertising response

Again, when advertising is processed, the main aim is to develop involvement, and interaction between the recipient and the advertisement. What is communicated is of secondary importance.

The mere fact of communication, and the design and tone of voice are more important than the actual advertising content. The key issue is contact, in the sense of a meeting of minds.

Product attributes are of secondary importance – they are mainly subservient to the principle of the dialogue. Neither is reasoning particularly important. A deeper level of processing is aimed for, with focused attention and activation of the memory content (as embedded in cognitions, emotions and tendencies to act). The objective is to get the brand stored in the memory more permanently. This produces higher awareness of the brand, though awareness alone need not lead to involvement.

Advertising characteristics

The relationship/involvement model entails a more intelligent and more entertaining form of communication. Interest is primarily activated by the form of the advertising. Use is made of mild humour, 'puzzles', play on words, mysteries, metaphors, mild exaggeration, gimmicks, suspense and surprise. Often activation of existing memory contents is applied, and a moment of 'mutual understanding' is built in, an implied wink: 'I know what you're thinking.'

A brand-specific advertising style and tone of voice are important.

Evaluation criteria

The emphasis with evaluation is on advertising involvement during exposure: the extent to which the advertisement is considered important or interesting because it ties in with the recipient's concerns, values or interests. In addition, the emotional closeness of the brand and the development of brand personality associations in the short and long term are important criteria for effectiveness.

No connection is made with short-term consumer behaviour.

The development of brand associations with instrumental product values is not essential. Recall of the campaign presentation is, however, and campaign likeability is crucial.

Notes

The relationship/involvement model usually selects communication that proceeds mainly along the 'peripheral route'. Product information plays only a minor part. As a result, presentation characteristics are more important than the factual content of the advertising.

The model is primarily applied to maintaining established brands in markets where products remain the same for many years, and to brands entailing a personal relationship with consumers, as in the service and business-to-business sectors.

It is helpful to keep the brand interesting and at the front of the long-term memory, in a well-established position.

Research is mainly used at the campaign development stage, to establish whether there is advertising involvement.

5.3.7 Awareness/saliency model

Key effect

The awareness/saliency model is based on the close connection in many markets between brand awareness and buying behaviour. Axelrod established in 1983 that 'first brand awareness' (these days generally termed TOMA, or top-of-mind awareness) was most closely connected to brand switching, and the best way of predicting short-term developments in buying behaviour.

Brand salience is assumed, in this model, to have substantial direct influence on buying behaviour: the choice need not be preceded by a (measurable) change in attitude. The model aims mainly for a short-term effect.

In this way it differs considerably from the hierarchical models, in which the steps between awareness and buying behaviour are indeed important. Attitude change can occur in this model, because of usage experience, but is not a primary communication objective.

Mental brand response

Brand saliency is the primary response to aim for. It is expressed in top-of-mind brand awareness. When the brands involved are younger ones, or ones for which the aided and spontaneous recall is below par, an increase in all awareness levels is aimed for, with TOMA as the ultimate goal. A close, intense association with the product category is important, so that when the need arises for the product, the brand is immediately recalled. Brand saliency relates to the brand's ability to differentiate itself from other brands in the same category thanks to the nature of the memories it evokes. The brand should be in the foreground of the consumer's perception of the category; it is perceived first and most clearly. Focused association development is considered less important than the raising of awareness.

Mental advertising response

The advertising response which is considered most functional in achieving top-of-mind awareness is a high level of attention during processing (high impact), leading to a high recall of the advertisement and high 'advertising recall' as a response to the campaign.

Advertising primarily aims to stimulate. It is a sign of success if recipients talk about it. Less importance, if any, is attached to communicating the message, or to activating product-related emotions. Brand registration is, of course, important.

Advertising characteristics

In the awareness/saliency model the characteristics of the advertising itself are central. The major requirement is advertising saliency – meaning that the stimuli stand out very distinctly from the immediate surroundings during exposure. In addition, lively advertising recall must differentiate them in the memory from generic, product-related advertising associations. The most important requirement is that the advertising be new, different and unexpected. Existing conventions must be broken, and advertising must deviate from the pattern of expectations for the category.

Mechanistic means can also be very practical in attracting attention: format, colour, movement, sound. It is important to integrate brand signals properly into the ad. This is why continuity is so important, in the sense of sticking to the foremost campaign elements over the years – like a particular actor or a mnemonic device (something unusual enough to stick in the memory).

Evaluation criteria

The main criterion is the extent to which communication succeeds in distinguishing itself from what is customary in the product category, and from more common forms of advertising in general.

Recall and advertising awareness are the chief advertising criteria, and the most important brand response criterion is an increase in the brand awareness (TOMA) linked to the product category. Attitude change based on exposure to advertising is not one of the model's aims.

Notes

The awareness/saliency model is very different from the persuasion and involvement models, but is similar in design to the likeability model. It is particularly suitable for products which are bought on impulse, and for which choice is not based on functional product attributes or specific emotional or symbolic associations, as well as for products which are not perceived to be different from the alternatives. This model can also be useful when brand awareness is being built up during the launch of a new product. When purchases are planned in advance or made by a non-user, TOMA may result in the brand's inclusion on the shopping list. There is often a strong correlation between TOMA and buying behaviour in the food markets.

5.4   HOW DOES A PERSON-TO-BRAND RELATIONSHIP DEVELOP?

In 'Brand stages of mind' (section 4.2.8, Chapter 4) the stages in which person-to-brand relationships develop were described. This division implies a connection with the evolution of a consumer's buying behaviour in terms of the brand. Figure 5.6 summarises this evolution, falling into five distinctive stages:
1   no brand experience;
2   one or more trial purchases;
3   brand in repertoire;
4   most purchased brand;
5   only brand purchased.

It is useful to outline the development of the brand stages of mind, based primarily on research by Ehrenberg. In 1974 he had already introduced his ATR model describing the development of brand choice behaviour:
1   gaining *awareness* of a brand;
2   making a first *trial purchase*;
3   being reinforced into developing and retaining a *repeat buying habit*;
4   in the 1990s he added a fourth stage, ATR became ATR&N, with N standing for *nudging* – being nudged into buying the brand more frequently.

In a series of articles he examines the development of brand associations and brand attitudes in connection with the development of brand buying behaviour. His basic premise is that behaviour is more likely to precede than result from attitude development, and that the formation of associations also largely proceeds from usage behaviour. His arguments are based on empirical research covering the past 30 years, largely relating to frequently purchased, low-involvement product categories. So the sequence of effects he assumes is also one of low involvement, starting with purchases, after which cognitions and attitudes develop. Obviously he endorses the view that the

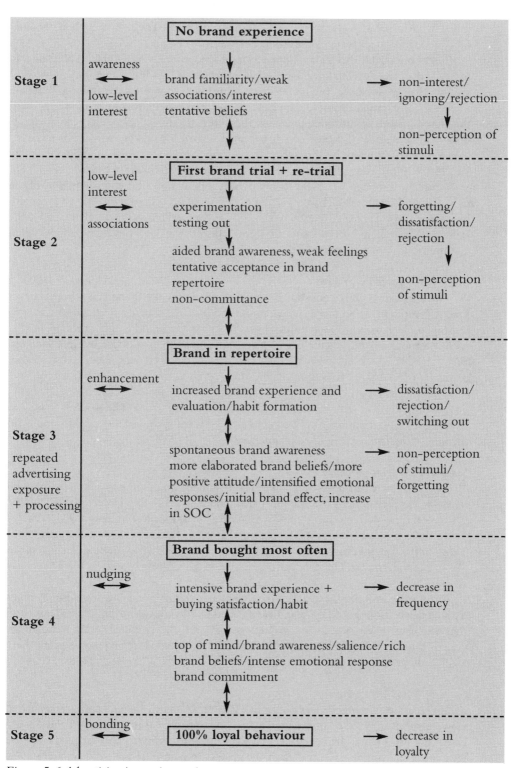

Figure 5.6 Advertising/usage interaction

initial behavioural response is preceded by some awareness. The sequence then becomes CEAC (cognition, experience, attitude, cognition).

Ehrenberg claims that his model is more or less generally applicable, at all events in markets that are developed, stable and homogeneous (undifferentiated). However, I assume that, at least for high-involvement product categories with long purchase intervals (for example, domestic appliances, hi-fi equipment, furniture, clothing, cars), the development of attitudes precedes the ultimate choice. Ehrenberg also has his doubts: 'The choice of motor cars is between virtual lookalikes with different brand names on their bonnets' he maintains. That may be true – but these brand names carry very different meanings. People buy the whole: the product and the brand.

Figure 5.6 on page 201 presents my own interpretation of the development of the person–brand relationship, based partly on Ehrenberg's findings. This diagram can also be used as a basis for segmentation of category users as regards buying behaviour for the individual brand. It is important to know the relative size of these groups when communication objectives and strategies are being developed.

Stage 1: No brand experience

This stage starts with a consumer who does not know the brand and who has never used it. It is the situation of every new brand and of new generations of consumers with respect to older brands. The consumer gets to know the brand name, although to start with it is more a matter of the brand 'seeming familiar' than of active brand awareness. The consumer discovers what product category is involved, and also perceives other brand features, such as packaging in the shop or an ad in the media. On the basis of these very first, superficial impressions, the consumer makes the first tentative check: does the brand tie in with his/her overall attitudes and fundamental values? Is it a brand that might merit attention, or is it immediately rejected – 'this isn't a brand for me' – on account of the first superficial acquaintance?

Stage 2: First trial purchase

The consumer can develop a low level of interest based on early impressions, and tentative expectations may result in a first purchase. Ehrenberg states: 'No dramatic persuasion is needed, anything "new" will tend to be noticed' (Ehrenberg et al., 1997).

So there is no need to develop a strong interest followed by a desire for possession, and then the first purchase – AIDA is not at issue here. The first purchase can also mean the end of the process. The product may prove to be nothing special or the brand may be quickly forgotten.

But some consumers have a positive experience of the brand and conclude: 'I might try that again sometime.' The brand is included in the consideration set, and a second trial purchase may result. Brand awareness increases, the consumer may have mildly positive feelings towards the brand and get to know the product better. But as yet there is certainly no active brand preference.

Stage 3: Brand in repertoire

Repeated trial use may lead to an inclination to buy the brand more often 'when convenient'. It is included in the brand repertoire, possibly as the second or third brand below the top brand. The consumer thinks: 'I think I might buy that again.' He or she buys the brand occasionally, and gradually grows more familiar with and appreciative of it. Spontaneous brand awareness develops and brand associations increase.

Barnard and Ehrenberg (1997), having examined a great many markets, concluded:

There is little or no reported evidence that consumers change their brand-choice behaviour as a result of changes in their attitude to a brand (especially a brand which they have so far not tried). Instead there is converging evidence that attitude change follows behaviour change – for example, that having tried a new brand one may come to like it (or not) … For a new brand (or a brand new to that consumer), advertising and hearsay etc. can create and/or reinforce brand awareness, brand reassurance, and a somewhat favourable predisposition, followed perhaps – usually rather later – by a somewhat doubtful first or second trial purchase. This may then lead to a real change of attitude, from inexperienced ignorance and lack of feeling for the brand to familiarity, brand assurance, and salience.

A degree of brand buying habit thus evolves.

Stage 4: Brand bought most often

Shifts can occur within the brand repertoire with respect to the probability of the various brands being bought, for instance, from relative frequencies of 0.6, 0.3 and 0.1 for three brands, to 0.5, 0.4 and 0.1. The second brand is bought a little more often than the first. That brand's share of customer has increased. A little later on, the second brand may move up to first place (nudging). Feelings for the brand gradually intensify, and the brand is recalled first in the category (TOMA). The consumer is satisfied with the brand, trusts it and now exhibits considerable brand loyalty: it has become the brand he or she buys most often.

Stage 5: 100% (or almost 100%) brand loyalty

At some stage, some consumers want nothing other than the brand in question. If a retailer does not have it in stock, they will postpone purchase or go to another shop. These are always a small number of all brand buyers, usually no more than 10%. (The number of 'near loyals', with a share of customer of 80%, also accounts for a small percentage only.) Now a real relationship exists – deeper emotions, greater emotional closeness. Consumers have a bond with the brand and feel they cannot do without it ('commitment').

Ehrenberg constantly reiterates that 100% brand-loyal buyers are primarily light users, who stick to one brand more for convenience. This is certainly true but it does not preclude the existence of really committed brand buyers, even among the medium and more heavy-use categories. Ehrenberg is unconvinced of this: he thinks there is no 'hard core' of brand-loyal buyers, and that 100% loyals occur as it were 'by chance'.

Much research shows that some brands succeed in building up a real relationship with, admittedly, a limited group of their buyers.

This description is based on a gradual, positive development in the relationship between a consumer and a brand. Obviously this development is not always so positive in reality. The initial impressions of a brand can cause a consumer to reject it immediately; initial product experience can be mediocre or even disappointing; development of brand awareness can stagnate, causing the consumer to 'forget' to buy the brand in question; new competing brands can have a negative effect on the brand; competitors' advertising pressure can have a negative effect on buying frequency, and so on.

So at every stage possible negative developments, as indicated in Figure 5.6, must be taken into account.

A new sequence of effects can therefore be traced, based partly on Ehrenberg's analyses. This does not take the form of a summary of the effect of an advertisement or series of ads (campaign), as was the case with AIDA, but represents the stages in a brand's evolution over a longer period, under the influence of continued communication, among other things.

This sequence is:

1   *Awareness*

Consciousness of the brand's existence and what it stands for.

2   *Interest*

A mild form of interest, with no dramatic influence – 'What might the brand mean to me?' Rossiter and Percy (1987) describe it as an 'attitudinal inference about the brand's likely quality, prior to purchase ... sufficient to investigate a trial purchase – "Maybe I'll try it".'

3   *Trial*

Uncertain purchase accompanied by doubt, sometimes leading to a second trial purchase.

4   *Reinforcement*

The strengthening of brand awareness and the initial (positive) product experience. The influencing of association development, particularly of the core meanings (brand essence).

5   *Nudging*

Step-by-step reinforcement of brand saliency and ensuring of the brand's constant presence, in such a way that the likelihood of the brand being chosen in the next category purchase increases. The result is a gradual increase in buying frequency and share of customer.

6   *Bonding*

Stimulation of users' affective, emotional feelings of emotional closeness and bonding towards the brand. Promotion of the identification with the brand: 'This is my brand.'

As Farr and Hollis (1997) state:

In most categories a consistent relationship can be identified between survey measures such as brand awareness and claimed trial, between familiarity and brand consideration and between claimed trial and recent usage. To some extent the nature of the relationship is that of the chicken and the egg. But brand awareness tends to precede trial.

Weaker relationships are observed where brands are fundamentally differentiated (on the basis of instrumentals, price, origin).

5.5   THE STRONG AND THE WEAK THEORIES

The next questions that need to be asked are:
- Where does a brand's growth come from?
- What advertising strategies are necessary to achieve growth?

As seen earlier (Exhibit 4.11, page 148), Ehrenberg believes that growth mainly results from increased penetration, and, in conjunction with that, increased frequency (double-jeopardy effect). Studies by Leo Burnett in the US (Sylvester *et al.*, 1994) also seem to confirm this: 75% of the growth of 95 growing brands resulted from increased penetration, 25% from increased frequency. Some of the increased frequency is an autonomous consequence of increased penetration (double-jeopardy effect). Smaller brands still depend more on increased penetration. So advertising will, in general, have to be geared primarily to generating trial purchases via the stages of awareness–interest–trial. The bigger the brand becomes, the more important reinforcement, nudging and bonding are, especially with a view to preventing decreased buying frequency resulting from competing brands' campaigns.

But what strategies are necessary to achieve these effects? Two opposing views exist; they are referred to as the 'strong' and the 'weak' theories.

Strong theory

This theory presupposes that advertising has a forceful, direct influence on consumer buying behaviour. Advertising followed a sequence from brand awareness to brand knowledge to brand buying behaviour. Attitude formation was thought to precede selection behaviour and result from knowledge of differentiating brand attributes. So, according to the strong theory, advertising is able to persuade people who have not previously used the brand to start buying it – conversion. New insight into the correlation between advertising exposure and buying behaviour based on analyses of single-source research (in particular Jones' STAS effect) began to convince people that the persuasion effect not only implied converting non-users of the brand, but also affected the buying frequency of actual users.

As seen in Chapter 1, there is no empirical backing for a sleeper effect. Most experts who have devoted a great deal of time to studying the connection between short and long-term effects believe that the occurrence of direct effects is a prerequisite for achieving long-term effects.

Jones (1997) claimed in this respect that advertising was able to exert a powerful direct influence on consumers' buying behaviour. As he put it: effective advertising sells, although this is not, by any means, always a 'hard sell', in the conventional sense. However, something must be communicated about the brand that is significant to the consumer. If this is done in an amusing, entertaining way it can be amazingly effective, even when the strict criteria of the STAS effect are applied.

Figure 5.7 provides an idea of the connection between brand buying behaviour and advertising exposures.

The short-term effect is merely a cumulation of the direct effect. It should be remembered that the average share of customer of a brand is usually around 30%. In other words, on average, users of a brand buy a competing brand two out of three times, and are thus open to the influence of these brands' advertising.

The STAS effect of competing campaigns can neutralise the direct effect of a brand's campaign, with the result that an initially positive STAS effect evaporates within a year.

Repetition is needed to achieve a positive short-term effect. As Jones (1997) said, if a brand is to free itself from the counter-pressure of competing advertising, you not only need advertising which achieves a direct effect, but also sufficient media pressure over a longer period than that within which the competition succeeds in neutralising the initial campaign effect. The race is won by the brand with the strongest ad (message plus creative concept), which also manages to hold out the longest.

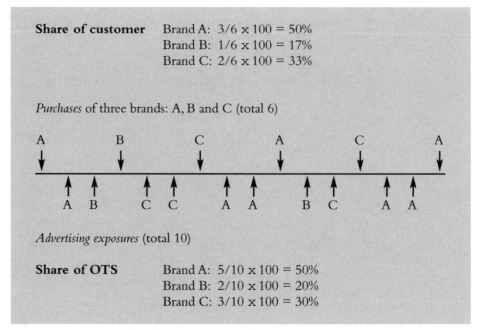

Share of customer   Brand A: 3/6 x 100 = 50%
Brand B: 1/6 x 100 = 17%
Brand C: 2/6 x 100 = 33%

Purchases of three brands: A, B and C (total 6)

A   B   C   A   C   A

A   B   C   C   A   A   B   C   A   A

Advertising exposures (total 10)

Share of OTS   Brand A: 5/10 x 100 = 50%
Brand B: 2/10 x 100 = 20%
Brand C: 3/10 x 100 = 30%

Figure 5.7 Example of brand buying behaviour and advertising exposures at an individual level

Relative advertising weight (expenditures, shares of voice) therefore plays a crucial role in the successful development of brands. An analysis of 138 brands in the US over a three-year period, from 1990–92 (Coalition for Brand Equity), revealed that the biggest difference between equity gainers and equity losers is the way they advertise. Brands that gained steadily advertised at levels that produced an average share of voice 2.7 times their market share. Brands with steadily declining equity had a SOV:SOM ratio of 1.6 (Longman, 1998).

Weak theory

The essence of the theory of weak advertising frameworks, which is inextricably linked with Ehrenberg, is that brand choice behaviour does not primarily result from the perception of differentiating brand attributes ('different', 'better'), but is a function of brand saliency. In Ehrenberg's view (Ehrenberg *et al.*, 1998): 'Differentiation which is successful in terms of sales asks to be copied and generally it is (e.g. PCs with Pentium chips; shampoos for oily hair). There are only rare exceptions (e.g. patents). Otherwise any advantage which is of sales importance is seldom sustainable. And any advantage which is sustained is seldom important.'

He adds to this Professor Tom Robertson's (1996) summary: 'The last few demanding years have drilled into us all the vital need to innovate – to gain the competitive edge. But when we really do steal a lead, we find the advantage is only temporary. Why? Because our competitors have been working to the same pressures, usually with similar resources.

'So we rapidly lose our edge and off we go again, striving to get ahead once more. Thus the battle of the brands continues, *with broad competitive parity over time and natural state of most of our markets*' [condensed, my emphasis].

Ehrenberg continues: 'Even a revolutionary product change mostly differentiates only briefly (for example, laundry soap being replaced in turn by detergents, biologicals, Greens, high-density liquids, and then also high-density powders). Me-tooism remains the dominant force in competition. Being competitive means cashing in on one's competitors' successes. Such imitation is not just restricted to minor product developments (baking soda in toothpaste, or guaranteed-money-back long-term investments), but even more to the major product characteristics (all mainstream cars have to be speedy, safe, fairly economical, washing powders wash white or whiter, etc.) This is not new: "The trends in our technology lead to competing products becoming more and more alike" (the 1920s guru James Webb Young).'

So Ehrenberg believes that brand choice is not primarily based on differentiating brand attributes, but on brand salience. He suggests that:

'Salience is broader than any single measure of brand performance. It depends on virtually all the different possible measures of performance correlating. Compared with Brand B, if Brand A has more salience than B, it has more people who:
- are aware of it (for just about any awareness measure);
- have it in their active brand repertoires (for frequently-bought products);
- and/or have it in their considerations sets (ie, brands they might buy);
- are familiar with the brand;
- feel it has brand assurance (for example, retail availability, after-sales service);
- have positive attribute beliefs about brand A;
- regard it as value for money;
- harbour intentions to buy and/or to use it in the future (and do so);
- would buy A if their usual brand was not available;
- choose A in a named product test;
- note and recall its advertisements (by and large);
- talk more often and more richly about it in focus groups;
- are "loyal" to A (by any measure of loyalty).

'For directly competitive and substitutable brands, all the different measures tend in practice to correlate well. Being in the consumer's consideration set is perhaps the simplest single conceptualisation of "salience". The measures then also go with the consumers' propensities to buy the brand and with their actual buying and usage (ie, with the actual repertoire), and with sales. And hence in turn also with how users say subsequently that they like the brand (familiarity leads to liking).

'Brand A being salient to more people than B is then usually also linked with whether A has, if anything, wider distribution perhaps; more and better shelf-space and display; more sales-people; more promotions; more word-of-mouth; more media mentions; more advertising; and probably bigger absolute profits. There are also remarkable feed-back loops and marketing-mix synergies in these relationships. The bigger brands are so much bigger because the promise of more advertising leads to more shelf-space and display; to higher and more profitable sales; hence to bigger advertising budgets (and possibly less price-cutting); and to more shelf-space, etc. again. The benign spiral means that the more marketing activity and display there is for brand A, the more noticing the brand can again help. Just seeing the brand around can reinforce its memorability and hence again its salience.

'Salience is not about how strongly the users of a brand feel about it – not ten times more strongly about A than about B (for example, ten times "Kinder to the hands").

'For some 100 attribute beliefs about brands in nine US and UK product categories, 48% of users of the top brand say "Kind to the hands" etc. about it, and 49% about the smallest of the eight itemised brands (with less than a quarter of the number of users).

'Nor does the much bigger brand A have to be "valued" much more by its many users than brand B is by its fewer users (apart again from the typical but relatively small "double-jeopardy" trends with market share).

'There is also no systematic evidence of big differences in "brand equity" or the like, or in strengths which can be associated with particular brands. As we see in the evidence, there are no strong brands and weak ones, only big brands and little ones.'

Ehrenberg is also of the opinion that advertising an established brand to experienced consumers will rarely lead to perceived differentiation. In his view, it is unlikely that consumers' attitudes can be changed by advertising. Advertising is not strong enough to convert people to a brand if their beliefs do not coincide with the advertising claims: 'I don't see need for "desire" or "conviction" before the first purchase is made. The point is to familiarise more people with the brand, so that they buy it once, include it in their consideration sets, and gradually gain more relevant brand assurance. This theory leads to "Here I am" advertising ("Coke is it").

'The advertising copy has to be distinctive, to be noticed, and to leave memory traces.

'But in practice this is not in order to attach a different message or image to the brand (or certainly not necessarily). To change people's attitudes or feelings greatly and/or lastingly is, we think, quite widely accepted to be very difficult or near-impossible. Nor should the aim be to make the advertising itself memorable: with a few exceptions (such as well-established slogans), few people recall a brand's advertising from two or three years ago, although one may recognise the old ads again when one sees them. ("Coke is it" was 10 years ago; more recently "Always Coca Cola".)

'Instead, the aim is, or should be, for the advertisements to help publicise the brand itself, to leave idiosyncratic memory traces for it, and, possibly longer-term memory associations with it. The closer and more substitutable the brand is with its competitors, the easier it is for creative and impactful "Here I am" publicity to maintain, reinforce and/or nudge the brand's salience and the consumers' purchase propensities. There are then no differentiating functional (or emotional) values for the advertising to overcome (like greatly preferring Shredded Wheat to muesli, say). Only consumers' habitual brand-choice propensities (and their consequent feelings for brands A or B – "I use it therefore I like it") may inhibit moving between directly competitive brands.

'The less differentiated brands are, the more readily can advertising nudge choice behaviour, but the greater therefore also is the need for defensive reinforcement of your brand. To us this explains the great scope for advertising to try and nudge your brand's impact, and the even greater need to defend your customers from your many competitors' encroachments. Most advertising and marketing for established brands seems in practice to be geared to counter the competition and defend one's market share from its close competitors' (Ehrenberg et al., 1998).

Advertising is not the powerful force it is sometimes purported to be. This would seem to be confirmed by the high percentage of failed product launches (over 80%) and the small number of brands with growing market shares.

Table 5.1 compares the strong and weak theories of advertising frameworks. They are not necessarily mutually exclusive. The conversion of other brand loyals (see the section on the conversion model in Chapter 4, page 120–21) and the substantial rise in share of customer with a brand's repertoire buyers requires a highly persuasive campaign. Ehrenberg (1997) comments: 'Creating any such persuasive advertising would be difficult and can hardly be produced to order. This is borne out by there being relatively few markedly successful brand-building case histories for established brands.'

Jones (1997) also states:

I believe that the strong theory probably works in a small minority of circumstances in certain defined product categories and with advertising employing certain specific media … but it is going too far to suggest that the weak theory operates in the extreme way described by Ehrenberg; it is too much to claim that advertising is never a prime mover, never a dynamic force.

	Advertising as a 'strong force' (Jones)	Advertising as a 'weak force' (Ehrenberg *et al.*)
Consumer loyalty	Monogamous/promiscuous	Polygamous
Brand based on:	Product performance	Brand salience (symbolic meanings)
Products	Differentiated	Equivalent
Brand objective	Sales/growth	Consolidation/stability
Advertising objective	Conversion/'switching'	Confirmation/'holding'
Advertising strategy	'Selling'/persuasion	Advertising salience (symbolic)
Advertising message	'I'm different/better'	'Here I am/I'm a good example of the category'
Consumer response	'Interesting/perhaps I'll buy you again sometime'	'I know, I'll go on buying you'
Advertising effect	Penetration growth/ increased buying frequency	Slow increase/maintenance of penetration/buying frequency
Time horizon	Short term	Long term

Table 5.1 Advertising as a strong and weak force

Not surprisingly, the growth of brands as a result of conversion of other brand loyals does not occur very often in stable markets in which there are no important product developments and in which the budgets for individual brands are usually derived from existing sales. Equilibrium usually prevails in these markets, which is merely confirmed by advertising.

In stable markets campaigns for established (larger) brands primarily have a consolidating function: to protect the achieved position from pressure from competing brands. But that protection also requires a constant influence on the repertoire buyers' next purchases of the brand. Ehrenberg calls this 'nudging' (although he sees 'nudging' mostly in the form of extra buyers (penetration) and not in increased buying frequency), and Jones calls it 'short-term advertising strength' (STAS). The two need not be opposing factors.

Ehrenberg's nudging can also be expressed as a gradual increase in buying frequency among repertoire buyers, and therefore occurs in the STAS effect described by Jones.

However, a brand's growth is chiefly due to greater penetration: persuading non-users to buy the brand once. An analysis by Roberts (1998) of the single-source research started in the UK in 1996 under the name 'TVSpan' indicates that the greatest direct effect of advertising is achieved among buyers with a share of customer of 0–10%: non-users and those who had previously only bought the brand once (see Exhibit 5.1).

So, strategically, it is necessary to decide upon what kind of balance is needed between increasing penetration and increasing frequency. Both are necessary, and to a certain extent related to each other (double-jeopardy effect). The assessment is based on what position the brand has achieved.

So what advertising framework model (or combination of models) results from all this? What results in 'awareness and interest' and what in 'enhancement and nudging'? Is there room for the persuasion model, for the models geared to image differentiation (symbolism and emotions models) and for the relationship/involvement model of advertising? Relevant empirical material is hard to come by. Available research primarily relates to pre-testing and tracking (with which developments of brands' share of customer cannot be followed). Millward Brown (1991) concludes from these studies: 'A claim which is new, relevant and credible will always have a dramatic sales effect.' Millward Brown calls this advertising framework model 'Immediate challenge', and it coincides with the persuasion model described earlier. But Millward Brown continues: 'It is very hard to find something new, relevant and credible to say about many well-known established brands, especially in undifferentiated (homogeneous) product fields like coffee and beer.'

In this situation, where there is a lack of new benefits, the advertising may act to stimulate interest in the brand, which can then lead to trial and inclusion of the brand in the repertoire: 'This is what gentle, entertaining "soft-sell" advertising does: it channels random switching by making brands interesting as a result of involving advertising memories.'

Enhancement comes next, with advertising claims and visual images during use of the product being converted into associations with and beliefs about the brand. Like Ehrenberg, Millward Brown (1990) concludes that:

The big improvement in attitudes happens at the point when the brand is adopted. So it makes sense to shift the time frame and suppose advertising memories condition the encounters with the brand – particularly the early ones when the brand is being tried experimentally … Brand

Short-term sales effects of TV advertising

Roberts (1998) analysed the TVSpan single-source data for a period of one year for 61 brands in eight categories of fast-moving consumer goods. He ascertained that the number of purchases by consumers who had seen a commercial for the brand in question during a two-week period prior to purchase was on average 6.1% higher than purchases by those who had not watched the TV ad. In households which had not purchased the brand at all (or only once) in the last 12 months (share of customer 10% or less) the increase in purchases due to the ad was 25.4%. This can be interpreted largely as penetration growth. Among repertoire buyers too, with whom the brand had a 10–50% share of customer, a considerable increase of over 7% in the number of purchases was noted. Obviously, the increase was lowest among already loyal buyers (share of customer >50%). Figure 5.8 below shows the percentage increase in sales among the different loyalty groups as a result of the advertising.

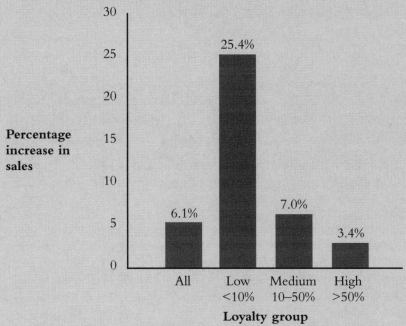

Figure 5.8 Incremental sales from advertising

Roberts concluded: 'Despite most of the researched brands being well established in mature markets, TV advertising does contribute to incremental sales in the short term. Its benefit is not confined to the argument that its role is purely defensive, only sustaining the brand in the longer term.'

Source: Andrew Roberts, Taylor Nelson AGB, 1998

Exhibit 5.1

attributes ('image') are the end result of a complex, largely non-rational process, rather than the starting point driving purchase decisions.

Millward Brown's view largely coincides with Ehrenberg's – except that research by the former also reveals that the strong theory (immediate challenge) can certainly exist alongside the weak theory. Ehrenberg does not believe that advertising works in as varied and complex a way as the seven frameworks described earlier in this chapter suggest. According to him the salience/weak theory is simply a matter of getting and keeping the brand in consumers' consideration sets and publicising the brand is the best way of doing so. This simplicity is one of the attractions of his weak theory, which is weak because it does not attempt to change people's brand perceptions. This is exactly what most advertisers believe in – as the seven frameworks demonstrate.

The seven models described earlier in this chapter have been plotted in Figure 5.9 on the time axis. Long-term effects are especially likely to occur with the models based on the process of classical conditioning.

	Direct effect	Short-term effect	Long-term effect
Mental brand response		• *Awareness/ Saliency (TOMA)*	• *Likeability* (positive brand attitude based on the entertainment function of the advertising) • *Relationship* (involvement in, relationship with the brand) • *Emotions* (positive feelings for the brand) • *Symbolism* (a brand that's me, expressive)
Brand behavioural response	• *Sales response* (sales, one ad) • *Persuasion* (STAS effect)	• *Persuasion* (penetration growth, share of customer)	

Figure 5.9 Seven advertising framework models

5.6   WHERE MODELS OVERLAP

It will certainly not always be clear which responses produced by a campaign are most forceful, and similarly in which model a campaign belongs. Research at the University of Amsterdam (van den Putte, 1998) indicates that several of the models are fairly unambiguous, but others tend to overlap. For instance, the awareness/saliency and the likeability models both lead to campaigns which strongly emphasise differentiating advertising, with all manner of entertainment forms. It is therefore often difficult to classify such campaigns in one of the two models. Might this not be one and the same model? However, brand saliency and likeability are two different strategic objectives, so it is wise to keep two different models. The fact that in practice they often produce the same type of campaigns (ie, generating both responses) does not alter this fact. Moreover, brand saliency has been pursued in recent years, with the use of forms of confrontational advertising (Benetton being the most obvious example) which have probably done little to promote a positive attitude to the brand in question.

The symbolism and emotions models also overlap here and there, partly because practitioners tend to refer to campaigns focusing on symbolic meanings as 'emotional advertising' – as opposed to 'functional (ie, rational) advertising'. However, symbolic meanings amount to cognitive associations – for example, between the brand and its users – as is the case with the persuasion model. The fact that users are often portrayed in an emotional usage context means that the difference between campaigns geared to these two models is not always clear.

The relationship model also proves difficult to identify on the basis of advertising characteristics. It primarily entails developing a brand personality and creating a feeling of the brand's emotional proximity. Perhaps there are (still) few campaigns focusing primarily on these responses. They are thought to be chiefly secondary objectives, expressed especially in style and tone of voice.

5.7   RESEARCH INTO RESPONSES

With each of the seven models, there is one central response category at the brand level. If one of these models is selected specifically, that category will also be the most important evaluation criterion. Two observations must be made in this respect:
*   Each model is partially defined at the advertising level by key responses which operate in achieving the brand response.
*   Other advertising responses are mainly facilitating in character – they influence the extent to which the key brand responses are achieved.

Figure 5.10 (overleaf) contains an overview of the key responses on which each advertising framework model is based, plus the facilitating advertising responses which mainly affect them.

A combination of models is often opted for, the aim being to produce several inter-related 'key responses'.

Advertising model	Key response at brand level	Key response at advertising level	Facilitating advertising responses
Sales response model	• Recorded buying behaviour • Fact-finding behaviour	• Interest in the proposition • Inclination to direct behavioural response	• Attention • Brand registration
Persuasion model	• Attitude change/ reinforcement • Brand–attribute association • Brand awareness – trial purchases • Share of customer	• Processing and storage (recall of the main message) • Interest in the proposition • Inclination to behavioural response	• Understanding of the message • Relevance of the message (buying interest) • Credibility of the message • Brand registration
Symbolism model	• User image • Brand personality • Attitude reinforcement	• Communication of symbolic meanings	• Ad likeability • Identification/ empathy • Advertising involvement • Brand registration
Emotions model	• Emotional brand associations • Attitude reinforcement	• Activation of specific emotion(s)	• Empathy • Identification • Brand registration • Ad likeability • Advertising involvement
Likeability model	• Liking for brand • Attitude reinforcement	• Ad likeability	• Assessment of originality • Experience of liveliness • Advertising involvement • Brand registration
Relationship/involvement model	• Brand involvement • Emotional proximity to the brand • Brand personality association • Share of customer	• Advertising involvement	• Empathy • Message likeability • Ad likeability • Brand registration
Awareness/saliency model	• Brand saliency (TOMA) • Emotional proximity of brand	• 'Impact' • Advertising recall (+ advertising awareness)	• Assessment of originality • Experience of liveliness • Differentiation of the advertising (advertising saliency) • Brand registration

Figure 5.10 Main evaluation criteria for advertising framework models

So the measurement of only one type of response will rarely suffice. In order to understand how a campaign works, several responses should preferably be measured, checked to see how they affect one another and efforts made to ascertain how to interpret the results in the light of the selected strategy. Prue (1994) suggests that at least three aspects should be examined in this respect:

- *Persuasion*
  Is there a direct influence on brand attitude? This mainly entails measuring attitude shifts, which is a typical procedure for much pre-testing in the US.
- *Salience*
  Does advertising contribute to getting the brand in a prominent position in the memory? With pre-testing this entails measuring advertising recall, for example, using the so-called clutter awareness test, and with the tracking method it is a matter of measuring advertising awareness (see Chapter 7, which deals with tracking).
- *Involvement*
  Does an advertisement contribute towards developing a more intimate relationship with the brand? Pre-testing seeks to establish this, using a method such as cognitive response analysis.

Prue calls the combination of these three responses '3-Dimensional testing'. However a fourth dimension should also be added: *likeability*.

Prue (1994) analysed several campaigns which received awards in the UK for effectiveness. He concludes that successful campaigns are often those that score in several dimensions: 'The créme de la créme campaigns tend to tap a wider range of responses, involvement, persuasion *and* salience.' Likeability undeniably also belongs in that list.

Likeability can be defined as an overall appreciation of the ad or the campaign. It has three essential underlying dimensions, each with a positive and a negative pole (Aaker and Stayman, 1990; Biel and Bridgewater, 1990; du Plessis, 1994):

- *Meaningfulness versus confusion*
  The main explanatory variable for advertising likeability. On the positive side, the advertising contains new information which is relevant to the recipient. On the negative side, the advertising is difficult to follow and understand, and causes confusion.
- *Amusement versus overfamiliarity*
  The entertainment function of the advertising. It succeeds in amusing the recipient with its originality and liveliness. But it can also be boring because dull or hackneyed forms of advertising are used.
- *Empathy versus offensiveness*
  The direct or indirect experience of warm human relationships, or alternatively the fact that recipients are put off by matters which they would prefer not to encounter (intimate products, unpleasant people, implausible situations, overfamiliar forms of advertising).

Likeability has both a tactical and a strategic significance. Likeability is the basis for sustained attention and deeper processing. This reveals itself in a strong correlation between overall likeability scores, and advertising awareness scores. A tracking study of 67 Dutch television campaigns (SPOT, 1998) in which viewers were asked to express their appreciation for commercials in marks from 0–10, displayed the relationship between likeability and awareness as shown in Table 5.2.

Ad appreciation	Advertising awareness (per 100 GRPs)
5	3%
6	10%
7	33%

Table 5.2 The relationship between likeability and advertising awareness (Source: SPOT, 1998)

So likeability is a key driver of advertising awareness, and an important response for six of the seven advertising frameworks (as stated before, the sales response model does not attach value to likeability).

The importance of the three underlying dimensions differs over the other six models, however. In the likeability model, which is based primarily on the entertainment function of the advertising, likeability is a strategic response. This model is based on the direct transfer of appreciation of the ad to appreciation of the brand.

In the other five models likeability has a tactical function: it mainly influences the amount of attention given to the advertising. In the persuasion model it is appreciation of the informative content which is especially important. In the emotions model, the relationship/involvement model and the symbolism model, likeability should be based foremost on empathy. For the awareness/salience model the entertainment dimension again is the most important underlying likeability factor.

It is obvious that in any circumstances a dislike response should be avoided: confusion, overfamiliarity and offensiveness lead to the early switching of attention to other stimuli.

6 Pre-testing

Mary Hoogerbrugge

6.1   INTRODUCTION

The accountability discussion has increased awareness, particularly among advertisers, of research methods that can be used for evaluating advertising effectiveness. Most advertisers would prefer to know beforehand how a television commercial, a magazine ad or billboard is going to affect sales figures (Weinblatt and Conway, 1996). However, it is not usually possible to make a direct link between investment in advertising and sales results. Various factors influence consumer buying behaviour simultaneously – price, distribution, in-store promotional activities, competitors' activities and other communications activities for the brand. Models are the only methods that can provide insight into the influence of these different variables. However, the possible effects of an advertisement can be assessed in advance by subjecting the finished (or almost finished) material to a quantitative pre-test.

Opinions differ in advertising practice on the extent to which such pre-tests can predict advertising effectiveness. There are those who expect to use test scores to predict exactly how advertising for the brand will work in the marketplace, while others claim predictions are impossible. Moreover, there are also different opinions on the objective of a pre-test. Is it a matter of identifying the problems which might obstruct communication with the target group, with the qualitative results forming the main focus, or is it a matter of discovering, at the earliest possible stage, what influence a commercial will have on sales figures?

These controversies mean that the pre-testing of advertisements generates many questions. It is impossible to answer them all here. After all, the question of whether and how pre-testing works is part of a far wider issue: the workings of the human brain. And even memory specialists have not yet managed to explain this. So the main aim of this chapter is to discuss which variables can be measured in a pre-test, and what the limitations of a pre-test are. The different responses which have been the focal point of pre-testing over the years will be reviewed against the background of developments in views on how advertising works. But first it is necessary to examine what pre-testing is.

What is a pre-test?

A final advertisement is the result of discussion between all the parties involved during the entire advertising development process. But will it perform as expected? A quantitative pre-test can measure respondents' direct individual reactions to ads which occur as a result of one or more exposures to the ad. Focus is primarily on the mental advertising responses (recognition, recall, likeability, personal relevance) rather than mental brand responses (persuasion, intention to buy). These direct effects are expected, in time, to lead to the desired mental brand responses, which in turn are linked to brand behaviour and sales figures. The diagram in Figure 6.1 presents the relationship between the responses at various levels (see Chapter 3 for a detailed discussion of the Advertising Response Matrix).

So which specific advertising or brand responses must be measured to predict the effect on brand behaviour? In recent decades a succession of different mental responses have been advanced as the most relevant for a quantitative pre-test. The best known are recognition, recall, persuasion, likeability, involvement and personal relevance. The opinions of the experts still differ greatly as to which really is the most relevant variable to measure in a pre-test. Jones (1996) is very much in favour of persuasion, du Plessis (1994b, 1994c) favours likeability and Biel (1996) prefers personal relevance, to mention

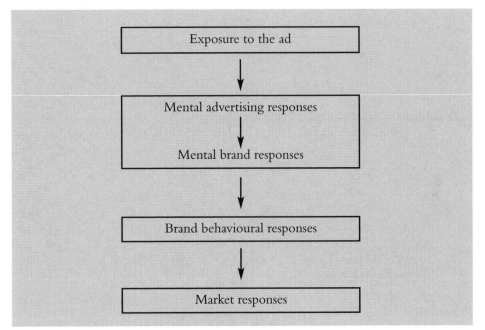

Figure 6.1 Summary of the Advertising Response Matrix

but a few. However, the most important question is whether there might conceivably be just one mental response which can tell us if advertising will be effective, in that it influences behaviour, regardless of which market and which brand is involved. Analysis of 389 split-cable tests in the US (Lodish *et al.*, 1995) reveals that there is often little connection between pre-test results and the eventual effects in the marketplace, irrespective of which response is being measured. In other words, no scientific proof was found that one of the variables (recall, recognition, persuasion, likeability) measured in a pre-test can forecast whether a certain commercial will work 'in real life'. Weinblatt and Conway (1996) argue that it is not possible to predict sales and market share unless pre-tests take into account competitive advertising and the behaviour of consumers in real life. Tracking results therefore might have much more predictive validity.

In looking at an analysis of 100 commercials Hollis (1995) found that (brand-linked) advertising awareness, measured in an ongoing tracking study, is most predictive of short-term sales. Likeability (enjoyability) in turn plays a critical role in creating advertising awareness and is therefore important to measure in a pre-test. Millward Brown uses the quantitative pre-test method LINK to predict brand-linked advertising awareness. This measures brand memorability by examining three elements:

- Is the ad involving and joyful?
- Is the ad linked to the right brand?
- Is the ad easy to follow?

Quantitative versus qualitative research

Those in favour of qualitative pre-testing are not inclined to believe that advertising effectiveness can be predicted. They stress that it is more important to understand what people do with advertising than what advertising does with people. For them the aim of a pre-test is to verify how the information in the ad is processed, or to check what message consumers extract from the ad and what interfering elements may hinder them. Do the values in the ad tie in with those of the target group and are its specific elements understood?

Gordon (1995) describes how qualitative research can provide valuable insight into communication and advertising in everyday (brand) marketing practice. Her chief recommendations are that we reconsider what fieldwork actually is and what form contact with respondents should take. This means:

- studying the relationship between the respondent and the product, brand or service at the moment the behaviour in question occurs. The researcher can, for instance, go shopping with the respondent, or 'take a look in the kitchen' to see whether a brand has been pushed to the back of the cupboard.
- developing a holistic approach in order to understand the brand relationship in various contexts in the course of time. For instance, a family might be 'adopted' and observed for a certain period. How do they go about buying a house?
- adopting an open approach to participants in the test, with co-operation as the key factor. Researcher and participant seek common views. Brainstorming and other workshop techniques may be used.

Concept testing

Before taking a closer look at the pre-testing of advertisements, and the interpretation and use of the results, it should be noted that pre-testing is not a form of research to aid ad development, which is the case with creative development research (for example, the concept test). The concept test amounts to assessing whether, and to what extent, the central creative idea might have the desired effects among the target group. In addition, its aim is to explain how the effects come about, to enable the creative team to develop and improve the concept further. The concept test is therefore an early check on the creative course and a means of optimising the end product. Creative development research and concept testing precede pre-testing. Some of the questions which are important for this evaluation of the concept are:

- Is the concept appealing (original, likeable, differentiating)?
- Does the concept convey the formulated positioning?
- Does it reflect the intended brand personality?
- Is there a 'big idea'?
- Does the concept present something new?
- Is it credible and in good taste?
- Is the idea 'campaignable'?
- Is the idea simple and clear?
- Does it make optimum use of the media?
- Is involvement sufficient?

6.2 EVOLUTION OF PRE-TESTING

The evolution of pre-testing is related to the evolution of ideas on how advertising works. The mental advertising response of recall in pre-testing was considered to be very important at a time when recollection of the advertisement was assumed to result in purchase. The mental brand response of persuasion became the key variable when the focus shifted from ad processing to the effect of the ad on the brand. Pre-testing is discussed here in the light of views on advertising frameworks. The three stages used by Hansen (1995) are taken as a guideline to designate the shift in focus in the central concepts within pre-testing, and are as follows:

- Stage 1 is the period characterised by the recognition versus recall debate (1930–70). In this period the main focus of interest was the direct effects of exposure to the advertisement, the so-called mental advertising responses.
- During Stage 2 (the persuasion era, 1960 to the present), researchers have been looking for variables which are directly related to sales figures, and their attention is now shifting from mental advertising responses to mental brand responses. 'Attitude towards brand' measurements are especially popular. This has led (and still leads) to pre-testing of the change in attitude towards the brand as a result of exposure to an ad. The ability of an advertisement to influence the consumer's attitude is expressed as a persuasion score.
- Advertising research has been attuned to advertising framework models from 1990 to the present day. Stage 3 is dominated by the assumption that not all advertising works in the same way. Consequently it does not seem likely that one single indicator can supply sufficient proof in all circumstances of the effectiveness of an advertisement. No one standard measurement exists which can predict the effectiveness of an ad. A combination of measurements has to be conducted, with the way advertising for the brand is expected to work determining the most important research variables within the pre-test. The test results must be interpreted in the light of the formulated objectives and assumptions on the effectiveness of the advertising for the brand (Gordon, 1996; Hodges, 1994).

6.2.1 Stage 1: recognition versus recall

The first model of advertising frameworks was the AIDA model, formulated in 1898 by St Elmo Lewis. The model represents the assumption that various steps have to be taken before the (rational) consumer proceeds to purchase. It assumes substantial consumer involvement when the brand is purchased. Over the years the hierarchical AIDA model has been continually adapted, most changes entailing the addition of different categories of effects. The DAGMAR model is one such example. It was developed in 1961 by Colley. In these models, awareness of the advertisement is the first step towards effective advertising, and consequently this mental advertising response was the most important in pre-testing for many years.

Recognition

The first quantitative measurement of an ad (in those days still prints only) was the recognition method, devised by Gallup/Robinson at the end of the 1920s (Hansen, 1995). Recognition entails measuring what the respondent recalls having seen, heard or read of the ad. The process of recognition is based on evoking impressions which have been stored in the memory in different ways.

For instance, the procedure for measuring a magazine ad is as follows. Respondents are shown the cover of a certain issue of a magazine. If they say they have read that particular issue, they go through the magazine page by page. Each time a page is opened which contains an ad to be tested, respondents are asked if they recognise the ad. They can also be questioned about elements in the ad which drew more or less attention. However, a drawback of the recognition method is that people tend to overestimate how much they remember. The opposite also sometimes applies: people can underestimate earlier exposure to unpleasant material (Dubow, 1994). At the end of the 1930s, as a reaction to this, Starch developed the recall method.

Recall

The recall method consists of asking respondents what they can remember having seen in a certain publication (in print), for example, yesterday's newspaper or last week's magazine. Researchers assumed that recall of an advertisement was directly connected with brand purchase. Advertising recall is ascertained by means of a verbal cue. The technique may differ in the amount of help the respondent is given to recollect the ad. Questions may be along the following lines:

- Which brands did you see advertised in yesterday's newspaper?
- Did you see an advertisement for coffee in yesterday's newspaper?
- Did you see an advertisement for Douwe Egberts' coffee in yesterday's newspaper?

It was felt to be especially important with the aided recall questions that respondents reproduced the central message of the ad before it could count as having been 'seen'. The Starch method provides information on:

- the percentage of people in the target group saying they have seen ('noted') the advertising message;
- the percentage of people in the target group saying they have seen part of the advertising message in which the brand name or 'sender' of the message was named ('seen/associated');
- the percentage of people in the target group saying they have read more than half the advertising message ('read most').

As radio and television gained in popularity, the Starch method was further developed by Burke into the 'day-after recall' method (DAR). In this method, a television commercial is broadcast in one or more local markets as part of the normal programmes. Different markets are worked in different ways (ie, the ad is broadcast at different times, around different programmes, and so on), facilitating comparison between a group which has seen the ad and a control group. This method is called the split-cable test. The next day, respondents are telephoned about what they have seen. The method ensures that while consumers are being exposed to the advertisements, they are not aware that they are taking part in viewing behaviour research.

Respondents are asked which advertisements they can remember having seen at the time in question, in the medium in question, for which brand, and what the ad's main message was. The respondent can be helped to a greater or lesser degree. The DAR method received a great deal of criticism from advertising practitioners, who doubted that recall (of an ad) is related to sales figures. Percy and Rossiter (1992, p 11) argued that recall measurements were related to a particular medium, a particular exposure, at a particular time. Recall scores cannot, they believe, be translated into behavioural responses, because those cues are not relevant to the consumer's selection process.

Another point of criticism is that recall is very much based on words (arguments), though much communication is non-verbal. Images and music often play an important part in brand communication. This primarily applies to advertisements geared to confirming consumers' existing brand choices rather than persuading them to buy a new brand. In such cases people have more problems putting into words what they can recall about the ad.

The fact that advertisement recall and sales figures have little to do with each other compounded the need for different measurements. Spontaneous brand awareness frequently proved to be related to brand buying behaviour. As the interest in brands grew, so did the importance of measuring mental brand responses (Hansen, 1995).

Brand salience

We think more often about people and things we consider important than about those we consider unimportant. The psychological term for items which are at the front of our memories is salience (Sutherland, 1993). Advertisers would like their brands to be salient for consumers. Salience means that a brand has the chance of being consciously present in a person's memory at a given moment. One way in which advertising can influence saliency is by repetition. We can easily remember brands that have been advertised for years, such as Nescafé, Pepsi, Philips and Adidas. Cues also determine what we think about at a given moment. Advertising can use cues by linking the brand to something which regularly occurs in everyday life. It can be anything: a word, an expression. The product category is an important cue. What springs to mind when the cue is 'soft drink' or 'chocolate bars'? If the product category is the cue, top-of-mind brands in that category nearly always come to mind, so with chocolate bars we might think of Mars, Snickers or Twix.

It is possible to measure a brand's saliency and the influence of advertising. Respondents are asked what brand first comes to mind when a product category is named. The order in which they name the brands tells us something about saliency in the category. However, not every brand in the product category succeeds in having a top-of-mind position or 100% spontaneous recall. Laurent and Kapferer (1989) believe that our limited memory capacity is the reason why only a few brands in a category enjoy high spontaneous awareness. In addition, it is unlikely that spontaneous brand awareness can still increase for large established brands after a consumer has been exposed directly to an advertisement in a test situation. This observation has led to a shift in focus from recall scores to providing information on the persuasive powers of the message.

6.2.2 Stage 2: the persuasion era

Many manufacturers use their advertising campaigns to try to convince consumers of the benefits of their products. Procter & Gamble commercials persuade consumers by showing them how a product can solve or prevent a problem. The commercial does not have to be particularly visually or verbally pleasing, as long as the message comes across clearly. Often a product demonstration supports the promise given. Practitioners expect a persuaded consumer to buy the product and go on buying it. These assumptions are also described in the persuasion model (see section 5.3.2, page 192).

Persuasion

In the 1940s Schwerin introduced the persuasion method in the US for measuring an advertisement's persuasiveness. The focal point is the change in attitude towards the brand rather than recall of the ad or awareness of the brand. To ascertain the persuasiveness of a commercial according to the Schwerin method, respondents are invited to go and watch a television programme, usually in a test location like a cinema or movie theatre. This is why such tests are referred to as 'theatre tests' in America. Before the programme starts, the respondents are asked which brands they would choose if they could win certain branded articles in a lottery. They are then shown a television programme, interrupted by a commercial break. After the audience has been exposed to the advertisement, they are again asked to say which brand they prefer. The question is generally posed in terms of attitude towards the brand, preference or intention to buy. The aim of the test is to ascertain brand preference before and immediately after exposure to the commercial, to enable comparison between the two responses. The persuasion test measures how exposure to an ad affects brand preference. This change in preference is thought to reflect a change in actual buying behaviour. In addition, the measured change in attitude in a test situation is assumed to be a valid criterion for subsequent attitude change generated by the campaign.

The persuasion score is still a popular and much-used measurement in the US. The Research Systems Corporation, following in Schwerin's footsteps, provides pre-tests which still concentrate on the attitude shift. In this system, termed the American Research System (ARS), a persuasion score is reached by deducting the percentage of people choosing the brand prior to exposure to the ad from the percentage choosing it after exposure. Jones is a great advocate of attitude-shift measurement (Jones, 1996). He is convinced that the persuasion score for every campaign indicates how successful it will be in the marketplace, regardless of which framework model applies (although clearly this takes no account of the influence of competing brands and other external factors). Analysis of various cases reveals that a persuasion score of seven or higher guarantees a rise in sales figures (Ashley, 1994).

However, in the UK especially the persuasion method has come in for a great deal of criticism, the chief point being that it assumes advertising works after only one exposure. Hodges (1994) also suggested that, when interpreting persuasion scores further, one should bear in mind that the persuasion score alone, measured as explained above, is not enough to forecast the effectiveness of an ad. The actual score depends on several factors. One factor is the number of competing brands in the product category. The more alternatives, the smaller the chance the consumer will choose the brand in question. A second factor is the extent to which consumers already chose the brand prior to exposure to the commercial. If that brand was already largely preferred, there is little room for growth. The strength of brand preference is also important. A consumer's inclination to buy a brand again when making a choice varies from one product category to another. The puddings and biscuits markets, for instance, are characterised by a desire for brand variation. Consumers exhibit greater brand loyalty when buying products like detergents and coffee.

Apart from the above-mentioned methods, various preference scales have been developed to ascertain shifts in attitude. The advantage of scales is that it is fairly easy for researchers to process the results. Their disadvantage is that very large samples are needed to obtain statistically significant results. After all, shifts in preference with fast-moving consumer goods, if they actually occur in the short term, are often very small. If there is high brand preference in the sample, it is unlikely that changes in preference will be noted after exposure to one advertisement only. Moreover, these measurements are usually carried out in 'unnatural' surroundings, which also affects the reliability of the results (Hansen, 1995).

6.3 NEW VIEWS

At the end of the 1970s criticism began to be levelled at the assumptions on which the traditional advertising framework models were based. The theory of the rational human being was abandoned. After all, not every purchase is carefully reviewed. There is a big difference between purchasing a consumer durable involving a financial risk (a washing machine, a house) and the daily shopping (coffee, soft drinks). Emotions are decisive in many choice processes (cigarettes, clothing, perfume). In 1984 Petty and Cacioppo presented the Elaboration Likelihood Model (ELM) in a reaction to the 'premise of the rational human being', as a means of processing information. 'Elaboration likelihood' refers to the probability that the recipient of persuasive messages processes the presented arguments rationally. Consumers are not always willing to pay attention to the advertisement and carefully digest the arguments. The word 'carefully' incorporates processing the arguments, deliberating on them and adapting one's attitude towards the brand as a result of that deliberation. In the ELM, Petty and Cacioppo (1986) refer to very careful processing of arguments as the 'central route' of information processing.

However, for many products attention is very low and their presentation characteristics are processed only superficially. Less attention and time are usually given to purchases of sandwich fillings and detergents than to the purchase of a microwave oven or washing machine. People consult a consumer magazine when buying durables; they deliberate extensively, while they can do the weekly supermarket shopping in less than an hour. The next section examines more closely these mental brand responses, which are also known as 'processing effects'.

A concept which should not be overlooked in this context is involvement in the buying process. The consumer is willing to pay far more attention to some products than others, because he or she is more involved in the purchase. For instance, people usually spend a great deal of time planning a holiday. They procure brochures and compare various offers to ensure they have the best possible chance of a good holiday. If consumers are involved in purchasing a product they are very likely to be willing to pay more attention to relevant communication. So the recipient's attitude partly determines the extent to which the message is processed.

In the 1980s it was becoming clear that many products were definitely not purchased for their functional attributes, but only for the symbolic function they perform. Since then products have been categorised as being either instrumental or expressive (Franzen, 1994). In addition, willingness to pay attention to an advertisement was found to depend on an emotional evaluation at the very first moment of exposure. First and foremost, advertising must attract attention and generate a positive emotional reaction. Van Raaij (1984) calls this the primary affective reaction (PAR). This reaction need not mean that consumers are positively inclined towards the brand, but that they are considering whether further processing would be useful, interesting or necessary.

Likeability (attitude towards the ad)

Biel (1990) is of the opinion that people watch ads longer and more often if they like them. Likeable advertisements therefore have more chance of communicating their messages. This means that likeability influences the reach of advertisements and can help to deepen the level of information processing. Du Plessis (1994b) believes that in situations when television viewers pay less attention to advertising, it is the likeability variable that most affects possible storage in the memory. In this approach likeability is a condition for advertising effects, though it says nothing about the effectiveness of an ad.

A distinction is made in the likeability context between ad content (message likeability) and ad presentation (execution likeability). After all, it is not only respondents' opinions about ad content that is important; their attitude to message presentation can also influence attention-holding (Franzen, 1994).

Respondent profiles such as Schlinger's (1979) and Wells' (1964) (see Appendix III of Chapter 3, pages 81 and 82) can be used to measure the direct emotional reactions of individual consumers to advertisements, thus determining what the major explanatory factor is for ad likeability. The 'meaningfulness' of the ad proves to be the most important factor (Biel and Bridgewater, 1990). This can also be expressed as 'personally relevant information' (Aaker and Buzzone, 1981). Meaningfulness is primarily determined by the information in the advertisement (message content), which not only includes product facts, but, more especially, 'novelty'. Vividness also plays an important part.

It is important for the advertiser to know what motivates the audience in transferring attention from a certain activity to the ad, or vice versa, and what causes attention to the ad to wane and the audience to focus on another activity. Du Plessis (1994a) refers in this context to the Supervisory Attention System (SAS), which denotes the stopping power of an ad.

The results of the Advertising Research Foundation validation test of copy-testing (Haley and Baldinger, 1991) suggest that likeability is the value which best predicts the ultimate selling results of an ad. The study reveals that likeability has a significant link with sales figures, but that the relationships between recall and sales figures, and persuasion and sales figures, are not significant. It is worth noting that the study examined only five brands, involving two commercials for each.

One conclusion of the study was that advertisements which respondents assess more positively are, in general (there are exceptions), better able to elicit positive reactions concerning the brand than commercials which are less appreciated. So ad likeability can be an important factor of ad effectiveness. The results of the above-mentioned studies have meant that, since 1990, likeability has become a much used variable in the pre-testing of advertisements.

The opposite of likeability is irritation. A debate about irritation is currently taking place, and whether the measurement of irritation should be carried out in the future. This would entail asking respondents how irritating they find the ad, and could be measured in the same way as ad likeability, ie, respondents giving marks expressing their evaluation. Scale techniques can also be used.

6.3.1 The active recipient

Hierarchical advertising framework models implicitly assumed that the consumer received the advertisers' messages passively, without actively taking part in the communication process. Advertisements were thought to 'inject' the central message straight into the recipient. Advertising practitioners have meanwhile realised that the consumer does not absorb all the offered information in its 'pure' form. Information is not stored away 'unadulterated', but is interpreted by recipients, using associations, beliefs and brand attitudes which are present in their memories. Information that does not tie in with existing knowledge is not assimilated into the memory, or is interpreted in such a way that it does tie in with existing knowledge. Consequently, consumers do not always draw the intended conclusions from the ad. Added to which, each recipient will interpret the information in his or her own way.

As a result of the growing concentration on the recipient of communication, various models were devised focusing on message processing by the recipient. The TRIADE model (Poiesz and Robben, 1994) is one such model. It stipulates three conditions for the successful transfer of information. First, opportunity – for the recipient to receive and assimilate the information. Second, ability – the recipient must be able to process the information. And third, interest.

Self-relevance

Work by Research International (Blackston, 1994) shows that a good score for perceived relevance of the message, the execution or the sender increases the chance of a successful campaign. Consequently, Research International's CRA (Cognitive Response Analysis) concentrates on the relationship or interaction between the consumer and the actual ad. This method determines the extent to which consumers are really involved with an advertisement. The greater the self-relevance, the greater the ad's chance of producing a shift in attitude towards the brand.

The CRA method proceeds as follows: after respondents have seen the test commercial, they write down all the thoughts, ideas and reactions which came to mind while they were watching. They then indicate whether each thought was positive, neutral or negative. All the responses are analysed as to processing, evaluation (positive, neutral, negative) and content. The extent of processing is determined from respondents' reactions that suggest the advertising was self-relevant. When evaluating content, a distinction is made between product, brand or service message, execution and sender.

6.3.2 Advertising, corroboration and attention for brands

Not only has the independent role of the recipient been recognised, but also better insight has been developed into the function of advertising itself. It is not always aimed at convincing consumers of the functional value of the product or brand by supplying them with rational arguments. One major role of advertising is to corroborate the behaviour of existing product or brand users. Trial purchases generally result from in-store activities or from special promotions. Advertising is geared to confirming and reinforcing the initial product experience and helps to keep brand awareness alive.

Corroborative advertising is also of importance for a brand with a large group of loyal users. Advertisers employ their advertising to communicate with people who use their brand several times a week, and sometimes have been doing so for years. The intention is to enhance and reinforce brand experience, and confirm functional product experience and brand use.

Consumers often choose a brand that appeals to them, without having made a detailed evaluation of its functional attributes. A brand's emotional meaning can even be more important than the instrumental functioning of the product. Since the 1980s growing emphasis has been given to the contribution of advertising to the emotional significance of brands. Brands greatly influence the way consumers perceive products and experience product use (emotions model). They represent lifestyles, act as symbols in communication between people and can colour usage experience (symbolism model). People attribute personal characteristics to some brands and develop brand relationships which can be compared to relationships with friends or loved ones (relationship/involvement model).

Transfer of symbolic meaning

Consumers assess the meaning of different brands in order to see whether they give off the right information about themselves. They look at what brands symbolise in order to add their meaning to their lives. Symbolic meaning is, among other things, the result of interaction with other members of the reference group. Other people's actions are interpreted and reacted to accordingly. In such cases brands serve as non-verbal means of communication. There are various ways in which the brand can have a symbolic meaning – it may have an expressive, a socially adaptive or an impressive function (Franzen and Hoogerbrugge, 1996).

It is possible to measure the symbolic meaning of a brand using statements which the respondent must evaluate according to a scale. Relevant literature contains little, if anything, on the measurement of the transfer of symbolic meaning. Exploratory research (van der Pol and Laskaris, 1994) and recent developments from research agencies show that association tests with verbal concepts are certainly an option.

Attitude towards the brand

Research by Mitchell (1991) and Shimp (1981) reveals that attitude towards a brand can be influenced by a positive attitude to the ad. So, apart from factors like duration of and intensity of attention to the ad, likeability can also directly affect feelings about (ie, attitude towards) the brand. Likeability is purely a form of classical conditioning (Biel, 1990). This observation suggests that it is, undeniably, the most important variable measured in the pre-test.

However, different studies show that likeability is not important for every brand. With instrumental products, characterised by high involvement (stereo equipment, cars, financial services) there would seem to be hardly any connection between likeability of the ad and advertising processing. But with brands in which symbolic associations play a part there is a distinct connection between likeability and advertising effect (Saupe, 1992). Rossiter and Percy (1987) reach the conclusion that likeability may or may not affect brand choice, depending on purchasing motives and the degree of involvement. They base their arguments on two purchasing motives: 'informational' and 'transformational'. Informational purchasing motives relate to 'avoidance' (ie, problem-solving) products. Transformational motives relate to 'approach' (ie, pleasure-providing) products. The authors suggest that likeability can be extremely important for problem-solving products with low involvement.

Attractive advertising is a way of creating liking for the brand (this is how the likeability model works). Obviously it is not the only solution. One criterion for liking the brand is that the user does not have a disappointing experience with the brand.

Franzen (1994) has represented in diagram form (see Figure 6.2) how the priorities of advertising, depending on high versus low product involvement, and symbolic versus instrumental brand values, can be expressed in objectives.

In this respect readers are referred to Chapter 5 (Figure 5.10, page 214), which contains a brief summary of the important responses that should be measured for each different framework.

Instrumental values	–	+	–	+
Symbolic values	–	–	+	+
High product involvement		• Message • (Believability) • Message likeability	• Feelings • (Identification) • Executional likeability	• Message • Feelings (believability and identification likeability)
Low product involvement	• Awareness (recall) • Execution likeability	• Message • Awareness (recall) • Message likeability	• Feelings (conditioning) • Awareness • Execution likeability • (Identification)	

Figure 6.2 High versus low involvement and symbolic versus instrumental brand values in relation to objectives (Source: Franzen, 1994)

6.4 MEASURING SEVERAL RESPONSES

As yet it has not been shown whether one mental response can be isolated which predicts whether advertising will affect behaviour. Experts differ widely in their views and it is debatable whether an unequivocal answer will ever be possible. Biel still sticks to 'self-relevance', Jones advocates an attitude shift and du Plessis swears by likeability. In practice, most research agencies do not opt for one specific variable but include several in the pre-test, assuming that one variable cannot forecast campaign effectiveness and that advertising can work differently for every brand in every market. If several responses are measured it helps us to understand how the campaign works and how the different responses interact.

The UK research agency Hall & Partners developed a pre-test method called 'Presponse'. It, too, is based on the various advertising framework models. This tool stresses the way in which advertising affects the consumer's relationship with the brand, which is termed the brand relationship. In addition, Presponse tests every ad for persuasive power (saliency, persuasion and involvement), because almost all commercials contain elements of the three concomitant models. An ad can hardly ever be covered by one model alone. Hall & Partners believe that if persuasion, involvement and saliency (at the advertising and the brand level) are measured for each ad, they can discover the main way in which the consumer is influenced by the advertising. Only then is it possible to ascertain how the advertising works or, more particularly, why it does not work. The way in which the advertiser and the advertising agency expect advertising to work determines which variables will be valued most when the advertisement is assessed. During an interview in 1996, Hardie of Hall & Partners explained in this context that in the past advertising was assumed to work according to the persuasion model, and that pre-testing was based only on that model. However, Hall described other models, and advertising research was adapted accordingly. After all, Hardie claimed, the assumptions concerning how advertising works must be the starting point for advertising research. Consequently, when the aim is to involve people with the brand through advertising, a pre-test must measure whether the advertisement is able to involve consumers with the advertising and the brand. So, as Hardie explained, Hall & Partners has not renounced the persuasion model, but does not see it as being sufficient on its own.

Another UK research service, Millward Brown, also bases its research methods on the view that advertising can work in different ways. The company supports its observations with years of tracking research, concluding that advertising with something new to communicate (a new brand, a new product, a new attribute, a new campaign concept) works differently from advertising which says nothing new (advertising for familiar, established brands, using a familiar concept). A new brand, a new product attribute, which is personally relevant and believable, or a new campaign, can be of direct influence on (trial) buying behaviour. Millward Brown calls this 'immediate challenge'.

Advertising for established brands often has nothing new to say and rarely produces direct results for consumer behaviour. For these brands, long-term mechanisms operate, namely interest/status and enhancement. Interest relates to advertising ensuring the consumer does not lose interest in the brand. Status entails advertising supporting the brand's status, and keeping it vivid. Enhancement represents the strength of advertising in colouring expectations concerning product experience in advance. These mechancisms coincide with the persuasion model as described in Chapter 5 (section 5.3.2).

Millward Brown's LINK test ties in with the three advertising mechanisms described. When testing an ad it takes into account the assumptions concerning the period in which effects are expected and the fact that advertising can aim to produce several effects at the same time. The decision on which effects are to be the principal objectives and which the intermediate variables depends on the strategic framework that is opted for – immediate challenge, interest/status or enhancement.

6.5   CONDITIONS FOR SUCCESS

If the test results suggest that the ad can convey the desired message, how is it possible to prove that this actually happens? Before advertising can do its work and influence the consumer, in whatever way, the message must be processed. First of all, the processing of advertising requires the viewing or reading audience to pay serious attention to the ad, think about it and forget their own prejudices about the product category. Understanding and relevance of the message, brand registration and (emotional) reactions to the advertisement are all facilitating responses. A closer look is taken below at the facilitating advertising responses which may be included in a pre-test. Depending on which advertising framework model is used, some responses are more important than others.

Attention

Today it is becoming increasingly difficult for advertising to gain attention. People are exposed to ever more stimuli. Attention-paying is the process in which we select one sensory input out of many, and transfer it to our consciousness (Glass and Holyoak, 1986). The attention-paying process can, in fact, only be measured at the actual moment that attention is paid. Since it is (practically) impossible to establish whether and how much attention people pay to an ad in natural circumstances, such measurements can be carried out only in experimental situations. Various physiological and semi-physiological tools can be used to measure the physical phenomena indicating the occurrence of attention, perception or arousal. Well-known examples are EDG (skin resistance), EEG (brain activity) and EMG (muscular tension) (Franzen *et al.*, 1996).

These physiological methods have been available for some time, yet they have never been widely used. They are characterised by their simplicity and their ability to cut out defensive reactions, but it is often unclear what exactly is being measured. If the heart beats faster, the respondent starts to sweat or the pupils dilate, is this an indication of a good or a bad ad? As a result, results are hard to interpret. It might be a solution to ask respondents themselves to explain the responses measured. The use of thought verbalisation would seem to be fair and permissible. However, it is not certain which mental events can and will be put into words by respondents (Wright, 1980). Moreover, the researcher triggers off a cognitive process that does not necessarily occur with natural processing.

For practical considerations, the customary procedure is to ascertain after exposure if the respondent paid attention to the ad. Memory tests are used, such as the measurement of aided and spontaneous recall. If recognition or recall of an ad is ascertained, it is in fact a matter of checking, after the event, whether the respondent registered the words, pictures and/or sounds.

Recently, Verify International in the Netherlands introduced the Verify method (Parker Brady, 1997). In this method eye movements are registered to determine whether the eyes are drawn to the ad, for how long they focus on the ad, on which elements and in what sequence they focus, and whether they also focus on the brand.

Transfer of meaning or message

When the advertising content is stored in the memory, the important thing is the content of what is registered – the knowledge the consumer has acquired and the feelings he or she has formed and stored away on the basis of that registration. Several studies have shown that, when processing time is very long and attention good, 30–55% of advertisements (both commercials and print ads) are still misunderstood (Franzen, 1994; Gordon, 1995). This is due firstly to 'shallow' processing of the advertising message. People do not pay enough attention to all the incoming sensory stimuli in order for them to be stored in the memory. In addition, people do not perceive objectively. What we see is always a mixture of perception and interpretation. We often misinterpret things because they do not tie in with what we already know, and we invariably misunderstand things because we are prejudiced. Consequently, many pre-tests are used to determine whether the intended message has been conveyed correctly. Respondents are asked about the ad's central message or about how easy it was to understand what was taking place in the commercial (Millward Brown, 1990). This question is particularly important with the persuasion model.

Brand registration

If the ad is to be effective, the consumer must of course link it with the right brand. This is termed brand registration. Tests show that ad-to-brand linkage often misfires. In over 40% of exposures no brand registration occurs (Franzen, 1994). Initial validation tests of the Verify method show that if people pay attention to the ad for longer than three seconds, there is a greater chance they will 'register' the brand.

With television commercials, brand registration is largely determined by the way in which the brand is presented in the advertising. If it is shown at the start of the commercial, the chance of brand registration is greater. It is also important for attention to be greatest at the very moment the brand is shown. It is a simple procedure to measure brand registration in a pre-test, by asking to which brand the commercial relates. Measurement of brand registration is especially important for the salience, relationship/involvement, symbolism and emotions models (see Chapter 5).

Advertising involvement

The recipient can process the information from the ad at six different levels, depending on involvement with the product, the brand, the attitude towards the ad content, the presentation of the ad and advertising in general (see Exhibit 6.1). Thorough processing ensures better recall, and that, in turn, can influence consumer choice.

Advertising involvement can be determined during exposure to the ad by means of handsets which record the respondent's reaction by the second. PEAC (Program Evaluation Analysis Computer) is an example of a continuous research system ascertaining, as respondents watch the ads, individual responses resulting from exposure to an advertisement. The PEAC method entails asking a respondent to hold a handset. The handset contains five buttons, A to E (A = very positive, B = positive, C = neutral, D = negative and E = very negative). Respondents have to use the buttons to indicate the extent of their liking for the ad (not the brand). Their reactions are recorded every two seconds. In this way it is possible to check appreciation of the different elements in the advertisement. Afterwards, focus group discussions are held to find out why certain elements are assessed positively or negatively. In the UK a few research services (including Millward Brown) ascertain involvement with the ad during exposure (Gordon, 1995).

Emotional responses

These responses relate to how people experience advertising subjectively. Emotions occurring as a result of exposure to an advertisement can have a tactical function, since they facilitate ad processing by the consumer. In such cases emotions activate attention, the persistence of attention and deeper processing. That in turn leads to better recall and greater persuasiveness of the ad.

Sometimes emotions have a strategic function. In such cases the emotion is seen as an important, differentiating benefit of brand use. Douwe Egberts' coffee is seen to bring about a feeling of solidarity and caring in the home, Coca-Cola to bring pleasure and happiness. If a brand succeeds in getting specific emotions linked with it, those emotions can form the foundations for positioning. This does not entail experiencing emotional responses as a result of exposure to an ad, but the emotional responses which are linked (associated) directly with the brand. This association of the brand with

Six levels of advertising processing

Franzen (1994, pp 74–82) describes six levels of advertising processing. Their occurrence depends on:

- the intensity of the attention paid to an advertisement;
- the extent to which existing associative networks in the memory are activated and used to decode the presented stimuli;
- the depth of understanding of the presented stimuli;
- the way in which new information is fitted into existing 'knowledge structures'.

Level 1: Pre-attentive processing
The unconscious processing of stimuli from our environment. Eyes and ears receive the stimuli, but the brain is scarcely activated, if at all.

Level 2: Minimal secondary processing
The processing of a few general characteristics which force themselves upon us because they are very dominant or stand out from their surroundings.

Level 3: Divided processing
Attention is divided between two matters. For example, while we are watching a commercial, our thoughts return to something that happened the day before.

Level 4: Passive primary processing
Attention is focused primarily on the commercial, but our senses continue registering other stimuli from our environment. The commercial is processed generally.

Level 5: Active primary processing
Attention is focused primarily on the advertisement. We assimilate the information with interest and form an opinion on it.

Level 6: Primary processing with identification
The commercial is about something that really interests us. Our attention is considerable. We even identify with what is happening in the ad.

Exhibit 6.1

specific feelings results from repeated exposure to the brand and the emotion together (in a process of classical conditioning).

Direct emotions that occur as the result of exposure to an ad can be measured by verbal scales and non-verbal techniques alike. The Beaumont Emotion Battery (Zeitlin and Westwood, 1986, p 39) is one verbal scale. Respondents are asked to sit in a simulated sitting room and are twice shown the advertisement which is being tested. The ad in question is included in a television programme with five other commercials. The aim is to measure the subjective emotions during exposure to the ad. The respondents evaluate 40 items concerning the ad. They consist of cognitive opinions on the ad based on subjective emotions like happiness, excitement, fear. Each item is evaluated on an emotional intensity scale. The respondent indicates the extent to which the item describes the ad: not at all, a little, to an average extent, well or extremely well.

An example of a non-verbal technique for measuring brand-related emotions is the 'photo-sort'. This uses portrait photographs depicting certain emotions. Respondents are asked to place what they think are the most appropriate photos beside a number of competing brands. In this way they can express themselves without having to put their emotions into words.

Another non-verbal method for measuring emotions is the self-assessment manikin (SAM). It is based on the idea that emotions have three independent and bi-polar dimensions: pleasure–displeasure; extent of arousal; dominance–submission. These dimensions can occur independently of one another when people look at an ad (Mehrabian and Russel, 1977). In SAM each dimension is represented in a series of drawings (see Figure 6.3). Pleasure begins with a happy, smiling manikin and ends with an unhappy, frowning one. Arousal begins with a sleepy manikin, with closed eyes, and ends with an agitated manikin with open eyes. Dominance is represented by a series of drawings beginning with a large, powerful, influential manikin and ends with a small submissive one (Morris, 1995). Respondents indicate by means of the drawings the intensity of their feelings with each dimension.

According to Haley et al. (1994), direct emotional responses are missing in most pre-tests, although they largely determine the variance in persuasion scores (pre–post shift in attitude) and saliency scores (TOMA). Music especially affects the viewer's mood and evokes emotions. Haley et al. believe that when an advertisement is pre-tested, respondents should not just be asked about the central message. Questioning should also be aimed at the direct responses to the ad which enable the message to be conveyed.

Figure 6.3 Self-assessment manikin (Source: Morris, 1995)

6.6 DIAGNOSTIC RESEARCH

Research into the connection between advertising responses and the characteristics of an advertisement is called diagnostic research. Respondents are exposed to a television commercial or print ad, and then asked to give their opinions, based on appropriate scales. Well-known scales used for diagnostic purposes are those devised by Zaichowsky (1985) for television or radio ads and Wells (1964) for print (see Chapter 3, Appendices II and III). Diagnostic research is useful because it can provide insight into the relationship between the processing of an ad and its characteristics. In other words, if the results of diagnostic research could be tied in with those of tracking research, it might be possible to understand why a commercial has worked.

This idea has been elaborated on further by Bruzzone Research Company, using the Advertising Response Model (ARM). This is a method which records the direct reactions to a commercial and links them to the mental advertising responses, which, in turn, are tied in with the mental brand responses. So the model charts how a

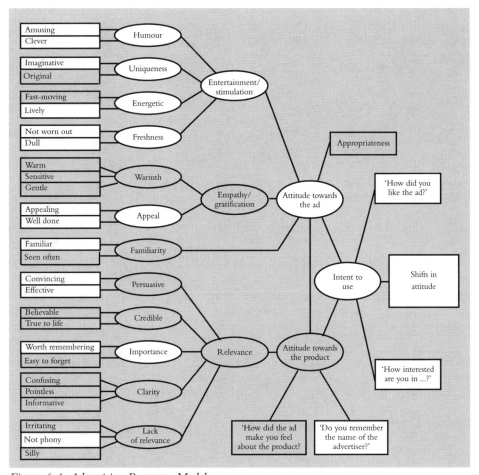

Figure 6.4 Advertising Response Model

commercial works at various levels. It is based on Petty and Cacioppo's ELM model (1986) and distinguishes between the peripheral and the central routes of influence.

The Advertising Response Model

The left-hand side of Figure 6.4 lists the direct reactions to a commercial which result in an overall attitude towards it. The emotional, affective reactions representing the peripheral route of the model are shown in the upper half. The lower left-hand side shows the more rational reactions leading to overall attitudes towards the product. The list of 27 characteristics is based on Wells', Leavitt's and McConville's reaction profiles of 1997. On the right-hand side the mental advertising and brand responses can be found.

The model can pinpoint exactly what driving force is behind a commercial, by indicating how the commercial scores on the different characteristics. It shows, with each characteristic, whether the commercial scores better than average (white), average (grey) or below average (black) compared with the norm. Figure 6.4 relates to a commercial which works via the central route, with the emphasis on empathy, and has no below-average scores.

One of this model's advantages, compared with many other pre-testing methods, is that it provides insight into the way the different responses interact, clarifying which advertising framework model has contributed to the working of the commercial. Thanks to this insight it will probably be easier to come up with effective commercials in the future.

6.7 ISSUES RELATING TO PRE-TESTING

In the previous sections several forms of pre-testing have been reviewed and the various effects and diagnostic variables which can be measured in pre-tests have been examined. Each method proves to have its pros and cons, but how does one decide which research method to use and which variables to measure? In theory, the question is easy to answer: a method can be chosen based on the test objectives and the validity and reliability of the measuring method. In practice, however, these criteria are not the only ones involved. Matters such as political agendas, time and money are also important. Here the chief issues which play a part in the choice of a pre-test are discussed, preceded by a brief review of what the terms 'validity' and 'reliability' mean in the pre-test context.

Validity

The main focus with validity is the way in which data are collected. In other words, is the variable being measured the desired measurement? In order to be in control of the validity of a research tool the tool must meet two requirements. First, there must be *empirical validity*, and second, *construct validity*.

Empirical validity relates to whether the measuring tool can indeed ascertain the required characteristic. If empirical validity is to be determined, the results of the measurement must correspond with results known to be valid. For example, it can be checked whether the scale used differentiates between people who are known, from other sources, to represent a little or a lot of an attitude or other characteristic in question.

Construct validity relates to whether the measurement tool measures *only* what is required, without any confusing factors being involved. It is impossible for other variables to influence the measured construct (the way the measurement is organised). So the important thing is whether the measuring tools used are criteria for the constructs in question.

There are more forms of validity, besides construct and empirical – internal and external validity, for instance. The internal validity of an experiment constitutes the controllability of the variables in the test environment. It concerns the way in which the researcher reaches conclusions about the effect of the independent variables. With pre-testing this relates to the relationship or correlation between ad exposure as an independent variable and the dependent variables or (intended) advertising effects.

External validity focuses on whether the test conditions correspond with reality, meaning that the results can be assumed to reflect what will occur under natural circumstances. Laboratory tests are sometimes so artificial (for example, respondents may be asked to pay attention while watching a television commercial) that they have little in common with 'normal' television viewing. The validity of such research should be questioned, since the test situation is too far removed from reality. Care should be taken not to view test results as applying to the entire population (Fletcher and Bowers, 1988).

Reliability

Reliability relates to the question of whether the testing methods are so reliable that they come up with the same results when measurements are repeated under similar conditions. The idea is to find out whether the different aspects of the research and the resulting data represent variations in reality rather than measuring errors, coincidences or procedural errors. In other words, reliability indicates whether the results are accidental or not; it is about the consistency and stability of the measuring tools.

6.7.1 What is the aim of a pre-test?

If pre-testing is aimed at assessing the effectiveness of the advertisement, quantitative research is the obvious choice, using standardised measuring tools. However, pre-testing of commercials in order to predict whether they will have a positive effect on sales figures is still a questionable and controversial issue. So far there is no scientific proof of a connection between the responses measured in pre-tests and effects in the marketplace (Lodish *et al.*, 1995). If the parties concerned decide beforehand on the objectives of the pre-test and the implications of the results, it can prevent problems. Do they expect the advertising to influence sales figures directly or do they intend the ad to have intermediate effects, thus increasing the value of the brand?

Disaster check

For advertisers, who invest huge sums of money in different advertisements in a campaign, it can certainly be worth testing which of the ads is most effective before deciding which ads to insert and/or broadcast. After all, the advertisers have to make media investments – and the media take the lion's share of the investments. Often, however, the results of creative development research will already have given clear indications of the development of an effective commercial. Consequently, many advertisers decide, based on experience and conviction of the agency's expertise, that no further research is necessary other than the measurement of effects in a post-test or tracking study (Stewart-Hunter, 1992).

It has been suggested that, since the pre-test is implicitly situated between copy-testing and tracking, it is superfluous. The strategic starting points are based on consumer information, and the dos and don'ts of the execution could have already been dealt with in concept development testing. Also, the parties involved have sometimes already committed themselves fully to the advertising (Schweitzer, 1983). However, it is conceivable that in certain circumstances the client and the advertising agency will want greater certainty and extra backing for their choices, for example, in the following situations:

- creative development research has come up with dualistic results;
- the original advertisement has been substantially altered during the production process;
- the test material proves, in retrospect, to be a poor reflection of the final ad;
- the qualitative technique is not felt to be an adequate basis for financial decisions;
- the advertiser is uncertain about the ad's effectiveness.

Comparison of two 'ready-made' advertisements

A pre-test is sometimes held to compare whether two or more advertisements achieve the desired advertising effect. The test results make it possible to choose the most promising ad. If, for instance, three commercials have been made and the advertisers can afford to drop one of them, they could opt to use the best two only. In practice, however, this does not often happen. In view of the costs already incurred, an advertiser generally decides to adapt the less good commercial and ensure it is ready on time to be broadcast in the second burst of advertising (Stewart-Hunter, 1992). When two advertisements are to be compared, it should be asked on what the comparison is based. In what respect does one ad function better than the other?

Standards

Quantitative research enables us to compare test results of alternative ads and verify them with standards. That is why large advertisers test every ad using the same method. In this way a data bank of test results can be compiled. The average of all test scores can be taken as the norm, and individual ads compared to this. The deviation of the score compared with the norm is supposed to predict how effective the ad will actually be.

Research services also use standard scores, with which specific ads are compared. These criteria can be attuned specifically to the product category, but it is more usual for the research service to use its own norms based on past pre-tests. These norms are in fact merely average scores from previous tests. When comparing the test results with these standard scores, it is wise to consider whether they are relevant to the ad in question. After all, the standard scores are not specifically geared to the target group and product category being tested.

6.7.2 Exposure conditions

Ideally an ad should be tested in natural surroundings for the respondent or in conditions which imitate the natural surroundings as closely as possible. However, most pre-tests entail 'enforced' exposure, generally in a laboratory situation, or else the respondent's memory is challenged (as in the day-after recall test). With enforced exposure it is impossible for the respondent to skip or avoid advertisements, there are no 'competitive' surroundings, no influence from programmes or adjoining editorials, and only one or two exposures take place, meaning that the results can never exactly predict what will really happen. Interpretation of the test results should take account of the influence of programme or editorial context, among other things. Research has shown that the likeability of a television programme influences the recall of the ads which are aired with it (Clansky and Kweskin, 1971). Similarly, research conducted by Burke (1978) reveals that the type of programme shown affects scores of concomitant commercials. For instance, spontaneous recall of advertisements shown with feature films is higher than those shown with news programmes.

In a clutter-reel experiment (a series of ads included one after the other on a tape, including the ad to be tested) the audience is asked to watch the commercials, or a programme accompanied by commercials. That is also the case with theatre tests, in which respondents are asked to watch a special show. Efforts are in fact made to distract respondents from the real aim of the test by suggesting that the test relates to the television programme in which the commercials have been included, but the fact remains that they behave differently in test situations. Conclusions drawn from laboratory tests should therefore be treated cautiously.

In-market recall experiments are tests which are conducted in the market, without the respondents knowing in advance that they are taking part in the test and being exposed to the ad in a forced situation. In some countries test markets are used to this end. In South Africa, in-market recall of television commercials is measured by asking people by telephone if they remember having seen a commercial for brand X. Various studies, including those by Millward Brown (1991) and du Plessis (1994a), show that there are big differences in test results between enforced exposure to the commercial and the 'in-market' tests. This might be explained by the fact that under natural conditions the commercial first has to gain the audience's attention.

Multiple versus single exposures

Most pre-testing methods are designed so that the respondent is exposed to the commercial once only. They do not allow for the so-called 'wear-in effects' (described below under 'effective frequency'). With an advertising campaign, however, it is generally assumed that optimum results are achieved only with multiple exposures to an ad. Accordingly, conveyance of an average commercial's message improves after two exposures (Weinblatt and Conway, 1996, p 44).

Research by McCollum and Spielman (1978a, 1978b) has shown that after one exposure, respondents recall the brand's usage characteristics which are already known, but they can only partially remember new characteristics, even when clearly evident in the commercial. The research results reveal that two exposures to new usage characteristics do communicate the new characteristics.

This increase in communication transfer does not apply with every commercial, however. With some, two exposures produce a slight increase in recall of only 4%, while with others, two exposures more than double communication transfer (Weinblatt and Conway, 1996). Whether repeated exposure increases the effectiveness of the ad depends, among other things, on the accessibility of the message and the type of topic. It is necessary to repeat vague, complicated, abstract, symbolic or other difficult messages more often for the intended message to be grasped.

Effective frequency

One exposure to the advertisement is not usually enough to achieve the maximum effect. This occurrence is termed the wear-in effect, which describes increased ad effectiveness after repeated exposure to the ad. When a pre-test design is being developed, it is as well to bear in mind how many exposures are expected to be necessary. In the advertising profession the prevailing wisdom, on psychological grounds, is that the consumer must be exposed to the ad at least three times if the ad is to be effective.

Krugman (1968) suggested that the first exposure produced a cognitive response of: 'What is it?' He described the response to the second exposure as a personal evaluation: 'What do I think about it?' He suggested that the third and subsequent exposures served as reminders. This assumption came in for a lot of criticism, as did the idea that there might be a general, optimum frequency. McDonald (1995) declared that most advertising is assumed – generally incorrectly – to be a matter of 'learning'. He stated that it invariably helps the consumer to remember a brand, and that this 'learning' is thought to require fewer exposures.

Krugman's findings were used by Research International as a basis for their reel-test for pre-testing television commercials, which entails including the ad to be tested within a sequence of ads. Respondents are shown the sequence twice and the impact of the ad in question can thus be established. The ad is repeated once more and then respondents are asked to reiterate its message. In this way it is possible to ascertain whether the intended message has been conveyed.

Wear-out

The opposite of the wear-in effect is the wear-out effect. This relates to the decrease in effectiveness of an ad after repeated exposures to it. In order to establish the optimum number of exposures, something of the ad's wear-out must also be known. These effects prove very difficult to determine in practice. Jones (1995) believes that wear-out depends, among other things, on the type of medium (print or television) and the quality of the ad. Insight into wear-out can, he believes, only be obtained with single-source research. This establishes which ads for which products consumers are exposed to, within households. The technique compares these results with consumers' actual purchases of the same brands shortly after the exposures. It makes it possible to compare the buying behaviour of consumers who were exposed to the relevant advertising with the buying behaviour of those who were not. Incidentally, Jones is also of the opinion that, with fast-moving consumer goods, one exposure to an ad is sufficient to achieve effects.

The Media Partnership (TMP) in France has devised a post-test tool which provides the necessary insight to reach an optimum and so economical insertion/airing schedule: the Media Observer (Faasse, 1992, 1996). The Media Observer determines the optimum contact frequency for campaign X for brand Y, taking account of the objectives of the advertising campaign. The effectiveness criteria used by TMP are: advertising awareness, spontaneous brand recall and aided brand recall. These criteria are related to the number of actual contacts with advertising, and this is thought to give insight into the effective frequency for the ad in question. This is highly topical for television advertising. Other media, such as radio, print and outdoor, are included in the test in order to establish optimum media mix alongside optimum contact frequency.

Duration of exposure

With print campaigns it is not only important to know what the effective frequency is, but also the duration of exposure. Readers decide for themselves how much time they spend on a particular page (internal pacing): usually no longer than four seconds. They then continue turning the pages or get sidetracked.

In recent decades the time spent on reading has been dropping substantially. The reading of newspapers, books or magazines has decreased markedly among young people in particular, having been ousted by television viewing and other leisure pursuits.

Readers spend on average two seconds looking at a full-page advertisement in a magazine, regardless of whether it is in colour or black and white. On average 1.5 seconds of that is spent on the visual (pictures) and 0.5 seconds on the text (Franzen, 1994).

Consequently the duration of exposure is an essential factor when the effect of print ads is being measured in forced test situations. Too long an exposure results in an unnatural ad-exposure situation, which may mean that the results differ greatly from normal circumstances. If the duration of exposure is varied during the test, it is possible to get an idea of its influence on the processing of the ad. Another possibility is to allow respondents to decide themselves how long contact will last. This can be done by inserting the ad for testing in a medium (magazine or newspaper) and allowing respondents to leaf through it.

Lack of competition

There are only a few examples of advertisers who are not faced with competing campaigns in the media. Generally, competitors with similar product characteristics tend to advertise at the same moment (according to Carter and Atkinson (1994), more than 60% of advertisers do so). However, most pre-testing methods are based on the assumption that there is little active competition, thus failing to allow for its possible neutralising or negative effect on the ad (Weinblatt and Conway, 1996). The British research agency, The Research Business, seeks to counteract this when testing commercials by using a clutter reel that also contains commercials by direct competitors. In a competitive setting, with all the ads making the same claims, it is possible to check whether the commercial might indeed work. The disadvantage of this procedure is that it is far removed from real life, because two competitors are never aired in the same break.

Sequence of ads

The ad's position in the advertising break greatly influences recall scores (Franzen, 1994). The first three commercials have higher scores on average than those in the middle of the break. The fact that the commercials at the beginning and end of the break are better remembered is described as the primacy or recency effect.

When different advertisements are being evaluated, it is as well to present them to respondents in a changing sequence ('randomised'), in order to avoid primacy or recency effects. A concept with a negative evaluation might, after all, affect the assessment of subsequent ads. Consequently, in a pre-test the main focus is on the first ad, because it is evaluated in the most unbiased way. The number of concepts to be evaluated must be limited, as respondents have a limited capacity for assessment and comparison. If more concepts are added, the sample used must be bigger (de Ruyter and Scholl, 1995).

The questionnaire

The questionnaire itself should be reviewed critically. Firstly, its length can influence the results. If a respondent has to spend too much time on the questionnaire, it can affect recall. In addition, the sequence in which the questions are dealt with influences the test results. Earlier questions can affect the answers to later questions. Figure 6.5 represents a proposal by Percy and Rossiter (1992, p 65) with respect to the sequence in a questionnaire.

Effectiveness

It takes a great deal of understanding and experience to interpret test results. For instance, research has shown that the recall (awareness) of a certain advertisement can vary tremendously, depending on a number of conditions (Percy and Rossiter, 1992).

- Is exposure to the ad on-air or off-air? On-air means the test is fitted into a real broadcast. Off-air means the recipient is shown the ad in a test situation.
- Is the ad included in a clutter reel in a programme context?
- When a clutter-reel test is held, it is worth bearing in mind that the test results partly depend on the other ads on the reel.
- In the programme context the content of a specific programme also proves to affect recall.

Pre-testing is nearly always an artificial method, be it in the form of a clutter reel including commercials for other categories or only commercials for competing products within the category, be it a reel with five, seven or nine commercials, or a folder test (ie, with print ads) with ten or twenty advertisements. All these research methods call on the consumer's short-term memory. As stated earlier, there is as yet

Control group	Experimental group
• No exposure to the stimulus (ad) • The control group is used to check whether the ascertained effects can be attributed to exposure to the ad	• Exposure to the ad to be tested

• Communication effects
  – category needs
  – brand awareness
  – intention to buy (if objective)
  – attitude towards brand
  – brand 'benefit beliefs'
	• Points of attention (with print ad)
	• Mental ad responses
	  – acceptance (high involvement)
	  – learning
	  – adjectives checklist
	• Mental brand responses
	  – category requirement (if objective)
	  – inclination to buy (if objective)
	  – attitude towards brand
	  – brand 'benefit beliefs'
	• Attention diagnoses

Figure 6.5 Proposal for test design (Source: Percy and Rossiter, 1992, p 65)

no watertight proof of a correlation or relationship between acceptance (of the brand name or content of advertising presentation) in the short-term memory (as measured by awareness measurements) and advertising effectiveness in terms of behavioural responses (Lodish *et al.*, 1995).

6.7.3 'Ready-made' advertisements versus concepts

Test material that has been fully worked out can generally give a better idea of the end results or be evaluated more precisely than a rough version. However, when comparing the results of alternative ads they should really be at the same stage of development. A disadvantage of rough concepts (sketches, loose texts, moving storyboards) is that they require the respondent to make an 'interpretation leap'. On the other hand, the input can easily be adapted and there is less pressure on the researchers. The decision as regards 'readiness' of the test material can, to some extent, be based on the way in which the ad is expected to work (de Ruyter and Scholl, 1995). With informative advertisements two rough concepts will sometimes be enough; it is fairly easy for the researcher to assess the informative value of the ad from respondents' reactions, even if the ad has not been fully worked out. However, for image-forming advertising, finished test material is essential, as much of its persuasiveness is derived from the way in which visual images, music and text, and the pictorial rhythm are harmonised. Harmonisation requires precision, with colours and composition playing an important part in conveying the right mood.

Animatics

Animatics, or simulations of a commercial that still has to be finalised, are sometimes used to test an advertisement. This constitutes a last check on the ad concept, prior to final production. The advantage is obvious. The test is carried out prior to production and so can prevent expensive advertisements from being made which in the end are not used. It also means that improvements can be made at an early stage. The disadvantage of animatics is that not all commercials are easy to present in this way, though it is claimed that even the most difficult of subjects can be turned into an animatic if the client is prepared to pay enough.

Humour, mood, the use of well-known personalities, unique visual images and music are examples of basic advertising formats which can reinforce attention for the ad, recall of the advertising or brand association formation. Such things are almost impossible to simulate, as their ultimate production and focus are decisive in influencing their effect. Consequently, Gordon (1995) believes that the pre-testing of animatics can be very misleading. She suggests that it can indicate whether viewers understand a scenario and the brand's place within it, but that it cannot indicate whether the final commercial has more than a 50% chance of success in 'real life'. The only person, in Gordon's view, who can make a decision on this is the creative director, and not many clients will be prepared to base their decision-making on one person's verdict.

6.7.4 Representativeness of the sample

Existing attitudes and brand use

When analysing the results, a distinction should be made between users and non-users of the brand. After all, brand users have formed an opinion about the brand in question which is often more fundamental than that of non-users. Moreover, a positive attitude towards the brand ensures that a person is more inclined to pay attention to the brand's advertising and to process the message at a deeper level.

Sample make-up

The individuals who take part in a test should be representative of the target group for whom the advertisement is intended. In other words, the sample should be taken from a relevant population if conclusions are to be drawn for the entire population. The sample must contain a proper balance of the characteristics of the target group. This primarily involves the respondents' relationship with and attitude towards the brand, but geographical dispersion, age dispersion, education, sex and so on also play a part. With random samples the product and brand use should be recorded to facilitate comparison of the scores. It goes without saying that respondents should have no prior knowledge of the planned test.

Sample size

The size of the selected sample affects the chance of its representing the population as a whole. In general, the more respondents involved, the more solid the foundations on which conclusions can be based. In practice, however, the selected sample size tends to be one where every pound invested supplies a maximum of additional information (de Ruyter and Scholl, 1995). The eventual sample size also depends on sample homogeneity. If there are big differences between the individuals, for instance, in age, geographical dispersion, knowledge or use of the brand or product, a larger sample is needed, or they should be divided into separate samples.

Nomograms

If a sample is used to reflect a population, there are always 'random fluctuations' in the results. In other words, observed changes are not by definition caused by the commercial or print ad. The size of the margins within which the scores fluctuate depends on the size of the sample and required reliability. Such margins can be deduced from a nomogram. Table 6.1 and the example below explain how a nomogram works.

Look in the first column of the matrix for the line with the sample size (n) closest to the actual sample size being used. Then check in which column the result percentage (p) belongs. The appropriate margins of deviation can be read from the matrix cells.

For example, a test shows that 79 out of 97 respondents (81.4%) spontaneously name Grolsch as a brand of beer. Therefore n = 100 (closest to 97), column = 19–22/ 78–81 (81.4%), matrix cell = 8.4. Therefore the number of people spontaneously knowing Grolsch with a chance of 9.5 in 10 will be between 81.4% minus or plus 8.4%, so between 73% and 89.8%.

6.7.5 Qualitative research

Over the years qualitative research has been further developed, alongside quantitative research (Hansen, 1995). In 1950 traditional motivational research was conceived, after which standard depth and focus research was developed. Later, semiotic approaches also became popular.

When advertisements are being developed, qualitative research is frequently used. The same variables can be measured as in quantitative research, but whereas quantitative research is geared to determining the extent to which a particular response occurs,

Table 6.1 Deviation margins with normal distribution and 95% reliability

p = found percentage

n = size of sample	0.2 / 99.8	0.5 / 99.5	1 / 99	2 / 98	3 / 97	4 / 96	5 / 95	6 / 94	7–8 / 92–93	9–10 / 90–91	11–12 / 88–89	13–15 / 85–87	16–18 / 82–84	19–22 / 78–81	23–26 / 74–77	27–31 / 69–73	32–40 / 60–68	41–59
22	–	–	–	–	–	13.5	13.9	14.4	15.0	15.7	16.4	17.2	18.0	18.8	19.5	20.2	20.9	21.3
24	–	–	–	–	12.1	12.6	13.1	13.5	14.1	14.9	15.6	16.3	17.1	17.9	18.7	19.3	20.0	20.5
27	–	–	–	–	11.1	11.6	12.0	12.5	13.1	13.8	14.5	15.2	16.0	16.8	17.5	18.2	18.9	19.3
30	–	–	–	–	10.2	10.7	11.2	11.6	12.2	13.0	13.6	14.4	15.1	15.9	16.6	17.2	17.9	18.4
33	–	–	–	–	9.5	10.0	10.5	10.9	11.5	12.2	13.0	13.6	14.3	15.1	15.8	16.4	17.1	17.5
36	–	–	–	8.4	8.9	9.4	9.9	10.3	10.9	11.6	12.2	12.9	13.7	14.4	15.1	15.7	16.4	16.8
40	–	–	–	7.7	8.2	8.7	9.2	9.6	10.2	10.9	11.5	12.2	12.9	13.6	14.3	14.9	15.5	16.0
45	–	–	–	7.0	7.6	8.0	8.5	8.9	9.5	10.1	10.7	11.4	12.1	12.8	13.4	14.0	14.6	15.1
50	–	–	–	6.5	7.0	7.5	7.9	8.3	8.9	9.5	10.1	10.8	11.4	12.1	12.7	13.3	13.9	14.3
55	–	–	–	6.0	6.5	7.0	7.4	7.8	8.4	9.0	9.6	10.2	10.9	11.5	12.1	12.6	13.2	13.6
60	–	–	–	5.6	6.1	6.6	7.0	7.4	7.9	8.6	9.1	9.7	10.4	11.0	11.6	12.1	12.7	13.0
66	–	–	–	5.2	5.7	6.2	6.6	7.0	7.5	8.1	8.6	9.2	9.8	10.4	11.0	11.5	12.1	12.4
73	–	–	4.3	4.9	5.4	5.8	6.2	6.6	7.1	7.6	8.2	8.7	9.3	9.9	10.4	10.9	11.5	11.8
80	–	–	4.0	4.5	5.0	5.5	5.8	6.2	6.7	7.3	7.8	8.3	8.9	9.4	9.9	10.4	10.9	11.3
90	–	–	3.6	4.2	4.6	5.1	5.4	5.8	6.2	6.8	7.3	7.8	8.3	8.9	9.4	9.8	10.3	10.6
100	–	–	3.3	3.9	4.3	4.7	5.1	5.4	5.9	6.4	6.9	7.4	7.9	8.4	8.9	9.3	9.8	10.1
120	–	–	2.9	3.4	3.8	4.2	4.6	4.9	5.3	5.8	6.2	6.7	7.1	7.6	8.1	8.5	8.9	9.2
140	–	–	2.6	3.1	3.5	3.8	4.2	4.5	4.8	5.3	5.7	6.1	6.6	7.0	7.4	7.8	8.2	8.5
170	–	1.9	2.2	2.7	3.1	3.4	3.7	4.0	4.3	4.8	5.1	5.5	5.9	6.3	6.7	7.1	7.4	7.7
200	–	1.7	2.0	2.4	2.8	3.1	3.4	3.6	4.0	4.4	4.7	5.1	5.5	5.8	6.2	6.5	6.8	7.1

qualitative research deals in more depth with the elements of the advertisement, helping to explain the occurrence or the absence of responses.

Qualitative research can make use of different methods, the two best-known being:
- the individual (informal) interview;
- the group interview (or group discussion).

Both have the advantage of personal contact between researcher and respondent, but also their disadvantages. The individual interview, for instance, forces the respondent to think extensively about an ad on which he or she might not normally spend more than four seconds. This greatly increases awareness and can cause respondents to exaggerate positive and negative aspects. Moreover, they will concentrate on elements in the ad which in real life would not have been noticed.

The use of group interviews with focus groups to test ads at an individual level proves to be extremely risky, because it activates processes that the individual does not experience in real life. This does not really matter with research on behalf of advertising development, but when the advertising effects are being measured it is a real threat to validity. Percy and Rossiter (1992) suggest that when focus groups are used, discussions arise, which make individual processing of the advertising impossible. In addition, test reliability is at risk, in view of the small sample and the concomitant risk of mistakes. If a commercial has been shown and discussed at an earlier stage in a group discussion, its advertising effectiveness can no longer be ascertained with the same respondents at an individual level (Gordon and Langmaid, 1988).

6.8   CONCLUSIONS

When the decision is taken to hold a pre-test, all parties involved must agree on the test objectives, consequences of the results and the action that follows. There must be agreement on how the advertising should work and the relevant criteria for effectiveness. Various research procedures have shown that no one variable can predict the results of the campaign in the marketplace. Campaigns can be conducted in different ways and work in several dimensions at the same time. It is therefore worth measuring different responses in a pre-test. Advertising framework models can aid the selection of the variables to be measured. (See Chapter 5 for the most important responses to be measured with the various models.) However, not all responses can be included in the same test; some are more suited to qualitative testing, others to quantitative. So there is certainly a case for quantitative pre-testing with qualitative adjuncts.

A pre-test will only be valid if the testing method meets the appropriate requirements. In practice, however, time and resources are often in short supply, meaning that the design of the pre-test can never meet the demands which would be made in a scientific context. Consequently, test results should be handled with care, and evaluated accordingly. Currently pre-test results tend to be taken as 'truths', even though test validity or reliability may be slight. Exhibit 6.2 summarises the basic principles of pre-testing. The overview is based on PACT (positioning advertising copy-tests), which was drawn up in 1982 for ARF by Yuspeh et al., and is still relevant today.

A summary of the basic principles of pre-testing

- A good pre-test should carry out measurements which are relevant to the formulated advertising objectives. A good copy-test is based on the explicit advertising framework model used. This entails including variables in the test which are expected to be important for measurements concerning the brand. If, for instance, the likeability model is used, the likeability factor will logically play an important part in the copy-test.

- A good pre-testing system requires agreement between the advertiser and the advertising agency, before the test is carried out, about how the results will be used.

- In a good pre-test several measurements are carried out to ascertain an effect, since advertising effectiveness cannot be established with only a few measurements. The many effects of advertising can only be revealed if several measurements are taken.

- A good pre-test allows for the fact that attention and understanding are required if effects are to occur in the target group.

- It should be considered whether the respondent should be exposed to the ad more than once during the test.

- It should be realised that material which has been worked out in full can be evaluated more precisely than rough material. Furthermore, it is only possible to compare advertisements in the same stage of development.

- In a good pre-test the distracting factors of the surroundings are kept under control. Recall of the same ad depends on the circumstances in which the ad is tested:
    - Is the ad included in a clutter reel or in a programme context?
    - It should be remembered, with a reel test, that test results are affected by other ads on the reel;
    - In a programme context, the content of a specific programme may influence recall.

- In a good pre-test the basic principles of a good sample are taken into consideration. So:
    - the test should be carried out among the target group of the brand in question;
    - the sample must be representative of the target group;
    - proper geographical dispersion should exist;
    - the sample should be big enough to be used as a basis for a decision.

- A good pre-test is a valid and reliable test. This means researchers must be aware of the theoretical demands of pre-testing, thus making it possible to assess the results properly.

Exhibit 6.2

7 Tracking research

Mary Hoogerbrugge

7.1 INTRODUCTION

The effectiveness of advertising communication has been very much in the limelight in recent years. More and more advertisers are expressing a preference for a rational approach, alongside intuition and emotion. And, since all the elements of company policy are scrutinised and appraised as to effectiveness, investments in communication cannot escape. Questions like: 'Is it worth it, at the end of the day?', and 'Might not the budget be used more efficiently?' are heard with ever greater frequency. This discussion of advertising effectiveness takes place at three levels (see Figure 7.1)

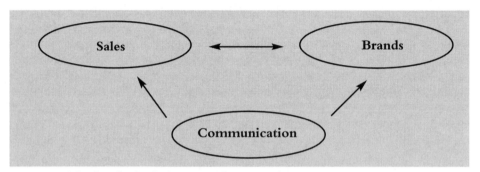

Figure 7.1 The three levels of advertising effectiveness discussion

The first level relates to direct sales figures. These can be obtained from agencies like Nielsen, AGB or GfK, and are the chief source of information on communication effectiveness for many advertisers. In the end, it all boils down to real money and hard figures. If sales figures go up, the advertising campaign must be working. By linking sales results or market shares directly to advertising expenditure, it is easier to understand advertising elasticity (the extent to which change in advertising budgets leads to a change in sales). It also means that all the other influencing factors must be taken into account. When all such factors are tied in with the market share, it is called market modelling, which is discussed in detail in Chapter 8.

Market modelling can provide insight into advertising elasticity, but it does not reflect developments in psychological brand responses. Advertising activities are generally aimed at strengthening the ties between brand and consumer and, by extension, increasing brand loyalty. It is therefore particularly important for brand builders to know what consumers are thinking or feeling. The second aspect of measuring advertising effectiveness looks at the effects of activities on behalf of the brand.

Lastly, it is important to look at the effectiveness of the actual communication activities – in other words, the campaign, advertisements and media deployment. How does a new campaign perform compared with the last one? Is it apparent that one ad in a run of commercials performs decidedly better than the others?

This chapter discusses how the first step towards understanding the effects of advertising can be taken, by continuously measuring the relevant mental advertising and brand responses – tracking research. The registration of sales is not taken into account here, because it does not measure consumer responses at an individual level, but only collects retail information. Such measurements do not provide insight into the intermediate advertising effects which might have led to buying behaviour. Consequently, they do not provide leads for the development of effective advertising campaigns. This chapter examines what tracking research entails exactly, and its advantages and disadvantages for advertisers.

It also looks at the difference between tracking studies, which focus on advertising effectiveness, and studies based on the relative position of the brand. The latter procedure is termed brand monitoring.

There is also a section reporting on exploratory research carried out in 1995 into European tracking practices. The overall conclusion is that few companies chart advertising effects continuously. Little change has been observed over the past few years in this respect, although more tracking models are available. However, increasing numbers of advertisers do seem to be seriously considering carrying out continuous research into effects.

Objectives

In order to gain insight into advertising effectiveness, it is not enough to follow consumer responses in the course of time. An important condition for accountability is the formulation of clear, specific objectives for judging a campaign or advertisement. Advertising can be aimed at a great many different effects. And similarly, a campaign can have several objectives.

However, research in the UK, the US and Norway has shown that advertising campaign objectives are rarely set, and, if objectives are set, they are invariably so general and vague that it is hard to measure whether they have been achieved (Britt, 1969; Majaro, 1970; Helgesen, 1992).

Hoogerbrugge *et al.* (1993) report that in the Netherlands, too, only a few of the 212 advertisers involved in their research set well-considered advertising objectives. Aims tended to be limited to 'increasing brand awareness' and 'improving the brand's

---

Well-considered advertising objectives

Hoogerbrugge *et al.* (1993) refer to 'well-considered' advertising objectives if they meet the following requirements:
- The advertising objective(s) must be written down, enabling all those involved to agree on what effects are aimed for, and to prevent misunderstanding on the direction of the advertising policy (Colley, 1964).
- The desired effect of the advertising campaign must be described (Floor and van Raaij, 1989).
- A target group within which the effect is to be achieved must be described (Floor and van Raaij, 1989; Franzen, 1992; Helgesen, 1992).
- A zero-measurement (preliminary test) should be carried out. This clarifies the situation in the market before the advertising campaign is started. A zero-measurement can be used as a benchmark with which advertising effects are compared (Floor and van Raaij, 1989; Helgesen, 1992).
- A period should be set within which the desired results are to be achieved.

Source: Hoogerbrugge *et al.* (1993)

Exhibit 7.1

image', though 'better' images were not indicated. According to these researchers, one of the main reasons for an absence of specific objectives is the fact that it is not often known exactly how advertising for the brand works. However, without clear and properly defined objectives, advertising will continue to be governed by intuition and irregularities. Exhibit 7.1 outlines the characteristics of well-considered advertising objectives.

7.2 TRACKING

Tracking research entails consistently measuring mental advertising and brand responses, over a long period of time (continuously), independently of specific advertising activities taking place at that time. 'Continuous' research involves an agreement with a research service to record and report on data periodically over this period. This provides some idea of developments of the responses over time. When measurements are carried out continuously, they result in time series. Consistent use of the same (quantitative) research methods and techniques facilitates comparison of the results. In tracking studies, measurements are carried out every week, every two weeks or every month within a sample, which is generally relatively small (and fresh) and is drawn from the target group. A sample of 100 respondents (per brand involved in the study) is usually sufficient for representative research (Percy and Rossiter, 1992). The sample size depends, on the one hand, on how far a significant difference between respondents has to be established and, on the other hand, on the margin of reliability used. It should be borne in mind that if a market is characterised by the presence of one or more small brands, the sample must be larger, in order to supply reliable measurements for these brands as well.

Admap (September 1998, p 49) indicates that the term 'tracking study' is used if a brand is tracked for a minimum of 12 months, and is or can be reported on at least four times a year.

7.2.1 Insight into the development of advertising effects

Continuous measurement gives a more dynamic and reliable picture of the development of advertising effects, compared with a post-test held once or twice only. After all, the results are less susceptible to incidental occurrences (Donius, 1986). Figure 7.2, showing the possible progress of spontaneous brand awareness of a new brand over 12 months, illustrates the importance of being able to view measurements over time.

This example shows how the choice of moments at which measurements are made influences the conclusions as regards the progress of brand awareness. If measurements are carried out in January and July, the results give the impression of an upward trend. However, it is quite a different matter if test results are based on measurements made in April and October. The true progress of awareness of brand X is only apparent if continuous measurements are made. Otherwise the course of the brand's progress can only be guessed at.

The development of spontaneous brand awareness is not only contingent on investment in advertising, but on a further series of factors, including media dispersion, share of voice, competitors' activities (marketing, for instance), other marketing activities on behalf of the brand and other (unforeseen) influences. Marketers can never know for sure whether the perceived results are the outcome of the advertising

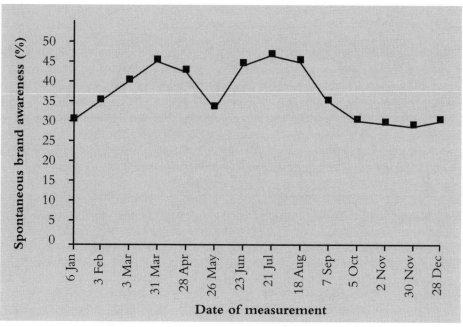

Figure 7.2 Advertising effects in the course of time: the progress of spontaneous awareness for a new brand

campaign (only), if all that is registered is advertising expenditure on their own brand. It is possible to discover what is at the bottom of a perceived development by comparing the ascertained results with the possible influences of the factors involved – for example, information concerning the media: which advertisers were operating during that week in the media, at what times and to what extent? (Sutherland, 1993, p 112).

7.2.2 Long and short-term effects

It is always difficult to decide when a post-test can best be held with traditional *ad hoc* measurements. Some effects will be apparent very quickly, others will take longer to emerge. On the one hand, the time taken for effects to emerge is due to the type of advertising campaign the advertiser conducts; to advertising pressure, dispersion, creativity, and so on. On the other hand, the test must take into account what effect is being aimed at. If brand associations are to be established or attitudes influenced, it generally takes longer than building up brand awareness.

If research is carried out over a longer period, the long and short-term effects need to be established. Information on the course of advertising effects, in the short and long term, will supply insight into the effect(s) of the current advertising campaign. This insight is helpful in formulating clear and specific advertising objectives in the future.

If the same advertising effects are charted continuously (every week, every two weeks or every month) and consistently, data series can be compiled. These allow comparison of the periodic results with those from past periods. When a tracking study is initiated, the first measurement is taken as the benchmark. Subsequent scores are compared with that benchmark, and the brand's progression can thus be charted.

Analysis of tracking data

According to Hankinson and Cowling (1992, pp 202–203), small samples are sufficient for tracking studies, as weekly samples can be combined when the results are analysed by adding up the weekly results. This creates a larger cumulative sample, the data for which have been collected at different times. Hankinson and Cowling believe that, ideally, tracking studies should use moving averages. A tracking study comprises at least 100 interviews, held every week, with a cumulative sample of n = 400, on a 'rolling' basis. Subject to the size of the weekly sample and the consistency of the results, the averages can be added up for four weeks, or for six weeks. These moving averages represent the results spread over the concentrated period. Figure 7.3 displays this in diagram form.

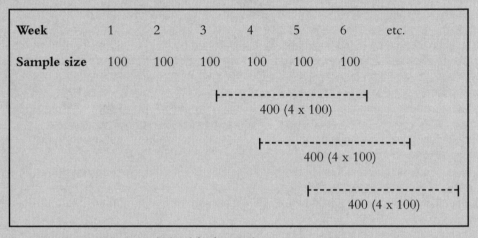

Figure 7.3 Moving averages calculated for four weeks

According to Donius (1986), if the figures are averaged in this way, reliable results are produced, as random fluctuations in the sample are evened out. The results reflect the effects of the campaign over time, in which the cumulative impact of the campaign is included.

This technique is especially relevant if continuity is expected in the variables. If that is not the case, moving averages can actually have an adverse effect, as their use can even out an incidental high or low in the data series. It means that the influence of certain events in the short term is not clearly expressed in the data series. If a marketer wants to know what effect a one-off in-store promotion has had on brand awareness, he or she must be able to see the results of that incidental activity. A second disadvantage of the use of moving averages is that a single high or low in the data series can influence the average for several weeks – something which can easily be misinterpreted.

Source: Hankinson and Cowling (1992)

Exhibit 7.2

If the tracking study continues for a longer period, such as three or five years, there is often little point in continuing to compare the results with an old benchmark. It is more sensible to compare them with more recent measurements (though this depends on the policy). In this way conclusions can be drawn on the development of the advertising and brand responses. Interested readers will find a more detailed discussion of the analysis of tracking data in Exhibit 7.2.

7.2.3 Establishing relationships

The series of data from tracking studies make it possible to work out relationships between the perceived changes in different variables. In this way possible connections between activities and effects can be tracked. If, for instance, a weekly record is kept of the advertising expenditure, expressed in the advertising budget or gross rating points (GRPs), and compared with the advertising awareness ascertained each week, conclusions can be drawn about the relationship between advertising presence and the measured results.

An example can be found in Figure 7.4, showing the relationship between advertising budget and advertising awareness, for campaign X for brand Y.

Here, again, it is impossible to state unequivocally whether the perceived changes are (only) the result of advertising expenditure for the brand in question without taking the other factors of influence into account – such as other communication activities and competitors' activities. The effect of competitors' activities can be demonstrated by comparing the results each week with the share of voice or percentage of total media spending in the market.

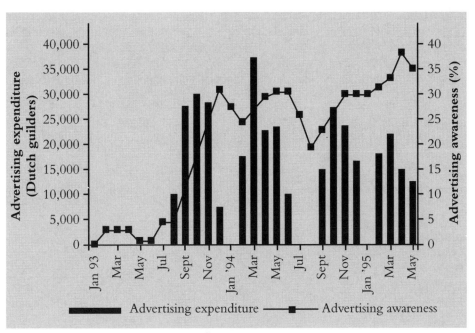

Figure 7.4 The relationship between advertising expenditure and advertising awareness (Source: Juchems, 1994b, p 4)

According to The Media Partnership (TMP), the advertiser's main concern is to determine the optimum advertising contact frequency per medium during a certain period of time. Appropriate questions in this context are:
- How often and at what intervals should the target group be exposed to the message?
- What happens when the campaign ceases?
- Which media best complement one another to obtain a synergetic effect?

Ideally, advertisers connect the data series of mental advertising and brand responses with advertising expenditure as well as with sales developments (results at the market level). A relationship can then be ascertained between consumer responses and purchasing figures which can be used as a basis for observations on the effectiveness of advertising activities at the market level.

However, no unequivocal verdict can be given on which intermediate advertising effects are connected with sales figures, and so should be measured in tracking tests. Usually discovering which variables supply the most information will be a process of trial and error. As shown in earlier chapters, this depends on different factors, like the hypotheses concerning advertising frameworks (ie, which advertising framework model is used) and the resulting advertising objectives. In the following sections two other factors will be discussed which play a part in the selection of research variables: the stage in a brand's life cycle and brand positioning. Brand positioning is considered in the section discussing the difference between advertising tracking and brand monitoring.

7.3 THE LIFE CYCLE OF A BRAND

Every brand starts out as a branded product, without awareness, positioning, market share and a consumer 'fan club'. When a brand is launched the main aim is to find customers for it. A great deal of money has to be spent to make people aware of it and persuade potential users to try it out (trial purchases). The brand has to be positioned. Advertising is used to create brand meanings and to clarify the brand's relative position in the market. In order to ascertain whether expenditure for the brand has been deployed correctly, tracking studies are used to measure whether the brand has developed according to plan. Has it generated trial? How is brand awareness progressing, and at what stage are brand associations? (Franzen and Holzhauer, 1991)

A branded product becomes a brand if it has a 'support group' who are prepared to put money down for it. An established brand is characterised by a market share. The brand becomes a success because it has built up a position in the market by differentiating itself from its competitors. Positioning within the market is one of the reasons for success.

At the growth stage, defence is more important than attack. The manufacturer must hold on to the growing number of consumers by keeping them satisfied and stopping them reacting to competitors' offers. Competing branders produce imitations in the hope of gaining from the new brand's momentum.

The success stage focuses on gaining the consumer's preference, resulting in commitment to the brand, which Ceurvorst (1994) describes as the psychological bond between the consumer and the brand. Preference can lead to brand loyalty. Brand preference depends on the strength and uniqueness of the brand associations. These must be supported and nurtured in order to keep preference intact. Insight into the differentiating brand associations compared with those of competitors (brand positioning) is therefore indispensable. During the brand's success stage it is not always necessary to track the progress of brand associations continuously, as established associations do not normally change quickly in a quiet market. It is probably enough to conduct a thorough qualitative study once every six months into the relevance, strength and uniqueness of the associations of the brand compared with those of its competitors.

Brands come in all shapes and sizes. Some have a very large associative network, others a small one. When asking consumers about brand meanings, it should be ascertained whether the associations mentioned are well-established or thought up on the spot. The associations will be many or few, according to the respondent's knowledge of and experience with the brand.

The most important associations to be measured will depend, among other things, on the brand's character (also termed identity). Brand identity relates to the 'brand's true self' – who the brand is. Readers are referred to Chapters 3 and 4 for a more detailed discussion of brands.

7.4   ADVERTISING TRACKING VERSUS BRAND MONITORING

There are two variants of tracking research. The first entails tracking methods that are aimed primarily at establishing a connection between advertising presence and consumer responses. This focuses on mental advertising responses and usually involves determining advertising awareness, advertising likeability and several brand responses. Some studies also include slogan awareness. This chapter has so far featured this type of tracking study.

Models of advertising expenditure and consumer responses can also supply relevant insight into the efficiency of media planning. Suppose a media drip strategy has been opted for, transmitting a sequence of impulses in the market. The fact that advertising awareness increases only slowly may cause those concerned to decide to raise the budget, facilitating continuous brand presence in the market and thus taking results to a higher level. Modelling can also assist strategic choices concerning the media mix – for instance, helping to chart the contributions from the different media.

Advertising tracking links the continuously charted consumer responses with advertising investment. One can observe (with the naked eye) whether there is a positive connection between mental advertising and brand responses, and sales figures and/or market shares, in this way ascertaining advertising accountability in the narrowest sense of the word. In this context, accountability means that the observer has an idea of the connection between investment in advertising and the results of the advertising activities. Ideally, the connection will be so clear that the effects can be predicted in advance, and the results can be established and explained in retrospect.

Insight into the connection between investment and returns also means that the optimum price:value ratio can be sought – ie, the ideal relationship between investment and returns.

The disadvantage of advertising tracking is that the measured consumer responses can only be related to advertising investments. But responses are not always generated by advertising alone. Promotional activities, product improvements, price changes and increased distribution can also have an effect. It is only possible to draw conclusions on the relative contribution of advertising if all the other factors are recorded, as is the case with brand monitoring. Only then is clear accountability a realistic prospect.

Brand monitoring

The focus of brand monitoring is the development of the brand. Since successful brands are very valuable, companies often base their policy on their brands. It is therefore important for branders to enhance all the elements of brand management: the analysis stage, the implementation stage, and the control of the entire process. In other words, it is just as important to control the whole process as it is to delineate brand strategies and implement brand policy. The focal point of a brand monitor is brand responses. Brand awareness, brand likeability, brand preference, brand perceptions, brand behaviour (as recorded by the respondent) are usually the most important, though advertising awareness and likeability are also generally determined.

Brand responses should be linked with other influential factors, including seasonal influences, price changes, changes in level of distribution, promotional activities, competitors' activities and so on. If an ongoing record is kept, a better understanding of the relative influence of advertising compared with other factors is provided.

The two tracking variants are not mutually exclusive. The difference is based on the focus of the measurements – is it advertising effects (advertising tracking) or the brand's position in the market (brand monitoring)?

7.5 THE PROS AND CONS OF TRACKING

Tracking results reflect the current situation of the brand. Consumer responses are followed continuously. Advertising tracking studies function as barometers, as it were; tracking records fluctuations and assists in the assessment of an altered situation. The results compiled over the years give an idea of advertising effects for the brand in question. Time series provide a wealth of information which can serve as a guideline when new campaigns are developed or operating campaigns are adapted. The average scores for mental responses covering different campaigns can, with time, be used as standard scores.

The chief advantage of tracking is possibly the fact that one can learn from the historical analyses. From that point of view, tracking has both a strategic and a tactical function. In terms of the former, tracking gives insight into the effects of advertising campaigns for the brand. The tactical function of tracking is the leads it provides on the effectiveness of specific elements in the message, media input, and so on.

A major advantage of tracking is that it can be used to determine effects in the short and long term. With long-lasting campaigns it is then possible, in theory, to adjust a campaign mid-course. Unfortunately, the scope for short-term intervention proves to be limited in practice.

Figure 7.5 gives an example of the development of advertising awareness for a new brand in the consumer durables sector. Advertising awareness clearly develops rapidly here (though this does not mean the brand is successful – a person might know about a new brand, but not necessarily want to buy it).

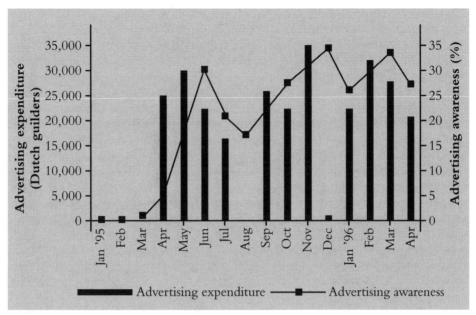

Figure 7.5 Relationship between advertising expenditure and advertising awareness for a new product (Source: Juchems, 1995, p 11)

The marketer can conclude from Figure 7.5 that advertising awareness is admittedly growing fast, but if the media budget is cut or the ad is omitted from the media, it drops fast too. Continuous dispersion of advertising investments might keep advertising awareness at the desired level.

If mental advertising and/or brand responses are ascertained continuously and related to the characteristics of the ads or the type of campaign being conducted, it is possible to obtain insight into which characteristics are, and which are not, of influence (see section 6.6, page 235). Prue (1995), suggests using a classification system with respect to the way in which the campaign expects to achieve the objectives. He makes a distinction between three functional advertising strategies, on which to base the classification of advertising campaigns, as presented in the persuasion, involvement and salience models. Persuasive advertising seeks to present product benefits, new uses or previously unperceived needs, which can be used to the consumer's advantage. Involving advertising entails linking more emotional values to the brand, by means of emotions which play a part or are evoked in the ad. Salience features striking advertising, which specifically differentiates the brand from its competitors. Figure 7.6 overleaf contains an example of a campaign which did not affect advertising awareness positively.

A tracking study can also reveal campaign wear-out (when an extra insertion/airing of an ad starts to have less impact on the effect objectives). Figure 7.7 shows that the campaign had good results to start with, but that as time went by advertising awareness started to drop, despite the investments made in that period.

Tracking research can be used not only for advertising effects on one's own brand, but also to determine the effects of competitors' advertising on their brands (brand monitoring). It enables marketers to compare the results of their own advertising strategy and those of competing brands.

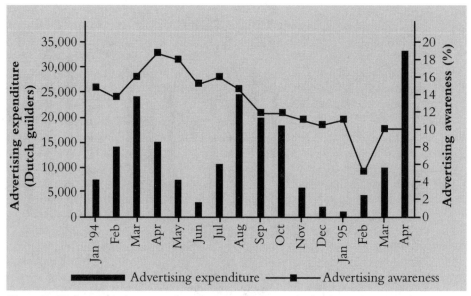

Figure 7.6 Relationship between advertising expenditure and advertising awareness for an inactive campaign (Source: Juchems, 1995, p 15)

Chapter 4 discusses how equilibrium models can be used to determine the influence of competitors on the brand in question. Models of this type show how one brand's profit can be the loss of one or more other brands. Registration of the characteristics and effects of competitors' campaigns increases knowledge of the effect of certain advertising strategies in the product field in question. In addition, it supplies insight into competitors' advertising activities and, accordingly, opportunities for taking swift counteraction. Information on competitors' activities also helps to interpret the results of our own activities.

The disadvantage of tracking research is that, compared with one-off measurements, it is a time-consuming, demanding method for charting the effects of advertising on the brand position. It is, consequently, classed as an expensive exercise. The price is relatively high, considering what is usually spent on advertising research, though, in absolute terms, it is in fact quite reasonably priced compared with advertising expenditure for major brands. Moreover, standard research design, automation of data collection and efficient reporting can keep costs down.

Tracking studies cannot, of course, find answers to all research questions. And so, ideally, there should be an integrated research system in which the different elements are interconnected and mutually reinforcing. Tracking studies are an excellent basis for additional research, which can examine the issues more specifically. Continuous measurements, for example, provide a framework for pre-testing. If the same (or very similar) variables are included in a pre-test as in the tracking study, the two studies can be compared and contrasted. Tracking research can also be used as a point of departure for more extensive brand equity research. Brand equity is measured using such variables as brand awareness, brand associations and perceptions, brand evaluations (attitude, affinity, preferences), brand use (penetration, loyalty), price elasticity of the brand, and stretch possibilities of the brand (new products, new markets). Many of these variables can be included in a tracking study, but additional data are also usually needed.

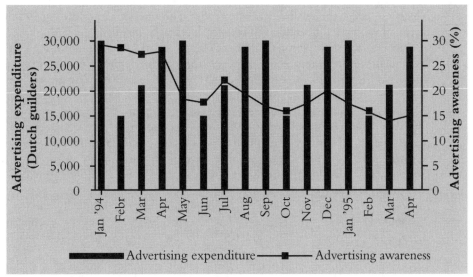

Figure 7.7 Relationship between advertising expenditure and advertising awareness: campaign wear-out (source: Juchems, 1995, p 15)

In-depth qualitative research into brand experience and likeability, aimed at gathering together the wealth of association networks and their meaning for people, will always be necessary. It is also advisable to ensure consistency so that studies which are held every one or two years can reflect a development in time.

Finally, the data series which tracking research produces form an important basis for modelling. The aim of tracking research is, after all, not just to register what takes place in consumers' minds. The ultimate aim is to produce something of value, in explanatory and predictive terms. If that is to be achieved, the data series should be related to market results on the one hand, and investments on the other.

This type of modelling can give an idea of the connection between advertising responses and brand responses, as well as the relationship between investments and sales results in the long run. Such insight helps to justify the fact that choices are made in advance and to demonstrate the results of activities in retrospect.

The following section examines which research methods are best suited for use in tracking studies.

7.6 CHOICE OF RESEARCH METHOD AND DESIGN

Tracking can be carried out with a variety of methods, each with its pros and cons. Consequently the method used should be decided by the specific measuring problems.

Tracking is usually carried out by telephone interviews, possibly using the computer (CATI – computer-assisted telephone interviewing). The advantage of such interviews is that they are not too expensive, and people who live far away and are hard to reach can easily be included in the sample. In America 80% of interviews are conducted on the phone (van Westendorp, 1996). A disadvantage of telephone surveys is that respondent involvement is lower than that of a personal interview, for example, which can affect the reliability of the replies. The interviewer must bear in mind that there is a substantial likelihood of socially acceptable answers.

Face-to-face surveys using CAPI are being carried out to an increasing extent. The respondent's involvement is often greater than with telephone interviewing, and the interviewer is more likely to notice socially acceptable answers. The greatest advantage of this method is that visual stimuli can be used, thus facilitating recall of the ads. If the focus of the study is to measure advertising responses, personal interviewing is advisable. The researcher must take into account that ad recognition is often overestimated, which can result in an overestimation of the actual reach of the ad. This is particularly true for campaigns that have been running for some time and so are firmly embedded in the memory. A disadvantage of personal interviewing is that it is expensive. Costs can be limited by recruiting respondents in a popular place, for instance, a shopping centre or station. The interview is usually carried out on the spot. However, this approach has the disadvantage that the composition of the sample can vary substantially from one measurement to another. Respondent selection criteria must be clearly specified. In addition, shopping centres differ in the type of people they attract. The town and the shopping centre must therefore be chosen carefully.

Written surveys are carried out less often when measuring mental advertising and brand responses. This method has its limitations for measuring spontaneous advertising and brand awareness (Donius, 1986, p 27). However, it is used to ascertain brand use (reported by the respondent). A great disadvantage of written surveys is the high risk of non-response.

7.6.1 Panels

When selecting the design of a tracking study, another consideration is whether to use a panel or a different population sample every time. A panel has the advantage that advertising effects can be isolated fairly easily, because the different relevant variables are measured in the same households each time. It is possible to tie in mental responses with behavioural responses directly. An obvious disadvantage is that a good panel is very expensive to build up and maintain – too expensive for one company. Another potential disadvantage is that 'sample bias' is sometimes prevalent in panels. It proves difficult in practice to keep up a representative panel (Francis, 1994, pp 101–116). Panels are subject to 'wastage' to some extent and cannot be restructured indiscriminately, in view of the requirement for representativeness. There is also a danger with panel research that respondents behave differently because they are on a panel.

In addition, many of the questions that have to be asked are not suited to panel research, since, in the end, respondents learn from the research itself. This is possibly the greatest drawback. If respondents are repeatedly asked the same questions, it is very likely that their answers will be influenced by the answers they gave for previous measurements. These are termed learning effects. According to market researchers, this risk is particularly great in the areas of brand awareness and brand attitude. Consequently, almost all research services select a new sample for every measurement. However, this means that the samples have to be properly matched each time to ensure the observed changes are not caused by differences in sample composition. An ideal solution would be to combine the panel and *ad hoc* methods to retain the advantages of both (Haley and Gattey, 1968). Such a design entails interviewing some respondents

The Silver Standard (Bronner, 1993)

In *The Silver Standard* (a report recommending guidelines for research into the effect of government campaigns) Bronner concludes that a combination of panel and *ad hoc* research is the best means of getting an idea of the possible effects of campaigns. Assuming that a group can be found that has not been in contact with the campaign, Bronner opts for a mock-experimental variant of Solomon's (1949) 'four-groups design', along with an *ad hoc* pre-measurement to ascertain questions that can spark off a learning effect among respondents. Solomon's design uses control groups who are not exposed to the stimulus, and/or are not included in the pre-measurement, in order to confirm whether differences in measuring results are caused by contact with the stimulus and not by the fact that a (pre-)measurement had been made.

Like Solomon, Bronner assumes that the effect of an advertising campaign is the same as the difference between the sample measurement and the pre-measurement for those confronted with the campaign, once any unexplained variables have been removed through comparison with the same difference for the groups who did not have ad contact (Bronner, 1993, p 110).

With this design it is also difficult to check whether, when an advertisement has featured in the media, respondents have been exposed to that ad or not, because they are invariably unaware if they have. So it continues to be difficult to attribute effects to a specific campaign.

Exhibit 7.3

from the old group at the same time as some new respondents. This reveals any learning effects. Exhibit 7.3 deals with this in more detail.

7.6.2 Single-source research and data fusion

According to Jones (1995c), panel methods are eminently suitable for determining the direct connections between media behaviour and buying behaviour at an individual level – the panel can help to tie exposure to advertising for a brand directly with the purchasing of that brand. This is termed single-source research (see section 2.2, page 30, for an explanation of how single-source research is carried out). Both media behaviour and buying behaviour are measured repeatedly with the same people in the course of time, enabling, in theory, the course of the causal relationship between seeing a commercial and buying a brand/product to be established. This might, in fact, provide an answer to the accountability question. However, this method does have some practical drawbacks (see Exhibit 1.1, page 19). The representativeness of the participating households is often slight, due to the pressure exerted on respondents. Neither do advertisers seem particularly keen on pure single-source research (Jones, 1996).

Fused data are sometimes used as an alternative for single-source research. This entails attributing the information supplied by one particular respondent in one particular study to respondents in another study. In the past, fusion techniques were mainly applied to the customary variables, like demographics (age, education, sex). It was assumed that behaviour variables could be applied to another set of data in the same way as the demographic variables. So when, for example, data for print and television were fused, it was thought that, given a certain age, education or sex, the chance that a person would read a magazine or newspaper was constant and not dependent on viewing behaviour. This has proved to be an exaggerated assumption, as there is unfortunately no single demographic variable that fully determines both types of media consumption (den Boon, 1996, pp 142–146). A woman who works full time, for instance, will have less time to watch television than a woman of the same age who does not work.

In an effort to meet the objections to data fusion, AGB Taylor Nelson use auxiliary variables which can serve as variables which link the various databases available (for example, social/career status data can be linked with brand buying behaviour). Demographics can predict television viewing behaviour only to a limited extent, so viewing behaviour has been added to the data on women in AGB Taylor Nelson's Superpanel (Roberts, 1996).

In the Superpanel, consumers record all their supermarket purchases using a bar code scanner. In addition, magazine and newspaper reading habits are ascertained and viewing behaviour recorded through a questionnaire. Television viewing is determined with great accuracy in the UK's BARB panel, by means of 'people meters'. Respondents are also asked about their print viewing behaviour, but no information is available on buying behaviour or other media use. Equivalent variables in the two sets of data mean that the viewing behaviour of one panel can be 'fused' with the print data in the buying panel (den Boon, 1996).

7.6.3 Multi-client research

Multi-client research is usually set up by the research agency and offered to its clients. Not only are there financial advantages to this, but such studies give advertisers information on the results of other brands. In theory, this information can serve as a benchmark. In practice, however, circumstances invariably differ so much from one market to another that the tracking results of brands in different categories cannot be used. The most valuable information for an advertiser concerns the specific category, the brands within it and their relative positions. Comparisons can also be made between the results of the various brands and expenditure on advertising for brands within the category. So these surveys are generally held within a product category or delineated market.

However, many advertisers consider it a great disadvantage that in multi-client research the competitive edge which fresh insight ought to provide is lost. Tracking is usually carried out for one specific client, in view of the tactical and strategic considerations for its use. This does not apply when clients are in different sectors.

7.7 MENTAL ADVERTISING AND BRAND RESPONSES

Tracking studies are used to ascertain intermediate advertising effects consistently, thus improving understanding of the relationship between advertising activities and sales developments. Listed below are the mental advertising and brand responses that can lead to buying behaviour. Chapters 3 and 4 discussed the measurement of the various responses at length, within the framework of the Advertising Response Matrix. Here the possibilities of including mental advertising and brand responses in tracking research are merely reviewed, highlighting the following responses:
- advertising recall;
- advertising likeability;
- brand awareness;

- brand associations and perceptions;
- brand evaluations (attitude, affinity, buying intention, preferences);
- brand use, self-reported (penetration, loyalty).

These are also the responses which are measured in most tracking research. However, it is not possible to make generalisations on the relevance of measuring certain responses, as this depends on the goal of the research and the objectives of the brand and advertising. Those objectives stem, in turn, from the stage in the brand's life cycle, the brand's position in the market and which advertising framework model applies.

7.7.1 Advertising recall

Spontaneous advertising recall refers to the respondent's ability to bring to mind the advertising for a certain brand, without information on the content or ad execution.

Questions which might be asked when measuring spontaneous ad recall are:
- Can you remember having seen advertising for detergents recently?
- And can you also remember having seen advertising for Persil?

Respondents may then be asked in what medium they had seen, heard or read the ad. However, the reliability of this question is debatable. The medium of television often predominates in the answers, even if other media have been used. It is therefore advisable to present the respondent with all media types, and examine recall for each. Research shows that weeks can pass before a certain magazine issue is read (Millward Brown, 1994b). So when measuring awareness of advertising in magazines, it should always be borne in mind that it builds up in time.

Aided recall is the term used when the respondent calls to mind the ad with the help of a cue. Cues facilitate matters and vary in character. For example, a description of the ad content can be given to trigger recall.

Advertising recognition

When ascertaining advertising recognition, visual stimuli are an obvious choice, though the stimuli used will depend on the research method. For example, only radio commercials and other auditive stimuli can be used with telephone interviews. Practically all types of ads can be shown in face-to-face interviews.

Opinions differ with respect to the importance of measuring advertising awareness in tracking research. Millward Brown sets great store by advertising awareness, since it helps to ascertain the 'awareness index' (increase in advertising – usually television – awareness based on 100 GRPs). It is possible, using this index, to relate advertising and sales figures, a process also known as sales modelling (Hollis, 1994b).

Du Plessis (1994b) sees advertising awareness as a relevant variable for media planning. Its development is, he believes, one of the factors which can be used to assess whether media planning has been effective. If the desired increase in advertising awareness does not occur, an extra 'burst' of advertising might be a solution.

Not everyone considers the measurement of advertising awareness to be worthwhile. After all, the main aim of advertising is not to be remembered, but to achieve a useful effect (Knecht, 1990, p 37). Sometimes advertising is remembered and the desired effect achieved, but this is not a causal connection – people especially remember the advertising of brands/companies they know and like. Sometimes the correlation between effects and attitudes actually proves to be negative: people remember the advertising because they dislike the brand/company.

Woodside and Wilson (1985) researched the correlation between advertising awareness and the brand's position in the memory. They discovered a positive connection between advertising awareness and brand awareness. It proves strongest with new brands, but is more difficult to determine with established brands. However, they do not feel there is reason to assume that those connections no longer exist with such brands.

Blair (1987, in Franzen, 1994) also discovered a strong connection between television advertising awareness and brand awareness. It could be concluded from these two studies that, in view of the correlation between the two variables, it is sufficient to continuously measure either advertising awareness or brand awareness in tracking research. However, when beginning tracking research, there is a danger that it will be based on the wrong assumptions. It is therefore advisable to include both variables at the initial stage. Analysis of the historical data series will then reveal which variable supplies most information.

7.7.2 Advertising likeability

The attitude towards an advertisement or campaign relates to what is referred to as 'likeability' in advertising literature. This term refers to a positive attitude concerning the ad and can relate to message or presentation. Likeability of an advertisement or campaign can be ascertained in tracking research by means of attitude scales or 'report marks'. Figures 7.8 and 7.9 contain examples of a Likert scale and semantic differentials (Osgood scales), respectively.

The Likert scale is a multiple-item scaling technique, devised by Likert, with which a respondent's attitude, for instance, can be measured by working out per respondent a sum of scores for a number of Likert items. A Likert item is a statement formulated in the negative or the positive, for which respondents must indicate, using a five-point scale, the extent to which they agree or disagree with that statement. The items must be relevant to the construct which is being measured (NIMA, 1993, p 126).

A semantic differential is a scaling technique designed by Osgood for measuring a respondent's opinion on an object (product, brand, company, person), using a number of bipolarities (good–bad, fast–slow, hard–soft, and so on). A seven-point scale is generally used (NIMA, 1993, p 139).

I like the commercial for brand X very much:

```
|----------------|----------------|----------------|----------------|
Absolutely        Don't            Neither          Agree            Absolutely
don't agree       agree            agree nor                         agree
                                   disagree
```

Figure 7.8 Example of a Likert scale

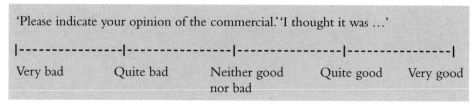

'Please indicate your opinion of the commercial.' 'I thought it was ...'

|----------------|----------------|----------------|----------------|

Very bad   Quite bad   Neither good   Quite good   Very good
                                 nor bad

Figure 7.9 Example of a semantic differential

According to du Plessis (1994a), likeability is the key to success for an advertising commercial. Whether viewers or readers like it (or not) is the factor that guarantees a commercial will get their attention and be remembered (or not). Recall of the commercial (linked to the correct brand) is, in turn, a condition for achieving other advertising objectives.

Impact Information, the South African research company, has been conducting research for the past 12 years into the likeability of more than 15,000 commercials in South Africa. Each week 200 respondents are asked whether they can remember a commercial that has been aired for two to three weeks, and if they consider it to be 'likeable'. Reactions to the commercials continue to be surveyed for another six weeks, for continued measurement of recall and likeability.

The results of this research are used to optimise media planning, and as a basis for the decision to produce a new commercial if wear-out is observed.

7.7.3 Brand awareness

It is particularly useful to track brand awareness in the course of time for a new or not very well-known brand. However, brand awareness is relatively unimportant for established brands like Coca-Cola, Adidas and Levi's. What matters, in the end, are the associations with which a brand is linked in the consumer's memory: the brand meanings. Brand awareness is needed if the mental conception of the brand is to be kept vivid and brand preference generated (see sections 3.3.2, page 53; 3.3.8.2, page 67; and section 4.2.1, page 101).

When brand awareness (spontaneous or aided) is measured, it is difficult to check to what extent the advertising campaign has contributed to the level of awareness. The researcher can try to solve this problem by asking appropriate questions or linking brand awareness scores to advertising awareness scores. However, it will always be difficult to establish what is cause and what effect. Brand awareness is included in almost all tracking studies. First, because increased brand awareness is one of the objectives of many brands, or is seen to be necessary for achieving other objectives. Second, presumably because brand awareness is relatively easy to ascertain.

7.7.4 Brand meanings

Many advertising campaigns for new and established brands are aimed at establishing, changing or reinforcing brand associations (often termed 'image' in practice). Research into the brand's meanings for consumers is needed to verify whether the campaign has been successful. Sometimes brand personality will be the focus of attention, sometimes the linking of specific emotions or values to the brand (see sections 3.3.3, page 55, and 4.4.2 to 4.4.4, pages 158–169).

Important associations tied in with the brand are those to do with the product category, the perceived price and perceived quality. If a person is considering buying a new car, that person, in the opinion of Volkswagen dealers, should think of their make immediately. The perceived price and quality are important points of differentiation – the decision to buy a brand (or not) is often based on these two criteria.

However, quality and price perception often provide too little insight into the core meanings of a brand. To discover which brand associations are most important for the consumer, additional, in-depth research is needed. Its results can be a basis for setting up tracking research. In Exhibit 7.4 several qualitative research methods are discussed in brief.

The fact that only a small amount of associations can be measured with tracking research makes it important to know which are the foremost associations for consumers and which play a part when they are considering buying a brand. Probing questions run the risk of generating brand associations on the spot, so it is wise to determine first of all which brand associations are mentioned spontaneously.

It is debatable whether it is necessary to carry out quantitative appraisals of meanings and perceptions of brands continuously. Strongly embedded brand associations are often difficult to change in the short term. Moreover, it is impossible to determine fully the wealth and range of the brand associative network in quantitative research. It is often more worthwhile, therefore, to subject established brands to extensive qualitative research twice a year. If the same research design is used consistently, the results can be compared and developments tracked in time.

Continuous tracking of associations is certainly relevant for new, still unknown brands. As yet the consumer has no embedded mental image of the brand. Continuous research can track whether the brand image is developing according to plan. Additional qualitative research is, in these circumstances, intended to provide more in-depth information.

Qualitative brand research

Brand associations can be measured by qualitative research (brand diagnostics) in the target group. This is one of the major sources of information on the relationship between the brand and its consumers. Research companies and advertising agencies have developed their own methods and techniques for charting all the associations, attitudes and values which consumers have in their minds concerning the brand. Qualitative methods include free association, in which the respondent is faced with an open question to which he or she must react, and projective techniques. The latter include:
- a 'collage' – respondents are asked to express their ideas and opinions about a brand by making a collage of images usually taken from magazines;
- 'photosort' – respondents seeks to clarify their associations with the brand by selecting a number of photos from an existing set;
- role-play – an 'acted' conversation in which the moderator gives participants a particular role to play;
- personification – respondents are asked to describe the brand as if it were a person;
- psycho-drawings – associations or projections connected with a brand are expressed in a drawing by the respondent.

Exhibit 7.4

7.7.5 Brand evaluation

Brand attitude

Apart from measuring brand awareness and brand associations, it is also necessary to chart the consumer's attitude to the brand, which is closely related to behaviour. It can predict behaviour, but also result from it. A consumer with a negative attitude will not be inclined to buy the brand. The ultimate decision on whether or not to do so depends partly on situational circumstances (presence and place in the shop, price). The consumer can develop a positive attitude towards the brand as a result of regular use.

Not all brands within a brand repertoire have the same position (of preference). Preference is a relevant aspect to be measured because it is thought to have a positive relationship with the size and stability of the market share. With small brands especially, it is important to measure the consideration set. Smaller brands require relatively more advertising activities to maintain brand awareness, as they enjoy less support from brand use – in other words, because they are bought less often than big brands, brand awareness is supported less in that way.

Van Westendorp (1996, p 32) states that national market leaders, like Douwe Egberts and Heineken in the Netherlands, often have more brand awareness than their market share justifies. They cannot improve their brand awareness, and must therefore improve the structure of their franchise (the strength of their relationship with consumers), to ensure that more people have a greater preference for the brand, and, in the end, demand it (van Westendorp, 1996) (see sections 3.3.6, page 62, and 4.2.5, page 117).

Buying intention

Buying intention is a mental characteristic; it is not actual behaviour, but the inclination to buy in a certain way. Actual purchase will depend, among other things, on the situation during purchase. Competitors' activities in the shop can persuade the consumer to choose a different brand after all. Actual purchase also depends on price. This is why the term 'usage intention' is sometimes used.

It has already been commented in Chapter 4 that, for fast-moving consumer goods, buying intention is not particularly relevant. It would seem to coincide more with consumer buying behaviour in the past than to predict behaviour in the future.

7.7.6 Brand use

Eventual advertising objectives are generally geared to influencing consumer buying behaviour, either immediately or within several months or years. In order to appraise the connection between advertising activities and buying behaviour, it must be possible to tie in mental advertising and brand responses with consumer buying behaviour. This enables a judgment on how advertising has worked for the brand (or not). So the determination of buying behaviour is an important element of much tracking research. Readers are referred to Chapter 4 for further information on the subject.

7.7.7 Designing tracking research

A design for good tracking research is summed up in ten steps (adapted from Speath, 1993a).

Step 1

Use a design containing data which relate to all stages in the advertising process. This should start with media reach figures for each individual ad and end with ultimate buying behaviour. The following variables should be taken into account:
- accurate media reach figures, GRPs, SOV, advertising expenditure;
- valid test measurements;
- brand awareness – TOMA, spontaneous brand awareness, aided brand awareness;
- advertising awareness – recognition and recall of ad and content of the message (Has my advertising been seen? And, more importantly, what do consumers deduce from the message?);
- brand associations (which associations are unique, differentiating, relevant?);
- brand attitude (preferences, relationship with brand);
- intention to buy the brand;
- brand buying behaviour;
- promotional environment.

When selecting variables, the ultimate aim in measuring them should be borne in mind. The important issue is how the brand develops in the marketplace. Questions must therefore be asked that are relevant to marketing.

As van Herk (1994) comments, the chief focus of advertising is to create brand awareness plus a growing market share, or the creation of brand preference or a close relationship with the brand.

Step 2

For every measurement, methods should be used that are as valid and reliable as possible. The validity and reliability of the individual measurements determine in the end the value of the entire tracking tool, and the resulting market models.
- Brand awareness should preferably be measured weekly.
- Ideally ad recognition should be established by means of clear visual stimuli.
- Relevant brand associations are produced by qualitative pre-testing and tie in with the advertising objectives.
- Scanner data are needed (involving a panel) to determine buying behaviour.

Step 3

Data should be integrated as early as the research design stage. Samples will not be identical, as different sources will be used. Misleading conclusions may therefore result. Different data should be adapted to facilitate comparison.

Step 4

Models of relationships between variables should be constructed. Comparison of the various individual measurements is the only way to gain insight into the effect of advertising on the brand in question.

Step 5

The researcher should realise that sales figures are vital. Seasonal influences, and the influence of price and promotional activities, must be separated from rough sales figures before a correlation can be ascertained between advertising and sales figures.

Step 6

Advertisers can try to understand the correlation between copy and media choice by examining whether and how the advertising message has come across in the target group (with the different media). These analyses can enable them to draw conclusions about media choice, copy, scheduling, and so on.

Step 7

It should be considered how the advertisement should influence brand awareness, brand associations or behaviour. How does advertising for the brand in question work in the product category?

Step 8

The results of the pre-tests should be integrated with those of tracking studies. The combination of the dynamics of the advertising process and the effect of the specific ad provides a broader insight, on which decisions can be based regarding advertising budget, repetition of advertisements and scheduling of the advertising campaign.

Step 9

A focus on the sales figures is not, in the end, sufficient. The research focus should be about the brand's financial value. The value of the brand for the consumer, in terms of brand awareness, relevant, differentiating and strong brand associations and brand preference, results in financial value for the brand's owner.

Step 10

The tracking study must be attuned specifically to the brand in question (life cycle, postioning, character), the presumed advertising framework model and the concomitant objectives, if optimum results are to be obtained.

7.8 TRACKING IN PRACTICE

In recent years, interest in continuous effectiveness research has been growing. More and more research services and marketers are becoming convinced of the necessity of ascertaining advertising effects on a continuous basis, in order to get an idea of the correlation between advertising and sales developments. The overview of tracking research facilities published each year by *Admap* shows that the supply of tracking research is quite substantial in the UK. In Germany it is growing (Pulch, 1995), and Biel (1995) reports that in the US too more tracking research is being initiated, leading to better developed methods. In the Netherlands, growing numbers of market research companies provide tracking research, but in practice effects measurements still prove to be mainly *ad hoc*, if they are carried out at all.

The repertoire of tracking methods is growing. How, one wonders, are studies carried out in practice? Methods prove to differ considerably within one country, and between countries. This is partly due to the way people expect advertising for a certain brand to work, which is most apparent in the difference between American and European tracking methods. Europeans focus primarily on intermediate advertising effects in order to provide a plausible explanation for advertising effectiveness, whereas the Americans stress the correlation between advertising and sales figures. Stavely (1993) describes this difference as 'added values focus' versus 'sales focus'.

The difference in repertoire is also due to the fact that most tracking methods are specifically attuned to clients' wishes. A client's research budget, for instance, has to be taken into account. In addition, assumptions concerning advertising effect, advertising objectives, relative brand position in the market, the stage in the brand life cycle and the goal of tracking affect the content of the tracking study.

The next section describes the tracking research situation in Germany, the UK and the Netherlands, on the basis of an extensive literature study and examination of research companies' brochures. In this context, it refers to European tracking practice.

7.8.1 European tracking practice

Data collection and reporting

Advertisers' needs for up-to-date information vary. Advertising budgets, the frequency with which advertisers themselves and their competitors change campaigns, and the regularity with which new brands are launched in the market are some of the factors that affect their needs. Consequently, the frequency of data collection and reporting can vary from one market to another. Information from British, German and Dutch research services shows that they do not all collect and report on data every week; some conduct their measurements every week, others every two weeks or every month. In Germany they frequently collect data in six or four-week intervals, or even less frequently per year. Some services make their reports once a week, others once a month or once a quarter.

The researcher should consider, depending on the number of brands in the study, what the most reliable sample size is (Percy and Rossiter, 1992). In the UK and Germany, sample size is determined by the frequency of the measurements, among other things. The more frequent they are, the smaller the sample size tends to be with each measurement. However, if, with quantitative research, the sample is too small, there is a risk that the results will not be representative of the population as a whole. When, in particular, smaller brands are included in a study, the sample must be large enough to give a representative reflection of small brands with low penetration.

If the budget does not permit a large enough sample for weekly interviews, the client should consider whether the size of the sample should suffer, or whether measurements might be carried out less frequently, such as every two weeks or every month. Such decisions should take account of their effect on the survey's representativeness. Another solution might be to increase the sample for a certain period of time if reliable conclusions concerning the results have to be made at some stage.

Sample size ranges from n = 5000, divided over four survey moments a year, to n = 2600, with n = 50 per week. Figure 7.10 contains an illustration of different tracking frequencies and corresponding sample sizes.

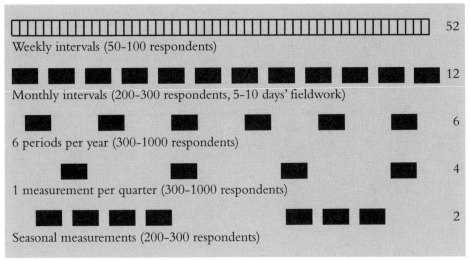

Figure 7.10 Different tracking frequencies (Source: Juchems, 1995, p 2)

The *Admap* review (September 1998) indicates that around two-thirds of the research companies in Britain specifically attune the sample to the target group in the product category; the remaining third use a standard selection, for instance, housewives up to the age of 55, or adults aged 15 and above.

Data collection methods differ widely in the countries reviewed. By and large, British and German research companies collect information by telephone and/or in personal interviews. Personal interviews are necessary if brand awareness of relatively unknown brands or new campaigns (or ads) is being researched. Consumers prove to make mistakes easily, which can be prevented if, for example, visual stimuli are used. Some companies use written surveys; some use panels.

Many clients in the Netherlands prefer telephone interviewing, for financial reasons. However, the time available and the complexity of the questionnaire also affect the choice of research method. All research companies design their own questionnaires. The questions will depend on the data collection method (phone, face-to-face or written). The sequence of questions is also determined by the response on which the survey focuses. The most important response is often the first to be measured, to prevent it being influenced by preceding questions.

Effectiveness criteria

Tracking research measures mental advertising and brand responses with a view to understanding the effectiveness process. The choice of variables to be included in the research depends on the test objectives and the brand. So the responses included in tracking research can vary greatly from one brand to another. In general, the following mental advertising and brand responses are included in tracking measurement, in both Germany and the UK (*Admap*, 1998; Pulch, 1995).

- Mental advertising responses:
  - advertising awareness (spontaneous, aided);
  - advertising likeability;
  - recall of ad content (spontaneous, aided).

- Mental brand responses:
  - brand awareness (TOMA, spontaneous, aided);
  - association with the brand (in practice, referred to as image measurements and/or the measurement of attitude towards the brand);
  - brand preference or 'brand ranking' (including intention to buy).

In Germany, the terms 'direct' and 'indirect' advertising effects are also used, the former referring to the effects directly resulting from exposure to advertising, the latter to the effects concerning the brand.

To obtain insight into the effect of advertising on the brand, it might be expected that the correlation between mental advertising and brand responses would be ascertained. Measurements are carried out at both levels but no effort is made to establish how the advertising and brand responses are connected or how such connections come about.

Input data

Ideally, noted mental advertising responses (invariably advertising awareness) are linked with input data, such as advertising expenditure, gross rating points (GRPs) and share of voice (SOV). Clients are interested in finding out more about the influence of their advertising investments on the established advertising effects. If the measured mental advertising effects can be connected up with the input data, an understanding of the influence of advertising on these effects can be obtained.

In the UK, 18 out of 30 companies involved in *Admap*'s study in 1998 linked media activity, expressed in GRPs, with the ascertained advertising effects (some as a standard service, others as an optional request).

Germany has a particular propensity to relate advertising effects directly to advertising expenditure. If the correlation between advertising investment and achieved advertising awareness can be established for many different advertising campaigns, standard scores can be worked out. According to various German research services, comparison of the individual campaign scores and these standard scores supplies insight into the relative performance of the campaign in question. Steps can then be taken to continue, adapt or end the campaign on the basis of that information (Juchems, 1995). It is known from pre-testing, however, that scores depend on the specific product category, brand awareness and current brand positioning in the market. It can therefore be dangerous to judge a campaign on the basis of such general information.

Admap notes that, in the UK, 19 out of 30 companies involved in the study report on figures concerning media contact. This information can be obtained through tracking research, by asking respondents about their media behaviour. The advantage of measuring media behaviour directly is that it helps to determine optimum advertising frequency, thus enabling the media plan to be improved. However, respondents often have difficulties remembering their exact media behaviour, especially if it relates to what they did one or two weeks earlier (see Belson (1986) for a more extensive discussion of the validity and reliability of reported behaviour). Another disadvantage is that media research requires extensive questionnaires. The growing number of television and radio channels and so on makes it increasingly difficult to establish media behaviour exactly.

The Media Observer

How often should the consumer be exposed to the advertising message to achieve the best possible result? TMP Research France has designed a measuring tool to provide the necessary insight for an optimum and economical media use schedule: the Media Observer (Faasse, 1992; 1996). The Media Observer determines the optimum contact frequency for campaign X for brand Y, taking into account the objectives of the advertising campaign. The effectiveness criteria it uses are: advertising awareness, spontaneous brand recall and aided brand recall. By tying in the effectiveness criteria with the number of actual contacts, insight is obtained into the effective frequency for the ad in question. This is especially relevant to television advertising. The other media types are included in the survey to enable the optimum media mix to be determined alongside the optimum contact frequency.
Since it links media behaviour with effectiveness criteria, the Media Observer can be seen as an advertising effectiveness programme. However, it has the drawback of only having one post-measurement.

Exhibit 7.5

The Media Partnership (TMP – a European venture of several large advertising agencies originating from the US) created the Media Observer research model, which determines the optimum contact frequency needed for an advertising campaign to achieve its objective. In the Media Observer a connection is made between the number of medium contacts and various mental advertising and brand responses. Media behaviour can be ascertained by means of self-reported behaviour. The principles of the Media Observer are described in more detail in Exhibit 7.5.

Sales figures

Information on sales figures is obtained from specialised agencies like Nielsen and GfK, or in an in-house statistical programme. Many advertisers have direct dealings with Nielsen or GfK. Research services in turn obtain the figures from their clients.

In order to gain an idea of the entire advertising process, it is as well to tie brand responses in with sales figures. The influence of advertising on buying behaviour can be explained by continuously and consistently charting the intermediate advertising effects. It is, however, difficult to find a direct correlation, as many factors affect the consumer's ultimate buying behaviour. This aspect is not a set part of tracking in British, German and Dutch research companies; they do not seek to establish correlations between brand attitudes and brand use, or between sales figures and brand responses.

Only half the British companies in the *Admap* survey say they do actually measure sales figures as part of tracking. McDonald (1995a, p 4) sees this as a drawback:

This is perhaps the weakness in the UK approach, which may have to be corrected; in the US they are more hard-nosed, and it is there that serious attempts are now being made to demonstrate relationships between (for example) advertising awareness fluctuations and short term sales changes.

7.9 CONCLUSION

This chapter has demonstrated how continuous measurement of mental advertising and brand responses can provide insight into how advertising works. At the end of the day, tracking research does not aim to merely register what takes place inside consumers' minds. It should also have an explanatory and predictive value. To achieve this, data series should be tied in with market results on the one hand, and with advertising investments on the other. Modelling in this manner can provide insight into how advertising responses and brand responses interconnect, as well as how investments ultimately relate to sales results. The resulting information means that choices can be better accounted for in advance, and the results of advertising activities demonstrated.

However, accountability requires more than frequent research and use of the right research methods and analysis techniques. Accountability is a process, a mentality. Research among practitioners on the agency and client sides in the Netherlands has shown that accountability requires discipline, more than anything else. 'First of all, accountability requires discipline and agreement on the objectives, on what to measure and on which methods are suitable for doing so' (Platform '95, 1997).

Only once this has been achieved will accountability be a realistic prospect.

8 Market simulation

Reint Jan Schuring
Marnix Vogel

8.1   INTRODUCTION

'This ground-breaking book demonstrates for the first time the link between advertising and consumer behaviour.' These are the words with which the publisher of *When Ads Work* by John Philip Jones (1995) opens his introduction. Judging from this quote, it must be concluded that, prior to the book's publication, it was merely *believed* that advertising influenced consumer behaviour. Yet that belief has formed the foundation for a 300-billion-dollar business (1997). Advertising agencies, not to mention all the spin-off companies, like media agencies, sponsorship consultancies, film producers and commercial television stations, live off the belief in the added value of advertising for brands, products and services.

It might therefore seem odd that, despite these substantial interests, the effects of advertising had not been examined in depth earlier. How on earth could it have taken until 1995 to demonstrate the link between advertising and consumer behaviour? Some cynics will argue that this very business, based as it is on the belief in the impact of advertising, is not served by research into the true effects, and that the absence of fundamental research is therefore hardly surprising. The advertising industry did not encourage such research either. It could manage without 'advertising proof' as long as a decent living could be made from the belief. Broadbent (1989, p 9) states: 'DAGMAR became an apparent success ... because it let advertising off the hook.'

The clients of advertising agencies have certainly made serious attempts to get a better grip on how advertising (and other marketing and communication tools) works. In the 1960s, multinationals made several bids to demonstrate marketing (and advertising) effects. PIMS (Profit Impact of Market Strategy) is the best-known example (Buzzell and Gale, 1987). PIMS works according to the principle of benchmarking: the scores obtained by a brand, product or service on a great many marketing variables are compared with averages of a great many comparable brands, products or services. In that way ROI (return on investment) can be forecast, and in turn compared with the actual ROI. Brand performance is the difference between the two. In 1987 the PIMS Database contained around three thousand business units.

It was a while before PIMS results cropped up in discussions on advertising effects. But then the argument ran as follows: there is a high correlation between business units with a high ROI and those with a high advertising budget, so a lot of advertising ensures a high ROI. However, this *post ergo propter* reasoning proved to be unreliable. First, the PIMS Database contains relatively few 'failures' and so does not form a representative reflection of reality, and second, the presence of a high correlation is still not always sufficient proof that there is a causal relationship (Day, 1986, p 150 *et seq.*).

PIMS may have supplied little insight into the impact of advertising, but scientists and, more especially, econometrists made several attempts in the 1970s to pinpoint advertising effects (Aaker, Blattberg, Ehrenberg, Kotler and Little). This did not result in extensive use of econometric models in marketing and communication. That can partly be explained by the complexity of the material. The substantial investments in time and money required by such research were also a drawback; analysis of advertising effects could easily take six months to a year, as well as the necessary programming time. Lastly, the results of the econometric studies were not spectacular, leading to the conclusion that not even econometricians were able to reveal advertising effects.

'Econometric modelling has shown that, while there is usually an advertising effect, it is usually very small: in most cases if you run a scenario without advertising, you lose a little bit of sales, but you make quite a lot of money' (McDonald, 1997, p 9). Obviously the econometric results could not count on a warm reception in an industry which has so much vested interest in the perception of advertising as a moneymaker.

8.1.1 The long-term effect

The defence (by the advertising industry) rested on the term 'long-term effect', a kind of bonus effect occurring alongside advertising's very modest short-term effect. The way in which that long-term effect should be measured is still a controversial subject. In fact, no single clear answer has ever been provided, and various participants in the discussion maintain that it is impossible to measure long-term effects. Broadbent (1997) sees the long-term advertising effect as the isolated influence of one or more years' advertising pressure on market share, for instance; Hollis (1996) sees brand equity as the long-term effect – a view endorsed in this book.

Why have not other involved parties like clients of advertising agencies embraced the results of econometric analysis and lowered advertising budgets accordingly? This is simply because the demonstrated marginal short-term effects of advertising do not tally with developments in various markets which are plain for all to see. For instance, years of advertising would seem to enable brands to create a distinctive position in the minds of consumers, which ensures long-lasting market leadership. There are examples of advertising campaigns which are generally considered to be responsible for the success of brands/products: the Volkswagen campaign in the US, Marlboro advertising, the Nike campaign and Heineken advertising.

If advertising has only a marginal effect, what is it that has enabled major brands like Coca-Cola, Heineken, Nike, Marlboro and the rest to maintain their strong position for so long? The success of these brands is not due to their price: they are more likely to be more expensive than their competitors. Neither can distribution always be an explanation, or quality, even in the instance of the beer market, where the inveterate beer drinker can in no way distinguish between the various brands.

Strong brands are valuable. The sums paid in takeovers involving such brands exceed the profits by twenty times. If managed well, they can keep income flowing in for many years. The brand equity or added value of the strong brand is recognised and acknowledged in business dealings. The results of econometric analysis could not explain that added value.

The emphasis of advertising research has been shifting. In Europe, at least, more focus has been given to how advertising works than to its effects. The formation of psychological theories (Beijk and van Raaij, 1989), connotation research and image research took over from research into quantitative effects. 'Depth' (ie, the strength of associations; the extent of associative ramifications for consumers) was intended to explain what 'length' (simple quantitative registration) had failed to do. All these efforts have indeed resulted in qualitative research in various shapes and sizes, but have not brought the answer to the question of advertising effects any closer.

8.2 NEW POSSIBILITIES

The accountability of advertising is once more a topical issue. As companies are becoming more focused on effectiveness and rationality, the unproven contribution (to profits) of expensive advertising has not been passed over and once more constitutes a controversy. So research is resuming the course it was pursuing prior to 'psychologicalisation': charting advertising effects, and the effects of other marketing and communication tools, by means of quantitative data and statistical (mathematical) techniques. There is every reason to assume that this renewed attempt will provide more results than the earlier efforts of clients and econometrists:

- computers are hundreds of times more powerful and faster than they were, and can process much more data;
- far more data are available (including scanning data), making it possible to record the individual consumer's buying behaviour daily;
- more money is now being spent, not only on scanning data, but also on tracking surveys, measuring consumer response to marketing and communication activities;
- statistical techniques are more sophisticated. New, non-linear methods in particular are proving eminently suited to the analysis of market dynamics.

More and more accurate data, vastly improved computers and more precise techniques should enable us to do today what many econometrists sought to do in the 1960s and 1970s: to demonstrate advertising effects, both in the short and in the long term. Jones (1995) proves that new possibilities can lead to new insight.

Several other authors even refer to a revolution in marketing (information) (Tapscott and Caston, 1993; Blattberg *et al.*, 1994). They predict radical rationalisation of the marketing process, in which the control of knowledge and the efficiency of knowledge acquisition play a crucial part. Blattberg *et al.* (1994) suggest in *The Marketing Information Revolution* that such rationalisation need not be at the expense of creativity or entrepreneurial spirit, but, on the contrary, can be very stimulating in that respect.

This section examines the new possibilities for revealing advertising effects. What conditions must be met and what results can be expected? More far-reaching consequences of accountability and, accordingly, of rationalisation in marketing will only be discussed in the context of research into advertising effects.

8.2.1 More and better data

If we wish to determine the effectiveness of marketing tools by means of time series analysis, applying either traditional variables or target variables/tool objectives, objective data will have to be collected on a continuing basis. Apart from the problem of the level at which data has to be collected (ie, the period etc. on which it should be based), data collection also entails a large investment for many organisations. Since there is a tendency in practice to underestimate the importance of ongoing data collection, we are of the opinion that, if insight is to be gained into the effectiveness of the application of marketing tools, such investments cannot be emphasised too much.

(Leeflang and Beukenkamp, 1981)

Leeflang and Beukenkamp's appeal has at last been heard. More and more large companies are investing in ongoing research into consumer perception and behaviour, and sales data.

Time has not stood still with respect to the latter category. Sales data such as market share, sales, turnover, price, promotions, promotion price, and (weighted) distribution have been available on a weekly basis for foods markets for some years now (scanning data are available through Nielsen or GfK Foodscan). Distribution sales data (not obtained by scanning) were available only on a two-monthly basis three years ago (and for atypical two-monthly periods at that), but now it is supplied on a monthly basis.

In other markets, too, the data-supply situation has improved considerably. This is partly due to the fact that companies and organisations in services, consumer durables and retailing sectors have set up and improved their databases with consumer information. Another contributing factor is the development of tracking research. Various research agencies offer survey products supplying ongoing charting of consumer perception and attitude regarding brands, products and services. There are other companies which are more geared to bridging gaps in their own databases (for instance, consumer perception of marketing activities) and they are seriously collecting such data on a continuous basis.

Jones (1995) carried out his research using a single-source technique. It looked for some time as though advertising effects could, in fact, only be pinpointed if single-source data were available. However, that is a mistaken assumption. Jones has submitted single-source surveys as an alternative for multi-source data combined with econometric analyses (Jones, 1995, p 8 *et seq.*, Broadbent, 1997, p 206 *et seq.*).

8.2.2 Techniques

Statistical techniques used to examine correlations in data are applicable only if specific conditions have been met. These conditions depend on the technique itself and, most especially, on the volume and complexity of the data. Zwart, for example, gives a number of conditions (in Leeflang and Beukenkamp, 1981) for the application of both simple and multiple correlation and regression analysis. The most important ones are listed below.

- In order to conduct regression analysis it must be possible to indicate, for each relationship, which variables are independent and which dependent.
- The relationship between the variables must be linear in the parameters.
- The correlation must be theoretically arguable (not nonsensical).

The third condition, for instance, precludes a correlation between the presence and/or number of storks and the number of births. The second condition, preventing the application of multiple linear regression to problems in which a non-linear correlation can be surmised in the parameters (assessors), is important. It means, for instance, that if a non-linear or curved relationship (ie, not a straight line) is suspected to exist between price or media and market share, multiple linear regression is not a good technique for revealing this curved correlation. Various authors (Dasgupta *et al.*, 1994, p. 10; Kumar *et al.*, 1995, p 4; Refenes, 1995) have already demonstrated that such a condition should not be dismissed lightly.

Refenes (1995), referring to Steiner and Wittenkamp's survey, commented that:

This study shows that ANNs [Artificial Neural Networks] outperform comparable statistical techniques for estimating the return of a single stock. Normally applied regression techniques allow only a coarse modelling of the underlying relations in the capital market. ANNs build a more precise model of the interdependencies based on historical sample data than when based on economic considerations. The resulting model of the relationship between the return of a stock and factors of the capital market is usually non-linear, may contain dependencies in time and multiple connections between several influencing factors. Therefore ANNs can give more reliable forecasts for stock returns than the comparable statistical techniques.

Use of linear techniques for non-linear problems gives results that lack accuracy or are even incorrect. Market dynamics (the gamut of relationships between market share and variables like price, media, promotion, image, and so on) are characterised by substantial non-linearity. Every retailer knows that the correlation between price and sales is not a straight line, but that there are what are called 'price points'. For example, £2.00 is quite different from £1.99 – more than the actual difference of 1p. Every media agency knows a certain media threshold is necessary if an advertising campaign is to be effective, and also that, with too much media expenditure (too high a frequency) 'wear-out' (loss of advertising attention value) can occur – adversely affecting the campaign's effectiveness. Even the influence of distribution on sales is far from linear. Here, too, threshold values can often be observed, as well as diminishing returns when the 100% mark is approached.

So, as a rule, the dynamics of markets can be represented only by non-linear relationships, which means that techniques must be applied which are capable of 'discovering' or, in econometric terms, 'estimating' them. There is a problem, in that, in order to continue using linear techniques, the non-linear correlations must be altered (transformed) in such a way that they become linear. This is no simple matter. After all, the object of the exercise is to multiply relations between variables (ie, not the variables themselves) – curved relations, the curvature of which is not known exactly – by a function which makes them linear, or straight. That is only possible if the scores on the variables are multiplied by a specific function, in the hope that the parameters (the relations between the variables) will become straight as a result. It is a process of trial and error, which certainly takes time and requires very specialised econometric know-how.

Fortunately a new generation of techniques has become available, making the use of non-linearity far easier. Neural networks, for instance, can carry out the search process described above 'automatically'. They enable us to estimate all non-linear relationships between variables as well as possible. (For a succinct discussion of neural networks, readers are referred to Adriaans and Zantinge, 1996, p 68 *et seq.*; Baestaens *et al.*, 1994, Chapters 1 and 2. The standard work on neural networks is by Simon Haykin, 1994.) For an average problem, the whole process takes no more than a few minutes. So work which until recently took weeks, even months, can now be done in a fraction of the time.

Another advantage of this new technique is the possibility of working simultaneously with several variables requiring explanation. This may sound abstract, but, in concrete terms, it means, for instance, that a model can be created which supplies answers about market shares for various brands at the same time. If brand A advertises more often, what are the consequences for the market share of brand A, brand B or brand C, and so on?

The handling of non-linearity and several variables requiring explanation (target variables) are also features of techniques like genetic algorithms and induction algorithms (Adriaans and Zantinge, 1996, p 47 *et seq.*). The nomenclature of these techniques is closely connected to the disciplines in which they were developed (those of evolutionary and mathematical biology, respectively). Originally they were developed as simulation models for the human brain (neural networks) or for evolution (genetic algorithm). Meanwhile, claims suggesting that the human brain works in the same way as neural networks have been dismissed. However, these techniques continue

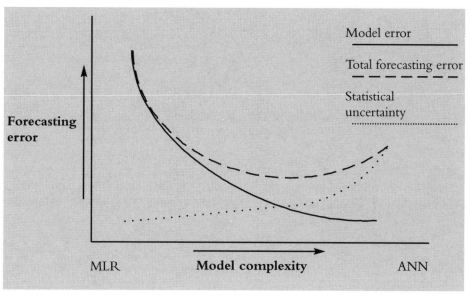

Figure 8.1 Errors in forecasting

to be of use as powerful, non-linear methods for mathematical analysis (Edelman, 1991).

The use of non-linear mathematics in simulating advertising effects has two important consequences. First, far greater accuracy can be achieved. Second, far more complex dynamics can be analysed. Of course, these non-linear techniques also have certain drawbacks. However, the disadvantages can largely be resolved and the remaining inconveniences are more than offset by the tremendous advantages the non-linear techniques entail.

Figure 8.1 represents the scope for model error using models with different levels of complexity. A less complex technique (multiple linear regression, MLR) will provide a high model error with a complex problem. A more complex technique (artificial neural networks, ANN) will provide a much lower error, though the greater the complexity, the greater the statistical uncertainty.

8.2.3 Computers

The advantage of the microprocessor will continue to grow. The capacity of traditional semiconductor computers is growing at around 20% per year. The number of transistors on a microprocessor chip, however, has grown from around 30,000 in 1980 to an anticipated 100 million by 1999 – a compound annual growth rate of over 150%. In addition, we can anticipate that well before the end of the 1990s, a single microprocessor chip will pass today's mainframe in raw power.

(Tapscott and Caston, 1993, p 19)

The greatly increased power of personal computers cut the time needed for an extensive analysis of advertising effects from six months to a year, down to one or, at most, a few weeks. That week also includes time for preparing data and compiling the report. So costs have easily been cut by a factor of 10. Not only the power, but also the memory of PCs has grown tremendously. A personal computer can now analyse extensive problems, with many records and columns, for instance, 100,000 records with 80 variables, almost effortlessly. Ten years ago that was unthinkable.

In addition, developments in the software field have had the effect of greatly reducing costs and increasing speed. Standardisation of software has helped to make various databases very accessible and to greatly promote data compatibility.

These hardware and software developments have not only aided analysis, but actually at last facilitated the registration of large amounts of data (the installation of many databases, scanning). It was just not possible in the 1970s or early 1980s to chart advertising effects for a reasonable price and within a reasonable time.

8.3   THE IMPORTANCE OF EFFECTS RESEARCH

It is by no means a waste of time to analyse advertising effects or to make advertising 'accountable'. To start with, it can save money, or make that money earn more.

However, this is certainly not the only, and perhaps not even the greatest benefit. Of far more importance is the contribution to the necessary innovation of a company's or organisation's marketing. In Figure 8.2 and Table 8.1 Tapscott and Caston (1993) outline the development from a high performance team to, ultimately, an extended enterprise.

Traditional hierarchical organisations are characterised by a centralised organisation of data and knowledge, and by a number of levels of management, responsibilities and bureaucracy. The first step of business process redesign, to form high-performance teams, has been facilitated by huge strides forward in technology. Instead of a rigid structure, a highly modular organisation comes about, in which teams operate as a network of client and server functions. Teams act as clients and service (product) providers for other teams, inside and outside the organisation. Teams have a multi-disciplinary make-up and have new responsibilities and tasks. Communication between teams is characterised by a cooperative attitude. (More information can also be found in Quinn Mills, 1991, or Keen, 1991.)

Growing turbulence in markets forced the development towards more open organisations. The traditional firm is unable to stand up to growing local and international competition quickly and adequately. A new organisational form is necessary to counter this.

Tapscott and Caston (1993) predict, at a subsequent stage, the combining of high-performance teams within the integrated organisation. Companies will need to operate as one single enterprise rather than a collection of highly autonomous teams. Integration through a comprehensive strategy for market operations is necessary for the organisation of work, information and technology.

The last step is referred to as the extended enterprise stage. This is when 'walls' between companies are broken down by facilitating co-operation – especially by means of information technology (including such forms of co-operation as cash dispensers, shared reservation systems and the Internet/Intranet). 'Virtual' organisations result, made up of alliances. The virtual organisation enables companies to work with other companies with which they have common interests. This increases competitive strength tremendously, companies can develop markets which had previously not been feasible,

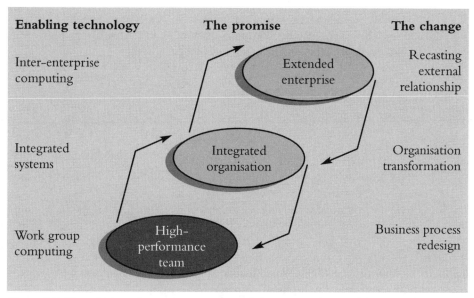

Enabling technology	The promise	The change
Inter-enterprise computing	Extended enterprise	Recasting external relationship
Integrated systems	Integrated organisation	Organisation transformation
Work group computing	High-performance team	Business process redesign

Figure 8.2 From high-performance team to extended enterprise (Source: Tapscott and Caston, 1993, p 32)

and consumers benefit from the supply of a more integrated products and services package.

It is necessary to sketch the development of the integrated organisation (which has also been described in different terms by Blattberg *et al.*, 1994; Drucker, 1988; Moss Kanter, 1989; Quinn Mills, 1991, and others) if the importance of research into advertising effects is to be properly assessed. Blattberg *et al.* (1994) conclude from their outline of this development: 'Perhaps the greatest casualty of the information revolution will be advertising.' Their prime argument is that companies will enter more directly into the dialogue with consumers in the course of the development outlined above, and, as a result, these companies will turn their backs on traditional media. In addition, alliances and the information technology they use will bring about new channels of communication, facilitating more direct communication with consumers.

The integrated enterprise	The shifts
• Technology applications	• Organisational restructuring
• System islands	• Integral systems
• Three classes of systems addressing the three resources	• Integrated computing environments
• Single-form systems	• Integration of data, text, voice and image
• Cost reduction	• Enterprise effectiveness

Table 8.1 The shifts towards an integrated enterprise (Source: Tapscott and Caston, 1993, p 86)

The role of marketing communications will shift from target group marketing, based on the needs of the consumer and of brand advertising, to managing the information flow between consumer and company.

If information management allows every customer to have a unique relationship with the firm, then each customer effectively becomes a segment, and the concept of dividing up the market into homogeneous subgroups becomes obsolete. Furthermore, most competitive strategies and marketing mix decisions are developed for and conducted at the segment level, and therefore we should expect to see profound changes in the nature of marketing strategy and marketing mix decisions as well.

(Blattberg *et al.*, 1994, p 12)

The growing dialogue with consumers also implies that they will have growing influence on the product or service. Adriaans and Zantige (1996) state: 'We suggest that those firms that are able to achieve sustainable marketing advantage in the information age are those that do the best job of "controlling" the customer.' They see the pursuit of knowledge through databases and 'data warehousing' as an initial practical step towards the use of information in creating product development and assembly.

Clearly, the use of traditional media, as has been customary up till now, does not fit in with these new developments. However, the authors do not believe that the biggest casualty of the information revolution will be advertising. But traditional media are bound to lose popularity if no research is carried out into how they can fit into tomorrow's form of marketing. The importance of research into advertising effects is not only in the interests of the efficiency and effectiveness of advertising. This research also – primarily – seeks to fit the possibilities of advertising into changing marketing practice, characterised as it is by vigorous dialogue with the consumer.

8.4 MARKET SIMULATION: TECHNIQUES

8.4.1 Introduction

A model can be described as a stylised representation of the ideas one has concerning that part of reality which is being studied.

(Leeflang and Beukenkamp, 1981, p 215)

Suppose a retailer knows from experience in recent years that suntan products have been selling well in the summer, especially in a good summer. Suntan product sales could be rewritten as a function of time (months 6, 7 and 8 in the year) and the number of hours of sunshine. The function of sales of suntan products in time is non-linear; it follows a parabolic course, as sales will gradually start to increase in spring towards a peak in the summer, to drop to almost zero in the autumn. The height of the summer peak will mainly depend on the number of hours of sunshine. Let us assume, with the retailer, that the more hours of sunshine, the more will be sold; so there is a linear relation between suntan products sales and hours of sunshine. If the functions of time and sunshine hours obtained in this way are plotted against the sales of suntan products, a mathematical model of the retail market of suntan products is created. In other words, a mathematical model has been formulated which can simulate the retail market for suntan products.

So market simulation (and process dynamics simulation) entails the formulation of a mathematical model which can simulate part of reality. The more accurately the model is able to estimate reality, the more reliable it is considered to be. All parts (or almost all) of reality can be modelled. Adriaans and Zantinge (1996) mention the following examples:

- simulation of buying behaviour of clusters of consumers;
- prediction of the steps in a pilot's career;
- reconstruction of relations between and/or in relational databases.

A long list can be added from personal experience (BrandmarC bv; see section 8.5):

- simulation of development in extent of customer satisfaction (retail);
- simulation of market dynamics (market share, sales, turnover) in food and retail markets, as well as in the service sector and in consumer durables markets;
- simulation of television viewing behaviour at an individual level;
- prediction and explanation of the likelihood of damage (insurance);
- shipping forecasts (water levels) based on weather forecasts;
- simulation of fluctuations in interest rates;
- simulation of effectiveness of advertising campaigns;
- simulation of consumer response behaviour;
- simulation of turnover of (new) outlets.

Simulation can also be used for:

- tracing fraud with credit cards;
- simulation of parts of the evolution process;
- simulation of behaviour relating to refrigerator use (Gielen, 1995);
- simulation of polyester manufacture (de Weijer, 1995);
- simulation of pathogenesis.

As the example of the retailer has shown, market simulation requires a number of essential ingredients. Before the retailer established his theory connecting time, temperature and turnover of suntan products, he kept a record of sales of that category in the store for a few years. He discovered repetitive sales patterns in the course of a year. Admittedly, the sales peaks did vary from one year to the next but that led him to conclude that differences in temperature could be the explanation. He made enquiries at the meteorological institute, only to discover a decided linear connection between temperature and sales of suntan products (in the summer months).

So the retailer had data (sales figures, temperatures) at his disposal, and went on to draw up his theory, on the basis of which he formulated his mathematical model. After the following summer, he added time and temperature data to the model, thus obtaining a forecast of sales figures. The figures predicted by the model proved to tally nicely with actual sales. The retailer concluded he had made a reliable model and, provided he had reliable temperature data in the following year, he would be able to attune his purchasing policy exactly to expected sales.

Therefore, the necessary ingredients for simulation are:

- an objective (improvement of purchasing policy);
- a tentative theory;
- available data;
- mathematical techniques.

8.4.2 Objectives

Market research supplies data on the consumer's behaviour, knowledge and attitude. The more market research, the more data. The amount of data on market dynamics is growing to such an extent that many marketers are complaining about the complexity of information they are receiving, partly because of the associated technological requirements. The information flow must be compressed and made more manageable.

Market simulation can make a structural contribution to solving the problem. Simulation gives marketers a grip on developments in the marketplace and provides information to help them optimise their marketing. Simulation is not only a technique and a method, but also a philosophy. It is based on the fundamental assumption that 'rationality' is the most successful pacesetter for marketing in the long term. It also requires a willingness to arrange the organisation according to that rationality.

Market simulation is aimed at extracting knowledge from data that have been obtained by market research but are not visible to the naked eye and cannot be 'read' by limited statistical techniques.

The objective of market simulation − to formulate, *a priori*, relevant knowledge − has great influence on the way the model is arranged. The average advertising effectiveness of an average brand requires a different model from the competitive 'clout' of brand A's advertising (the extent to which advertising for brand A can be considered responsible for winning market share from competitors).

Market simulation has four main aims:
* optimisation;
* prediction;
* explanation;
* evaluation.

The optimisation of advertising can, for instance, relate to absolute expenditure, the number of gross rating points (GRPs), and the effectiveness of media plans and campaigns. The prediction of advertising effects can be useful in determining what effects (on market share, for instance) an unchanged advertising policy would have with unchanged competitive pressure. It can also be useful to work out the consequences of time scenarios. One might choose to examine which strategy is best: continuity or bursts of advertising. Copy length, advertising likeability, broadcasting moment and choice of television station can play an important part in explaining advertising effect.

Evaluation of advertising policy is a matter of answering questions which can also be classified under optimisation, prediction or explanation. More specifically, all advertising variables are assessed with respect to their contribution to market share, sales and image. Advertising pressure, advertising likeability, advertising continuity, advertising moment, advertising format − all these variables can influence market share, sales or image. The individual contribution of each variable plus predictions and optimisations are together decisive in advertising policy evaluation.

8.4.3 Modelling

Market simulation should be seen as an exploratory process; it starts with the formulation of a rough theoretical model and ends with an exact theoretical model with practical validation. An initial, rough model of market dynamics might look like Figure 8.3.

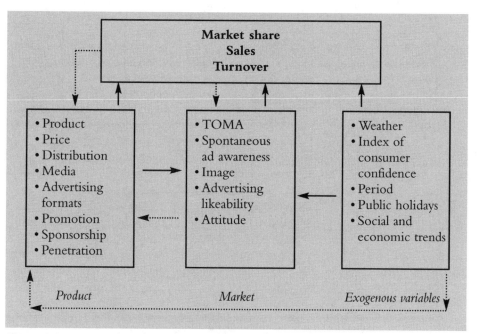

Figure 8.3 A statistically explanatory model of market dynamics

This basic model can be applied to foods and consumer durable markets, as well as to the retail and service (for instance, financial services) sectors. Obviously each of the variables has to be worked out (operationalised). In the (financial) services sector, information on clients and their behaviour (as filed in the administrative systems) can be used instead of the market variables in Figure 8.3. It is not necessary to describe all the links within the model in detail, nor is it necessary to indicate the required weight of a variable's influence. Mathematical techniques are used to determine both factors when the model is being constructed.

The relations between variables become clearer if the time factor is introduced into the model and the assumption made that a product or service starts with a price, distribution, promotions and media, and that a market position (and/or market share) is obtained in this way, which in turn influences product and market variables, and so on. This is also dependent on the exogenous variables playing their part during this process (see Figure 8.4 overleaf).

The interesting thing about this type of presentation is that it provides scope for the development of premium, as well as private label brands. If the market has considerable influence (premium brands, image-sensitive markets), the direct influence of the product on market share and turnover will be slight. If the influence of the market is slight (private label brands), the product's direct influence on market share and turnover will be substantial. Exogenous variables, including the influences of competition, affect both processes.

At the same time, the dynamic model of market dynamics suggests that product variables or market variables alone will not be able to predict market share, turnover or sales adequately. Product variables must be accompanied by at least one market variable or at least the market share, turnover or sales of the previous period. Market variables

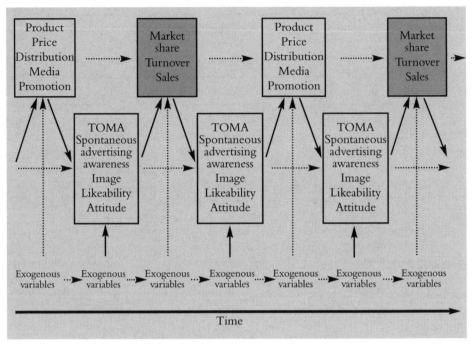

Figure 8.4 A dynamic model of market dynamics

must be accompanied by at least one product variable or at least market share, turnover or sales, and in practice that proves to be the case (see section 8.5).

The effects of advertising can be simulated both statically and dynamically. The 'static conceptual model' supplies information on the average effect of market, product and exogenous variables on the average brand. The variance in influences of these variables on the specific brand, compared with those on the average brand, gives an idea of the strength of the specific brand. Time and competitors' activities are included implicitly (and as averages).

In the dynamic model of market dynamics, time and competitors' activities are included explicitly. Brand A's product and market variables apply alongside those of competitive brands as explanatory variables which influence brand A's market share. The total market dynamics can be simulated by means of a collection of brand models. However, it is not necessary to create separate models. Mathematical calculation techniques enable us to combine several brand models.

In the two models discussed here, advertising is a variable that both requires and provides explanation. Media weight is always an explanatory variable. Spontaneous advertising awareness and advertising likeability can also be taken as providing and requiring explanation.

Separate models containing only advertising variables are, by necessity, always sub-models. For example, the media product variable can be computed according to variables like copy length, format, GRPs, adstock (a term used to refer to the amount of media activity for a brand, taking into account the decreasing effect of media activity over time) and campaign.

Additional factors such as market share, top-of-mind awareness or image are also necessary. In this case, only spontaneous advertising awareness and/or advertising likeability can be used as variables to be explained. A sub-model like this can be used to simulate sub-effects of advertising. For more extensive analysis, which examines the advertising effect on market share, turnover, sales or image, other explanatory variables, such as price, promotion and distribution, are required, if only for theoretical reasons.

The operationalisation of the market, product and exogenous 'blocks' (Figure 8.4) is affected by the state of theory and market research. How can terms like image, price perception, price, quality ratio, and so on be used, and how can they be measured in a valid and reliable way? Such knowledge is crucial when setting up tracking studies.

The models described are aimed at presenting marketing and communication as a comprehensible process. It must be possible for marketers to influence the variables on which the process is modelled. Variables which have too little scope for manoeuvre (for instance, because they are insufficiently unambiguous or cannot be steered by a marketer) should be replaced by suitable ones. Clearly, process simulation must not suffer as a result, so the reliability and precision of the model must be the same, at the very least. This principle is known as 'Ockham's razor-blade'. According to the fourteenth-century philosopher, William van Ockham, the simplest explanation is the best. 'Simplest' in this context means that no more entities are included in the explanation than strictly necessary.

8.4.4 Data

The crucial concept with respect to data is information content. The more information contained in the data, the better. The information content is determined by:
- measuring frequency;
- sample size;
- survey validity;
- precision and scope;
- independence of variables;
- questionnaire length.

Measuring frequency and sample size

Higher measuring frequency will usually go together with a smaller sample size. It might, at first sight, look as if that reduces survey reliability. However, upon closer examination, it proves possible, with a series of measurements, to assess the reliability of each individual measurement satisfactorily. This is not the case if there is only one measurement, partly because 'chance' errors (measuring errors caused by chance – external factors) cannot be precluded if there is only one measurement. When there is a series of measurements, a chance 'extreme' can be identified and removed.

Consequently, a series of measurements has a higher information content than a one-off measurement. As Blalock (1960, p 412) comments: 'The total error is thus a function of two independent sources of error and cannot be substantially reduced unless both types are simultaneously controlled.' There is no point taking a large sample if an effort is not made at the same time to curb errors which are not related to the sample (for example, interviewing errors, non-response, leading questions, survey effect, chance errors, and so on).

There is a limit to how much measuring frequency can be increased at the expense of sample size; this can be calculated using simple techniques (Swanborn, 1981). Moreover, the smallest population for which a result is required must be taken into account. The requirement of representativeness, together with that smallest population, in fact means that the total sample is still sizeable. That can often be avoided quite simply by dropping the demand for representativeness, which is often mistakenly required. A 'biased' sample may well contain more information than an 'unbiased' one.

Validity

The validity of a survey can be examined in various ways. To start with, the results can be related to valid measuring tools. If earlier research has shown that viewing behaviour, for instance, can be measured correctly, the new operationalisation of viewing behaviour can be linked to the former procedure (it is assumed that the previous operationalisation will also be measured). In that case, the new should predict the old.

Another method uses qualitative research to examine the terms and context in which respondents discuss certain topics. This can be used to indicate the validity of the questionnaire.

A third method focuses on previous research, preferably on a series of comparable measurements, studying the consistency of the pattern of answers. Moreover, researchers can examine theory and, when possible, econometric modelling in which the relevant information has proved to be of importance. In that way validity is ascertained indirectly. It goes without saying that low validity is responsible for low information content of data.

Precision and scope

These are two traditional conflicting concepts when surveys are being set up: the wider the scope, the lower the precision. In marketing and communication research, it is important to curb both. The scope of a survey must be restricted pragmatically to commercially relevant target groups (as opposed to being representative of the total population). The requirement for precision must be consistent with the inadequate communication during the survey. Generally speaking, the greater the scope, the lower the information content.

Independent variables

The independence of variables can be easily checked by simple statistical techniques like the correlation matrix (a measure of the relationship between two variables) and x–y plots (graphic presentations of the relationship between two variables). Principal components analysis or factor analysis are more complicated. If the research results display relatively high correlations with replies to questions, this research will contain relatively little information. After all, answers with high correlation contain the same information.

Questionnaire length

The length of the questionnaire is important in connection with the independence of the scores on variables. The longer the questionnaire, the greater the average correlation coefficient will be between questions. Information content drops accordingly. In other words, it is inefficient, expensive and hardly more informative to have a longer questionnaire than strictly necessary, quite apart from the mistakes which will be caused by respondent fatigue.

Required number of measuring points

Many variables which can be important when establishing advertising effects have already been examined. However, the number of measuring points required to come up with reliable models and simulations still has to be discussed. Demands are higher with non-linear techniques than with linear, which is easy to envisage: only two points are needed to define a linear line, but at least three for a non-linear or curved line.

The rule of thumb is that the number of measuring points should be at least 2.5^n where n is the number of variables. (This applies, at any rate, to the dynamic model. The number of measuring points can be much lower for the static model, if competing brands are measured as well.) This means, for instance, that for a simulation with six explanatory variables, at least 244 measurements of the same brand, or at least 24 measurements of ten different brands are needed to arrive at a statistically reliable model. However, the acid test of simulation reliability occurs when datasets are predicted that were not used for training.

8.4.5 Analysis techniques

Multivariate analysis (as opposed to univariate analysis), taking into account more than one explanatory variable, can distinguish between the effects of different marketing activities. In multivariate analysis it is assumed that a certain characteristic Y (for example, market share, turnover, sales) depends on variables $X_1, X_2, X_3, X_4 \ldots X_n$ (for example, price, media weight, distribution, shelf position). Characteristic Y is caused by the specific data structure in $X_1, X_2, X_3, X_4 \ldots X_n$, and by (measurement) interference:

Characteristics = data structure + interference

The measurement error or interference in research results in the marketing or communication field is nearly always unknown. So when a model is constructed with which the market is to be simulated, specific precautions must be taken to prevent interference playing an explanatory and/or predictive part in the simulation. Interference must be removed as far as possible during modelling.

When a multivariate technique is selected, the complexity of simulation and the precision of the available techniques must be taken into account. A relatively simple technique like multiple linear regression will provide a high prediction error if applied to a complex problem. The use of too simple a technique with a complex problem is termed 'underfitting'. Complex techniques, like an artificial neural network, tend to 'overfit' a problem. They analyse the problem too well, which detracts from the model's general nature. Usually complex techniques such as partial least squares, artificial neural networks and genetic algorithms will have to be used to explain and predict the effects of advertising (see Adriaans and Zantinge, 1996; Baestaens *et al.*, 1994; Dasgupta *et al.*, 1994).

The choice of simulation technique is preceded by the formulation of a modelling method. Data cannot be presented to a technique for analysis 'just like that'. Some data may well be missing, correlations between variables may be high, 'outliers', or unusual data due to errors in research, for example, may be present, there may be constant variables or variables with a very distorted distribution, and so on. So data must be pre-processed before a data structure can be found which explains Y. That modelling method comprises a series of necessary steps (or operations). For each step or operation several techniques are available. The method is reproduced in diagram form in

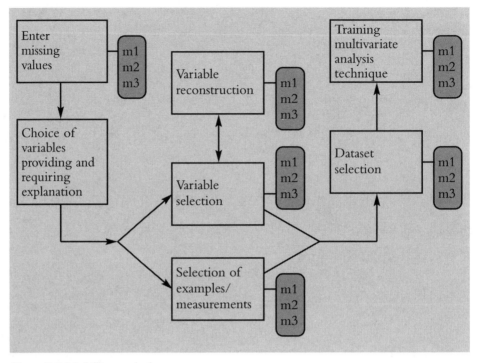

Figure 8.5 Modelling methods

Figure 8.5 ('m' represents the various techniques). Missing values can be added in various ways. The intended technique should be such that the empty cells are filled with values which either affect the modelling process as little as possible or provide the best possible estimate of expected actual (measured) values.

8.4.6 Selection of variables

A selection of variables requiring and providing explanation is needed. In addition, constant variables, variables which theoretically do not belong in the model and variables with highly deviant statistical characteristics, which cannot be improved through transformation techniques, must be removed. (For further information on these and other statistical techniques mentioned, see *Introduction to Multivariate Analysis* (Chatfield and Collins, 1980), or, for more advanced studies, *Applied Regression Analysis* (Draper and Smith, 1998)).

The selection of variables has various purposes. It reduces the number of variables making up the eventual simulation. It ensures 'orthogonalisation' (the use of variables that are totally independent of each other) within the explanatory space created by the variables. It also contributes to good representation of all available information. These three characteristics of variable selection are crucial for the reliability and usability of simulation models.

Various techniques are available for selecting explanatory variables only. Correlation matrix, principal component analysis, auto-associative neural networks and the Kennard and Stone algorithm can all be used. (These techniques are available in AIMM

(Advanced Information Modelling Method), a software package developed by BrandmarC bv which focuses specifically on market and process simulation.)

An auto-associative neural network can be used to verify whether variable selection has been carried out correctly. It must be possible for the selected variables to predict all the dependent variables correctly within certain margins. If that is the case, variable selection can be concluded to contain (almost) as much information as the total set of explanatory variables. Selection is then correct.

Objects (one measurement of all available variables for a brand) must also be selected. This entails checking whether all objects belong to the same class, ie, whether they can all be taken together as a coherent whole. They might break up into two segments, each of which behaves differently. In that case it is worth making two simulations – one for each segment. In addition, the objects of one particular brand, such as the market leader, may be located far outside the (measuring) area of the objects of all other brands. Then, too, one might decide to split the objects. Some examples may come so far outside the range of other examples of that brand that they must be seen as outliers, and must be removed.

Object selection can be reached by principal component analysis, x–y plots and leverage points. Selection of datasets entails distributing the previously selected objects among the calibration (training) set, the validation set and the prediction (forecast) set. The validation set is used to check whether the model overfits, the prediction set is used to see how correct the model is in its forecasting.

8.4.7 Choice of analysis techniques

After all these preliminaries, a multivariate analysis technique may be selected. Generally neural networks or, for very few examples, partial least squares, will be chosen for explaining and predicting advertising effects. Partial least squares is a linear technique which is particularly well suited to application to datasets with many correlations between variables which have to be included in the simulation.

The neural network technique can take into account the interactions between linearly independent variables (for example, interactions between television advertising and promotions), can visualise non-linear relations between variables providing and requiring explanation, and deal with several variables requiring explanation. The neural network can be adjusted to the complexity of the problem, and deal with time series, as well as assuming nothing a priori about the data structure. This makes it an extremely effective technique for research in the market dynamics field. After all, the effects of advertising are still largely unknown. The correlation between price and market share is assumed to be non-linear, and the same applies to that between media and market share. Interactions between media and promotional activities, for instance, have been recorded more often. Such observations make out a case for an exploratory technique, which can simulate non-linear problems, deal with a higher order of interactions and provide insight into the structure of the selected simulation model. Adriaans and Zantinge (1996, p 71) see several disadvantages, alongside the advantages, of neural networks. They describe them (as do many other authors, as it happens) as 'black boxes', which are unable to reveal the structure of the model. That accusation can only be based on unfamiliarity with application of the technique. A data structure found by a neural network can easily be represented using normal statistical techniques.

The partial least squares technique, which, like multiple linear regression, assumes linearity in the parameters, is particularly suited to use on datasets with very few objects and a great many variables. It can be a great help, especially for dynamic models which only have a limited number of available measurements.

The construction of the simulation model does not mean that the job is finished. Analysis techniques must now help to read the simulation and convert it into usable knowledge. The choice of analysis techniques depends to a limited extent on what modelling technique is used (neural network, partial least squares, multiple linear regression, genetic algorithms). Of far greater influence however is the area in which market simulation is applied. Different analysis techniques will be chosen for classification problems – for instance, the explanation and prediction of response to direct mail – than for continuous problems, such as the explanation and prediction of advertising effects. For reading classification models, techniques may include the calculation of customer profiles, a gains chart (response result percentage) and information retrieval via queries. For continuous problems the following analysis techniques are widely used:

- *Sensitivity*
  Variation in an explanatory variable and the effect on a variable requiring explanation.
- *Forecast*
  The prediction of the effect on a variable requiring explanation of changed scores on several or all explanatory variables.
- *Main effect*
  The average effect of the explanatory variables on a variable requiring explanation.
- *Point elasticity*
  The effect of a (minor) alteration on the explanatory variables from a specific position on a variable requiring explanation.
- *Strategy*
  The search (search process using a genetic algorithm) for optimum strategies in order to obtain a certain score on a variable requiring explanation (or certain scores on variables requiring explanation).

These analysis techniques, as well as statistical reliability measures, can be used to provide a good understanding of the correlations on which simulation is based.

8.4.8 Rational marketing philosophy

Models, data and techniques will be insufficient if at least one other important condition is not met: the company in question must adhere to a rational approach in marketing. It is still quite common practice in marketing and communication circles to base decision-making on intuition, or gut feeling. This has a number of drawbacks:
- intuitive knowledge is the prerogative of one person;
- when that person leaves the company, his or her intuition is lost;
- it is hard for others to penetrate intuitive knowledge;
- the company cannot control the decision-making process;
- situation-specific 'arguments' (emotions) can play too big a part;
- the decision-making process is not systematic;
- decision-making can experience serious delays if several experts with conflicting intuitive knowledge are involved in the process.

Market simulation in a company with a rational marketing philosophy does not have these drawbacks. Every new experience contributes to the company's knowledge. That knowledge is readily available, in general, for interested parties and can be easily consulted. It is not lost when the person with the right 'intuition' leaves. The decision-making process can be controlled because all participants have the same information at their disposal. This helps to speed up the process considerably. *Ad hoc* arguments (ie, those related to a specific situation) are almost exceptional.

A company with a rational marketing philosophy recognises the advantages of market simulation. It prefers a systematic learning process to short-lived success. After all, no one will deny the possibility of obtaining good results with gut feeling – certainly in the short term – despite the above-mentioned drawbacks. A decision-making process in which gut feeling plays an important role cannot, however, be reconciled with the use of market simulation techniques. First, because it is impossible to work systematically and intuitively at the same time; second, because management which believes in intuition will baulk at the use of systematic techniques. A leading marketer was noted to have made the following remark: 'If I can't do it better than that computer, they should fire me tomorrow.' These words were not meant as a challenge, but were referring to the inferred superiority of intuition, based among other things on experience and talent.

8.5   AN ANALYSIS OF 100 BRANDS

8.5.1 Survey description

BrandmarC bv (founded in 1993) has specialised in the simulation of markets and processes using non-linear multivariate techniques. It has developed a method to that end comprising different techniques (see section 8.4.5). BrandmarC has accumulated expertise in the simulation of many consumer markets in Europe, in the consumer durables, retail, financial service-provision and food sectors. It has experience in other, more process-based fields too. These include individual viewing behaviour, prediction of individual damage risk and reliable shipping forecasts. All simulations are commissioned by international enterprises or national governments. The principals have provided the appropriate data, for their own brand/brands, as well as for competitors (where relevant).

Specifically for studies concerning the explanation and prediction of advertising effects, the simulation 'stock' was screened with respect to comparability. Some 20 simulations of foods markets met that requirement. Around 100 brands were involved in the analyses. All the simulations related to national markets within Europe. Data were available for all markets relating to a period of at least two-and-a-half to three years. This data generally applies to the 1993–96 period, sometimes to an earlier period as well. The focus is on short-term effects, to use the terminology of the Advertising Response Matrix. Dependent variables (those requiring explanation, such as market share) as well as independent variables (those providing explanation: media weight, for instance) were measured on a weekly basis (the average or the total in a particular week). So it could be indicated on a weekly basis for all brands the media activities that were carried out, the average price in that week, the sales obtained, and so on.

The information used for these 20 simulations comprised at least market shares, sales, prices, distributions, promotions and media activities. Sometimes information on such variables as shelf position, image, awareness (TOMA, name, brand), advertising recall or advertising likeability was also available. However, this information could not be involved in the comparison of the different markets (or simulations) because it was not available for all markets. Distribution is not important for some simulations, in view of the high degree of distribution which all players may have already achieved. Consequently the comparative study related only to price, promotion and media effects. This decision was determined in part by the fact that BrandmarC's clients required guaranteed confidentiality concerning the exact results of the simulations.

Market share as a dependent variable

In the simulations, market share was selected as a dependent variable, to be explained and predicted. Often more than one dependent variable is defined – sales, turnover and image, for example. The report contains a description of the influence on market share of several independent explanatory variables, or resulting combinations. This has the additional advantage that, for market simulation, no problems occur from markets which grow or decline in their entirety. If, for instance, a brand in a plummeting market segment manages to drop less than its competitors thanks to media activities, a positive effect of media on sales will still not be found, even though it can be demonstrated for market share. The market share variable enables us to assess the performance of one brand compared with others, without the necessity of additional information on seasonal influences, market size or weather conditions. However, these variables are assumed to be of equal importance for all brands in the market. If not, the addition of these variables to the simulation model will still heighten the accuracy of the explanation and forecasting of market share. Where necessary, this has been done in the simulations discussed in this chapter.

Three explanatory variables

In all models the price, GRPs and/or adstock and weighted distribution of sales promotions (a measurement of the distribution of promotions in terms of which outlets generate the most market share) are present as independent variables. Although the simulation model always contains other variables, the discussion is confined to the influences of these three variables and/or combinations of them for various groups of brands (see section 8.4.3, Figure 8.3, for a list of other possible independent explanatory variables).

A variable which gives the (weighted) distribution of promotional activities in their entirety provides an understanding of the use of promotions. That variable will chiefly consist of the weighted distribution of price promotions, possibly supported by displays or features. After all, these promotions dominate almost all consumer markets. If promotions (or their weighted distributions) are represented by several variables (weighted distribution of price promotions, weighted distribution of promotions with display, weighted distribution of promotions with leaflets, weighted distribution of promotions with display and leaflets), the total effect of these variables is recorded jointly. It should be borne in mind that the effects of promotions as discussed here should primarily be seen as the effects of distribution, alongside the content and/or form of these promotions. If, for instance, an optimum is found for the weighted distribution of promotions, it may be because higher promotion distribution does not add any extra sales, or because the content or form of the promotions (on shelf, on display, leaflets) leaves something to be desired. It might even be a combination of the two. In making this comparison, it was assumed that the content and form of the promotions was reasonably well distributed in the various markets and that market comparison was therefore possible.

Price was usually measured as price per standard purchasing unit, which facilitates comparison of prices of differing packs and products within a market. The price variable, measured on a weekly basis, also includes the effect of price promotions (on the average price). A big price cut with limited weighted average distribution will only have a limited effect on the average price. A limited price cut with high weighted distribution will have the same effect.

Media activity is represented in the models by the GRPs or adstock variables. GRPs are calculated using the following formula (where reach is the percentage of people who see a commercial):

Frequency x *reach of a commercial*

One GRP stands for a one-off reach of 1% of all inhabitants of the country in question aged 13 and above, or a one-off reach of 1% of any more specifically defined target group (see, among others, Floor and van Raaij, 1993).

The representation of media activity by the GRP variable has great advantages compared with that by media expenditure (in monetary terms). If media expenditure is used, there is a danger that expenditure in one year cannot be compared with another year on account of inflation corrections and other price adjustments. If the analysis period covers a number of years, it can cause a great deal of 'interference' in the simulation. If the GRP variable is used to represent media activity, the media activity effect in different countries can be compared reliably over a longer period. The value of the GRP variable is always linked to the measurement period. Thus, if variables are provided per month, the GRP variable refers to the GRPs obtained each month. If the measuring unit is one week, the GRPs indicate how many were achieved in one week.

The adstock variable is also used to render, with diminishing weight, media activities (in GRPs) in the measuring period prior to the relevant period in the simulation. The further in the past media activities are, the lower their weight. In this way, a variable is calculated which represents the cumulative effect of media activity over a longer period. In the 20 different markets an initial estimate was made on theoretical grounds of the possible lag effect of media activity, for which buying frequency was the main guideline. If buying frequency is known to have an average of around once a month (consumers buy the product once a month on average), calculation of the adstock variables can be based on the assumption that the media activity of one month previously may also influence (some of the) consumers' buying frequency in the next measurement period of a month. The different logical alternatives (media activity for five, six, seven and eight weeks) and the additional contribution they made in explaining the variation on market share were checked. The variable which better explained that variation was eventually included in the model. To prevent any misunderstanding: adstock represents cumulative media activity of weeks or months, not years. The latter is out of the question, for various reasons. These include problems with the availability of data on other variables, the long time needed to obtain sufficient examples, and radical changes in context. Broadbent (1997, p 153 *et seq.*) also discusses working with adstock.

8.5.2 The average effect of media activity on the average brand

If 20 market simulations are to be compared, the first thing to be calculated is the average effect of media activity on an average brand under average market circumstances. This requires an extensive, yet, in mathematical terms, relatively simple calculation.

The starting point for the calculation is the average score of each variable. If all the scores on all the explanatory variables of all the brands in a market are added up and divided by the number of measurements performed, this gives the average score on every dependent explanatory variable. The simulation model can now be 'asked' for the corresponding score on market share. It means that in a cola market, for instance, the Coca-Cola and Pepsi cola scores are added up and then divided by the number of measurements, which gives an 'average cola brand' – a brand with average scores only, and a corresponding market share.

There are a number of conditions for the average effect of a variable for an 'average' brand in 'average' circumstances:

- the situation (and market share) in which the scores average out on all explanatory variables should be taken as the starting point and the score on an explanatory variable varied upwards and downwards;
- this must be carried out for constant scores on all other explanatory variables, as well as varying these scores, in such a way that a great many possible combinations are calculated;
- the effects on market share of every change in the explanatory variables (ie, all scores on the market share with every combination of explanatory variables) must be added up and divided by the number of combinations of 'experiments' that have been calculated.

The standard that is obtained in this way (the main effect) forms a benchmark for the influence of an explanatory variable on a specific brand. The calculation of a point effect (the effect for one brand) for a specific brand is obtained in a similar way, though the starting position is not the average (for all explanatory variables) for all brands in the market, but the scores on the explanatory variables of the brand in question in a specific measuring period. The explanatory variables are also varied in a narrower area. The point effect can be compared with the main effect. For each brand it can be examined in this way whether the explanatory variables have a greater or lesser effect on the market share than the average brand.

Figure 8.6 gives an example of how the main effect can be represented. In order to add significance to the average influence of a variable, the main effect is always calculated for all the explanatory variables at the same time. The influence of a variable on the market share is shown as a column. The height of the column indicates the maximum influence on market share of the explanatory variable in question. So the market share is found on the Y axis of Figure 8.6. If an explanatory variable has a negative effect on market share, as is the case with the variable price, the column points downwards. Here, the column indicates that the difference between a minimum (lowest price measured in the market) and a maximum (highest price measured in the market) is eight points in market share for an average brand. For weighted distribution, an average brand can acquire 10.4 percentage points of market share if it can move from minimum to maximum distribution.

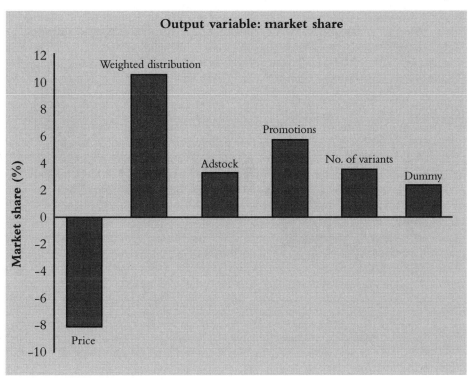

Figure 8.6 Main effect for a food market

It is clear from Figure 8.6 that weighted distribution (WD) is the greatest explanatory factor for market share (10.4 percentage points or 32% of the total change in market share), followed by price (25% of the total change in market share, or −8 percentage points) and promotions (18% explanatory variance or 6 percentage points). Media weight (represented here by adstock) accounts in this market for around 3.5 percentage points, on average, of market share – which corresponds with 10% explanation of the total change in market share. So in this market, media weight can add, on average, around 3.5 percentage points of market share if weight is raised from a minimum to a maximum (as measured in the market).

The number of variants has a somewhat greater explanatory effect than media weight and an added dummy variable a little less (dummy variables are added in order to represent unavailable information, to indicate market segments and denote consumer franchise).

8.5.3 The average effect in 20 European food markets

To gain insight into the average influence of media weight for an average brand in an average food market, all the main effects of all 20 food markets were aligned. Media weight influence on market share proved to vary between 5 and 11% in these markets. It means that for an average food brand in the 20 markets examined, 5–11% of the fluctuations in market share can be explained by (changes in) media expenditure. If the average of all main effects is then calculated, average media effect proves to be 7.6%. With a standard deviation of 5.9, media weight influence for the average brand can actually vary considerably around that 7.6% – which is apparent from the difference in

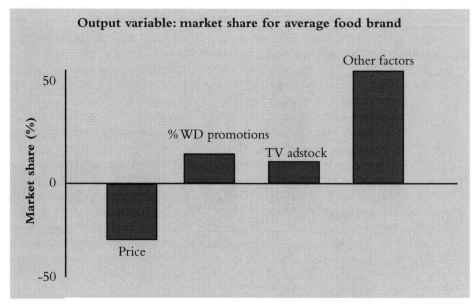

Figure 8.7 Main effect on average food brand (price = average price; %WD promotions = percentage weighted distribution of promotions; TV adstock = media activity in present and past periods; other factors = the variance in market share explained by other variables than the three previously mentioned)

media weight influence in the various markets. The differences in media effectiveness with brands will be further discussed later in this chapter (section 8.6.1).

The influence of the weighted distribution of promotions for an average food brand varies even more, accounting for between 2% and 20% of the variance in market share with an average of almost 10%. The vast range of 2–20% means that the influence of the weighted distribution of promotions largely depends on the specific context. Not surprisingly, standard deviation is high (8.6).

As far as the price variable is concerned, influence on market share also varies greatly according to the context. The explanatory variance in market share varies from 5% to over 30%. The average is 22% explained variance. This means that the influence of price in a few food markets is considerably lower than in most of the others. Usually the price variable is very much an explanatory variable for market share.

	Media	Promotions	Price	Other
Main effect (%)	7.6	9.6	21.9	60.90
Standard deviation	5.9	8.6	12.5	

Table 8.2 Average main effect for food brands in percentage of explained variable of market share (total variance in market share = 100)

The average influence of the above-mentioned explanatory variables in market share for the average food brand is reproduced in Figure 8.7 and Table 8.2.

So for an average food brand, media weight has somewhat less influence on market share than use (weighted distribution) of promotions. A higher or a lower price has at least three times the effect on market share with the average food brand. However, no hasty conclusions should be drawn from this. The following analyses will show that a few subtle distinctions are needed. Variables other than price, weighted distribution of promotions and media weight account for a good 61% of the variance in market share. Those other variables are, for example, weighted distribution, image and awareness.

8.5.4 Market leaders, upwardly mobile brands and secondary brands

Marketing literature often differentiates between different groups of brands. Kopp *et al.* (1991) speak, for instance, of the difference between large and small, young, freshly-launched and more established brands and line extensions. Floor and van Raaij (1993) also make a clear distinction between brands in various stages of the 'life cycle'. It was decided, in keeping with that literature, to focus the study of media, price and promotions effects on market leaders, 'upwardly mobile' brands (those that rise in keeping with trends) and secondary brands separately.

It is often claimed that with market leaders it is less a matter of growth due to weight of media than of media weight being necessary to hold on to the buying public. This explains the special interest in the effect of media weight for market leaders.

Upwardly mobile brands can also be described as 'runners up' – young, popular brands which are said to benefit far more easily from media weight than market leaders. The restriction to young, fast-growing brands proved difficult to apply in practice. Since too few brands met both requirements (young and fast-growing), it was necessary to drop the 'young' aspect. An upwardly mobile brand is thus one that rose in keeping with the trend in market share in the period under analysis.

Secondary brands – those that are second or third in the market – are claimed to benefit less from media weight than market leaders and runners-up. This group of brands was also examined separately.

A further division of the market leaders and the secondary brands into two more categories was based on *ad hoc* reasons. The main consideration was a reduction in standard deviation of media, price and promotion influence on market share, in order to obtain the most coherent group possible.

8.5.5 Elasticity of market leaders

If the comparison of the influences of the explanatory variables in the 20 markets is restricted to the market share influence of market leaders only, a different picture emerges from that of the average food brand. The effects of media activity, price and promotions can again be examined, but the average scores on all variables of the market leader are taken as the starting point, not varying the scores more than the lowest and highest measured score. The point effect is also calculated (the same calculation will be used for the point effect of upwardly mobile and secondary brands).

The point effect can be compared with the main effect. Both serve to indicate the sensitivity of market share to changes in the variable in question. The point effect is a measurement of the influence of variables over a provided range. The point effect indicates what effect media weight, for example, would have on market share, if that effect, as measured in a restricted area, were spread evenly throughout the entire range of media weight. So a sensitivity measured from the average and varying from lowest score in the market to highest, is compared with a sensitivity measured from a specific position (for example, market leader) in a limited area (lowest and highest score of market leader). It is assumed, to aid comparison, that the latter applies to the entire area. If the point effect is greater than the main effect, it shows that sensitivity of the variable in question in the specific area (of, say, the market leader) is higher than the average over the entire range of the variable in the market. Figure 8.8 represents the point effect of an average food market leader.

As with the average brand, price also best explains the variance in market share (followed by promotions and media) for the average food market leader.

Price does not have a significantly bigger effect on market share of the average food market leader than on the average brand (21.9% explained variance compared with 23.9%).

However, the weighted distribution of promotions does have a more explanatory effect for variance in market share of the food market leader: 16.5% as opposed to 9.6% for the average brand. Media weight also clearly accounts for a greater part of market share fluctuations for the food market leader than for the average brand (15.9% compared with 7.6% on average). This means that, for the average food market leader, media weight contributes twice as much to variance in market share compared with the average brand.

Yet the standard deviation of media weight effect for the average food market leader is relatively large (13.6%); there are apparently big differences in media effectiveness between market leaders.

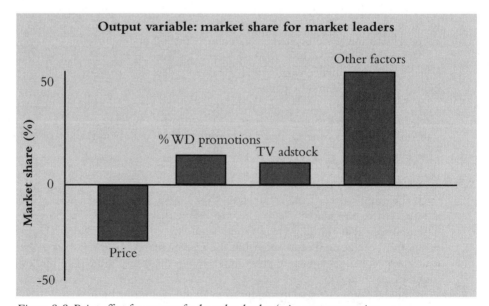

Figure 8.8 Point effect for average food market leader (price = average price;
%WD promotions = percentage weighted distribution of promotions; TV adstock =
media activity in present and past periods; other factors = the variance in the market
share explained by other variables)

		Media	Promotion	Price	Other factors
Total	Point effect (%)	15.9	16.5	21.0	46.6
	Standard deviation	13.6	7.3	9.2	
<10%	Point effect (%)	4.5	17.7	18.9	58.9
	Standard deviation	1.2	9.8	9.5	
>20%	Point effect (%)	29.5	15.6	23.0	31.9
	Standard deviation	9.3	6.3	9.5	

Table 8.3 Point effect for the average food market leader (total = all market leaders; <10% = food market leader with an explanatory effect of media on market share variance of less than 10%; > 20 % = food market leader with an explanatory effect of media on market share variance greater than 20%

Further study of the point effects of food market leaders shows that there are two different groups of market leaders:
- those for which media activity has an explanatory effect on market share variance of between 3% and 10% – group A;
- those for which media activity has an explanatory effect on market share variance of more than 20% – group B.

Table 8.3 shows that the standard deviations of media effect within these groups are considerably lower than for the total group of market leaders. It is worth splitting them into two groups, since these groups display great similarity in media effectiveness.

The first group of market leaders, group A (media sensitivity of less than 10%), mostly contains larger market leaders (market share of 20–30%). There is relatively little more for them to gain, or to gain much more would require considerable effort. Media weight accounts for less than 5% of the variance in these leaders' market share. Standard deviation is low, only 1.2. Market leaders with a market share of less than 20% are not found in this group.

The second group of market leaders, group B (media sensitivity larger than 20%) contains a number of relatively small market leaders (market share 15% or less), together with some larger ones. It is interesting to note that with this group media weight is the most important explanatory variable for the variance in market share. In this market leader group, with media sensitivity of 20% or more, there are also a few larger market leaders - whose market share is 20–30% or more.

Evidently some market leaders with a high market share are quite capable of increasing their market share even more, through increased media weight. Why do some large market leaders succeed, while other large ones do not? At all events, it is clear that context is a decisive factor for the effect of media weight on market share of the large market leader. Further research will have to show which contextual variables or combinations of variables can explain this phenomenon. As yet, it must be assumed that several variables (combined) can play a part. These might include the content of advertising, the message, duration of the dominant position, product launches, product attributes, market structure and presence of and/or type of competitors.

It is striking that no single small market leader (less than 15% market share) is placed in group A – the group of market leaders with low media sensitivity. It might seem like a logical conclusion that small market leaders can grow faster precisely because they are still small, but that can be only a partial explanation. After all, a number of larger market leaders have equally high media elasticity. Further research into the similarities and differences between the large market leaders with high media elasticity versus large market leaders with low elasticity, and small market leaders is needed to round off the explanation.

Several other interesting differences can be noted, apart from the difference in media sensitivity between the two groups of market leaders. The most obvious one is the almost 60% variance in market share of group A which is explained by other variables than media weight, price and promotion. For group B the variance is no more than 32%. The cautious conclusion can be drawn that the A group of market leaders are boosted mainly by the carry-over effect of their market position (their brand equity). The sensitivity of group A to promotions is slightly higher, but price sensitivity is a little lower than that of group B. So additional promotions might help to increase market share a little, but a structural price reduction results in a smaller contribution to market share (compared with the B group). The hypothesis can be advanced that market leaders in group A cannot communicate meaningfully (any more) with the consumer. Or that communication is only affirmative – ie, information is communicated that the consumer already knows (one-sided communication) or is no longer interesting. Established image, routine buying behaviour and competitors' communication determine the A group's market share. The fact that size cannot be the only explanatory factor is demonstrated by the large market leaders in group B with high media sensitivity.

8.5.6 Elasticity of upwardly mobile brands

Upwardly mobile brands, some of which are runners-up and some of which are brands that have existed for a longer period of time and are rising during the period under study in accordance with the trend, reveal greatest media elasticity of the groups under examination. Market leaders, even if they present a rise in market share in keeping with the trend, are not allowed in this category. But a few brands are represented which may well take over the market leader's position within the foreseeable future.

The variance in market share of the average upwardly mobile group as explained by media weight is 24.4%. Media weight explains, with one exception, 20% or more of the shifts in market share of the upwardly mobile brands. After correction for this low score (an outlier), the average works out at over 26% – considerably more than for average brands, the A group of market leaders and the secondary brands (see section 8.5.7).

In other words, media weight is the most important factor in the success of upwardly mobile brands. The other variables account for only 35–38% of total variance in market share, as opposed to around 60% for the average brand, and on average 47% for the average market leader.

Weighted distribution of promotions has an almost equally explanatory effect for variance in market share as media weight. However, a substantial difference can be noted in the very high standard deviation in the influence of weighted distribution of promotions. It means that some upwardly mobile brands do grow considerably thanks

		Media	Promotions	Price	Other factors
Total	Point effect (%)	24.4	23.9	13.5	38.2
	Standard deviation	9.4	15.9	12.1	
After	Point effect (%)	26.2	25.1	14.0	34.7
correction	Standard deviation	7.9	18.1	12.4	

Table 8.4 Point effect on market share of the average upwardly mobile brand (total = all upwardly mobile brands; after correction = all upwardly mobile brands minus an atypical brand)

to the weighted distribution of promotions, but others scarcely benefit from promotions at all. So far the reason for this large difference in promotion elasticity with upwardly mobile brands has not been investigated.

As can be seen in Figure 8.9 and Table 8.4, price accounts for relatively little variance in market share of upwardly mobile brands. Their growth is evidently not occasioned by price propositions but by media weight and promotions. In other words, they are less sensitive to price rises than other brands. This is backed up by the observation that the higher media sensitivity of upwardly mobile brands is not based on quantity – so upwardly mobile brands do not, on average, do more in media terms than other brands (market leaders, secondary brands), but they do benefit more from every GRP they deploy.

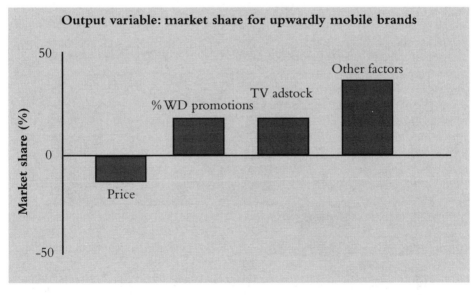

Figure 8.9 Point effect on the market share of the average upwardly mobile brand (after correction; price = average price; %WD promotions = percentage of weighted distribution of promotions; television adstock = media activities in present and past periods; other factors = variance in market share explained by variables other than the three above-mentioned)

It is worth noting the similarities and differences of point effect results of upwardly mobile brands compared with the point effect scores of group B of the market leaders (high media sensitivity). The latter may be practically the same for both, but the upwardly mobile brands are more sensitive to promotions than the market leaders. It is once more worth bearing in mind that the standard deviation for weighted distribution of promotions is very high for the average upwardly mobile brand (15.9). So promotions cannot be said to be an effective tool for all such brands to increase their market share. The price sensitivity of upwardly mobile brands is far lower than that of market leaders. But in that respect too standard deviation is very high for upwardly mobile brands (12.1). So those brands also differ greatly among themselves with respect to the influence of price. Nevertheless, a tentative conclusion emerges, suggesting that upwardly mobile brands chiefly benefit from communication activities, either in media or in promotions. For the B group of market leaders a structural price reduction, alongside media weight, can be said to affect market share positively, when compared with upwardly mobile brands.

8.5.7 Elasticity of secondary brands

Secondary brands have the least media sensitivity of all the groups of brands (see Figure 8.10).

The foremost explanatory factor of the variance in market share of secondary brands is the use of promotions. For secondary brands a substantially larger part of market share fluctuations is accounted for by the percentage of weighted distribution of promotions (33%) than for other groups. The percentage of variance on market share explained by price is comparable with the average, but media weight accounts for

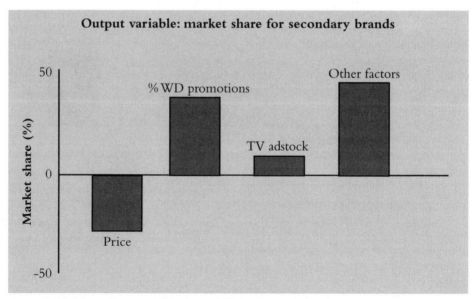

Figure 8.10 Main effect on market share of the average secondary brand (price = average price; TV adstock = media activities of present and past periods; other factors = variance in market share explained by variables other than the three above-mentioned)

		Media	Promotions	Price	Other factors
Total	Main effect (%)	7.2	33.1	21.7	38.0
	Standard deviation	9.7	20.4	18.1	
0–5%	Main effect (%)	2.1	27.2	24.3	46.4
	Standard deviation	1.0	16.6	19.6	
>18%	Main effect (%)	22.8	62.7	14.0	0.5
	Standard deviation	4.8	0.1	10.7	

Table 8.5 Main effect on market share of the average secondary brand (total = all secondary brands; 0–5% = all secondary brands with 0–5% explained variance in market share due to media weight; > 18% = all secondary brands with more than 18% explained variance in market share due to media weight)

relatively little of that variance for secondary brands. The standard deviation is even greater than the percentage of explained variance. For some secondary brands media weight has negative effects on market share. These results lead us to conclude that media weight for the average secondary brand has no significant effect on market share.

Secondary brands, like market leaders, can be divided into two distinct subgroups (see Table 8.5):
- secondary brands with media sensitivity between 0 and 5% – group A (the vast majority);
- secondary brands with media sensitivity of more than 18% – group B (five brands).

In group B, market share is greatly influenced (62.7% of explained variance) by promotions. Media sensitivity is relatively high, but this is most probably due to the media weight in supporting promotions. Price sensitivity is relatively low (at the same level as upwardly mobile brands). This means that little additional market share is achieved by a structural price reduction. Other variables do not account for more than 0.5% of the variance in market share. So these brands have to rely fully on promotions and promotions with media support.

Group A is not only characterised by very low media elasticity, but also by the relatively high percentage of explained variance in market share by variables other than media weight, promotion and price.

Price sensitivity is high (the same level as market leaders with high media sensitivity – group B). Sensitivity to promotions is also high (a little higher than that of upwardly mobile brands, though it is less than half that of the B group).

The point effect of group A of secondary brands greatly resembles that of group A of the market leaders (low media elasticity). In comparison, the promotion and price sensitivity of group A of the secondary brands is a little higher. However, the category of other variables accounts for somewhat less than with the market leaders in group A. A cautious hypothesis can be formulated that these secondary brands cannot communicate meaningfully with consumers (any more), but that they have built up a certain position based on past performance.

8.5.8 Elasticity depending on market position

Table 8.6 provides a complete overview of the main effect and point effect of all the different groups.

The main effect of the average brand is extremely misleading as regards the influence on market share of various marketing and communication tools. Their influence is decidedly non-linear, meaning that, depending on the score of variables, the influence of media weight on market share can vary greatly. Non-linearity of media weight, as well as of weighted distribution of promotions and price, is easy to demonstrate by indicating the difference in percentage of explained variance in market share caused by the same variables for the different groups of brands.

The above observation may also explain the results found by econometrists in the 1960s and 1970s (see section 8.1). After all, media sensitivity of the average brand is very low and, once it has been corrected with the standard deviation, scarcely any media effect remains. It is very different if the average brand is subdivided into market leaders, upwardly mobile brands and secondary brands. In the 1960s and 1970s linear techniques were used, which supply results that are comparable with those of the average brand.

			Media	Promotions	Price	Other factors
Average brand		Average (%)	7.6	9.6	21.9	60.9
		SD	5.9	8.6	12.5	
Market leaders	Total	Average (%)	15.9	16.5	21.0	46.6
		SD	13.6	7.3	9.2	
	<10%	Average (%)	4.5	17.7	18.9	58.9
		SD	1.2	9.8	9.5	
	>20%	Average (%)	29.5	15.6	23.0	31.9
		SD	9.3	6.3	9.5	
Upwardly mobile brands	Total	Average (%)	24.4	23.9	13.5	38.2
		SD	9.4	15.9	12.1	
	After correction	Average (%)	26.2	25.1	14.0	34.7
		SD	7.9	18.1	12.4	
Secondary brands	Total	Average (%)	7.2	33.1	21.7	38.0
		SD	9.7	20.4	18.1	
	0–5%	Average (%)	2.1	27.2	24.3	46.4
		SD	1.0	16.6	19.6	
	>18%	Average (%)	22.8	62.7	14.0	0.5
	SD	4.8	0.1	10.7		

Table 8.6 *Main effect and point effects for the average food brand, market leaders, upwardly mobile brands and secondary brands*
Market leaders with less than 10% and more than 20% variance in market share explained by media, secondary brands with 0–5% and more than 18% variance in market share explained by media (SD = standard deviation)

This report on research into 20 different European markets using non-linear simulation models demonstrates conclusively that non-linear techniques are essential to pinpoint correctly the effects of marketing and communication tools on market share. The same applies for the effect of marketing and communication tools on turnover or sales.

The margin of error in predicting the effect, for instance, of media weight for a group B market leader (high media sensitivity) based on media influence for the average brand is 300%, no less (7.9% for the average brand as against 29.5% for the group B market leader). The margin of error is even greater with respect to the influence of (weighted distribution of) promotions on the market share of secondary brands. If the effect of weighted distribution of promotions of the average brand had been taken as the starting point, the effect of promotions on the market share of, at any rate, five secondary brands would have been estimated 500% too low.

8.5.9 Conclusions

It can be concluded that the effect of media weight, weighted distribution of promotion and price depends greatly on the brand's position in the market. Average effects, obtained by averaging out the results of different brands, are misleading. Media weight is one of the most important cornerstones of upwardly mobile brands. Moreover, a number of market leaders, especially those with lower market shares (though not only these), can grow thanks to media weight. Promotions are chiefly an effective tool for secondary and upwardly mobile brands. Price is a less important tool for the latter – in other words, upwardly mobile brands lose little market share if they raise their prices. However, group B market leaders in particular can grow as prices change (are reduced). This also applies to group A of the secondary brands.

Causalities

Although the simulation models of the 20 European markets are of a causal nature, ie, causal relationships are assumed to exist between variables providing and requiring explanation (market share in the latter case), causality cannot be guaranteed. There may well still be some unknown variables which have a greater explanatory capacity and which are only partly represented by the known explanatory variables. In addition, each explanatory variable may be representative of a combination of activities. For instance, the use of newspapers for advertising may have a positive effect on market share, but that variable may in fact convey that product launches (in newspapers) are beneficial for market share. One should be constantly vigilant about the causality of perceived correlations.

However, it is difficult to construct a simulation model with variables that reflect only one independent, and, more especially, unequivocal parameter which addresses only one unequivocal aspect of a marketing activity. It would mean, for example, that media weight would have to be represented by a great many variables instead of just one, in such a way that each variable is completely unequivocal. Apart from the question whether, in terms of scientific philosophy, this is possible for reasons of polysemy (several meanings for a single word), there are practical objections to such an endeavour. The number of variables becomes so great that it is extremely difficult to construct a reliable model, in view of the limited number of measuring moments. Nor is it easy for a marketer to interpret such a model, with huge numbers of variables. The concomitant costs and time required to collect those data increase exponentially.

These are good reasons to permit polysemic variables, provided one is aware of the variety of meanings. As far as the unknown explanatory variables with considerable explanatory power are concerned, first, the margins of error of the simulation model give an idea of the used variables' explanatory capacity; second, the validity of the simulation model, in the course of time, must be regularly checked. A market simulation model may well prove to be less accurate in explaining market share two years after it was set up. After all, models like this are created with data relating to a very short period (usually not more than five years). The model's field of operation is in fact also limited to that period and an extrapolation for that period. It is impossible to establish beforehand how far ahead the model will be able to extrapolate. This must be checked repeatedly. As far as the simulation models for the 20 European markets were concerned, the validity of several models was tested at a later stage. In addition, a great many policy recommendations based on analyses of these simulation models are still proving very successful today – in other words, response is moving in the predicted direction. Both observations are reassuring as regards the causality and reliability of the models.

Theoretical implications

Several conclusions can be drawn on the basis of the research results recorded above:

- the general opinion that media weight for market leaders is primarily to 'maintain' the relationship with consumers (to retain users) must at least be modified;
- market leaders with a high market share (20–30% or higher) generally have a lower effect with media activity than market leaders with a low market share (15% or less);
- however, some market leaders with a market share of 20–30% or more do manage to achieve a high contribution from media weight;
- market leaders with both high market share and high media sensitivity depend less on the carry-over effect of their past market position (their brand equity);
- in general, it is incorrect to claim that the contribution of media weight to market share is very limited. That may apply to an average, non-existent brand, but not to specific groups of brands;
- the rising market share of upwardly mobile brands is largely thanks to media weight;
- with secondary brands, media weight can also make a substantial contribution to market share, but probably mainly combined with the use of promotions;
- the contribution of media weight to market share can be correctly estimated only if relevant context variables are included in the analysis.

It can also be concluded that research into the effects of media weight cannot be carried out with linear techniques. Single-source analysis is definitely not necessary for research into the effects of the various marketing and communication tools.

Analysis of quantitative data using the correct techniques can supply a vast amount of information. This information can be compared with that obtained from qualitative research, the difference being that the simulation model can also serve as a measure of reliability and a quantitative forecaster.

8.6 RESPONSE CURVES FOR MEDIA WEIGHT

If a brand's position at moment X is taken as the starting point, sensitivity analysis can be used to indicate the relationship between media weight and market share at moment X. This relationship should be interpreted as the expected effect on market share if the media–weight score changes, while the scores remain the same on all other variables.

In Figure 8.11 the relationship can be seen between market share and media weight (adstock) for a group-B market leader (high media sensitivity) in one of the markets analysed. Media response functions given for market leaders, upwardly mobile brands and secondary brands (Figures 8.11, 8.12, 8.13, 8.14 and 8.15) are examples. These functions occur several times with the brand groups in question. This does not mean that in individual cases no other media response functions may be found. Media response can alter with time and changing circumstances.

It is plain that media weight in the area between 50 and 180 (X axis) has a pronounced effect on market share (Y axis). When media weight is above 180, the

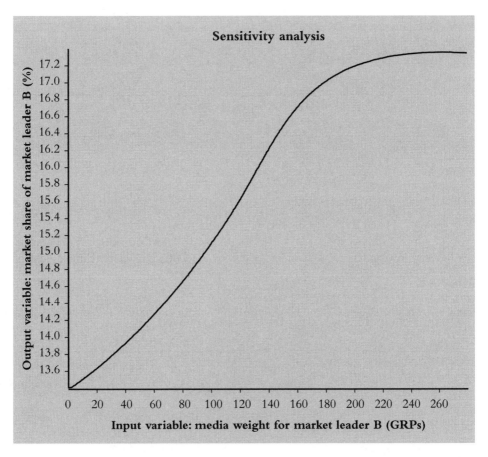

Figure 8.11 Relationship between market share and media weight for a group B market leader (high media sensitivity)

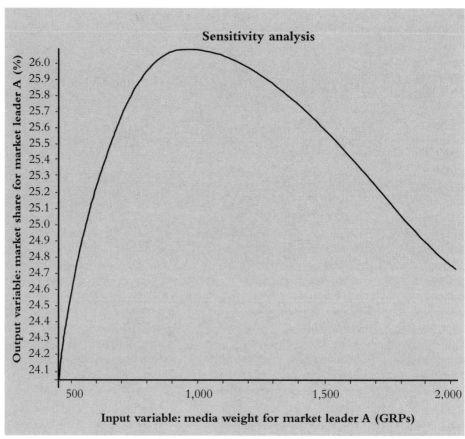

Figure 8.12 Relationship between market share and media weight for a group A market leader (low media sensitivity)

increased yield of the additional activity drops substantially. Above 240, additional media activity has no more effect on market share.

When media weight is below 50, the media effect on market share also decreases. Very low and very high media activities are both less effective than average media expenditure, at least for this group B market leader.

In several markets, an inclining S (as in Figure 8.11) has been found to be a good approximation of the relationship between media weight (adstock) and market share for a group B market leader (high media sensitivity).

For market leaders with low media sensitivity (group A market leaders), a media response function has an entirely different appearance. To start with, the market share reacts closely to media activities; however, an optimum effect is achieved relatively quickly and higher media weight even leads to a loss of part of that optimum effect (see Figure 8.12).

Optimum media activities are found at a media weight of 900. The maximum effect on market share is no higher than 2%. The group B market leader clearly achieves a far higher effect on market share with media weight (around 4%).

The media response function of an upwardly mobile brand most resembles a linear function. The media effects on market share are equal, in relative terms, for each activity. The more media activities, the higher the market share (see Figure 8.13). The effect of media weight on market share is almost the same as that of the group B market leader (3–3.5% of market share), but can be achieved with a far lower level of market share.

An almost linearly positive media response function was also found for a group A secondary brand (low media sensitivity). However, it must be pointed out that the observed media effect was not significant. The range on the Y axis, in market share points, is no more than 0.11%. Such a limited change does not overstep the criteria of error used to check reliability and accuracy of the simulation model. So it is safe to say that media weight for the group A secondary brand in Figure 8.14 (overleaf) does not have a significant effect on market share.

An entirely different media response function is found for a group B secondary brand (see Figure 8.15 on page 317). If media weight for that brand is to be effective, relatively sizeable investments will be required. The threshold value above which media weight starts to have an effect on market share is high. Media response rises steeply

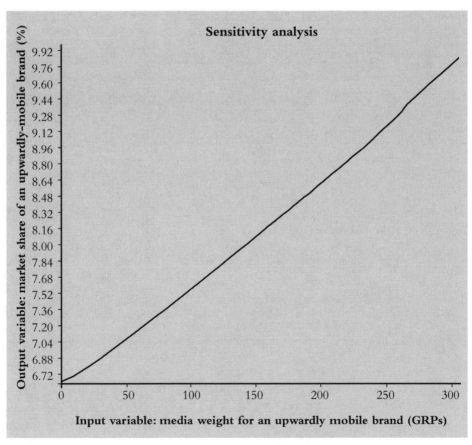

Figure 8.13 Relationship between market share and media weight for an upwardly mobile brand

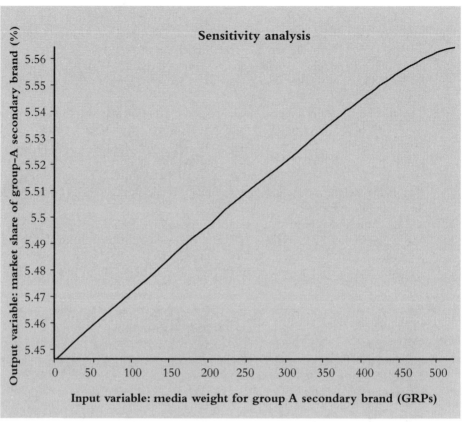

Figure 8.14 Relationship between market share and media weight for a group A secondary brand (low media sensitivity)

above 800. However, in absolute terms, the media effect is limited (1.7 %; though admittedly this is a big effect in percentage of explained variance).

8.6.1 Negative advertising effects

An explanation for when relationships with consumers become negative (loss compared with the optimum) can be found in wear-out effects (irritation caused by repetition), perceptions of advertising campaigns (of competitors), content of commercials, or variations of a brand that take some of its market share. Surprising numbers of marketers have problems noting or even considering the possibility that media weight might be damaging to a brand's market share, and result in a loss for the brand rather than a profit. However, they are able to accept that media weight may have no effect on market share. On theoretical grounds, the possibility of media weight having a negative effect can be justified.

If competing brand Y has very high media elasticity, and a private label X has very low media elasticity, it is quite feasible that if both brands advertise heavily, brand X will lose market share. Brand X's media weight will have a positive effect for a group of more or less established users, but is more likely to generate rejection than acceptance in brand switchers. After all, brand Y's media activities are far more appreciated and rate well with switchers. In this way, the less appreciated media weight of brand X reinforces

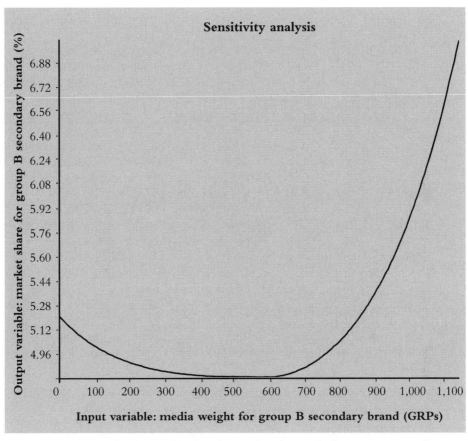

Figure 8.15 Relationship between market share and media weight for a group B secondary brand

the much more appreciated weight of brand Y, not only leading to a higher market share for brand Y, but also to a lower market share for brand X (See Jones (1995, p 44) for a similar argument).

Keeping in mind the media response function for group A market leaders (see Figure 8.12), it is possible to imagine that this function will tilt forward to such an extent that the optimum is lowered and a situation will soon come about in which high media weight even leads to a lower market share than there was initially. In practice, with simulation model building, these effects are often encountered. Media weight was also observed to have a negative effect during the launching period of a new food product. In spite of extensive consumer trials, the effect of media weight on acceptance proved to be negative; media activities only contributed to its rapid demise. This is an example of how media weight can reinforce the consumer's bad memories and the way in which communication is affected.

In section 8.6.1 a few results of the relationship between media weight and market share are indicated. It should be borne in mind that these results can change in time, with the position of the brand and its competitors. Different commercials can generate completely different response functions. Our results were all obtained on the basis of the average effect of all media executions used for the brand in the period under examination. A price rise or cut can also affect the relationship between media weight and market share.

The relationship between media effect and context also confirms the importance of seeing media and advertising policy as an integral part of the overall marketing policy. Once a successful combination of marketing tools (including media weight) has been found, this combination must be managed competently in order to hold on to that success. A change in one ingredient (one of the variables in this effective combination) can terminate success. On the other hand, in view of the worrying position of a number of market leaders, it should be remembered that communication with the consumer must be possible at all times. And communication with the consumer is not the same as merely deploying media, as can be seen from the media sensitivity of group A market leaders and group A secondary brands.

The context-specific character of the media effect can also be a good explanation for the fact that marketing successes and marketing failures can usually only be explained with hindsight. Writers on marketing are not inclined to think in combinations of variables and generally seek to explain failure and success contextually, in such a way that combinations of variables can be taken as the divining force. It is not easy to apply an explanation like this as input on how to act in a following situation, simply because the assumed causal relation was not independent enough from the context. Research into successful combinations of variables which are understood within a specific context and, for that very reason, can be taken out of it, is still in its infancy. It is hoped that the research this chapter has been reporting on constitutes a good start.

8.7 APPLICATION OF SIMULATION MODELS TO ADVERTISING

There are many different variables, other than the GRPs and adstock discussed above, which can represent media weight. The choice of how to represent information greatly depends on what data are being sought. One may, for instance, opt to look for the correlation between media weight and advertising awareness effects, rather than try to find directly the correlation between media weight and market share response. Other explanatory (independent) variables, such as copy length and GRP execution (the number of GRPs achieved by a specific commercial), plus other variables, can also be used to explain the variance in market share and/or advertising awareness or image.

Simulation models can imitate various parts of market dynamics. Figure 8.16 provides an overview of:
- variables that can represent media weight;
- possible variables requiring explanation;
- the hoped-for data from the simulation.

Variables that can represent media weight

The most important variables which can represent media weight are located on the left-hand side of Figure 8.16. These are, besides GRPs and adstock, which provide information on media expenditure, copy length, advertising formats, advertising likeability, advertising awareness and advertising knowledge (brand and campaign content).

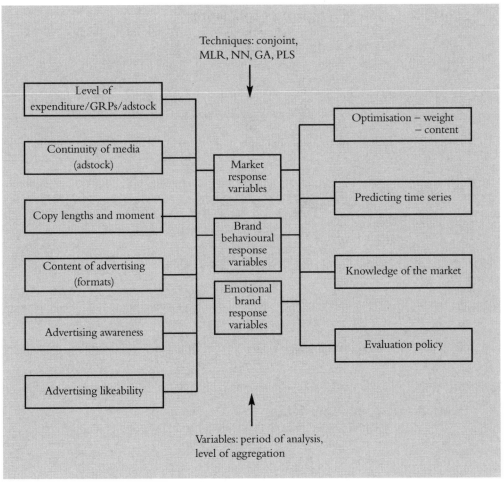

Figure 8.16 Modelling relating to advertising effect: forms of media representation (left), variables requiring explanation (centre) and data to be obtained (right)

If media weight is represented by the number of GRPs per copy length of the commercial (length in seconds of aired commercials) or by the number of GRPs per broadcasting moment, some information can be obtained on the difference in effectiveness of advertising spots of different lengths or with different broadcasting schedules. The number of GRPs per advertising format (such as testimonials from consumers or celebrities, product advertising, lifestyle advertising, news formats, and so on) can help to describe the content of commercials, permitting representation of advertising creativity in the simulation model. Advertising awareness reflects the consumer's familiarity with and knowledge of the advertising for a product or brand. Advertising likeability is an expression of the consumer's perception as regards a certain commercial or campaign for a product or brand. If advertising awareness or advertising likeability is included as an explanatory variable in a simulation model, it provides insight into that variable's contribution to a change in market share.

Possible variables requiring explanation

It is necessary to select, depending on the problem definition, which variables best represent media weight. In the central part of Figure 8.16 the variables (to be explained) that can be expected to be influenced by media weight are shown. These are the variables requiring explanation (the dependent variables) in the model. These variables are the criteria by which media effect can be measured. Advertising effect can be expressed in terms of market share (an increase in activities by a number of GRPs results in an increase in market share of x points), but also in terms of awareness or image. The variables to be explained can be divided into three categories (also dealt with in Chapter 4 on brand equity): *market response variables, brand behavioural response variables* and *emotional brand response variables*.

- *Market response variables*
  A product's financial/economic performance in the market (sales, turnover, market share, profit).
- *Brand behavioural response variables*
  Variables which describe consumers' customary or consciously loyal purchases of a brand: penetration, brand loyalty, premium price (the connection between consumer buying behaviour and consumer perception).
- *Emotional brand response variables*
  All variables which describe consumers' knowledge and perception of products: brand or product awareness (TOMA, spontaneous and aided advertising awareness, consideration set), product and brand knowledge, attitude and image (quality, price, reliability, satisfaction, perceived level of service, customer-friendliness, uniqueness, innovation), preference and affinity.

Hoped-for simulation data

The right-hand side of Figure 8.16 presents the knowledge that can be obtained with the various simulation models. Possible applications of market simulation with respect to advertising effect are diverse, for example: to obtain information on market and advertising effect, to optimise media activities and advertising content, to predict the effects of future media weight or to evaluate policy measures.

A model can be made, for instance, using the effect of advertising likeability, copy lengths, advertising formats and GRPs to explain variance in market share and to maximise it (optimisation of the market response variable). We can also try to analyse, using the same explanatory variables, the effect on brand or advertising awareness in order to discover the effect of these awareness variables (to acquire knowledge on emotional response variables).

9 Evolutionary campaign management

Cees Kappert

9.1 INTRODUCTION

The current discussion on accountability mainly concentrates on the measurability of and responsibility for marketing activities. Such accountability is generally assessed *after* commercial results have become available. From marketing management's viewpoint, it is far more interesting and important to have a reliable assessment of the measurable effect of marketing activities upfront. The effective registration of (historical) marketing activities and the associated results, combined with modelling methods and the possibilities for steering media, target groups and concept in the right direction, enable us to support decisions concerning marketing activities in advance, and to optimise them at the implementation stage. Evolutionary campaign management – in the Darwinian sense – sheds a different light on accountability, and produces knowledge, step-by-step (or generation after generation), on the commercial feasibility of marketing activities.

9.2 ACCOUNTABILITY

Accountability is sometimes described as the ability to justify commercial expenditure on various marketing activities. The pressures of cost control and disappointing results are forcing marketers to take an objective look at their actions, and rationalise or, preferably, optimise their operations.

The accountability debate currently focuses on the concept of measurability. It is an almost philosophical discussion; can marketing expenditure and returns be measured? The first step in the process is to record activities and results. In other words, what is needed is a concrete, quantified translation of 'gut feeling' and the marketer's – and customer's – emotions.

This is in fact possible, to a greater or lesser degree, and at different levels of accuracy – for example, there are differences between direct and indirect marketing techniques regarding measurement of important variables. Measuring problems can arise, however, because some factors are measured indirectly, not all factors are measured, or the influence of factors in time is hard to identify (Rossiter and Percy, 1987; Sissors and Bumba, 1996).

The present discussion of measurability only contributes to the accountability issue to a limited extent. Accountability has several aspects (see Figure 9.1). An additional issue is whether there is a causal connection between activities in retrospect and perceived returns. Can the results be 'explained' by considering the characteristics of a campaign?

Most marketing successes, in which a clear relationship can be demonstrated between activities and returns, tend to be discussed after positive results have been achieved. Looking in the rear-view mirror, marketers observe the relationship between activity and result, without going into cause-and-effect relationships very deeply. Incidentally, with less successful activities, the rear-view mirror tends to steam up: discussions on campaign failure are unpleasant, and rarely held. In any case, the success or failure of marketing activities often remains unexplained.

There is another question from management's viewpoint that needs answering. Can the marketer consciously manage (in advance) an increase in commercial returns? Is the marketer able, with the available knowledge on the effectiveness of marketing tools, to

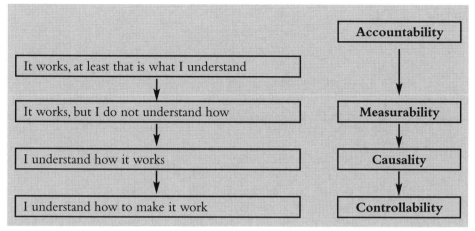

Figure 9.1 Stratification of accountability

reach *a priori* sound, optimal choices on which marketing resources to deploy, which target groups are relevant and what content/form the communication should have?

The question of whether the success of marketing activities can be predicted (with reasonable certainty) in advance often remains undecided in practice. Obviously a marketing activity may have 'felt' right, otherwise that action would not have been taken, but all unsuccessful activities would also have felt right at the time.

The definition of accountability is somewhat time-dependent in focus, even if it is assumed to be a term with different levels. Every campaign is judged on an individual basis, without looking at its interaction with other campaigns or at a logical development in a succession of campaigns.

9.3 LACK OF MEMORY

In general, marketing management has a distinctive characteristic, which might be termed 'evolutionary action-focus'. In a Darwinist race, marketers and advertising and direct marketing agencies are searching for the holy grail of the optimum commercial activity or advertisement. After a generation of campaigns, they decide 'what is hot and what is not'. Success, in this sense, is success here and now. Response and conversion figures for separate marketing activities are important. Specific campaigns are only occasionally related to longer-term communication and client objectives. Similarly, learning effects are rarely achieved by thorough evaluation of the results of different (successive) campaigns.

What causes this short-sighted view of marketing activities and results issues, what are its drawbacks, and what are the consequences for the interpretation of accountability?

Biological evolution provides some interesting parallels with accountability. If the Darwinist approach is adhered to, the key problems when developing successful marketing activities resemble the characteristics of the biological evolution of life forms, namely slowness and inefficiency (see Barash, 1987). It may take several generations of campaigns to produce a good-scoring marketing activity. Few companies have long-lasting success with their marketing activities.

Biological evolution is slow and inefficient. This is caused by a lack of memory; every generation is a random variation of genes, which leads to certain functional characteristics. These characteristics enable the individual to survive, if that individual is adapted to the environment – the survival of the fittest. 'Random' indicates that evolution is not forward-looking, but that the characteristics, or the combination of genes, are, in essence, determined by chance when copying (reproduction) takes place. No 'looking ahead' to future circumstances occurs – circumstances which might steer the development of genes in the direction of the greatest chance of survival. This type of looking ahead could be based on the memory of successful adaptations in the past. However, it does not exist, meaning that adaptation to changing circumstances is reactive and relatively slow (see Dawkins, 1986; Dennet, 1995).

Marketing departments and agencies can also be relatively 'lacking in memory'. Marketers and product managers change jobs or companies, companies change their advertising agencies. Knowledge is taken along and lost to the original employer or client. Knowledge can also be concentrated in specific parts of an organisation, without proper exchange of knowledge taking place (for example, in product management functions). As a result, every campaign seems to be a semi-random (chance-driven) variation on concepts, target groups and media. It is only possible to attribute differing degrees of success (fitness) to any combination of these elements in retrospect.

As long as the variation in concepts, target groups and media does not tie in with developments in the marketing environment, successes and failures will have to be considered as accidental (lucky or bad shots). There is no prospect of future success at the moment. Past successes do not guarantee success in the future.

Yet every campaign that does not achieve its goal is 'sub-optimal', and, to some extent, a waste of money. Good marketing activities often remain after a number of poor campaigns have petered out. If every campaign is taken individually, it is hard to decide whether it was in fact 'good'. Perhaps it met its objective, but was that set too low? This is hard to ascertain if there is no insight into historical figures.

The price of varying target groups, media and concepts with a relative lack of memory is slowness and inefficiency, sometimes leading to commercial sub-optimalisation. The only way to stay in the race, in evolutionary terms, is to create a large number of campaigns, thus increasing the chances of a 'successful' campaign. But that, even in test situations, is a very expensive business.

9.4   EVOLUTIONARY CAMPAIGN MANAGEMENT

One way of increasing the chance of marketing activity success is to create memory. If success can be traced, in a sequence of marketing activities covering the different campaigns it might be possible to adapt future marketing activities upfront, thanks to that acquired knowledge. Marketing activities are thus improved in the evolutionary context. Success factors in campaigns are recognised. Certain critical combinations of media, target groups and concepts are linked to commercial successes. Causal relationships are formed and connections understood. It is no longer necessary to reinvent the wheel time and again. Knowledge is exchanged between different campaigns and forms of campaign. Insight into how different campaigns might reinforce one another can also be obtained: this is the definition of integral communication management (Verbeke and Mosmans, 1990).

It is difficult to find commercially attractive combinations if a great many different types of campaign are being developed at the same time. New, interactive media and the tendency towards the individualisation of target groups into 'customers' and 'prospects' do not simplify matters. The human memory often fails in this respect, and the computer, and in particular database technology, can provide support.

Not only must marketing management and the agencies identify and understand the successes of the past, they must also be able to use that knowledge in adapting future campaigns. This was implied in the third layer of accountability – 'controllability'. This means that marketing managers must have choices, technically and commercially, in terms of media, target group and concept.

This combination of understanding historical successes in a wider context than campaigns themselves, through a strengthened memory function, together with the possible choices within controllability, is decisive for the way in which accountability and evolutionary campaign management are shaped. Evolutionary campaign management 'improves' the results of campaigns (in the future) by recording and analysing the success and failure of campaigns (in the past). With the knowledge acquired in this way, profitable variations can be made to the marketing tools and target groups. So, in systems terminology, there is feedback: deviations between achieved results and desired results are reduced by making adjustments (Gosling, 1994).

9.5   TRANSLATION INTO EVERYDAY PRACTICE

If this is translated into practical terms for the marketer, it means, first and foremost, that information on successes, failures and circumstances of campaigns should be stored. Perhaps a pattern can be recognised in the data, facilitating the steering of future campaigns towards commercial yields which exceed expectations. The correlation between historical successes and campaign elements, represented in concrete terms in a (media) model, serves as a searchlight for future successes.

This means, specifically, that agencies and organisations should compile proprietary databases, in which the chief aspects of campaigns (including concepts, target groups, circulation figures, results of response and conversion) are specified in as much detail as possible. In that context, models should be designed which describe these causal relationships (patterns) between the data. The importance of relationships between the variables (under the marketer's control) of campaigns and the criteria for success should be recognised. Models of this type shape the controllability criterion of accountability. They facilitate purposeful, intelligent action; it is possible to predict the commercial environments in which certain campaigns will be successful. Optimum campaign strategies, given the existing level of knowledge, are facilitated. Moreover, correlations between campaigns, or elements of long-term campaigns, can be investigated. And this enables integral communication management to acquire a knowledge base.

An advantage is that a 'memory' like this, in the form of databases and models, is cumulative. In other words, in constant conditions, insight increases. Every campaign, be it a success or a failure, forms a 'learning event'. Failures produce fresh insight and adapted models, taking the apparently changed circumstances into account. Successes confirm the rationality behind the pursued strategy.

It is tempting to think that this is the holy grail of campaign management and accountability, but as yet its practical implementation has not been perfected. That is why so many activities are still doomed to fail or do not come up to expectations.

In any event, three essential steps are needed in order to give substance to the concept of accountability for evolutionary campaign management:

1 Record all relevant data concerning planning, implementation and results of campaigns.
2 Create the possibility of ascertaining causalities, in particular between operations variables and result (ie, model relationships between the data gathered in step 1, especially between controllable marketing variables and the concomitant outcomes).
3 Create the possibility of controlling (in advance) the planning and implementation of future campaigns, applying the knowledge acquired in step 2. This also implies the possibility of simulation (testing) in order to fill gaps in knowledge.

Accountability is a stratified concept, comprising layers of measurability, causality and controllability. These terms acquire substance in steps 1 to 3. As can be seen, step 3 still leaves much to be desired. However, the present debate focuses on the scope of steps 1 and 2, which are both crucial. There is still a long way to go on the evolutionary road to solving the accountability issue.

10 Source literature

CHAPTERS 1 AND 2. RESEARCH INTO ADVERTISING EFFECTIVENESS; ADVERTISING EFFECTS AND RESEARCH METHODS

Books

Franzen, M.P. (1992) *Hoe Reclame Echt Werkt*. Deventer: Kluwer Bedrijfswetenschappen.

Franzen, M.P. (1994) *Reclame: Geloofshandeling of Verkoopinstrument*. Genootschap voor Reclame Monografie.

Jones, J.P. (1995) *When Ads Work: New Proof that Advertising Triggers Sales*. New York: Lexington Books.

Lodish, L.M. (1991) *Key Findings from 'How Advertising Works'*. The Advertising Research Foundation.

Marder, E. (1997) *The Laws of Choice: Predicting Customer Behaviour*. New York: The Free Press.

McDonald, C. (1997a) *Monitoring Advertising Performance*. Henley-on-Thames: NTC Publications Ltd.

Articles and other sources

Baker, C. (1984) 'The evaluation of advertising effects: philosophy, planning and practice', *Admap*, April, pp 192–199.

Biel, A.L. (1996) 'Advertising research: time for new paradigms?', Genootschap voor Reclame Presentation, Amsterdam.

Bloom, D. (1989) 'Do we need to worry about long-term effects?', *Admap*, October, pp 49–52.

Broadbent, S. (1996) 'Advertising effects: more than short term', *Journal of the Market Research Society*, 35(1), pp 37–49.

Broadbent, S. and Colman, S.(1986) 'Advertising effectiveness: across brands', *Journal of the Market Research Society*, 28(1).

Broadbent, S. (1996) 'The gatekeeper takes the lie-detector test', *Admap*, December, pp 34–39.

Feldwick, P. (1989) 'The use (and abuse) of market research on the evaluation of advertising effect', Market Research Society Annual Conference Papers.

Freeman, P. (1996) 'Defending advertising through market modelling', *Admap*, September, pp 27–29.

Gibson, L.D. (1996) 'What can one TV exposure do?', *Journal of Advertising Research*, March/April.

Haley, R.I., and Baldinger, A.L.(1991) 'The ARF Copy Research Validity Project', *Journal of Advertising Research*, 31, April/May.

Hall, M. (1997) 'Testing to oblivion or testing to win?', *Admap*, April.

Hollis, N. (1994) 'Television advertising awareness and sales', a paper from the 1994 European Advertising Effectiveness Symposium. An ASI Conference.

Hollis, N. (1995a) 'The link between TV-ad awareness and sales', *Journal of the Market Research Society*, 36(1), pp 41–55.

Hollis, N. (1995b) 'How to show the influence of advertising on sales', *Admap*, March, pp 75–78.

Jones, J.P. (1996a) 'Latest advertising research developments from the USA', Speakers' papers of the Admap & The Advertising Association seminar on Monitoring Advertising Performance.

Jones, J.P. (1996b) 'Look before you leap', *Admap*, November, pp 18–22.

Jones, J.P. (1996c) 'Getting it right the first time', Research Systems Corporation.

Jones, J.P. (1998) 'Rational arguments and emotional envelopes', *Admap*, April 1998.

Kuse, A.R. (1990) 'Continuing useful validation into the 1990s', ARF Key Issues Workshop, The OmniPark Central hotel, 11 July.

Lodish, L.M. (1995) 'How TV advertising works: a meta-analysis of 389 real world split-cable TV advertising experiments', *Journal of Marketing Research*, XXXII, May, pp 125–139.

Lodish, L.M. (1997) 'J.P. Jones and M.H. Blair on measuring advertising effects – another point of view', *Journal of Advertising Research*, September/October.

Lodish, L.M., Abraham, M., Kalmenson, S., Livelsberger, J., Lubetkin, B., Richarson, B. and Stevens, M.E. (1995) 'How advertising works: a meta-analysis of 389 real world split-cable television advertising experiments', *Journal of Advertising Research*, 17, May, pp 125–139.

McDonald, C. (1992) 'The limits of accountability', *Admap*, May, pp 27–32.

McDonald, C. (1996a) 'Advertising sales effects', *Admap*, April, pp 39–43.

McDonald, C. (1996b) 'How frequently should you advertise?', *Admap*, July/August, pp 22–25.

McDonald, C. (1997b) 'Short-term advertising effects: how confident can we be?', *Admap*, June.

Plessis, E. du (1994a) 'Understanding and using likeability', ARF, *Journal of Advertising Research*, September/October, pp 3–10.

Plessis, E. du (1994b) 'Likeable ads work best, but what is "likeability"?', *Admap*, May.

Schroeder, G., Richardson, B.C. and Sankaralingam (1997) 'Validating STAS using BehaviourScan', *Journal of Advertising Research*, July/August.

Tellis, G.J. and Weiss, D.L. (1995) 'Does TV advertising really affect sales?', *Journal of Advertising*, XXIV(3).

CHAPTER 3. THE ADVERTISING RESPONSE MATRIX

Books and theses

Aaker, D.A. (1991) *Managing Brand Equity. Capitalizing on the Value of a Brandname.* New York: The Free Press.

Aaker, D.A. (1996) *Building Strong Brands.* New York: The Free Press.

Aaker, D.A. and Biel, A.L. (1993) *Brand Equity & Advertising – Advertising's Role in Building Strong Brands.* Hillsdale, NJ: Lawrence Erlbaum Associates.

Aans, N. (1996) *Emoties en Reclame. Associatievorming Tussen Merk en Emotie.* Amsterdam: doctoral thesis, University of Amsterdam.

Baldinger, A.L. *What CEOs Are Saying About Equity: A Call to Action for Researchers.*

Binnendijk, N. (1995) *Q-methodologie. Een Oplossing Voor of Bevestiging van de Problematiek Tussen Adverteerders en Hun Reclamebureaus.* Amsterdam: doctoral thesis, University of Amsterdam.

Bouwman, M. (1996) *Vlinders Vangen. Op Zoek naar een Manier om Merkimago's te Onderzoeken en te Wegen.* Amsterdam: doctoral thesis, University of Amsterdam.

Bremer, D. (1996) *Merkrelaties. De Ontwikkeling van een Theoretisch Model Rond het Begrip 'Merkrelatie' en de Toepassing Ervan op het Merk Robeco van de Robeco Groep.* Amsterdam: doctoral thesis, University of Amsterdam.

Broadbent, S. (1988a) *The Advertiser's Handbook for Budget Determination.* Boston, MA/Toronto: Lexington Books.

Clawson, C.J. (1994) *Secrets of Attracting More Customers.* Lake Arrowhead Publications, p 143.

Engel, J.F., Blackwell, R.D. and Miniard, P.W. (1990) *Consumer Behavior.* Orlando: The Dryden Press.

Fishbein, M. and Ajzen, I. (1975) *Belief, Attitude, Intention and Behaviour: An Introduction to Theory and Research.* Reading, MA: Addison Wesley.

Fournier, S.M. (1994) *A Consumer–Brand Relationship Framework for Strategic Brand Management.* Florida: dissertation, Florida University.

Franzen, M.P. (1984) *Mensen, Produkten en Reclame. Een Handboek voor Strategische Reclameplanning.* Alphen aan den Rijn: Samson Uitgeverij.

Franzen, M.P. (1992a) *Hoe Reclame echt Werkt. Bevindingen Uit Empirisch Onderzoek.* Deventer: Kluwer Bedrijfswetenschappen.

Franzen, M.P. (1994) *Advertising Effectiveness.* Henley-on-Thames: NTC Publications Ltd.

Franzen, M.P. and Bouwman, M. (1999) *De Mental Wereld van Merken*: to be published.

Frijda, N.H. (1986) *The Emotions.* Cambridge: Cambridge University Press.

Frijda, N.H. (1993) *De Psychologie Heeft Zin.* Amsterdam: Prometheus.

Glass, A.L. and Holyoak, K.J. (1986) *Cognition.* Singapore: McGraw-Hill Book Co.

Goessens, C. (1994) *Attitude Toward the Ad.* Amsterdam: doctoral thesis, University of Amsterdam.

Heusden, W. (1994) *On-line Registratie van Emotionele Reacties op Televisie-Reclames: Validatie van Q-Vision.* Rotterdam: doctoral thesis, Erasmus University.

Hoogerbrugge, M. (1994) *Reclame (on)Meetbaar? Meting (on)Misbaar! De Relaties Tussen Reclamewerking, Effectmeting en het Formuleren van Weloverwogen Reclamedoelstellingen.* Amsterdam: doctoral thesis, University of Amsterdam.

Keller, K.L. (1991) *Conceptualizing, Measuring, and Maintaining Consumer-based Brand Equity.* Cambridge, MA: Report no. 91–123, Marketing Science Institute.

McDonald, C. (1992b) *How Advertising Works.* Henley-on-Thames: NTC Publications Ltd.

Millward Brown International (1991) *How Advertising Affects the Sales of Packaged Goods Brands: A Working Hypothesis for the 1990s.* Warwick, UK.

Nawas, M.M. (1986) *Inleiding Tot de Persoonlijkheidsleer.* Assen: van Gorkum.

Pauli, H. and Smeth, F. de (1994) *Kapitaliseren op het Merk.* Groningen: Adformatie/Samson Bedrijfsinformatie.

Pieters, R.G.M. and Raaij, W.F. van (1992) *Reclamewerking.* Leiden/Antwerpen: Stenfert Kroese.

Pol, I. van de, and Laskaris, A. (1994) *Waarden in Kaart.* Amsterdam: doctoral thesis, University of Amsterdam, pp 62–64.

Pröpper, S. (1994) *Principes, Politiek en Politici – De Dimensies van de Imago's van de Vier Grote Politieke Partijen.* Amsterdam: doctoral thesis, University of Amsterdam.

Riezebos, H.J. (1994) *Brand-added Value. Theory and Empirical Research about the Value of Brands to Customers.* Delft: Elburon Publishers.

Schiffman, L.G. and Kanuk, L.L. (1987) *Consumer Behavior* (third edition). New Jersey: Prentice-Hall International, Inc.

Sutherland, M. (1993) *Advertising and the Mind of the Consumer*. St Leonards, Australia: Allen & Unwin Pty Ltd.

Vries, H. de (1997) *'Het Draait om de Kern', een Onderzoek Naar Kernassociaties die Consumenten Hebben met Merken*. Amsterdam: doctoral thesis, University of Amsterdam.

Articles and other sources

Aaker, J. L. (1997) 'Dimensions of brand personality', *Journal of Marketing Research*, August.

Abraham, M.A. and Lodish, L.M. (1990) 'Getting the most out of advertising and promotion', *Harvard Business Review*, May/June, pp 50–58.

Achenbaum, A.A. (1972) in: Franzen, M.P. (1984) *Mensen, Produkten en Reclame. Een Handboek voor Strategische Reclameplanning*. Alphen aan den Rijn: Samsom Uitgeverij, p 68.

Adams, A.J. and Blair, M.H. (1992) 'Persuasive advertising and sales accountability: past experience and forward validation', *Journal of Advertising Research*, March/April, pp 20–25.

Ajzen, I. (1991) 'The theory of planned behaviour', *Organization Behaviour and Human Decision Processes*, 50.

Alt, M. and Griggs, S. (1988) 'Can a brand be cheeky?', *Marketing Intelligence Planning*, 4, pp 9–16.

Ashman, S. and Clarke, K. (1994) 'Optimising ad effectiveness', *Admap*, February, pp 43–56.

Baker, C. (1984) 'The evaluation of advertising effects: philosophy, planning and practice', *Admap*, April, pp 192–199.

Baker, C. (1991) *Advertising works series* (ed), New York, Advertising Research Foundation.

Barnard, N. (1978) 'On advertising effectiveness measurement: an idiosyncratic view', *Admap*, July, pp 381–369.

Barnard, N. (1990) 'What can you do with tracking studies and what are their limitations?', *Admap*, April, pp 21–26.

Barz, E.I. (1993) 'How to know if advertising generates sales: a new method of measuring the sales effectiveness of print advertising', ANA seminar, *The Advertiser*, Fall, pp 32–42.

Batra, R. and Stayman, D.M. (1990) 'The role of mood in advertising effectiveness', *Journal of Consumer Research*, 17, September, pp 203–214.

BBDO Worldwide (1992) *Typen van Emotionele Responsen* (internal document).

Biel, A.L. (1990) 'Strong brand, high spend: tracking relationships between the marketing mix and brand values', *Admap*, November, pp 35–40.

Biel, A.L. (1991) 'Coping with recession: why budget-cutting may not be the answer', The third Advertising Research Foundation advertising and promotion workshop, New York, February.

Biel, A.L. & Associates (1991) 'Keeping spend up in a downturn and other insights from the PIMS database'.

Biel, A.L. & Associates (1991) 'The Brandscape: converting brand image into equity', *Admap*, October.

Biel, A.L. & Associates (1992) 'How brand image drives brand equity', *Journal of Advertising Research*, 32(6).

Blackston, M. (1993) 'Beyond brand personality. Building brand relationships', in: Aaker, D.A., and Biel, A.L. *Brand Equity & Advertising: Advertising's Role in Building Strong Brands*. Hillsdale, NJ, Hillsdale: Lawrence Erlbaum Associates, pp 113–124.

Bloem, S. (1992) 'Van confrontatie naar effect: vier modelllen van reclamewerking', *Adformatie*, 20(36), pp 3–5.

Bloom, D. (1976) 'Consumer behaviour and the timing of advertising effects', *Admap*, September, pp 430–438.

Bloom, D. (1978) 'Budget determination and the problem of long-term effects', Esomar seminar: The business of advertising, Barcelona, 14–17 June.

Bloom, D. (1989) 'Do we need to worry about long-term effects?', *Admap*, October, pp 49–52.

Bogart, L. (1989) 'Advertising: art, science, or business?', *Journal of Advertising Research*, December 1988/January 1989, pp 47–52.

Brinberg, D. and Hirschman, E.C. (1986) 'Multiple orientations for the conduct of marketing research: an analysis of the academic/practitioner distinction', *Journal of Marketing*, 50, October, pp 161–173.

Britt, S.H. (1969) 'Are so-called successful advertising campaigns really successful?', *Journal of Advertising Research*, 9(2), pp 3–10.

Broadbent, S. (1979) 'One way TV advertisements work', *Journal of the Market Research Society*, 21(3), pp 139–166.

Broadbent, S. (1980) 'Price and advertising: volume and profit', *Admap*, November, pp 532–540.

Broadbent, S. (1984) 'Modelling with Adstock', *Journal of the Market Research Society*, 26(4), October, pp 295–312.

Broadbent, S. (1986) 'Two OTS in a purchase interval – some questions', *Admap*, November, pp 12–16.

Broadbent, S. (1988b) 'Advertising effects: more methodological issues', *Journal of the Market Research Society*, 30(2), pp 224–235.

Broadbent, S. (1988c) 'Wait and measure: advertising effectiveness', *Marketing*, September, pp 22–23.

Broadbent, S. (1989a) 'Monitoring advertising performance in tightening markets. Are your ways of evaluating too restrictive?', *Admap*, May, pp 28–31.

Broadbent, S. (1989b) 'Point of view: what is a "small" advertising elasticity?', *Journal of Advertising Research*, August/September, pp 37–39.

Broadbent, S. (1990a) 'Modelling beyond the blip', *Journal of the Market Research Society*, 32(1), pp 61–102.

Broadbent, S. (1990b) 'The deadly cutbacks trap: the short-term damage to brand profits caused by cuts in ad spending', *Campaign*, 3, October, p 15.

Broadbent, S. (1992a) '465 views of how advertising works – and what, if anything, they tell us', *Admap*, September, pp 34–36.

Broadbent, S. (1992b) '465 views of how advertising works – and what, if anything, they tell us, part 2: The findings', *Admap*, November, pp 17–20.

Broadbent, S. (1993) 'Advertising effects: more than short term', *Journal of the Market Research Society*, 35(1), pp 37–49.

Broadbent, S. and Colman, S. (1986) 'Advertising effectiveness: across brands', *Journal of the Market Research Society*, 28(1), pp 15–23.

Broersma, H. and Hees, A. van (1993) 'Brutus, wat heb je met mijn miljoenen gedaan?', *Bedrijfsdocumentaire*, May, pp 36–38.

Bronner, F. (1993) 'Het double jeopardy effect en de merkmonitor', *Study*, April.

Brown, G. (1986) 'Modelling advertising awareness', *The Statistician*, 35, pp 289–299.

Brown, G.H.A. (1993) 'Werbeforschung: Aktuell brennende Fragen und Zukunftperspectiven', *Planung und Analyse*, May, pp 56–60.

Celsi, R.L. and Olson, J.C. (1988) 'The role of involvement in attention and comprehension processes', *Journal of Consumer Research*, 15, September, pp 210–224.

Ceurvorst, R.W. (1994) 'A brand equity measure based on consumer commitment to brands', ARF workshop transcript proceedings, 15–16 February, pp 189–207.

Chow, S., Randall, L.R. and Clarke, D.G. (1992) 'Sequence: structural equations estimation of new copy effectiveness', *Journal of Advertising Research*, July/August, pp 60–72.

Coleman, L.G. (1991) 'Massive funding urged for ad research', *Marketing News*, 27 May, p 15.

Conference report (1992) 'Relationships: "advertising accountability" and the double bind of the full service agency', *Admap*, April, pp 17–18.

Corlett, T. (1976) 'How we should measure the longer-term effects of advertising on purchasing', *Admap*, September, pp 422–430.

Corlett, T. (1977) 'How can we monitor the influence of advertising campaigns on consumers' purchasing behaviour?', MRS Conference Papers.

Corlett, T. (1985) 'Modelling the sales effects of advertising: today's questions', *Admap*, October, pp 486–500.

Coutts, C. and Auton, R. (1990) 'Brands across boundaries – deconstructing and reconstructing the core relationships', Esomar seminar papers *(Countdown to 1992: Which issue at stake? Which strategies in the single market? Which needs in research and consultancy?)*, Brussels, 9–11 May.

Crosier, K. (1983) 'Towards a praxiology of advertising', *International Journal of Advertising*, 2, pp 215–232.

Darby, N. (1979) 'Never mind the theory – only connect', presentation to the Advertising Planning Group, July.

Davis, E., Kay, J. and Star, J. (1991) 'Is advertising rational?', *Business Strategy Review*, Fall, pp 1–23.

Dhalla, N.K. (1978) 'Assessing the long-term value of advertising', *Harvard Business Review*, January/February, pp 87–93.

Dittus, E.C. and Kopp, M. (1990) 'Advertising accountability in the 1990s: moving from guesswork and gut feelings', *Journal of Advertising Research*, 30, December 1990/January 1991, pp 7–12.

Dutka, S. (1992) 'Measuring advertising accountability', The 83rd annual meeting of the Association of National Advertisers, The Homestead, Hot Springs, VA, 10–13 October.

Edell, J. and Chapman Moore, M. (1991) in: Franzen, M.P. (1992) *Hoe Reclame Echt Werkt. Bevindingen uit Empirisch Onderzoek*. Deventer: Kluwer Bedrijfswetenschappen, p 138.

Ehrenberg, A.S.C. (1974) 'Repetitive advertising and the consumer', *Journal of Advertising Research*, 14(2).

Ehrenberg, A.S.C. (1991) 'New brands and the existing market', *Journal of the Market Research Society*, 33,(1), pp 285–299.

Ehrenberg, A.S.C. (1992) 'Comments on how advertising works', *Marketing and Research Today*, August, pp 167–169.

Ehrenberg, A.S.C. (1996) 'Brand loyalty under the microscope', presentation for the Genootschap voor Reclame, Amsterdam, 3 April.

Ehrenberg, A.S.C., Goodhardt, G.J. and Barwise, T.P. (1990) 'Double jeopardy revisited', *Journal of Marketing*, 54, July, pp 82–91.

Eisenhart, T. (1990) '"Guaranteed results" plan may suit business marketers', *Business Marketing*, July, p 32.

Elliot, J. (1985) 'How advertising frequency affects advertising effectiveness: indications of change', *Admap*, October, pp 512–515.

Fajer, M.T. and Schouten, J.W. (1995) 'Breakdown and dissolution of person–brand relationships', *Advances in Consumer Research*, 22, pp 663–667.

Farquhar, P.H., Han, J.H., Herr, P.M. and Ijiri, Y. (1992) 'Strategies for leveraging master brands: how to bypass the risks of direct extensions', *Marketing Research*, September, pp 32–42.

Farr, A. (1996) 'Proof that advertising works'. Speakers paper from the Admap & the Advertising Association seminar on Monitoring Advertising Performance, London, 24 January.

Feldwick, P. (1989) 'The use (and abuse) of market research on the evaluation of advertising effect', Market Research Society Annual Conference Papers, 15, pp 267–286.

Franzen, M.P. (1985) *Productattributen en Prestaties*, BBDO Europe, internal document.

Franzen, M.P. (1987) 'Hoeveel reclame is er nodig?', *Nieuws Tribune*, 4(18), pp 28–29 (Part 1), 19, pp 12–14 (Part 2), 20, pp 30–31 (Part 3).

Franzen, M.P. (1992) 'Agencies and effectiveness-research: some personal observations and remarks', presentation at BBDO College, November.

Franzen, M.P. (1996) 'Het merk in het geheugen', Naarden Vesting, Giep Franzen and Company (not published).

Franzen, M.P. and Hoogerbrugge, M.C. (1996) 'Het merk op weg naar de eenentwintigste eeuw', *Tijdschrift voor strategische bedrijfscommunicatie*, 2(1), pp 78–95.

Fulgoni, G.M. (1986) 'Advertising weight testing: the Behavior Scan Experience', *Admap*, March, pp 136–144.

Gordon, W. (1992) 'Accessing the brand through Research', in: Cowley, D. *Understanding Brands*. Kogan Page, UK, pp 33–56.

Gordon, W. and Corr. D. (1990) 'The ... space ... between ... words: the application of a new model of communication to quantitative brand image measurement', *Journal of the Market Research Society*, 3(3), July, pp 410–434.

Gordon, W. and Restall, C. (1992) 'Brands – the missing link: understanding the emotional relationship', Esomar seminar: The challenge of branding today and in the future, Brussels, 28–30 October.

Greig, I. (1991) 'Quant pretesting; preference and image shifts', *Admap*, June, pp 31–35.

Haley, R.I. (1992) 'What we know and what we should know about copytesting', 38th Annual conference of the Advertising Research Foundation, Open Forum, New York.

Hall, M. (1992) 'Using advertising frameworks: different research models for different campaigns', *Admap*, March, pp 17–21.

Hall, M. and Maclay, D. (1991) 'Science and art. How does research practice match advertising theory?', MRS Conference Papers.

Higie, R.A. and Sewall, M.A. (1991) 'Using recall and brand preference to evaluate advertising effectiveness', *Journal of Marketing Research*, 31(2), April/May, pp 57–63.

Högl, S. (1977) 'Werbewirkung und ihre Messkriterien', *Planung und Analyse*, pp 104–106.

Hollis, N.S. (1990) 'Separating advertising from promotional effects with econometric modeling', *Journal of Advertising Research*, 30(3), June/July, pp 6–12.

Hollis, N.S. (1993) 'The link between TV ad awareness and sales: new evidence from sales response modeling', *Journal of the Market Research Society*, 36(1), pp 41–55.

Holman, R.H. and Hecker, S. (1983) 'Advertising impact: creative elements affecting brand saliency', *Current Issues and Research in Advertising*, pp 157–172.

Honomichi, J.J. (1988) 'Winning the bottom line', *Advertising Age*, November, pp 12, 36.

Hoogerwerf, A. (1984) 'Beleid berust op veronderstellingen: de beleidstheorie', *AP*, 4.

Jain, K. and Srinivasan, N. (1990) in: Bearden, O., Netemeyer, R.G. and Mobley, M.F. (1993) *Handbook of Marketing Scales: Multi-item Measures for Marketing and Consumer Behavior Research*. Newbury Park, CA: Sage Publications, pp 146, 162–163.

Jones, J.P. (1988) 'How much is enough? Getting the most from our advertising dollar', *Advertising Age*, November, pp 45–56.

Jones, J.P. (1989) 'How to shape effective advertising: worldwide!', ADASIA Conference Papers, February.

Jones, J.P. (1990a) 'Advertising: strong force or weak force? Two views an ocean apart', *International Journal of Advertising*, 9, pp 233–246.

Jones, J.P. (1990b) 'The double jeopardy of sales promotions', *Harvard Business Review*, September/October, pp 145–152.

Jones, J.P. (1990c) 'Ad spending: maintaining market share', *Harvard Business Review*, January/February, pp 38–42.

Jones, J.P. (1991) 'Over-promise and under-delivery', *Marketing and Research Today*, 19(4), November, pp 195–204.

Joyce, T. (1991) 'Models of advertising process', *Marketing and Research Today*, November, pp 205–213.

Juchems, A. (1993) '"Werbe-Awareness" muss nach Inhalt und Qualit't differenzieren', *Wissenschaft und Forschung, Media Mix*, 49, pp 64–66.

Juchems, A. (1994) 'Tracking and the "black hole" – learning what goes on between ad exposure and product purchase', *Admap*, May, pp 15–19.

Keidan, B.M. (1986) 'Achieving the full potential of your company', The ANA Advertising Financial Management Conference, Palm Beach Gardens, Florida, 5 May.

Koks, L. (1994a) 'Op lange termijn is reclame "accountable"', *Nieuws Tribune*, 11(26), pp 20–22.

Koks, L. (1994b) 'Kwaliteit gewenste OMO-imago laat te wensen over', *Nieuws Tribune*, 11(24), p 6.

Krijnen, F. (1991) 'De reclamegulden op 'n gouden schaaltje – effectmeting steeds betrouwbaarder', *Management Team*, September, pp 34–39.

Kruijk, M. de (1994) 'Gewoon even lekker snoepen: candybars beoordeeld op fysieke eigenschappen', *Nieuws Tribune*, 11(26), p 19.

Kuin, H. (1994) 'Alleen trouwe klanten geven groei die ook winst oplevert', *Adformatie*, 22(13), p 5.

Krishnan, H.S. and Charkravarti, D. (1993) 'Varieties of brand memory induced by advertising: determinants, measures and relationships, in Aaker, D.A. and Biel, A.L. (1993) *Brand Equity, Advertising; Advertising's Role in Building Strong Brands*. Hillsdale, NJ: Lawrence Erlbaum Associates, pp 213–231.

Kuypers, K., Ware, R., Niekerk, P. van and Rodenburg, J. (1994) 'Effect & accountability', *Blad/Dossier*, 8, July.

Laurent, G. and Kapferer, J.N., (1985) in: Bearden, O., Netemeyer, R.G. and Mobley, M.F. (1993) *Handbook of Marketing Scales: Multi-item Measures for Marketing and Consumer Behavior Research*. Newbury Park, CA: Sage Publications, pp 144–145.

Lauterborn, B. and Anderson, M. (1992) 'The great divide: accountability and payment by results in the 1990s', *Admap*, April, pp 19–22.

Leavitt, C. (1970) 'Leavitt's Reaction Profile', in: Bearden, O., Netemeyer, R.G. and Mobley, M.F. (1993) *Handbook of Marketing Scales: Multi-item Measures for Marketing and Consumer Behavior Research*. Newbury Park, CA: Sage Publications, pp 203–204.

Leeflang, P.S.H., Nusmeier, H.N. and Olivier, A.J., Chapter 4, *Reclame-bekendheid, Reclame-uitgaven en de Responsmaatstaf Marktaandeel [Advertising Awareness, Advertising Expenditure and Market Share as Response Criteria]*.

Levin, G. (1992) 'Want accountability? Then go direct', *Business Marketing*, November.

Levin, G. (1993) 'Sponsors put pressure on for accountability', *Advertising Age*, 21 June.

Light, L. (1993) 'The role of advertising research in building brand equity', Advertising Research Foundation, March.

Lynn, L.Y.S. (1993) 'Brand equity, profitability, price elasticities and repeat rate', *Marketing and Research Today*, May.

McDonald, C. (1991) '"Intended response": respondents aren't things, but people, who don't always inhabit the same model', *Admap*, July/August, pp 26–27.

McDonald, C. (1992a) 'The limits of accountability', *Admap*, May, pp 27–32.

McDonald, C. (1993) 'Point of view: the key is to understand consumer response', *Journal of Advertising Research*, September/October, pp 63–69.

McQuarrie, E.F. and Munson, J.M. (1986) in: Bearden, O., Netemeyer, R.G. and Mobley, M.F. (1993) *Handbook of Marketing Scales: Multi-item Measures for Marketing and Consumer Behavior Research*. Newbury Park, CA: Sage Publications, pp 156–157.

McQueen, J. (1991) in Franzen, M.P. (1994) *Advertising Effectiveness.* pp 204–208. Henley-on-Thames: NTC Publications Ltd, pp 204–208.

Machleit, K.A., Allen, C.T. and Madden, T.J. (1993) 'The mature brand and brand interest: an alternative consequence of ad-evoked affect', *Journal of Marketing*, 57, October, pp 72–82.

Malhortra, N.K. (1981) in: Bearden, O., Netemeyer, R.G. and Mobley, M.F. (1993) *Handbook of Marketing Scales: Multi-item Measures for Marketing and Consumer Behavior Research*. Newbury Park, CA: Sage Publications, p 24.

Mano, H. (1996) 'Assessing emotional reactions to TV ads: a replication and extension with a brief adjective checklist', *Advances in Consumer Research*, 23.

Marchant, L. and Hutchinson P. (1990) 'Understanding consumer choice: a new approach?', MRC Conference Papers, The Market Research Society, 33rd annual conference, Brighton, pp 13–23.

Michels, W. and Defesche, F. (1993) 'De onmeetbaarheid van creativiteit', *Adformatie*, 21(14), pp 6–7.

Minekus, G. (1993) 'Voor wie geen doel heeft, heeft niets betekenis', *Adformatie*, 21(14), p 3.

Moran, W.T. (1994) 'Marketplace measurement of brand equity', *The Journal of Brand Management*, 1(5), pp 272–282.

Muehling, D.D., Russell, N.L. and Andrews, J.C. (1993) 'Defining, operationalizing and using involvement in advertising research: a review', *Journal of Current Issues and Research in Advertising*, 15(1), Spring.

Musiol, K.G. and Andresen, T. 'The key to brand equity or unlocking the future of your brands.'

Oherlihy, C. (1980) 'How to test the sales effects of advertising', *Admap*, January, pp 32–35.

O'Malley, D. (1991) 'Sales without salience? Small brands, advertising models and the "curse of television"', *Admap*, September, pp 36–39.

Pearch, A., Philips, N. and Terris, J. (1992) 'Accountability: economy with the truth – 16 common agency TV buying "crimes"', *Admap*, April, pp 23–26.

Pieters, R.G.M. (1989) 'Een nieuw ontwikkeling in segmentatie and positioneringsonderzoek: Laddering', *Tidjschrift voor marketing*, 23 October.

Pieters, R.G.M. and Raaij, W.F. van (1988) 'Functions and management of affect: applications to economic behavior', *Journal of Economic Psychology*, 9, pp 251–282.

Pieters, R.G.M. and Raaij, W.F. van (1993) 'Nieuwe antwoorden op oude vragen', *Adformatie*, 21(14), p 10.

Plessis, E. du (1994) 'Likeable ads work best, but what is "likeability"?' *Admap*, May, pp 10–12.

Plummer, J.T. (1984) 'How personality makes a difference', *Journal of Advertising Research*, 24(6), pp 27–31.

Plutchik, R. (1958) 'De acht basisemoties, functies en dominant gedrag', in: Aans, N. (1996), *Emoties en Reclame. Associatievorming Tussen Merk en Emotie*. Amsterdam: doctoral thesis, University of Amsterdam, p 46.

Pol, I.G.M. van der (1994a) 'Accountability is een zegen'.

Pol, I.G.M. van der (1994b) 'Accountability in praktijk'.

Poulsen, C.S. and Ussing, A. 'Testing effect hierarchy models by way of latent class analysis'.

Powell, C. (1994) 'Client-agency relationships', *Admap*, January, pp 32–34.

Prue, T. (1987) 'Where is the "scientific method" in the measurement of advertising effect?', *Admap*, December, pp 58–62.

Ratchford, B.T. (1987) and Vaughn, R. (1986) in: Bearden, O., Netemeyer, R.G. and Mobley, M.F. (1993) *Handbook of Marketing Scales: Multi-item Measures for Marketing and Consumer Behavior Research*. Newbury Park, CA: Sage Publications, pp 160–161.

Restall, C. (1990) 'What are a brand's values to the consumer and do they cross frontiers?', The 43rd Esomar Marketing Research Congress: Using Research for Marketing in the 90s, Monte Carlo.

Restall, C. and Gordon, W. (1994) 'Merken: inzicht in de emotionele binding', *Tijdschrift voor Marketing*, March, pp 72–79.

Rokeach, M.J. (1968, 1973), in: Bearden, O., Netemeyer, R.G., Mobley, M.F. (1993) *Handbook of Marketing Scales: Multi-item Measures for Marketing and Consumer Behavior Research*. Newbury Park, CA: Sage Publications, p 83.

Rossiter, J.R. (1993) 'Brand awareness and acceptance: a seven-set classification for managers', *The Journal of Brand Management*, 1(1).

Russel, D.A. and Starkman, D.L. (1990) 'Measuring the emotional response to advertising', in: Franzen, M.P. (1992) *Hoe Reclame Echt Werkt. Bevindingen uit Empirisch Onderzoek*. Deventer: Kluwer Bedrijfswetenschappen, pp 137–138.

Sampson, P. 'An examination of car image typologies using an implicit model of personality', Automotive Conference on Marketing Challenge for the 1990s, Geneva.

Sampson, P. (1993) 'A better way to measure brand image: positioning, segmentation and the dynamic attributes that drive brands', *Admap*, July/August, pp 19–23.

Schlinger, M.J. (1979a) 'A profile of responses to commercials', *Journal of Advertising Research*, 19(2), April, pp 37–46.

Schlinger, M.J. (1979b) 'Viewer Responses Profile', in: Bearden, O., Netemeyer, R.G. and Mobley, M.F. (1993) *Handbook of Marketing Scales: Multi-item Measures for Marketing and Consumer Behavior Research*. Newbury Park, CA: Sage Publications, pp 205–207.

Schlossberg, H. (1993) 'Marketing's "stepchild" gets respect', *Marketing News*, 27(6), pp 1–7.

Schroer, J.C. (1990) 'Ad spending: growing market share', *Harvard Business Review*, January/February, pp 44–48.

Sikkel, D. and Oppenhuisen, J. (1998) 'Values in the Netherlands: inventory of values in Dutch society', Research project of Stichting Wetenschappelisjk Onderzoek Commercial Communicatie, not published.

Simon, J.L. (1983) 'Advertising's sales effect can be measured and evaluated very well', *International Journal of Advertising*, 2, pp 331–341.

Simon, J.L. and Arndt, J. (1980) 'The shape of the advertising response function', *Journal of Advertising Research*, 20(4), August, pp 11–28.

Sloan, J. (1994) 'Ad agencies should learn the facts of life', *Marketing News*, 28 February, 4, pp 4, 14.

Smeth, F. de (1996) Discussion with the author.

Smit, E.G. (1994) 'Reclamestijl & campagne-effect', investigation into communication campaigns and the public, Amsterdam, University of Amsterdam.

Soffer, I. (1993) 'De effectiviteit van attitudecampagnes', *Nieuws Tribune*, 10(40), pp 18–21.

Southgate, P. (1990) 'Researching design: why quantitative old versus new evaluations are meaningless crap', MRS Conference Papers, 16, pp 161–164.

Spaeth, J. (1993) *Advertising and brand equity*, Advertising Research Foundation Annual Conference, New York, 23 March.

Spangenberg, E.R. (1997) 'Measuring the hedonistic and utilitarian dimensions of attitude: a generally applicable scale', *Advances in Consumer Resarch*, 24.

Steffenhagen, H. (1985) 'Ansätze der Werbewirkungsforschung in überblick', *Planung und Analyse*, May, pp 192–196.

Stewart, M.J. (1978) 'The long-term effects of econometrics', *Admap*, February, pp 64–70.

Team BBDO (1993) 'Research into market structure of detergents', Austria, not published.

Tellis, G.J. (1989) 'Point of view: interpreting advertising and price elasticities', *Journal of Advertising Research*, August/September, pp 40–42.

Thomas, R. (1993) 'The valuation of brands', *Marketing and Research Today*, May.

Triplett, T. (1994)' Brand personality must be managed or it will assume a life of its own', *Marketing News*, May.

Tuck, M. (1971) 'Practical frameworks for advertising and research', Translating advanced advertising theories into research reality, seminar.

Twyman, T. (1976) 'The long and short of advertising effectiveness', *Admap*, September, pp 420–422.

Twyman, W.A. (1978) 'Cost effectiveness of different media: are long-term effects possible or measurable?', Seminar on Cost Effectiveness, Barcelona.

Ulfman, A. (1990) 'Beoordeling op meetbare criteria', *Adformatie*, 21(21), pp 58–59.

Vaughn, R. (1986) 'How advertising works: a planning model revisited', *Journal of Advertising Research*, 26(1), pp 57–66.

Verbeke, W. (1989) 'Developing an advertising agency–client relationship in the Netherlands', *Journal of Advertising Research*, December 1988/January 1989, pp 19–27.

Verbeke, W. (1992) 'Advertisers do not persuade consumers; they create societies around their brands to maintain power in the marketplace', *International Journal of Advertising*, 11, pp 1–13.

Verhallen, T.M.M. (1985) 'Psycho-fysiologische methoden en het meten van reclame-effecten', *Tijdschrift voor Marketing*, June, pp 40–49.

Verleye, G. (1992) 'Chapter 2: Modellen rond de werking van reclame', in: *Attitude toward the ad*. Gent: University of Gent.

Wells, R.D. (1975) 'An empirical model of television advertising awareness', *Journal of the Market Research Society*, 17(4), pp 243–255.

Westendorp, P. van (1996) *Op weg naar accountability*, Genootschap voor Reclame Monografie, 9, Amsterdam, Genootschap voor Reclame.

Wicks, A. (1989) 'Advertising research – an eclectic view from the UK', *Journal of the Market Research Society*, 31(4), pp 527–535.

Yeck, J.D. (1993) 'Direct marketing means accountability', *Public Relations Agencies*, 24 June.

Yoon, C. (1991) 'Tears, cheers and fears: the role of emotions in advertising', Marketing Science Institute Conference, 14–15 February.

Young, M. (1993) 'Direct marketers should practise what they preach', *Direct Marketing International*, March, pp 18–19.

Zaichkowsky, J.L. (1985) 'Measuring the involvement construct', *Journal of Consumer Research*, December, pp 341–352.

Zaichkowsky, J.L, (1990), in: Bearden, O., Netemeyer, R.G., Mobley, M.F. (1993) *Handbook of Marketing Scales: Multi-item Measures for Marketing and Consumer Behavior Research*. Newbury Park, CA: Sage Publications, pp 154–155.

Zeldenrust, D. (1982) 'Psychologie en de emotionele werking van reclame', 29 October.

Zeldenrust, D. (1985) *Alles is emotie, maar dat zegt nog niks*, Presentation for Genootschap voor Reclame, 6 June.

Zinkhan, G.M. and Fornell, C. (1985) 'A test of two consumer response scales in advertising', *Journal of Marketing Research*, 12, November, pp 447–452.

CHAPTER 4. BRAND EQUITY: CONCEPT AND RESEARCH

Books and theses

Aaker, D. (1991) *Managing Brand Equity*. New York: The Free Press.

Aaker, D. (1996a) *Building Strong Brands*. New York: The Free Press.

Block, M. (1991) *Attitudinal vs. Behavioral Segmentation: A Methodological Perspective. An ARF Reference Series Book: Exploring Brand Equity.* New York: ARF.

Buzzell, R.D. and Gale, B.T. (1987) *The PIMS Principles: Linking Strategy to Performance.* New York: The Free Press.

Chernatony, L. de and McDonald, M.H.B. (1992) *Creating Powerful Brands: The Strategic Route to Success in Consumer, Industrial and Service Markets.* Oxford: Butterworth-Heinemann Ltd.

Donius, James F. (1986) *Marketplace Measurement: Tracking and Testing Advertising and Other Marketing Effects.* New York: Association of National Advertisers.

Ehrenberg, A. (1996) *Merktrouw? Een Empirische Studie naar Merktrouw Volgens het Dirichlet Model.* Amsterdam: Genootschap voor Reclame-Monografie.

Fournier, S.M. (1994) *A Consumer–Brand Relationship Framework for Strategic Brand Management.* Florida, US: dissertation, University of Florida.

Gordon, W. and Langmaid, R. (1988) *Qualitative Market Research: a Practitioner's and Buyer's Guide.* Aldershot: Gower.

Haigh, D. (1996) *Brand Valuation: A Review of Current Practice.* London: Institute of Practitioners in Advertising.

Hallberg, G. (1995) *All Consumers Are Not Created Equal.* New York: John Wiley & Sons Inc.

Heath, R. (1997) *Brand Commitment as the Predictor of Advertising Effect.* Taylor Nelson AGB.

Jones, John Philip (1995) *When Ads Work.* New York: Lexington Books.

Kapferer, J.N. (1995), *Strategisch Merk Management.* Schoonhoven: Academic Service (Dutch translation of *Strategic Brand Management*).

Keller, K.L. (1998) *Strategic Brand Management.* New Jersey: Prentice Hall.

Luik, J.C. and Waterson, M.J. (1996) *Advertising and Markets.* Henley-on-Thames: NTC Publications Ltd.

Pauli, H. and Smeth, F. de (1994) *Kapitaliseren op het Merk: Een Complete Methode voor Merkwaarde-Creatie en Merkenmanagement in de Onderneming.* Alphen a/d Rijn: Adformatie/Samsom Bedrijfsinformatie.

Pelsmacker, P. de and Kenhove, P. van (1996) *Marktonderzoek, Methoden en Toepassingen.* Garant uigevers: Apeldoom.

Steenkamp, J.B.E.M. (1989) *Product Quality: An Investigation into the Concept and How it is Perceived by Consumers.* Assen: Van Gorcum.

Stobart, P. (1994) *Brand Power* (ed). London: The Macmillan Press Ltd.

Vries, H. de (1997) *'Het Draait om de Kern': Een Onderzoek naar Kernassociaties die Consumenten Hebben met Merken*. Amsterdam: doctoral thesis.

Articles and other sources

Aaker, D. (1996b) 'Measuring brand equity across products and markets', *California Management Review*, 38(3), Spring.

Aaker, J. L. (1997) 'Dimensions of brand personality', *Journal of Marketing Research*, August.

Achenbaum, A.A. (1993) 'The mismanagement of brand equity', Measuring and managing brand equity: ARF Fifth Annual Advertising and Promotion Workshop, New York, ARF.

Agres, S.J. and Dubitsky, T.M. (1996) 'Changing needs for brands', *Journal of Advertising Research*, January/February 1996.

Ahlers, J. (1996) 'Mac & Maggie was nog lang niet uitgeput', *Adformatie*, 11, 14 March.

Ajzen, I. and Fishbein, M. (1977) 'Attitude behaviour relations: a theoretical analysis and review of empirical research', *Psychological Bulletin*, 84.

Ambler, T. (1995) 'Brand equity as a relational concept', *The Journal of Brand Management*, 2(60).

Anschuetz, N. (1997) 'Building brand popularity: the myth of segmenting to brand success', *Journal of Advertising*, January/February.

Bacon, L.D. (1994) 'Linking attitudes and behaviour', presentation to the American Marketing Association, San Francisco, September.

Baldinger, A.L. (1993) 'Measuring brand equity for enduring profitable growth: the research contribution', ARF Brand Equity Research Day, New York, ARF.

Baldinger, A.L. and Rubinson, J. (1996) 'Brand loyalty: the link between attitude and behavior', *Journal of Advertising Research*, November/December 1996.

Baldinger, A.L. and Rubinson, J. (1997) 'In search of holy grails: a rejoinder', *Journal of Advertising Research*, November/December.

Barnard, N. (1990) 'What can you do with tracking studies and what are their limitations?', *Admap*, April.

Blackston, M. (1993a) 'Brand equity in the age of mega brands and corporate brands', Measuring and managing brand equity: ARF Fifth Annual Advertising and Promotion Workshop, New York, ARF.

Blackston, M. (1993b) 'Measuring the meaning and value of a brand', ARF Brand Equity Research Day, New York, ARF.

Boer, D. de and Waarts, E. (1997) 'Verbondenheid als basis voor loyaal koopgedrag', *Tijdschrift voor Marketing*, June.

Bornard, N. (1990) 'What can you do with tracking studies and what are their limitations?', *Admap*, April.

Boschloos E. 'The Parfitt Collins Market Share Analysis; improving the model', Europanel.

Bronner, A.E. and Hoog, R. de (1979) 'Keuzemodellen en marktonderzoek', in: *Jaarboek van de Vereniging van Marktonderzoekers*, pp 223–239.

Bronner, F. and Rooy, C. van (1997) 'Mail en merkentrouw', PTT-Post Mediaservice.

Bronner, F. (1993) 'Het double jeopardy effect en de merkenmonitor', *Onderzoek*, April.

Bronner, F. (1993) *Naar een Zilveren Standaard. Een Aanzet tot Richtlijnen voor Effectonderzoek naar Campagnes van de Rijksoverheid*, research report, Veldkamp, commissioned by the Rijskvoorlichtingsdienst.

Dowling, G.R. and Uncles, M. (1997) 'Do customer loyalty programs really work?', *Sloan Management Review*, Summer.

Dyson, P., Farr, A. and Hollis, N. (1996) 'Understanding, measuring, and using brand equity', *Journal of Advertising Research*, November/December.

Dyson, P., Farr, A. and Hollis, N. (1997) 'What does the market team need, description or prescription? A response to comments by Andrew Ehrenberg', *Journal of Advertising Research*, January/February.

Ehrenberg, A. (1997) 'In search of holy grails: two comments', *Journal of Advertising Research*, January/February.

Ehrenberg, A.S.C. and Uncles, M.D. (1995) *Dirichlet-type markets: a review* (Part I: Patterns and Theory; November 1995; Part II: Applications and Implications; November 1995). Papers from GVR presentation, 'Brand loyalty under the microscope', 3 April 1996.

Ehrenberg, A.S.C., Barnard, N. and Scriven, J. (1998) 'Differentiation or salience', JOAB report, no. 5, South Bank University, London.

Ehrenberg, A.S.C., Goodhardt, G.J. and Barwise, T.P. (1990) 'Double jeopardy revisited', *Journal of Marketing*, 54, July, pp 82–91.

Ellis, G. and Gajula, S. (1993) 'Nielsen brand equity "ratings"', ARF Brand Equity Research Day, New York, ARF.

Farr, A. and Hollis, N. (1997) 'What do you want your brand to be when it grows up? Big and strong?', *Journal of Advertising Research*, 6, pp 23–36.

Feldwick, P. (1996) 'What is brand equity anyway, and how do you measure it?', *Journal of the Market Research Society*, 38(2), April.

Fornell, C., Johnson, M.D., Anderson, E.W., Cha, J. and Everitt Bryant, B. (1996) '"The American Customer Satisfaction Index": nature, purpose and findings', *Journal of Marketing*, 60, October.

Franzen, M.P. (1998) Notes for Communication Science Faculty, University of Amsterdam, not published.

GfK (1996) *GfK Foodscan*.

Haigh, D. (1996) 'A review of current practice: brand valuation', Institute of Practitioners in Advertising.

Haigh, D. (1997) 'Brand valuation or brand monitoring? That is the question', *The Journal of Brand Management*, 4(5).

Hofmeyr, J. (1990) 'The Conversion Model – a new foundation for strategic planning in marketing', Third EMAC/Esomar Symposium on New Ways in Marketing and Marketing Research.

Jancoby, J. (1971) 'Brand loyalty, a conceptual definition', Proceedings of the 79th annual convention, American Psychological Association.

Keller, K.L. (1991) 'Conceptualising, measuring, and managing customer-based brand equity', Stanford University, research paper.

Lazarus, D. (1997) 'This year's model: loyalty', *Marketing Week*, 12 June, 1997.

Light, L. (1989) 'The battle for brand dominance', The Advertising Research Foundation.

Light, L. (1998) 'Brand loyalty management – the new marketing basic', *Admap*, May.

Luyten, A.L.J.M. (1993) 'Merkartikelposities en koopgedrag bij low-involvement', *Tijdschrift voor Marketing*, December.

Luyten, A.L.J.M. and Hulsebos, W.H.L. (1994) 'Op weg naar geïntegreerde analyse van data', *Jaarboek 1994/95, Nederlandse Vereniging van Marktonderzoekers*, pp 103–115.

McQueen (1991) in Franzen, M.P. (1994) *Advertising Effectiveness*. Henley-on-Thames: NTC Publications Ltd, pp 204–208.

Moran, W.T. (1993) 'Conceptual framework for brand equity measurement and management', ARF Brand Equity Research Day, New York, ARF.

Moran, W.T. (1994) 'Marketplace measurement of brand equity', *The Journal of Brand Management*, 1(5).

Mosely, D. (1993) 'How to track customer satisfaction', *Admap*, September.

Netelbeek, M. and de Smeth, F. (1997) 'Brand management vanuit een financieel perspectief', *Tijdschrift voor Marketing*, June.

Nielsen (1997) *Pricing Optimization*, company brochure, the Netherlands.

NIPO (1996) *Het Conversie Model*, company brochure.

Parfitt, J.H. and Collins, B.J.K. (1968) 'The use of consumer panels for brand-share prediction', *Journal of Marketing Research*, V, May, pp 131–145.

Park, S.C. and Srinivasan, V. (1994) 'A survey-based method for measuring and understanding brand equity and its extendibility', *Journal of Marketing Research*, 31, May, pp 271–288.

Positioneringsgroep/A.C. Nielsen (Netherlands) BV (1994) *Studie top 3 merken*, conducted by A.C. Nielsen.

Putte, B. van den (1997) 'Serie onderzoeken naar de werking van de onderscheiden reclamewerkingsmodellen van Franzen', University of Amsterdam (not published).

Quelch, J. and Harding, C. (1996) 'Brands versus private labels: fighting to win', *Harvard Business Review*, January.

Reibstein, D. and Farris, P. (1995) 'Market share and distribution: a generalization, a speculation and some implications', *Market Science*, 14(3).

Roberts, A. (1998) 'Measuring the short-term sales effects of TV advertising', *Admap*, April.

Sloot, L.M. and Bunt, J. (1996) *Brand watcher, meetinstrument voor merktrouw*. Publication for Commercial and Government Communications Faculty, Erasmus University, Rotterdam.

Sloot, L., Peelen, E. and Bunt, J. (1997) 'Merktrouw: kwestie van gedrag èn attitude', *Tijdschrift voor Marketing*, June.

Spangenberg, E.R. (1997) 'Measuring the hedonistic and utilitarian dimensions of attitude: a generally applicable scale', *Advances in Consumer Research*, 24.

Srivastava, R.K. and Shocker, A.D. (1991) 'Brand equity: a perspective on its meaning and measurement', Report no. 91–124, Cambridge, MA, Marketing Science Institute.

Sylvester, A.K., McQueen, J. and Moore, S.D. (1994) 'Brand growth and "Phase 4 marketing"', *Admap*, September.

Taylor, J.A. (1992) 'Brand equity: its meaning, measurement and management', ESOMAR Seminar: The challenge of branding, now and in the future, Brussels, October.

Westendorp, P. van (1993) 'Leuk and Belangrijk', *Onderzoek*, March and April.

Westendorp, P van (1996) 'Op weg naar accountability', GVR publication, no. 9, Amsterdam, Genootschap voor Reclame.

CHAPTER 5. ADVERTISING FRAMEWORKS

Books and theses

Colley, R.H. (1961) *Defining Advertising Goals for Measured Advertising Results*. New York: Association of National Advertisers.

Ferguson, M. (1989) *The Aquarian Conspiracy*. Paladin: London.

Franzen, M.P. (1994) *Advertising Effectiveness: Findings from Empirical Research*. Henley-on-Thames: NTC Publications Ltd.

Lindblom, C.E. and Cohen, D.K. (1979) *Usable Knowledge*. Newhaven, Connecticut: Yale University Press.

March, J.G. and Simon, H.A. (1958) Organizations. London: John Wiley & Sons.

McDonald, C. (1992) *How Advertising Works*. Henley-on-Thames: NTC Publications Ltd.

Millward Brown International (1991) *How advertising affects the sales of packaged goods brands: a working hypothesis for the 1990's*. Warwick, UK.

Putte, B. van den (1997) 'Serie onderzoeken naar de werking van de onderscheiden reclamewerkingsmodellen van Franzen', University of Amsterdam (not published).

Rossiter, J.R. and Percy, L. (1987) *Advertising and Promotion Management*. New York: McGraw Hill.

Stappers, J.G., Reijnders, A.D. and Müller, W.A.J. (1990) *De Werking van de Massamedia, een Overzicht van Inzichten*. Amsterdam: De Arbeiderspers.

Articles and other sources

Aaker, D.A. and Stayman, D.M. (1990) 'Measuring audience perceptions of commercials and relating them to ad impact', *Journal of Advertising Research*, 30.

Barry, T. and Howard, D. (1990) 'A review and critique of the hierarchy of effects in advertising', *International Journal of Advertising*, 9(2), pp 121–135.

Biel, A.L. and Bridgewater, C.A. (1990) 'Attributes of likeable television commercials', *Journal of Advertising Research*, 30, June/July.

Cacioppo, J.T. and Petty, R.E. (1985) 'Central and peripheral routes to persuasion: the role of message repetition', in: Mitchell, A. A. and Alwitt, L.F. (eds) *Psychological Processes and Advertising Effects*. Hillsdale, New York: Lawrence Erlbaum Associates, pp 91–112.

Darby, N. (1979) 'Never mind the theory – only connect', presentation for the Advertising Planning Group, July.

Ehrenberg, A., Barnard, N. and Scriven, J. (1997) 'Justifying our advertising budgets', *Marketing and Research Today*, pp 38–44.

Ehrenberg, A., Barnard, N. and Scriven, J (1998) 'Differentiation or salience', JOAB report, South Bank University, London.

Farr, A. and Hollis, N. (1997) 'What do you want your brand to be when it grows up? Big and strong?', *Journal of Advertising Research*, 6, pp 23–36.

Hall, M. (1992) 'Using advertising frameworks: different research models for different campaigns', *Admap*, March.

Hall, M. and Maclay, D. (1991) 'Science and art: how does research practice match advertising theory?', MRS 1991 conference papers.

Hoogerwerf, A. (1983) 'Beleid berust op veronderstellingen: de beleidstheorie', *AP*, April.

Jones, J.P. (1997) 'Is advertising still salesmanship?', *Journal of Advertising Research*, pp 9–15.

Joyce, T. (1991) 'Models of advertising process', *Marketing and Research Today*, November.

Krugman, H.E. (1965) 'The impact of television advertising: learning without involvement', *Public Opinion Quarterly*, 29(3), pp 349–356.

Lannon, J. and Cooper, P. (1983) 'Humanistic advertising', *International Journal of Advertising*, 2(3), July, pp 195–213.

Lavidge, R.J. and Steiner, G.A. (1961) 'A model for predictive measurements of advertising effectiveness', *Journal of Marketing*, 25, October, pp 59–62.

Longman, K. (1998) 'If not effective frequency, then what?', *Journal of Advertising Research*, 37(4), pp 44–50.

Machleit, K.A., Allen, C.T. and Madden, T.J. (1993) 'The mature brand and brand interest: an alternative consequence of ad-evoked affect', *Journal of Marketing*, 57, October.

McDonald, C. (1993) 'Point of view: the key is to understand consumer response', *Journal of Advertising Research*, September/October.

McDonald, C. (1991) 'Intended response', *Admap*, July/August.

McGuire W. (1968) 'The nature of attitudes and attitude change', in: Lindzey, G. and Aronson, E. (eds), *Handbook of Social Psychology*, second edition, vol. 3. Reading, MA: Addison Wesley, pp 136–314.

Petty, R.E. and Cacioppo, J.T. (1986) 'The elaboration likelihood model of persuasion', *Advances in Experimental Social Psychology*, 19.

Petty, R.E., Cacioppo, J.T. and Schuurmann, D. (1983) 'Central and peripheral routes to advertising effectiveness: the moderating role of involvement', *Journal of Consumer Research*, 10, September, pp 135–146.

Plessis, E. du (1994) 'Likeable ads work best, but what is "likeability?"', *Admap*, May.

Prue, T. (1994) 'The 1994 IPA Advertising Effectiveness Awards, a "frameworkish" guide to some of this year's winners', *Admap*, November.

Roberts, A. (1998) 'Measuring the short-term sales effects of TV advertising', *Admap*, April.

Rossiter, J.R., Percy, L. and Donovan, R.J. (1991) 'A better advertising planning grid', *Journal of Advertising Research*, October/November, pp 11–21.

SPOT (Stichting Promotie en Optimalisatie TV-advertising) (1998) 'The effectiveness of TV advertising – results of 67 case histories in 10 product categories'.

Sylvester, A.K., McQueen, J. and Moore, S.D. (1994) 'Brand growth and "Phase 4 marketing"', *Admap*, September.

Vakratsas, D. and Ambler, T. (1995) 'Advertising effects: a taxonomy and review of concepts, methods and results from the academic literature', Centre for Marketing working paper no. 95–301, London Business School, October.

Vaughn, R. (1980) 'How advertising works: a planning model', *Journal of Advertising Research*, 20(5), pp 27–33.

Vaughn, R. (1986) 'How advertising works: a planning model revisited', *Journal of Advertising Research*, 26(1), pp 57–66.

Verbeke, W. (1992) 'Advertisers do not persuade consumers; they create societies around their brands to maintain power in the marketplace', *International Journal of Advertising*, 11.

Yoon, C. (1991) 'Tears, cheers, and fears: the role of emotions in advertising', *Marketing Science Institute Conference*, 14–15 February.

CHAPTER 6. PRE-TESTING

Books and theses

Aans, N. (1996) *Emoties en Reclame. Associatievorming Tussen Merk en Emotie*. Amsterdam: doctoral thesis, Communication Studies Faculty, University of Amsterdam.

Bearden, O., Netemeyer, R.G. and Mobley, M.F. (1993) *Handbook of Marketing Scales: Multi-item Measures for Marketing and Consumer Behavior Research*. Newbury Park, CA: Sage Publications.

Boer, D.J. den, Bouwman, H., Frissen, V. and Houben, M. (1994) *Methodologie en Statistiek voor Communicatieonderzoek*. Houten/Zaventum: Bohn Stafleu Van Loghum.

Bronner, F. (1993) *Naar een Zilveren Standaard. Een Aanzet tot Richtlijnen voor Effectonderzoek naar Campagnes van de Rijksoverheid*. Amsterdam: Veldkamp.

Colley, R.H. (1961) *Defining Advertising Goals for Measured Advertising Results*. New York: Association of National Advertisers.

Fletcher, A.D. and Bowers, T.A. (1988) *Fundamentals of Advertising Research* (3rd ed). Belmont, California: Wadsworth Publishing Co.

Franzen, M.P. (1992a) *Hoe Reclame echt Werkt. Bevindingen uit Empirisch Onderzoek*. Deventer: Kluwer Bedrijfswetenschappen.

Franzen, M.P. (1994) *Advertising Effectiveness*. Henley-on-Thames: NTC Publications Ltd.

Goessens, C. (1994) *Attitude Towards the Ad*. Amsterdam: doctoral thesis, Communication Studies Faculty, University of Amsterdam.

Gorden, W. and Langmaid, R. (1988) *Qualitative Market Research. A Practitioner's and Buyer's Guide*. Aldershot: Gower House.

Heijen, A.G. (1988) *Het Pre-testen van Reclame: Een Theoretische en Praktische Benadering*. Rotterdam: doctoral thesis, Faculty of Economics, Sociology and Psychology, Erasmus University.

Pieters, R. and Raaij, W.F. van (1992) *Reclamewerking*. Leiden: Stenfert Kroese.

Pol, van der and Laskaris, A. (1994) *Waarden in Kaart*. Amsterdam: doctoral thesis, Communication Studies Faculty, University of Amsterdam, p 62–64.

Rossiter, J.R. and Percy, L. (1987) *Advertising and Promotion Management*. New York: McGraw Hill.

Ruyter, K. de and Scholl, N. (1995) *Kwalitatief Marktonderzoek, Theorie en Praktijkcases*. Utrecht: Lemma.

Segers, J.H.G. and Hagenaars, J.A.P. (1990) *Methoden voor de Sociale Wetenschappen, deel 2. Technieken van Causale Analyse*. Assen/Maastricht: Van Gorcum.

Sutherland. M. (1993) *Advertising and the Mind of the Consumer.* St Leonards, Australia: Allen & Unwin Pty Ltd.

Swindels, A. (1986) *Advertising Development Research Yesterday, Today and Tomorrow.* Warwick: Millward Brown.

Tilburg, M.A.L. and Tuitert, A.B.A. (1995) *Kwalitatief Marktonderzoek in Nederland. Een Overzicht van Methoden en Technieken uit de Onderzoekspraktijk.* Brabant: Economics and psychology series, 1, Tilburg, Catholic University.

Articles and other sources

Aaker, D.A. and Buzzone, D.E. (1981) 'Viewer perceptions of prime time television advertising', *Journal of Advertising Research*, 21(5).

Admap (1995) 'Advertising pre-testing systems. An authorative guide to the UK's leading pre-testing services', *Admap*, December, pp 36–47.

Ashley, S. (1994) 'Can persuasion measurement predict sales?', Research Systems Corporation.

Baker, C. (1984) 'The evaluation of advertising effects: philosopy, planning and practice', *Admap*, April, pp 192–199.

Batra, R., Lehman, D.R., Burke, J. and Pae, J. (1995) 'When does advertising have impact? A study of tracking data', *Journal of Advertising Research*, September/October, pp 19–32.

Belson, W.A. (1986) *Validity in survey research*, Aldershot, Gower Publishing Company.

Biel, A.L. (1990) 'Love the ad. Buy the product?', *Admap*, September.

Biel, A.L. (1995) 'American developments in advertising pre-testing', *Admap*, April, pp 28–30.

Biel, A.L. (1996) 'Why copywriters don't like advertising research – and what kind of research might they accept', ARF Advertising and Copy Research Workshop, November 1995.

Biel, A.L. and Bridgewater, C.A. (1990) 'Attributes of likeable television commercials', *Journal of Advertising Research*, 30, June/July.

Blackston, M. (1994) 'Copy-testing and brand equity: what is the connection?', *Journal of Advertising Research*, Research Currents, pp 2–7.

Blackston, M. (1996) 'Can advertising pre-tests predict the longevity of advertising effects?', *Marketing and Research Today*, February, pp 11–17.

Bloom, P.N., Edell, J. and Staelin, R. (1994) 'Criteria for assessing research on the effects of marketing communications', working paper report number 94–123, Cambridge, MA, Marketing Science Institute.

Bogard, L. (1995) 'Is there an optimum frequency in advertising?', *Admap*, February, pp 32–34.

Branthwaite, A. and Swindels, A. (1995) 'The way forward for advertising research?', *Admap*, October, pp 31–34.

Brown, G. (1990) 'Copy testing ads for brand building', papers from the ARF 7th copy research workshop, OmniPark Central Hotel, 11–12 July, pp 250–277.

Burke, J. (1978), in: Franzen, M.P. (1992) *Hoe reclame echt werkt. Bevindingen uit empirisch onderzoek.* Deventer: Kluwer Bedrijfswetenschappen, p 50.

Burke Marketing Research (1986) 'Day-after recall. Television commercial testing.'

Carter, P. and Atkinson, S. (1994) 'What do clients need to know? How good is my advertising or how good is my advertising competitively?', MRS Conference papers, p 77–82.

Clansky and Kweskin (1971) 'Related recall results by program attitude', *Journal of Advertising Research*.

Cook, W.A. and Dunn, T.F. (1996) 'The changing face of advertising research in the information age, an ARF copy research council survey', *Journal of Advertising Research*, January/February, pp 55–71.

Downham, J. and Twyman, T. (1983) 'Can pre-testing be validated? A critical review of possibilities and evidence', Seminar on Effective Advertising. (Can research help?), Monte Carlo (Monaco), 26–28 January, pp 163–199.

Dubow, J. (1994) 'Recall first; but not recall alone', ARF Copy Research Workshop Transcript Proceedings, New York.

Ehrenberg, A. (1974) 'Repetitive advertising and the consumer', *Journal of Advertising Research*, 14(2).

Ehrenberg, A. (1996) 'Brand loyalty under the microscope', reading for the GvR, Amsterdam, 3 April.

Faasse, J. (1992) 'Media Observer. Effectiviteit verzekerd', Diemen, TMP, May.

Faasse, J. (1996) 'Campagneonderzoek', in Boon, A. den and Neijens, P.: *Media en Reclame*. Groningen: Wolters-Noordhoff, pp 117–132.

Farr, A. (1996) 'Proof that advertising works', Speakers' papers of the Admap & The Advertising Association seminar on Monitoring Advertising Performance, London, Cavendish Conference Centre, 24 January.

Feldwick, P. (1996) 'What evidence of how advertising works can the advertiser reasonably demand?', speakers' papers of the Admap & The Advertising Association seminar on Monitoring Advertising Performance, London, Cavendish Conference Centre, 24 January.

Fenwick, I. and Rice, M.D. (1991) 'Reliability of continuous measurement copy-testing methods', *Journal of Advertising Research*, February/March, pp 23–29.

Franzen, M.P. (1992b) 'Agencies and effectiveness-research. Some personal remarks.' (not published)

Franzen, M.P. (1994) 'Reclame: geloofshandeling of verkoopinstrument?', presentation to the Commercial Science Faculty, Amsterdam, University of Amsterdam.

Franzen, M.P. (1996) 'Merken in ons geheugen', Naarden-Vesting, Giep Franzen & Company (not published).

Franzen, M.P. and Hoogerburgge, M.C. (1996) 'Tijdschrift voor strategische', *Bedrijfscommunciatie*, 2(1), pp 78–95.

Franzen, M.P., Goessens, C. and Hoogerbrugge, M.C. (1996) *De Reclame Respons Matrix*, Naarden Vesting, Giep Franzen & Company.

Glass, G. and Holyoak, K.J. (1986) in: Franzen, M.P., Goessens, C. and Hoogerbrugge, M.C. (1996) *De Reclame Respons Matrix*. Naarden Vesting: Giep Franzen & Company.

Gordon, W. (1995) 'Advertisement pre-testing works – or does it?', *Admap*, March, pp 57–60.

Gordon, W. (1996) 'Pre-testing works', Speakers' papers of the Admap & The Advertising Association seminar on Monitoring Advertising Performance, London, 24 January.

Gorden, W. and Restall, C. (1992) 'Brands – the missing link: understanding emotional relationships', Esomar seminar, the Challenge of Branding Today and in the Future, Brussels, 28–30 October.

Gordon, W. and Swan, N. (1992) 'Facing the press', MRS Conference Papers, pp 211–219.

Greig, I. (1991) 'Quant pre-testing; preference and image shifts', *Admap*, June, pp 31–45.

Haley, R.I. (1990) 'The ARF research validity project: the final report', proceedings transcript of the 7th annual ARF Research workshop, New York, 11–12 July.

Haley, R.I. (1992) 'What we know and what we should know about copytesting', Proceedings of the 38th annual ARF conference on copy testing sales validity, New York, 23–25 November.

Haley, R.I. and Baldinger, A.L. (1991) 'The ARF copy research validity project', *Journal of Advertising Research*, April/May, pp 11–32.

Haley, R.I., Stafferoni, J. and Fox, A. (1994) 'The missing values of copy testing', *Journal of Advertising Research*, 34(3), pp 46–56.

Hall, M. and Maclay, D. (1991) 'Science and art: how does research practice match advertising theory?', MRS Conference papers.

Hall & Partners (1996) 'An interview with M. Hardie and C. McDonald', London, 23 January.

Hansen, F. (1995) 'Recent developments in the measurement of advertising effectiveness: the third generation', *Marketing and Research Today*, November, pp 259–269.

Hodges, A. (1994) 'Television pre-testing: getting the most out of television pre-testing – and the need to put enough behind it', *Admap*, December, pp 39–42.

Hollis, N. (1995) 'Like it or not, liking is not enough', *Journal of Advertising Research*, September/October, 7–15.

Jones, J.P. (1995) 'Advertising exposure effects under a microscope', *Admap*, February, pp 28–31.

Jones, J.P. (1996) 'Latest advertising research developments from the USA', Speakers' papers of the Admap & The Advertising Association seminar on Monitoring Advertising Performance, London, 24 January.

Kover, A.J. (1996) 'Why copywriters don't like advertising research – and what kind of research might they accept', *Journal of Advertising Research*, Research Currents, pp 8–10.

Krugman, H.E. (1968) in *American Psychologist*, April.

LaBarbera, P.A. and Tucciarone, J.D. (1995) 'GSR reconsidered: a behavior-based approach to evaluating and improving the sales potency of advertising', *Journal of Advertising Research*, September/October, pp 33–53.

Lannon, J. and Thompson, W.J. 'New techniques for understanding consumer reactions to advertising', *Journal of Advertising Research*, pp 6–9.

Laurent, G. and Kapferer, J.N. (1989) 'Threshold in brand awareness. Developments in advertising and communication research', Esomar congress papers.

Leckenby, J.D. and Plummer, J.T. (1983) 'Advertising stimulus measurement and assessment research', *Current Issues and Research in Advertising*, pp 134–165.

Lodish, L.M., Abraham, M., Kalmenson, S., Livelsberger, J., Lubetkin, B., Richardson, B. and Stevens, M.E. (1995) 'How advertising works: a meta-analyis of 389 real world split-cable television advertising experiments', *Journal of Advertising Research*, 17, May, pp 125–139.

McCollum, D.H. and Spielman, H.M. (1986) 'An exciting time to grow up', in: Lipstein, B. (ed) (1986) *Copy Research, A Historical Retrospective*, pp 81–98.

McCollum, D.H. and Spielman, H.M. (1978) 'The need for multiple exposure', *Topline*, 1(1), October, pp 1–2.

McCollum, D.H. and Spielman, H.M. (1978) 'A perennial question: 30s vs 60s', *Topline*, 1(1), October, p 3.

McDonald, C. (1995) 'Where to look for the most trustworthy evidence', *Admap*, February, pp 25–27.

McDonald, C. (1996) 'Sales measures of advertising', speakers' papers of the Admap & The Advertising Association seminar on Monitoring Advertising Performance, London, 24 January.

Mehrabian and Russel (1977) 'Evidence for a three factor theory of emotions', *Journal of Research in Personality*, 11, pp 273–294.

Metha, A. (1994) 'How advertising response modeling (ARM) can increase ad effectiveness', *Journal of Advertising Research*, May/June, pp 62–74.

Millward Brown International (1990) 'The Millward Brown Link Tests', Warwick, Millward Brown International.

Millward Brown International (1991) 'How advertising affects the sales of packaged goods brands. A working hypothesis for the 1990s'.

Mitchell, O. (1991) in: Hansen, F. (1995) 'Recent developments in the measurement of advertising effectiveness: the third generation', *Marketing and Research Today*, November, pp 259–269.

Moran, W.T. (1990) 'Brand presence and the perceptual frame', *Journal of Advertising Research*, October/November, pp 9–16.

Morris, J.D. (1995) 'Observations: SAM – The Self-Assessment Manikin. An efficient cross-cultural measurement of emotional response', *Journal of Advertising Research*, 6, pp 63–68.

Parker Brady, R. (1997) 'De registratie van onbewusthyken', *Nieuwstribune*, 16 October, pp 16–19.

Percy, L. and Rossiter, J.R. (1992) 'Measuring advertising ffectiveness: copy testing (pre-testing) ads and tracking (post-testing) the campaign', working paper, no. 92–020, Kensington, Australia, Australian Graduate School of Management, University of New South Wales.

Petty, R.E. and Cacioppo, J.T. (1984) 'The effects of involvement on responses to argument quantity and quality: central and peripheral routes to persuasion', *Journal of Personality and Social Psychology*, 46, 69–81.

Petty, R.E. and Cacioppo, J.T. (1986) 'The elaboration likelihood model of persuasion', *Advances in Experimental Social Psychology*, 19.

Plessis, E. du (1994a) 'Recognition versus recall', *Journal of Advertising Research*, 34(3), May/June, pp 75–91.

Plessis, E. du (1994b) 'Understanding and using likeability', *Journal of Advertising Research*, Research Currents, September/October, pp 3–10.

Plessis, E. du (1994c) 'Likeable ads work best, but what is likeability?', *Admap*, May, pp 2–4.

Poiesz, T.B.C. and Robben, H.S.J. (1994) 'Individual reactions to advertising; theoretical and methodological developments', *International Journal of Advertising*, 13, pp 25–53.

'Pre-testen, goed begonnen is half gewonnen' (1993) Rotterdam, IPM.

Prue, T. (1994) 'Where is the scientific method in the measurement of advertising effect?', *Admap*, December, pp 58–82.

Raaij, W.F. van (1984) 'Affectieve en cognitieve effecten van reclame', Amsterdam, November, preliminary research commissioned by the VEA.

Reynolds, T.J. (1991) 'Means–end based advertising research: copy testing is not strategy assessment', *Journal of Business Research*, 22, pp 131–142.

Rossiter, J.R. and Eagelson, G. (1994) 'Conclusions from the ARF's copy research validity project', *Journal of Advertising Research*, 34, May/June, pp 19–32.

Saupe, C. (1992) in: Franzen, M.P. *Hoe reclame echt werkt. Bevindingen uit empirisch onderzoek*. Deventer: Kluwer Bedrijfswetenschappen.

Schlinger, M.J. (1979) 'A profile of responses to commercials', *Journal of Advertising Research*, 19(2), April, pp 37–46.

Schweitzer, P. (1983) 'Wat is een pretest. Wat moeten we ermee en hoe moet het?', Amstelveen, FHV.

Shimp, T.A. (1981) in: Hansen, F. (1995) 'Recent developments in the measurement of advertising effectiveness: the third generation', *Marketing and Research Today*, pp 259–269.

Smith, A. (1989) 'Eye movement research', *Marketing and Research Today*, May, p 64.

Speath, J. (1991) 'Integrating evaluative and diagnostic measures: know more about how your advertising works, ARF Copy Research Workshop, New York, 11 September.

Spielman, H.M. (1987) 'Copy research: facts and fictions', *European Research*, November, pp 226–231.

SPOT (1996) 'Onderzoek naar schakelgedrag', Amsterdam/Hilversum.

Stavely, N.T. (1993) 'Is it right ... will it work? An advertiser's guide to pre-testing methods in the 1990s', *Admap*, May, pp 23–26.

Stewart-Hunter, M. (1992) 'Testing advertisements', in: Cowley, D. (ed) *How to Plan Advertising*, pp 132–150. London: Cassell, in association with the Account Planning Group.

Swinyard, W.R. and Patti, C.H. (1979) 'The communications hierarchy framework for evaluating copytesting techniques', *Journal of Advertising*, 3, pp 29–36.

Twyman, T. (1983) 'Can pretesting be validated? A critical review of possibilities and evidence', Seminar on effective advertising: can research help?, Monte Carlo (Monaco) 26–28 January.

Walker, D. and Dubitsky, T. (1994) 'Why liking matters', *Journal of Advertising Research*, 34(3), May/June, pp 9–18.

Weinblatt, L. and Conway, S. (1996) 'Can pre-tests really predict sales?', *Admap*, January, pp 44–46.

Wells, R.D. (1964) in: Bearden, O., Netemeyer, R.G., Mobley, M.F. (1993) *Handbook of Marketing Scales: Multi-item Measures for Marketing and Consumer Behavior research*. Newbury Park (Ca.): Sage Publications, pp 199–200.

Wright, R. (1980) 'How advertising works. A presentation that raises questions rather than gives answers.'

Yuspeh, S., Dunn, T. and Plummer, J. (1982) 'PACT: Positioning Advertising Copy Testing. Consensus credo representing the views of leading American Advertising Agencies', ARF Conference Understanding Copy Testing, proceedings transcript, New York, pp 93–120.

Zaichowsky, J.L. (1985) 'Measuring the involvement construct', *Journal of Consumer Research*, 12, December, pp 341–352.

Zeitlin, D.M. and Westwood, R.A. (1986) 'Measuring emotional response', *Journal of Advertising Research*, November, pp 34–44.

CHAPTER 7. TRACKING RESEARCH

Books and theses

Aaker, D.A. (1991) *Managing Brand Equity. Capitalizing on the Value of a Brandname*. New York: The Free Press.

Baker, C. (1995) *Advertising Works*. Papers from the IPA (Institute of Practitioners in Advertising) Advertising Effectiveness Awards. Henley-on-Thames: NTC Publications Ltd.

Bearden, O.W., Netemeyer, R.G. and Mobley, M.F. (1993) *Handbook of Marketing Scales: Multi-item Measures for Marketing and Consumer Behavior Research*. Newbury, California: Sage Publications Inc.

Belson, W.A. (1986) *Validity in Survey Research*. Aldershot: Gower Publishing Company.

Binnendijk, N. (1995) *Q-methodologie: Een Oplossing voor of Bevestiging van de Problematiek Tussen Adverteerders en Hun Reclamebureaus*. Amsterdam: doctoral thesis, University of Amsterdam.

Boer, D.J. den, Bouwman, H., Frissen, V. and Houben, M. (1994) *Methodologie en Statistiek voor Communicatieonderzoek*. Houten/Zaventum: Bohn Stafleu Van Loghum.

Boon, A. den and Neijens, P. (ed.) (1996) *Media en Reclame*. Groningen: Woltersgroep.

Bromley, D.B. (1993) *Reputation, Image and Impression Management*. West Sussex: John Wiley & Sons Limited.

Colley, R.H. (1964) *Vaststellen van Reclamedoelen voor de Peiling van Reclameresultaten [Defining Advertising Goals for Measured Advertising Results (1961)]*. New York: Association of National Advertisers.

Corkingdale, D.R. and Kennedy, S.H. (1975) *Measuring the Effect of Advertising*. UK: Saxon House, Teakfield Limited.

Corkingdale, D.R. and Kennedy, S.H. (1975) *Managing Advertising Effectivity*. UK: MCB Books.

Cowley, D. (ed) (1992) *How to Plan Advertising*. London: Cassell, in association with the Account Planning Group.

Dam, D. van (1989) *Het Post-testen van Reclame: een Praktische en Theoretische Benadering*. Rotterdam: doctoral thesis, Department of Economics, Sociology and Psychology: Erasmus University.

Donius, J.F. (ed.) (1986) *Marketplace Measurement, Tracking and Testing Advertising and Other Marketing Effects*. New York: ANA Inc.

Fletcher, A.D. and Bowers, T.A. (1988) *Fundamentals of Advertising Research*. Belmont, CA: Wadsworth Publishing Company.

Floor, J.M.G. and Raaij, W.F. van (1989) *Marketing en Communicatiestrategie*. Leiden: Stenfert Kroese, pp 266–286.

Franzen, M.P. and Holzhauer, F. (1991) *Merkartikel, Concurrentie en Strategie* (The brand, part 8). Deventer: Kluwer Bedrijfswetenschappen.

Franzen, M.P. (1994) *Advertising Effectiveness*. Henley-on-Thames: NTC Publications Ltd.

Gordon, W. and Langmaid, R. (1988) *Qualitative Market Research, a Practitioner's and Buyer's Guide*. Aldershot: Gower House.

Hankinson, G. and Cowling, P. (1992) *Branding in Action. Research Methodologies for Branding*. McGraw-Hill, pp 185–219.

Honkoop, M. (1993) *Reclame-onderzoek: Onontbeerlijk of Overbodig?* Amsterdam: doctoral thesis, University of Amsterdam.

Hoogerbrugge, M.C. (1994) *Reclame (on)meetbaar? Meting (on)misbaar! Een Onderzoek naar de Relaties Tussen Reclamewerking, Evaluatie-onderzoek en het Formuleren van Weloverwogen Reclamedoelstellingen*. Amsterdam: doctoral thesis, University of Amsterdam.

Jones, J. P. (1995a) *When Ads Work. New Proof that Advertising Triggers Sales*. New York: The Free Press.

Murphy, J. (1991) *Brand Valuation* (2nd edition). London: Business Books Unlimited.

Nylen, D.W. (1986) *Advertising Planning, Implementation and Control*. Cincinnatti, Ohio: South Western Publishing, pp 570–622.

Rossiter, J.R. and Percy, L. (1987) *Advertising and Promotion Management*. Singapore: McGraw-Hill.

Ruyter, K. and Scholl, N. de (1995) *Kwalitatief Marktonderzoek, Theorie en Praktijkcases*. Utrecht: Lemma.

Segers, J.H.G. and Hagenaars, J.A.P. (1990) *Methoden voor de Sociale Wetenschappen, Deel 2. Technieken van Causale Analyse.* Assen/Maastricht: Van Gorcum.

Solomon (1949) in Swarnborn, P. (1987) *Methoden voor Sociaal-wetenschappelijkonderzoek.* Meppel: Boon, p 6.

Sutherland, M. (1993) *Advertising and the Mind of the Consumer.* St Leonards, Australia: Allen, Unwin Pty Ltd.

Swindels, A. (1986) *Advertising Development Research Yesterday, Today and Tomorrow.* Warwick: Millward Brown International.

Zimbardo, P.H. and Leippe, M.R. (1991) *The Psychology of Attitude Change and Social Influence.* New York: McGraw-Hill.

Articles and other sources

(1998) 'A users' and buyers' guide to advertising tracking & monitoring services', *Admap*, September, pp 49–62.

AGB Dongen (Attwood)(1990), in: Franzen, M.P. (1995) *Merken en reclame.* Reader 1: Summary of the subject group, 1995/1996. Syllabus number: 95.10.63. Amsterdam: University of Amsterdam, Faculty of Communication Studies.

Andrews, J.C., Durvasula, S. and Akhter, S.H. (1990) 'A framework for conceptualising and measuring the involvement construct in advertising research', *Journal of Advertising*, 19(4), pp 27–40.

Archer, J. and Hubberd, T. (1996) 'Integrated tracking for integrated communications', *Admap*, February, pp 29–31.

(1990) 'Asspat-methode', Rotterdam, Research International Nederland, October.

(1994/1995) 'ATP: Advertising Tracking Programme', London, VA Research.

ATR (Awareness, Trial, Reinforcement), in: Franzen, M.P. (1995) *Merken en reclame.* Reader 1: Summary of the study material, 1995/1996. Syllabus number 95.10.63. Amsterdam: University of Amsterdam, Faculty of Communication Science, pp 7–25.

Axelrot, J. and Dindorf, J.R. (1993) 'The definition and measurement of brand equity', ARF Conference on brand equity, transcript proceedings, New York, 27 October.

Baker, C. (1984) 'The evaluation of advertising effects: philosophy, planning and practice', *Admap*, April, pp 192–199.

Baker, C. (1996) 'Factors behind success: the 1994 IPA Award winners', *Admap*, December, pp 9–13.

Baldinger, A.L. *What CEO's are saying about brand equity, a call to action for researchers.*

Baldinger, A.L. (1993) 'Measuring brand equity for enduring profitability growth: the research contribution', in ARF brand equity research day proceedings, New York, 27 October, pp 59–74.

Barnard, N. (1990) 'What can tracking studies do and what are their limitations?', *Admap*, April, pp 21–26.

Batra, R., Lehman, D.R., Burke, J. and Pae, J. (1995) 'When does advertising have impact? A study of tracking data', *Journal of Advertising Research*, September/October, pp 19–32.

Biel, A.L. (1990) 'Love the ad. Buy the product?', *Admap*, September.

Biel, A.L. (1995) 'American developments in advertising pre-testing', *Admap*, April, pp 28–30.

Biel, A.L. and Guillaume, L. (1993) 'A multidimensional approach to tracking brand equity: a progress report', in ARF brand equity research day proceedings transcript, New York, 27 October, pp 133–148.

Binnendijk, N. (1996) 'Bruisend geruis van betekenis', promotional presentation for the Communication Studies Faculty, for the benefit of the SWOCC, Amsterdam, University of Amsterdam, February.

Birkin, M. (1991) 'The benefits of valuing brands', in: Murphy, J. (ed.), *Brand valuation* (2nd edition). London: Business Books Ltd, pp 12–23.

Birkin, M. (1995) 'Why brands are valued. Brands are significant corporate assets and their licencing is more than a formality', *Admap*, March, pp 18–19.

Blackston, M. (1993) 'Beyond brand personality: in Aaker, D.A. and Biel, A.L. (eds.) *Brand Equity, Advertising; Advertising's Role in Building Strong Brands*. Hillsdale, NJ: Lawrence Erlbaum Associates, pp 163–180.

Blackston, M. (1993) 'Brand equity in the age of mega brands and corporate brands', in ARF 5th annual advertising and promotion workshop on Measuring and Managing Brand Equity, proceedings transcript.

Blackston, M. (1994) 'Copy-testing and brand equity: what is the connection?', in ARF advertising research workshop on New Advances in Advertising Research – Strengthening its Role in Accountability, proceedings transcript, New York, November, pp 169–182.

Blair, H. (1987), in: Franzen, M.P. (1992) *Hoe Reclame Echt Werkt: Bevindingen uit Empirisch Onderzoek*. Deventer: Kluwer Bedrijfswetenschappen, p 237.

Blair, H.M. and Rosenberg, K.E. (1994) 'Convergent findings increase our understanding of how advertising works', *Journal of Advertising Research*, May/June, pp 35–45.

Bochove, J. van (1993) 'Adverteerders aantoonbaar op zoek naar effectieve communicatie', *Nieuws Tribune*, 50, pp 30–31.

Bogard, L. (1995) 'Is there an optimum frequency in advertising?', *Admap*, February, pp 32–34.

Bohlander, G. (1996) 'Reclamebestedingen', in: *Media en reclame*. Groningen: Woltersgroep, pp 3–14.

Boon, A. den (1995) 'Nadruk op accountability leidt tot eenzijdig prijskopen', *Adformatie*, 11, p 48.

Boon, A. den (1996) 'Multimedia-onderzoek', in: Boon, A. den and Neijens, P. (eds) *Media en reclame*. Groningen: Woltersgroep, pp 142–149.

Branthwaite, A. and Swindels, A. (1995) 'The way forward for advertising research?', *Admap*, October, pp 31–34.

Britt, S.H. (1969) 'Are so called successful advertising campaigns really successful?', *Journal of Advertising Research*, 9(2), pp 3–10.

(1995) 'Britse accountants beginnen jaarlijkse merkwaardering', *Adformatie*, 31/32.

Broadbent, S. (1994) 'Advertising effectiveness', presentation at the International Advertising Association Education Conference, Milan, 28 October.

Broadbent, S. (1995a) 'Lessons from 1994 and from 1964–93', presentation at the Admap IAA Conference on Monitoring Advertising Performance, London, 25 January.

Broadbent, S. (1995b) 'Single source – the breakthrough?', *Admap*, June, pp 29–31.

Broadbent, S. and Burnett, L. (1992) '456 views on how advertising works, and what, if anything, they tell us', *Admap*, 9, pp 34–36 and 11, pp 17–20.

(1994) 'The brand barometer', *The Campaign Report*, 25 November, p 13.

Bronner, F. (1993) *Naar een zilveren standaard. Een aanzet tot richtlijnen voor effectonderzoek naar campagnes van de rijksoverheid*, inquiry report commissioned by the Rijksvoorlichtingsdienst.

Brown, G. (1986) 'Modelling advertising awareness', *The Statistican*, 35, pp 289–299.

Buck, S. (1995a) 'Evaluating the effects of advertising through the use of consumer panels', presentation at the Admap IAA Conference on Monitoring advertising performance, London, 25 January.

Buck, S. (1995b) 'The decline and fall of the premium brand. Is it really happening', *Admap*, March, pp 14–15.

Budner, D.M. (1994) 'Increasing the odds for marketplace success – advertising development at FCB/LKP', *Journal of Advertising Research*, May/June.

Byers, L. and Gleason, M. (1993) 'Using measurement for more effective advertising', *Admap*, May, pp 31–35.

Carter, P. and Atkinson, S. (1994) 'What do clients need to know? How good is my advertising or how good is my advertising competetively?', MRS conference papers, pp 77–82.

Cartwright, P.A. (1994) 'Advanced scanning applications. Paper from the 1994 European Advertising Effectiveness Symposium', ASI Conference papers.

Ceurvorst, R.W. (1994) 'A brand equity measure based on consumer commitment to brands', ARF conference on Exploring brand equity, transcript proceedings, New York, 15–16 February, pp 189–207.

Chan, Su Park and Srinivasan, V. (1994) 'A survey based method for measuring and understanding brand equity and its extendibility', *Journal of Marketing Research*, 16, May, pp 271–288.

'Choosing the right attitude measure', *Topline*, 38, McCollum Spielman Worldwide.

Colman, S. and Brown, G. (1982) 'Advertising tracking studies and sales effects', *Journal of the Market Research Society*, pp 165–183.

Crimmins, J.C. (1992) 'Better measurement and management of brand value', presentation at the ARF Advertising and Promotion workshop, New York, 12–13 February, pp 119–141.

Cuba, F. (1985) 'Fourteen things that make or break tracking studies', *Journal of Advertising Research*, 25(1), pp 21–23.

Day, G.S. (1986) 'Analysis for strategic market decisions', Chapter 5, in: *The Analysis of Pooled Business Experience, The PIMS Program*. St. Paul, US: West Publishing company.

Deighton, J. (1988) 'Persuasive effects that tracking studies may miss', ARF Tracking Marketplace Performance Workshop, Chicago, 3 June, pp 135–140.

Donius, J.F. (1985) 'Market tracking: a strategic reassessment and planning tool', *Journal of Advertising Research*, 25(1), February/March, pp 15–19.

Donius, J.F. (1987) 'Measuring the sales effect of advertising: the reality meets the promise', ARF Measuring Advertising's Sales Effectiveness workshop, New York, 18 June.

Donius, J.F. (1994) 'Brand equity: a holistic perspective', ARF proceedings transcript, workshop, 15–16 February, pp 125–133.

Duckworth, G. (1995) 'New angles on how advertising works, the universe and everything', *Admap*, January, pp 41–43.

(1994) 'Effect van reclame wordt steeds duidelijker: verslag van symposium over reclame-effectiviteit in Brussel', *Nieuws Tribune*, 24, pp 6–7.

Ehrenberg, A.S.C. (1974) 'Repetitive advertising and the consumer', *Journal of Advertising Research*, 14(2).

Ehrenberg, A.S.C. (1981) 'New brands and the existing market', *Journal of the Market Research Society*, 33(1), pp 285–299.

Ehrenberg, A.S.C. (1994) 'An academic's agenda for the nineties', *Admap*, September, pp 62–65.

Ehrenberg, A.S.C. (1996) 'Brand loyalty under the microscope', Reading for the Genootschap voor Reclame, Amsterdam, 3 April.

Elliott, J. (1992) 'Campaign evaluation', in: Cowley, D. (ed.) *How to Plan Advertising*, pp 151–176. London: Cassell, in association with the Account Planning Group.

Eubank, S.K. (1993) 'Understanding brand equity: a volumeric model', ARF Conference proceedings transcript, New York, 27 October, pp 165–176.

Faasse, J. (1992) 'Media Observer. Effectiviteit verzekerd', Diemen, TMP, May.

Faasse, J. (1996) 'Media and Merken Monitor', *TMP Nieuwsbrief*, February, pp 2–7.

Faasse, J. (1996) 'Campagne-onderzoek', in: Boon, A. den, and Neijens, P. (ed), *Media en reclame*. Groningen: Woltersgroep, pp 117–132.

Farquhar, P.H. and Herr, P.M. (1993) 'The dual structure of associations', in: Aaker, D.A. and Biel, A.L. (eds) *Brand Equity and Advertising; advertising's Role in Building Strong Brands*. Hillsdale, NJ: Lawrence Erlbaum Associates, pp 163–180.

Farr, A. (1994) 'From readership research to advertising effectiveness', paper for the Dutch Market Research Association.

Farr, A. (1996) 'Proof that advertising works', speakers' papers of the Admap & The Advertising Association seminar on Monitoring Advertising Performance, London, 24 January.

Feldwick, P. (1995) 'What evidence of how advertising works can the advertiser reasonably demand?', speakers' papers of the Admap IAA Conference on Monitoring Advertising Performance, London, 25 January.

Fenwick, I. and Rice, M.D. (1991) 'Reliability of continuous measurement copy-testing methods', *Journal of Advertising Research*, February/March, pp 23–29.

Flandin, M.P., Martin, E. and Simka, L.P. (1992) 'Advertising effectiveness research: A survey of agencies, clients and conflicts', *International Journal of Advertising*, 11, pp 203–214.

Francis, N. (1994) 'Panel data: friend or foe? How Royal Mail use panel data', ESOMAR seminar on the changing faces of panel research, Rome, 20–22 March, pp 101–116.

Franken, M. (1993) 'Continue campagne evaluatie verdient hernieuwde aandacht', *Nieuws Tribune*, 14, pp 24–25.

Franzen, M.P. (1992) 'Agencies and effectiveness-research: some personal observations and remarks', BBDO College, November.

Franzen, M.P. (1994) 'Reclame: geloofshandeling of verkoopinstrument?', oration by professors of Commercial Communication, Amsterdam, University of Amsterdam, Communication Science Faculty.

Franzen, M.P. (1995) '*Commerciële Communicatie: merken en reclame.* Part 1: Study group summary, syllabus number 95.10.63, Amsterdam, University of Amsterdam, Communication Studies Faculty, pp 146–151.

Franzen, M.P. and Hoogerbrugge, M.C. (1996) 'Het merk op weg naar de 21ste eeuw', *Tijdschrift voor strategische bedrijfscommunicatie*, 1, pp 78–95.

Franzen, M.P., Goessens, C. and Hoogerbrugge, M.C. (1996) *De Reclame Respons Matrix*, Naarden Vesting, Giep Franzen and Company.

GfK-Werbeindikator/ATS (1995) 'Internationales Kampagnen-Tracking', GfK Bureau brochure.

Gilles, L. (1993) 'A new vision: beyond the land of Oz', ARF Conference papers.

Gordon, W. (1992) 'Accessing the brand through research', in: Cowley, D. (ed.) *Understanding Brands.* London: Kogan Page, pp 31–56.

Gordon. W. (1994) 'Taking brand repertoires seriously', *The Journal of Brand Management*, 2(1), pp 25–30.

Gordon, W. and Corr, D. (1990) 'The ... space ... between ... words: the application of a new model of communication to quantitative brand image management', *Journal of the Market Research Society*, 32(3), July, pp 409–434.

Gordon, W. and Restall, C. (1992) 'Brands – the missing link: understanding the emotional relationship', ESOMAR seminar, The challenge of branding today and in the future, Brussels, 28–30 October.

Green, P.E. and Srinivasan, V. (1990) 'Conjoint analysis in marketing: new developments with implications for research and practice', *Journal of Marketing*, 4, October, pp 3–19.

Greene, C.S. and Nkonge, J. (1989) 'Gaining a competitive edge through conjoint analysis', *Business*, 14, April/June, pp 14–18.

Groller, J.P. (1992) 'Sterk merk: lust of last?', *FEM*, 8(4), April, pp 42–44.

Häcker, T. (1991) 'MerkTrack, of: Heeft de consument nog "trek" in mijn merk?', *NieuwsTribune*, 30, pp 18–19.

Häcker, T. (1996) 'Reclame moet vaker aan de monitor', *Tijdschrift voor Marketing*, March, pp 4–8.

Hall, M. and Maclay, D. (1991) 'Science and art: how does research practice match advertising theory?', MRS Conference papers.

Harding, C. (1994) 'Does advertising work? A paper from the 1994 European Advertising Effectiveness Symposium', ASI conference.

Helgesen, T. (1992) 'The rationality of advertising decisions: conceptual issues and some empirical findings from a Norwegian study', *Journal of Advertising Research*, November/December, pp 22–30.

Herk, M. van (1994) 'Is the tail of market research wagging the dog?', 47th ESOMAR Marketing Research Congress: Accountability in market research, pp 477–487.

Heylen, J.P., Dawson, B. and Sampson, P. (1995) 'An implicit model of consumer behavior', *Journal of the Market Research Society*, 37(1), pp 51–67.

Higie, R.A. and Sewall, M.A. (1991) 'Using recall and brand preference to evaluate advertising effectiveness', *Journal of Advertising Research*, 31(2), pp 57–63.

Hollis, N. (1993) 'Tracking in the 90s: where integration becomes reality', ARF conference meeting.

Hollis, N. (1994a) 'Copy research and brand equity: determining your brand's future today', ARF transcript of workshop proceedings, 15–16 February, 20, pp 249–269.

Hollis, N. (1994b) 'Television advertising awareness and sales', a paper from the 1994 European Advertising Effectiveness Symposium, an ASI Conference.

Hollis, N. (1994c) 'The effect of TV advertising on sales, *Journal of the Market Research Society*, 36(1), pp 41–55.

Hollis, N. (1995) 'How to show the influence of advertising on sales', *Admap*, March, pp 75–78.

Hollis, N. (1995) 'Like it or not, liking is not enough', *Journal of Advertising Research*, September/October, pp 7–15.

Hoogerbrugge, M.C., Vijlbrief, B. and Wink, M. (1993) *Onderzoek naar het formuleren van reclamedoelstellingen door adverteerders in Nederland*, investigation report, University of Amsterdam.

Ionides, C.L., Shine, P.J. and Solly, D.J. (1980) 'The market place of the mind', Market Research Society Conference, March, pp 275–290.

Inter/View (1994) 'ABLE tm. Assessing Brand Leverage', Amsterdam.

'Introducing ARM: An integrated marketing mix model. What it is, how it works', *Topline*, no. 43.

An introduction to Stochastic reaction Monitor, London, BJM Research.

(1995) 'Der IPA-Plus Werbewirkungskompass. Erste generalisierende Ergebnisse', Frankfurt, IP-Plus Vermittlung für Fernsehwerbung GmbH.

Jenkins, D. (1992) 'What are the components of recall and recognition which lead to effective advertising?', ARF Conference papers.

Jones, J.P. (1991) 'Over-promise and under-delivery', *Marketing and Research Today*, November, pp 195–203.

Jones, J.P. (1994) 'Does advertising produce sales today or sales tomorrow?', Education Conference, International Advertising Association, Milan, 28 October.

Jones, J.P. (1995b) 'Advertising exposure effects under a microscope', *Admap*, February, pp 28–31.

Jones, J.P. (1995c) 'We have a breakthrough. Single-source data is the key to proving advertising's short-term effects', *Admap*, June, pp 33–35.

Jones, J.P. (1996) 'Latest advertising research developments from the USA', speakers' papers of the Admap & The Advertising Association seminar on Monitoring advertising performance, London, 24 January.

Juchems, A. (1994a) 'Tracking and the "black hole". Learning what goes on between ad exposure and product purchase', *Admap*, May, pp 15–19.

Juchems, A. (1994b) 'Advertising tracking. The way forward', Hamburg, IVE Research International.

Juchems. A. (1995) 'Advertising tracking with TRACE. The state of art', Bureaubrochure GfK-Hamburg.

Keller, K.L. (1991) *Conceptualizing, measuring and managing customer-based brand equity*, Report no. 91–123, Marketing Science Institute, Cambridge, Massachusetts.

Knecht, J. (1990) 'Advertising tracking', *Reclame en Onderzoek*, 1(1), pp 33–37.

Koks, L. (1994) 'De commercial, het schuifje en de emotie', *Nieuws Tribune*, 42, p 25.

Koks, L. (1994) 'Op lange termijn is reclame accountable', *Nieuws Tribune*, 26, pp 20–22.

Koks, L. (1995) 'Op naar single source', *Nieuws Tribune*, 39, p 31.

Korver, A.J. (1993) 'Paths to brand equity and beyond. Measuring and managing brand equity', ARF 5th annual advertising and promotion workshop.

Krijnen, F. (1991) 'De reclamegulden op 'n gouden schaaltje: de effectmeting steeds betrouwbaarder', *Management Team*, September, pp 34–39.

Krishnan, H.S. and Charkravarti, D. (1993) 'Varieties of brand memory induced by advertising: determinants, measures and relationships', in: Aaker, D.A. and Biel, A.L. (1993) *Brand Equity, Advertising; Advertising's Role in Building Strong Brands*. Hillsdale, NJ: Lawrence Erlbaum Associates, pp 213–231.

Kuin, H. (1994) 'Makers van reclame willen steeds eerder effecten kunnen voorspellen', *Adformatie*, 44, pp 29–30.

Kuin, H. (1994a) 'In onderzoek gaat het draaien om goed voorgekauwd advies', *Adformatie*, 43, pp 3–5.

Kuin, H. (1994b) 'Het gaat om de nuance in het advies', *Adformatie*, 43, pp 6–7.

Kuin, H. (1994c) 'Kwaliteit van veldwerk kritisch bekijken', *Adformatie*, 43, p 8.

Kuin, H. (1994d) 'Onderzoekers steken maar weinig van elkaar op', *Adformatie*, 43, pp 12–15.

Kuin, H. (1994e) 'Summo waagt zich aan meting van campagne-effectiviteit', *Adformatie*, 49, p 43.

Kuin, H. (1995a) 'Effectiviteit', *Adformatie*, 11, p 72.

Kuin, H. (1995b) 'Gebrek aan onderzoek leidt tot ondergang themareclame', *Adformatie*, 11, p 20.

Kuin, H. (1995c) 'Korte termijn-verkoopkracht beste graadmeter voor effect', *Adformatie*, 19, p 40.

Kuin, H. (1995d) 'Planningsmodel Carat drukt nut media uit in reclamebekendheid', *Adformatie*, 20, p 46.

Kuin, H. (1995e) 'GfK meet verkopen in winkels én aankopen in huishoudens', *Adformatie*, 42, pp 56–57.

Kuipers, P. (1994) 'De komst van IRI staat absoluut los van Nielsens veranderingsproces', *Personality*, September, pp 4–5.

Kuse, A.R. (1994) 'Advertising effectiveness measures: empirical learning, application', a paper from the 1994 European Advertising Effectiveness Symposium, an ASI Conference.

Lannon, J. (1993) 'Asking the right questions: what do people do with advertising?', in: Aaker, D.A. and Biel, A.L. (1993) *Brand Equity, Advertising; Advertising's Role in Building Strong Brands*. Hillsdale, NJ: Lawrence Erlbaum Associates, pp 163–176.

Lannon, J. and Thompson, W.J., 'New techniques for understanding consumer reactions to advertising', ARF Conference papers, pp 6–9.

Leavitt, C. (1970) 'Leavitt's Reaction Profile', in: Bearden, O., Netemeyer, R.G. and Mobley, M.F. (1973) *Handbook of Marketing Scales: Multi-item Measures for Marketing and Consumer Behavior Research*. Newbury Park, CA: Sage Publications, pp 144–145.

Leckenby, J.D. and Plummer, J.T. (1983) 'Advertising stimulus measurement and assessment research', *Current Issues and Research in Advertising*, pp 134–165.

Light, L. (1993) 'The role of advertising research in building brand equity', ARF Conference proceedings transcript, New York.

Lodish, L.M., Abraham, M., Kalmenson, S., Livelsberger, J., Lubetkin, B., Richardson, B. and Stevens, M.E. (1995) 'How advertising works: a meta-analyis of 389 real world split-cable television advertising experiments', *Journal of Advertising Research*, 17, May, pp 125–139.

McCollum Spielman Worldwide, *ACCU Track: Recognition Tracking System*, New York.

McDonald, A. (1992) 'Modelling TV effectiveness: predicting ad awareness through reach and frequency', *Admap*, February, pp 3236.

McDonald, C. (1991) 'Intended response: respondents aren't things, but people, and don't always inhabit the same model', *Admap*, July/August, pp 26–27.

McDonald, C. (1993) 'De grenzen van accountability', *Adformatie*, 14, pp 4–5.

McDonald, C. (1993b) 'Point of view; the key is to understand consumer response', *Admap*, September/October, pp 63–69.

McDonald, C. (1995a) 'Where to look for the most trustworthy evidence', *Admap*, February, pp 25–27.

McDonald, C. (1995b) 'Breakthrough or bun-fight?', *Admap*, March, pp 35–38.

McDonald, C. (1995c) 'Accountability and Advertising – the view from Britain', text from the GVR Presentation, 9 March.

McDonald, C. (1996) 'Sales measures of advertising', speakers' papers of the Admap & The Advertising Association Seminar on Monitoring Advertising Performance, London, 24 January.

MAD: Media and Advertising Diagnosis System. Ein System der Werbeerfolgskontrolle (1995) Frankfurt, RSG Marketing Research.

Majaro, S. (1970) 'Advertising by objectives', *Management Today*, 1.

Marchant, L.J. (1978) 'Systematic analysis of market behaviour and attitudes', *Admap*, July, pp 348–354.

Martin, C.A. and Eubank, S.K. (1994) 'Linking tracking data and sales volumes', ARF meeting, New advances in advertising research – Strenghtening its role in accountability, New York, 17 November, pp 73–84.

Media Observer (1992a) 'Examples of what has been learned in 1991', Diemen, TMP Research Nederland.

Media Observer (1992b) *Effectiviteit verzekerd*, Diemen, TMP Research Nederland.

Mensing, W.C.J.J. (1994) 'De scanning-revolutie en retailpanels', *Tijdschrift voor Marketing*, January, pp 30–34.

Mensing, W.C.J.J. and Boonsman, A.M. (1990) 'Effectmeting van promoties', *Tijdschrift voor Marketing*, October, pp 42–52.

Merz, J. (1994) 'Target: integrating pre- and post-testing', paper from the 1994 European Advertising Effectiveness Symposium. An ASI Conference.

Metha, A. (1994) 'How advertising response modeling (ARM) can increase ad effectiveness', *Journal of Advertising Research*, May/June, pp 62–74.

Michiels, W. and Defesche, F. (1993) 'De onmeetbaarheid van creativiteit', *Adformatie*, 14, pp 6–7.

Millward Brown International (1990) 'How advertising affects the sales of packaged goods of brands. A working hypothesis of the 1990s', Warwick.

Millward Brown International (1994a) 'The Advanced Tracking Programme', Warwick, June.

Millward Brown International (1994b) 'IPC Adtrack interim report', Warwick.

Minekus, G. (1993) 'Voor wie geen doel heeft, heeft niets betekenis', *Adformatie*, 14, p 3.

Molen, M. van der and Robben, H. (1991) 'Reclame-onderzoek onderzocht: Hoe RRO en Impact reclame-effecten meten', *Dossier: Meetmethoden*, 2, pp 10–126.

Monkman, M. (1996) 'Modelling TV audience data', *Admap*, April, pp 18–19.

Moran, W.T. (1993a) 'Advertising performance and brand loyalty', ARF Conference proceedings transcript, New York.

Moran, W.T. (1993b) 'Conceptual framework for brand equity measurement and management', ARF Conference proceedings transcript, New York, 27 October, pp 33–58.

Moran, W.T. (1994) 'Brand equity: the durability of brand value', ARF workshop proceedings transcript, New York, 25–16 February, pp 137–163.

Mosely, D. (1993) 'How to track consumer satisfaction', *Admap*, 28(9), pp 43–44.

Munzinger, U. (1995) 'Advertising in Germany', presentation for the Genootschap voor Reclame, Amsterdam, 9 March.

(1993) 'Mystiek van reclame verdwijnt en dat bevordert onderzoek', *Adformatie*, 21(26), p 23.

Nielsen, A.K. and Andersen, L.C. (1983) 'Comparability in the measurement of advertising persuasion', Seminar on effective advertising: can research help?, Monte Carlo, 26–28 January, pp 127–147.

Der NIKO – Werbe-Index: Werbetracking und Mediaoptimierung (1994) Frankfurt: NIKO Media Research GmbH.

NIMA (1993) *Marketing lexicon: begrippen en omschrijvingen*, Groningen: Wolters Noordhoff.

NIPO Posttest meet de effectiviteit van reclame, Amsterdam, company brochure, NIPO.

(1995) *Voorbeeld van de opzet van een trackingstudie*, internal report, Amsterdam, NIPO.

Parfitt, J.H. and Collins, B.J.K. (1968) 'Use of consumer panels for brand-share prediction', *Journal of Marketing Research*, 5, May, pp 131–145.

Percy, L. and Rossiter, J.R. (1992) 'Measuring advertising effectiveness: Copy-testing (pre-testing) ads and tracking (post-testing) the campaign', working paper 92–020, Kensington, Australia, Australian Graduate School of Management, University of New South Wales.

Pieters, R.G.M. and Raaij, W.F. van (1993) 'Nieuwe antwoorden op oude vragen', *Adfomatie*, 14, pp 10–11.

Platform '95 (1997) 'Thema dossier accountability'. Amsterdam.

Plessis, E. du (1994a) 'Likeability ads work best, but what is "likeability"?', *Admap*, May, pp 2–4.

Plessis, E. du (1994b) 'Recognition versus recall', *Journal of Advertising Research*, May/June, 34(3), pp 75–91.

Plessis, E. du (1994c) 'Understanding and using likeability', *Journal of Advertising Research*, September/October, pp 3–10.

Poling, F. (1994) 'Measuring advertising's influence on brand health', ARF transcript of workshop proceedings, 15–16 February, pp 225–248.

Prue, T. (1994) 'The 1994 IPA Advertising Effectiveness Awards', *Admap*, November, pp 36–39.

Prue, T. (1995) 'How different assumptions about advertising function can affect the assessment of advertising', Conference papers of the Admap & The Advertising Association: Monitoring Advertising Performance, London, 25 January.

Pulch, B. (1995) 'Licht im schwarzen Loch', *Wissenschaft und Forschung*, 16, pp 130–132.

Research International (1995a) 'The Research International approach to brand image analyses', Rotterdam.

Research International (1995b) 'Een compendium van Research International technieken', Rotterdam.

Research International (1995c) 'B.R.A.V.E.: Brand relations zijn bepalend voor de MerkMeerWaarde', Rotterdam.

Restall, C. (1990) 'What are a brand's value to the consumer and do they cross frontiers?, The 43rd ESOMAR Marketing Research Congress, Using Research for Marketing in the 90's, Monte Carlo, pp 609–628.

Riezebos, H.J. (1987) 'Reclame-onderzoek', Rotterdam, Erasmus University (not published).

Riezebos, H.J. (1995) 'De consument als basis voor financiële merkwaardering', *MAB*, January/February, pp 50–59.

Riezebos, R. (1995) 'Unravelling brand value: a conceptual model on consumer and producer-based brand value', Management report series no. 213, Rotterdam, Erasmus University, Rotterdam, Professional information study group.

Roberts, A. (1994) 'Measuring advertising effects through panel data', paper from the 1994 European Advertising Effectiveness Symposium, an ASI conference.

Roberts, A. (1996) 'Evaluating the effect of advertising through the use of consumer panels', speakers' papers of the Admap & The Advertising Association seminar on Monitoring Advertising Performance, London, 24 January.

Rood, T. (1995) '3x zo effectief, 6x zo efficiënt', *Blad*, 1, pp 19–23.

Rossiter, J.R. and Eagleson, G. (1994) 'Conclusions from the ARF's copy research validity project', *Journal of Advertising Research*, May/June, 34(3), pp 19–32.

Rother, A. (1994) 'Kampagne auf Kurs?', *Absatzwirtschaft*, 2, pp 50–52.

Rother, A. and Link, K.H. (1994) 'Positionierung: Ausbruch aus drangvoller Enge', *Absatzwirtschaft*, 6, pp. 62–67.

Rubinson, J. (1992) 'Brand strength means more than market share', 4th Annual ARF Advertising and Promotion workshop, Researching the Power of Brands, New York, 12–13 February.

Rubinson, J. (1993) 'Tracking systems that manage brand equity', ARF Conference and Research Expo, 23 March.

Sampson, P. (1993) 'Positioning, segmentation and the dynamic attributes that drive brands', *Admap*, July/August, pp 19–23.

Schlinger, M.J. (1979) 'A profile of responses to commercials', *Journal of Advertising Research*, 19(2), April, pp 37–46.

Scholl, N. and Struik, S. in Groenland, E. (1994) 'Tussen basic en bombarie', *Nieuws Tribune*, 36, p 38.

Schumann, D.W., Petty, R.E. and Clemons, D.S. (1990) 'Predicting the effectiveness of different strategies of advertising variation: a test of the repetition-variation hypotheses', *Journal of Advertising Research*, 17, September, pp 192–202.

Schuring, R.J. (1994) 'Een doorbraak', BrandmarC, Amsterdam.

Schuring, R.J., (1994) 'BrandmarC', presentation for the Genootschap voor Reclame, Amsterdam, 1 November.

Schuring, R.J. (1995) 'Meten en verbeteren van uw marketing- en verkooprendement; accountability in marketingcommunicatie', presentation, September.

Semiometrische benadering van een doelgroep (1994) Trendbox BV.

Signicom (1994) Confidential inquiry report.

Sikkema, P. and Rood, N. (1991) 'Ad-visor en Campaign Tracking: andere vragen, andere antwoorden', *Dossier: Meetmethoden*, 2, pp 128–153.

Simon, C.J. and Sullivan, M.W. (1992) 'A financial approach to estimating firm-level brand equity and measuring the impact of marketing events', Working paper, Report no. 92–116, Cambridge, MA, Marketing Science Institute.

Smeth, F. de (1993) *Merkwaarde als uitgangspunt voor het beheer van merkoperaties*, Amsterdam, De Smeth en Co.

Smit, E.G. (1994) 'Reclamestijl en Campagne-effect', from inquiry report, *Communicatiecampagnes en het publiek*', for the Communication Science Faculty, University of Amsterdam, Amsterdam.

Smit, E.G. (1996) Technical report, 'Mediagebruik en reclame', Communication Studies Faculty, University of Amsterdam, Amsterdam.

Smith, A. (1989) 'Eye movement research', *Marketing and Research Today*, May, p 64.

Soffer, S. (1993) 'De effectiviteit van attitudecampagnes', *Nieuws Tribune*, 40, pp 18–21.

Spangler, D. and Gilles, L. (1994) 'Transitioning tracking to meet the need of the 90's', ARF Conference, New advances in advertising research; strengthening its role in accountability, New York, 17 November, pp 86–105.

Speath, J. (1991) 'Integrating evaluative and diagnostic measures: know more about how your advertising works', ARF Copy Research Workshop, New York, 11 September.

Speath, J. (1993a) 'Ten steps toward advertising tracking studies that work', ARF Conference, New York.

Speath, J. (1993b) 'Advertising and brand equity', ARF Annual Conference, New York, 23 March.

Srivastava, R.K. and Shocker, A.D. (1991) 'Brand equity: a perspective on its meaning and measurement', Report no. 91–124.

Stavely, N.T. (1993) 'Is it right … will it work? An advertiser's guide to pre-testing methods in the 1990s', *Admap*, May.

(1995) 'Der Stein der Weisen hat viele Facetten', *Wissenschaft und Forschung*, Background, 18, pp 60–63.

Stockman, L. (1995) 'Brand Asset Valuator geeft marketeer inzicht in merkposities en merkstrategie', *Nieuws Tribune*, 4, pp 22–23.

Sutherland, M. and Harper, W. (1994) 'The use of moving averages: a case study in extracting information from databases', *Australasian Journal of Advertising Market Research*, 2(2), July, pp 19–34.

Swan, N. (1995) 'News from the front line', presentation for the Genootschap voor Reclame, Amsterdam, November.

Swarte, G. de (1994) 'Kan het waar zijn?', *Nieuws Tribune*, 26, pp 23–24.

TABS: Tracking advertising, brand strength (1994) London, TABS Ltd.

Tauber, E.M. (1982) 'Editorial: Researching durables', *Journal of Advertising Research*, 22(3), pp 9–10.

The Media Partnership (1995) 'Het bestedingen bos: hoe worden reclamebestedingen gemeten?', *Nieuwsbrief*, September.

The Media Partnership (1996) Brochure: *Media en Merken Monitor*.

Tilburg, M.A.L. van and Tuitert, A.B.A. (1995) 'Kwalitatief marktonderzoek in Nederland. Een overzicht van methoden en technieken uit de onderzoekspraktijk', *Reeks Economische Psychologie*, 1, Tilburg, Catholic University Brabant.

Titford, R. (1993) 'New plans from old data. How the past can vividly reveal present and future marketing options', *Admap*, September, pp 20–25.

Traas, L. (1995) 'Scannen per winkelwagentje', *Foodmagazine*, 1, 13 January.

Twyman, W.A. (1978) 'Cost effectiveness of different media. Are long-term effects possible or measurable?', Seminar on Cost Effectiveness, Barcelona.

Twyman, T. (1984) 'Assessing the validity of pre-testing: part 1', *Admap*, February, pp 74–84.

Ulfman, A. (1990) 'Beoordeling op meetbare criteria', *Adformatie*, 21, pp 58–60.

Verhallen, Th.M.M. (1985) 'Psycho-fysiologische methoden en het meten van reclame-effecten', *Tijdschrift voor Marketing*, June, pp 40–49.

Verhallen, Th., Trijp, M. van and Steenkamp, J.E.B. (1989) 'Nieuwe methode voor image- en positioneringsonderzoek: Procrustus-analyse (I)', *Tijdschrift voor Marketing*, June, pp 18–26.

Vught, T. van (1994a) 'Dossier: Weg met de eigenheimer in onderzoek', *Adformatie*, 43, p 16.

Vught, T. van (1994b) 'Onderzoek trekt te vaak aan het kortste eind', *Adformatie*, 43, pp 18–19.

Walker, C. 'How strong is your brand?', *Marketing Tools*, January/February, pp 46–53.

Walker, D. (1990) 'Beyond validation: advertising research for the 1990s', ARF 7th annual copy-research workshop, New York, 11 July.

Walker, D. and Dubitsky, T.M. (1994) 'Why liking matters', *Journal of Advertising Research*, May/June, 34(3), pp 9–18.

Warrens, B. (1993) 'Testing to improve accountability (and be smarter)', ARF Conference proceedings transcript.

Watson, P.J. and Gatchel, J. (1979) 'Autonomic measures of advertising', *Journal of Advertising Research*, 19(3), June, pp 15–26.

Wells, R.D. (1964) in: Bearden, O., Netemeyer, R.G. and Mobley, M.F. (1993) *Handbook of Marketing Scales: Multi-item Measures for Marketing and Consumer Behavior Research*. Newbury Park, CA: Sage Publications, pp 199–200.

Wells, R.D. (1975) 'An empirical model of advertising awareness', *Journal of the Market Research Society*, 17(4), pp 243–255.

(1971) *Werbedosis – Werbewirkung. Untersuchung des Response-Funktionen von Anzeigen-Kampagnes* Konstanz, Delta Marketing Forschung.

Westendorp, P.H. van (1984) 'More value from research for less money: the KS-technique', 37th Esomar congress: What we have learned from the recession, Rome, September.

Westendorp. P.H. van (1989), 'NSS Target Monitor – An instrument to assess consumer franchise', pp 221–252.

Westendorp, P.H. van (1996) *Op weg naar accountability*, GvR document, no. 9, Amsterdam, Genootschap voor Reclame.

Willie, T. (1992) 'The evidence from continuous tracking on how advertising builds brands', 4th annual ARF Advertising and promotion workshop, Researching the power of brands, New York, February 12–13.

Woerden C. van, Boer, P.G. de (1994) 'Merken. Een literatuurstudie', MSA group.

Woodside, A.G. and Wilson, E.J. (1985) 'Effects on consumer awareness of brand advertising preference', *Journal of Advertising Research*, 25(4), August/September.

Wright, P. (1980) 'Message evoked thoughts: persuasion research using thought verbalisations', *Journal of Consumer Research*, 7, September, pp 151–175.

Yuspeh, S., Dunn, T. and Plummer, J. (1982) 'Positioning Advertising Copy Testing (PACT)', ARF Conference on Understanding copy testing, proceedings transcript, New York, pp 93–120.

Zachowsky, J.L. (1985) 'Measuring the involvement construct', *Journal of Consumer Research*, 12, December, pp 341–352.

Zachowsky, J.L. (1990) in: Bearden, O., Netemeyer, R.G. and Mobley, M.F. (1993) *Handbook of Marketing Scales: Multi-item Measures for Marketing and Consumer Behavior Research*. Newbury Park, CA: Sage Publications, pp 154–155.

Zalinge, D.E.C. van (1994) 'Planning en controle van merken', *Tijdschrift Financieel Management*, 6, pp 60–69.

Zalinge, D.E.C. van (1995) 'Waardering van merken', *Tijdschrift Financieel Management*, 1, pp 62–73.

Zaltman, G. and Moorman, C. (1989) 'The management and use of advertising research', *Journal of Advertising Research*, 28(6), pp 11–18.

CHAPTER 8. MARKET SIMULATION

Books and theses

Adriaans, P. and Zantinge, D. (1996) *Data Mining*. Harlow: Addison Wesley Longman.

Baestaens, D.E., Bergh, W. M. van den and Wood, D. (1994) *Neural Network Solutions for Trading in Financial Markets*. London: Pitman Publishing.

Beijk, J. and Raaij, W.F. van (1989) *Schemata: Informatie Verwerking, Beïnvloedingsprocessen en Reclame*. Amsterdam: preliminary research for the VEA, VEA.

Blalock, H.M. (1960) *Social Statistics*. Lujbliana, Yugoslavia: McGraw-Hill/Mladinska Knjiga.

Blattberg, R.C., Glazer, R. and Little, J.D.C. (1994) *The Marketing Information Revolution*. Boston, MA: Harvard Business School Press.

Broadbent, S. (1989) *The Advertising Budget*. London: McGraw-Hill.

Broadbent, S. (1997) *Accountable Advertising*. Henley-on-Thames: NTC Publications Ltd.

Buzell, R.D. and Gale, B.T. (1987) *The PIMS Principles, Linking Strategy to Performance*. New York: The Free Press.

Chatfield, C. and Collins, A.J. (1980) *Introduction to Multivariate Analysis*. Chapman & Hall.

Day, G.S. (1986) *Analysis for Strategic Market Decisions*. St.Paul, Minnesota, US: West Publishing Company.

Draper, N.R. and Smith, H. (1988) *Applied Regression Analysis*. New York: John Wiley & Sons, Inc.

Edelman, G.M. (1991) *Bright Air, Brilliant Fire: On the Mattor of Mind*. New York: Basic Books.

Floor, K. and Raaij, W.F. van (1993) *Marketing-communicatiestrategie*. Houten: Educatieve Partners Nederland.

Haykin, S. (1994) *Neural Networks*. Princeton, NJ, USA: Prentice-Hall.

Jones, J.P. (1995) *When Ads Work*. New York: Lexington Books.

Keen, P. (1991) *Shaping the Future: Business Design through Information Technology*. Cambridge, MA: Harvard Business School Press.

Leeflang, P.S.H. and Beukenkamp, P.A. (1981) *Probleemgebied Marketing, een Managementbenadering*, Leiden/Antwerpen, H.E. Stenfert Kroese BV.

Lilien, G.L., Kotler, P. and Moorthy, K.S. (1992) *Marketing Models*, New Jersey, USA, Prentice-Hall.

Little, J.D.C. (1975) *Brandaid: a Marketing-mix Model*.

McDonald, C. (1997) *Monitoring Advertising Performance*. Henley-on-Thames: NTC Publications Ltd.

Moss Kanter, R. (1989) *When Elephants Learn to Dance: Managing the Challenges of Strategy, Management and Careers in the 1990s*. New York: Simon & Schuster.

Naert, P.A. and Leeflang, S.P.H. (1978) *Building Implementable Marketing Models*. Leiden/Boston: Martinus Nijhoff.

Quinn Mills, D. (1991) *Rebirth of the Corporation*. New York: John Wiley & Sons Ltd.

Refenes, A.P. (1995) *Neural Networks in the Capital Markets*. Chichester: John Wiley & Sons Ltd.

Swanborn, P.G. (1981) *Methoden van Sociaal-wetenschappelijk Onderzoek*. Meppel: Boom.

Tapscott, D. and Caston, A. (1993) *Paradigm Shift*. New York: McGraw-Hill.

Weijer, T. de (1995) *Structure–property Relations of Semi-crystalline Yarns Obtained with Natural Computation*. Nijmegen: proefschrift KUN.

Articles and other sources

Dasgupta, C.G., Dispense, G.S. and Ghose, S. (1994) 'Comparing the predictive performance of a neural network model with some traditional market response models', *International Journal of Forecasting*, 10, pp 235–244.

Drucker, P.F. (1988) 'The new organization', *Harvard Business Review*, January–February.

Gielen, C. (1995) 'Wanneer zijn neurale netwerken toepasbaar', in: *Toepassing van neurale netwerken in marketing*, Henry Stewart conference studies, Amsterdam, 26 January.

Hollis, N. (1996) 'Integrating information sources to understand short and long-term advertising effects', AMA Attitude and Behavioural Research Conference, LaJolla, 22–24 January.

Kopp, M.A., Smith, R.S. and Tarshis, A. (1991) 'Breakthrough marketplace advertising research for bottom line results', ARF Key Issue workshop, New York, 6–7 November 1991.

Kumar, A., Rao, V.R. and Soni, H. (1995) 'An empirical comparison of neural networks and logistic regression models', *Marketing Letters*, 6(4), pp 251–263.

CHAPTER 9. EVOLUTIONARY CAMPAIGN MANAGEMENT

Books

Barash, D. (1987) *De Haas en de Schilpad – Cultuur, Biologie en de Aard van de Mens*. Amsterdam: Bert Bakker.

Dawkins, R. (1986) *The Blind Watchmaker*. Harlow: Longman Scientific & Technical.

Dennet, D.C. (1995) *Darwin's Dangerous Idea – Evolution and the Meanings of Life*. New York: Simon & Schuster.

Engel, J.F., Warshaw, M.R. and Kinnear, T.C. (1991) *Promotional Strategy – Managing the Marketing Communications Process* (7th edition). Homewood, Illinois: Irwin.

Gosling, W. (1994) *Helmsmen and Heroes – Control Theory as a Key to Past and Future*. London: Weidenfeld & Nicolson.

Rossiter, J.R. and Percy, L. (1987) *Advertising and Promotion Management*. McGraw-Hill Book Company.

Sissors, J. Z. and Bumba, L. (1996) *Advertising Media Planning* (5th edition). Chicago: NTC Business Books.

Verbeke, W. and Mosmans, A. (1990) *Marketing Communicatie en Chaos*. Kluwer Bedrijfswetenschappen.

Wells, W., Burnett, J. and Moriarty, S. (1992) *Advertising – Principles and Practice*. Englewood Cliffs, NJ: Prentice Hall.

INDEX

market simulation 293–4, 295–6
Animatics 243
Arousal 44
Artificial Neural Networks (ANN) 281
Association tests 57
Associative brand networks 52–3
Asspat method 109, 110
ATRN process 62
Attachment 126–7
Attention 41–3, 44, 227–9, 231
Attitudes
   see also brand attitude
   Achenbaum's attitude scale 64
   affective component 50
   and behaviour 50, 62
      correlation between 150–7
   cognitive component 49–50
   conative component 50
   existing, and brand use 243–4
   forecasting consumer buying behaviour 65
   three-component model 49–50
   towards advertisement or campaign 49–50
      measuring 50
      response profiles 81–3
      towards content 51
Auto-associative neural networks 295
Awards, advertising effectiveness 14, 15
Awareness of content of advertisement or campaign 48–9
Awareness/saliency model 188–91, 198–200
Awareness set 63

BAN *see* Brand Associative Network
Beaumont Emotion Battery 233
Behaviour
   and attitude 50, 62
      correlation between 150–7
   consolidating, advertising effectiveness 24
   forecasting 65
   research 138–40
Behavioural brand equity 75, 99, 170
   behaviour research 138–40
   behavioural brand loyalty 141–7
   correlation between attitude and behaviour 150–7
   penetration 140–1
   price premium 147–50
   strong brand characteristics 171–2

Behavioural brand loyalty 141–7
Behavioural effects
   advertising effectiveness 16–17
   buying frequency 16
   penetration 16
Benchmarking 278
BETA (Brand Equity or Price Trade-Off Analysis) 116
Binding interest 125–6
Brand Asset Valuator 103, 108, 110–11, 117, 126, 133
Brand association categories 58
Brand Associative Network (BAN) 53, 54, 182, 189
Brand attitude 61, 228–9
   brand preference 63
   overall evaluation and 117–22
   satisfaction 63–4
   tracking 269
Brand awareness 53–5, 101–4
   tracking 267
Brand behavioural responses
   Advertising Response Matrix *see* Advertising Response Matrix
   variables, market simulation 320
Brand behavioural tendency 64–5
Brand Builder 122–4
Brand builders 11
Brand duplication 143
Brand Dynamics Pyramid 129, 131–3, 152, 156
Brand equity 74–5
   advertising effects research 36
   behavioural *see* behavioural brand equity
   definitions 174–6
   financial/economic *see* financial/economic brand equity
   introduction 98–101
   mental *see* mental brand equity
   research; no one magic formula 172–3
   strong brands 170–3
Brand evaluation, tracking 269
Brand ideal 109–10
Brand image 109
Brand involvement 67
Brand knowledge 104–10
Brand-loyal buyers 70
Brand loyalty 63–4, 65, 71, 73, 121
   Hallberg 154
   and market share 149
   penetration versus 153–7

AUTHOR INDEX

ABOUT THE AUTHORS

Giep Franzen is the professor of commercial communication at the University of Amsterdam, in the Communication Studies department. In 1962 he founded the advertising agency, Franzen, Hey & Veltman, together with two fellow partners. They merged with BBDO in 1970 to form FHV/BBDO. Until 1990 Franzen was the chairman of the board of BBDO Nederland, the leading group of communication companies in the Netherlands, when he began lecturing at the University of Amsterdam and set up Giep Franzen & Company, specialising in the development of branding and advertising know-how. He has written and published extensively on both subjects.

Cindy Goessens graduated in 1993 from the University of Amsterdam in the Communication Studies department. She then worked for a year as an academic assistant with Giep Franzen & Company, helping to develop the Advertising Response Matrix.

Mary Hoogerbrugge graduated from the Communication Studies department of the University of Amsterdam in 1994. In September 1994 she took over from Cindy Goessens at Giep Franzen & Company. There she conducted an in-depth study into methods of and experience with tracking and pre-testing. She is currently working as a strategy manager at FHV/BBDO.

Cees Kappert has a degree in management science from Twente University. He has held various positions in the area of advanced information technology applications in marketing, in companies such as Shell, KPMG, Livingstones and Datamind.

He is currently working at Avero (a member of the Achmea group) and is preparing his thesis on new marketing concepts facilitated by advances in information technology. He has published work on the applications of neural networks in market modelling and the development of knowledge-driven, event-propelled marketing processes.

Reint Jan Schuring is the managing director of BrandmarC, the company he founded in 1993, which specialises in market simulation and process dynamics. He has also had strategic and marketing responsibilities in a number of leading advertising agencies and in the financial world (Direktbank). He began his career as a researcher at the University of Groningen, having first studied Western sociology.

Marnix Vogel studied business administration at Erasmus University, Rotterdam. In 1996 he rounded off his studies in the marketing management department with a course in modern modelling techniques in marketing. He then joined BrandmarC as a consultant.